Administering for Quality

Canadian Early Childhood Development Programs

SECOND EDITION

Karen Chandler

George Brown College

PEARSON

Prentice
Hall

Toronto

National Library of Canada Cataloguing in Publication

Chandler, Karen (Karen A. M.)
    Administering for quality : Canadian early childhood development programs / Karen Chandler.—2nd ed.

Includes bibliographical references and index.
ISBN 0-13-129000-2

    1. Child care services—Canada—Administration—Textbooks. I. Title.

HQ778.7.C3C373 2006   362.71'2'068   C2005-901439-3

0-13-129000-2

Vice President, Editorial Director: Michael J. Young
Acquisitions Editor: Dave Ward
Marketing Manager: Toivo Pajo
Developmental Editor: Michelle Harrington, Suzanne Schaan
Production Editor: Richard di Santo
Copy Editor: Trish O'Reilly
Proofreader: Anne Borden
Production Coordinator: Janis Raisen
Manufacturing Coordinator: Susan Johnson
Permissions Manager: Susan Wallace-Cox
Page Layout: Heidi Palfrey
Art Director: Julia Hall
Cover Design: Miguel Acevedo
Cover Image: Getty Images / The Image Bank / Tim Platt

    3 4 5   10 09 08 07 06

Printed and bound in the United States of America.

Contents

Preface

This second edition of *Administering for Quality: Canadian Early Childhood Development Programs* is designed to facilitate early childhood practitioners' understanding of administrative, professional, and advocacy responsibilities. Considering that each practitioner's influence on young children and families is so lasting, it is important to fully prepare oneself for this commitment.

Over many years—as an early childhood development specialist working with children, families, and professionals in a wide variety of settings; as a college professor of administration, professionalism, advocacy, sociology, and interpersonal communication; and as a writer on early childhood topics, including *Administering Early Childhood Settings: The Canadian Perspective* and *The Whole Child*—I have seen that thoughtful planning and administration are essential to the success of quality ECEC programs. This book is built on that conviction.

Readers are introduced to a range of administrative demands in different types of early childhood settings. Special attention is given to family child care, as it is the type of care the majority of Canadian parents use—and many ECE graduates, at some point in their careers, work in family child care.

Designed for programs at the post-secondary level, this book can also be used as a self-help aid in preparing for credentialling. A rich source of information for practicing directors, it includes up-to-date Canadian statistics, highlights current research, and identifies a variety of resources including some vital weblinks.

Terminology

A major struggle faces our profession: to attain recognition for our important work. In part, this struggle is reflected in an inconsistent use of terminology and nomenclature—the terms we use to describe ourselves and the titles others assign to us. For words such as "doctor," "lawyer," and "nurse," we generally have a set of images about what the profession does and what it stands for. We in the field of early childhood education and care have long debated what to call ourselves, and at times discussion of the title has been quite contentious. Among the terms used are "early childhood educator," "child care professional," "developmental worker," "teacher," "caregiver," "child care worker," "home child care provider," "day care staff," and "practitioner." One point of agreement: Don't call us "babysitters"! A task for our profession is to reach agreement on what we are going to call ourselves. In this book I chose to use the term "early childhood practitioner"; those who work as front-line practitioners are called "caregivers" and "family child care providers"; and "director" describes one who acts as an administrator and/or supervisor. I have used the pronoun "she" for directors and family child care providers because it is so very rare to find men in these roles.

Rather than "child care," I have used the term "early childhood education and care," which acknowledges a broader range of services, including services for children and families that foster health, safety, security, success at learning, and social engagement and responsibility.

New Features

This edition reflects some of the changes taking place in the field. Recently there has been increased focus on the early childhood practitioner with the development of Occupational Standards, and the endeavor to reach agreement on terminology has received attention in the paper "What's in a Name" by the Canadian Child Care Federation (CCCF 2004). The Child Care Human Resources Sector Council has been formed since the previous edition and has released its report *Working for Change: Canada's Child Care Workforce* (Beach et al. 2004) as well as other research into salaries and working conditions. The federal government has committed additional funds over five years to support provincial and territorial government investments in regulated programs for children under six. Many feel we are on the brink of achieving a national child care policy. Chapter 6 "Human Resources Management in an ECEC Environment" has been rewritten with co-author Nora Spinks, who specializes in Human Resources. My work with CCCF has enabled me to work with First Nations' representatives and SpeciaLink and reflect their values in a broader definition of quality.

Instructional features

The following pedagogical features are included in each chapter:

- *Objectives.* At the beginning of each chapter, learning outcomes are suggested. Individual instructors of a variety of courses can adapt these suggestions to their own focus for presenting material.

- *Exhibits/focus boxes.* Charts and tables are used to summarize research. Boxes highlight material, provide samples, and help organize, illustrate, and simplify information.

- *Standards.* Samples of quality standards from the *Partners in Quality* study and the Occupational Standards sponsored by the Canadian Child Care Federation are provided in many chapters.

- *Key terms and concepts.* These are identified in boldface type on first use, and definitions are located in a *glossary* at the end of the book. At the end of each chapter, key terms and concepts of particular relevance to the chapter are listed.

- *Activities.* Student activities follow a summary at the close of each chapter. Questions are designed to stimulate the reader to reflect, examine her or his beliefs, and take a look at practices.

- *Recommended readings.* Suggestions for further reading are given for each chapter.

- *Weblinks.* This feature links readers to a whole world of resources pertinent to chapter material.

- *Appendix.* A list of government and professional organizations, including Internet addresses, is given at the end of the book.

A special request to readers of this book: Please let me know how you like the book and how I can make it better. Here is how I can be reached at George Brown College:

Karen Chandler
Early Childhood Development Program
P.O. Box 1015, Station B
Toronto, Ontario
M5T 2T9

Acknowledgments

First of all, I would like to pay tribute to the students at George Brown College, who help me formulate my ideas about the field and who continue to teach me a great deal about life. They draw my attention to the need for current Canadian materials. The many children, families, and professionals I have worked with challenged my thinking and broadened my understanding. I have had endless opportunities to discuss new ideas and strategies with colleagues in the Early Childhood Development program at George Brown College. One of the most rewarding aspects of the field is the people I work with in a voluntary capacity, including my colleagues at the Canadian Child Care Federation—both staff and participants on member council and the Child Care Human Resources Sector Council.

This book could not have been written without the many organizations and colleagues in the early childhood development field who contributed through their research and publications, their recommendations and advice. To them, I proclaim my admiration and gratitude. To gain insight into the real world, I interviewed and shared resources with experienced practicing directors, family child care providers, former students, and leaders of national, provincial, and territorial organizations. Many individuals and reviewers contributed their time and expertise to the development of this book. Special thanks go to Nora Spinks, Work Life Harmony; Michelle Turiano, Childcare Resource and Research Unit; Lana Crossman, Canadian Child Care Federation; Elaine Ferguson, Child Care Connections, NS; Gabey Chavet, Association of Early Childhood Educators, Ontario; Jill Harvey, City of Toronto Children's Services; Kira Heineck, Ontario Coalition for Better Child Care; Michelle Lupa, Growing Up Healthy Downtown; Carol Rowan and Elisipee Inukpuk', Avataq Cultural Institute; Sharon Hope Irwin, SpeciaLink; Simmone Phillips, St. Lawrence Child Care; Libby Walters, OPSEU representative on Health and Safety concerns; Dorothy Kaytor, Assiniboine Community College; Joanne Morris, College of the North Atlantic; Fran Dobbin, University of Toronto Early Learning Centre; Pat Campbell, consultant; Mary Gross-Prowse, Association of Early Childhood Educators, Newfoundland and Labrador; and Maria Ciampini, Rachel Langford, and Zeenat Janmohamed of George Brown College.

I thank my family, who lived through the clutter of research reports and articles—particularly Rod, who supported me in meeting each successive deadline. Our cat Misha provided a welcome distraction and endeavoured to add her own editorial comments while walking on the keyboard.

This text makes significant reference to the four reports of the *You Bet I Care!* project, funded by Child Care Visions, covering both centre- and family-based early childhood settings serving children under the age of six (Goelman et al. 2000; Doherty et al. 2000a, 2000b, 2001). It also significantly references the study *Working for Change: Canada's Child Care Workforce* (Beach et al. 2004), which built on the 1998 study *Our Child Care Workforce: From Recognition to Remuneration* (Beach, Bertrand and Cleveland). *Working for Change* provides an updated profile of those who work in the regulated child care sector, the environment, and the opportunities and challenges they face in caring for the youngest members of society.

I would like to express my appreciation to Pearson Education Canada for inviting me to write this book: Michelle Harrington, who identified the need for more information; and Trish O'Reilly, who clarified my intentions.

Karen Chandler
George Brown College

Defining Quality Early Childhood Programs

Objectives

- Outline the benefits of early childhood education and care (ECEC) programs.
- Discuss the need for more ECEC programs.
- Identify what should comprise an ECEC system.
- Define quality ECEC programs.
- Identify factors that contribute to quality ECEC programs.
- Provide methods of achieving quality.
- Identify the relationship of regulation, accreditation, and program evaluation to program quality.

The creation and maintenance of quality early childhood education and care (ECEC) programs is a focus throughout this book. This chapter describes early childhood programs, explains the need for these programs, looks at what is meant by quality, and discusses the factors generally recognized as indicative of high quality programs. Today early childhood education and care refers to child care, nursery schools, and kindergarten, ideally delivered as one seamless program. The Organisation for Economic Co-operation and Development (OECD) noted that "'care and education' are inseparable concepts . . . the use of the term ECEC supports an integrated and coherent approach to policy and provision, which is inclusive of all children regardless of employment or economic status . . . such arrangements may fulfill a wide range of objectives including care, learning and social support" (OECD 2001). A high quality early childhood experience determines an individual's health and social success throughout his or her life (Canada 1996b). Quality programs benefit all children—those whose **parents** are in the paid workforce as well as those who are not. Canadian parents from all social, economic, and cultural groups and from all regions seek opportunities for their children to get the best start in life.

Benefits of Quality Early Childhood Programs

There is overwhelming evidence of the importance of early childhood experiences in determining health and social success throughout a person's life. Early childhood development programs that nurture, protect, and educate young children affect not only the children themselves but also their families, their communities, and the larger society. The *Benefits and Costs of Good Child Care* study concludes that for every dollar invested in high quality early childhood development, there is a two-dollar benefit to children, parents, and society (Cleveland and Krashinsky 1998). The social and economic benefits of quality **early childhood settings** reach into every segment of Canadian society—parents are able to work or attend school, while children receive the best nurturing and early childhood experience possible.

Significant economic and social changes over the past two decades—including increased global economic competition, a shifting economic base, changing demographics, and an influx of mothers into the workforce—have made the issue of children's early years and care one of national importance. Quality early childhood development is crucial to Canada's future economic prosperity (Cleveland and Krashinsky 2001). Quality early childhood development can provide members of the next generation of workers with a solid foundation of skills, competencies, attitudes, and behaviours that will ensure their success in a more technologically-based economic environment. This perspective has caught the attention of policy makers. At the same time, we must also recognize that children are citizens with their own rights and deserve the best start. This perspective is elaborated on in this chapter.

Quality early childhood development programs foster children's confidence and identity.

The reasons for investing in early childhood development are numerous. Increased workforce participation of both single mothers and mothers in two-parent families produces lower social spending on families, higher tax revenue to governments, and increased future economic security for women (Cleveland and Krashinsky 1998).

A child's ability to think, form relationships, and live up to his or her full potential is directly related to the synergistic effect of good health, good nutrition, and appropriate stimulation and interaction with others. There is substantial evidence that the quality of early childhood experiences has long-term effects on an individual's performance in the education system, behaviour, and risks for chronic disease in adult life (Canada 1996b). Recent human development research confirms how important the first five years of life can be for children's life-long abilities, health, and well-being. This is a crucial time for brain development, when the structure of children's brains is strongly influenced by the world around them. The quality of care that children experience affects the way they think and learn. Unhealthy physical, emotional, and social environments can have lifelong consequences. The brains of infants and toddlers develop quickly, and children can learn a great deal before kindergarten when they are in environments where they can discover and explore. In fact, children who have been well nurtured have brains that are physically different from those of children who experienced less favourable conditions in their early years.

We must invest in programs that lay the foundation for healthy cognitive and emotional development, which translate into tangible economic returns. Children who participate in quality early childhood programs tend to be more successful in school, are more competent socially and emotionally, and show higher verbal and intellectual development during the early years than children who do not participate in these programs. Recent public policy research reports point to the need to support early child development as a lever to improve school performance. As well, there is clear evidence that the first six years of life are crucial for the development of the language, interpersonal, and intellectual skills that will determine adult competence (Steinhauer 1999). Ensuring healthy child development, therefore, is an investment in a country's future workforce and capacity to thrive economically and as a society.

The National Children's Agenda

Early childhood development programs are a powerful tool for breaking the intergenerational cycle of poverty. Under the right conditions, these programs have significant economic benefits for all children—most particularly for the poor. But the poor, almost by definition, are unable to pay for the considerable costs of ECEC programs. Poor nutrition during childhood, exposure to unsafe environments, and lack of stimulation damage children for the rest of their lives. ECEC programs aim at preventing this damage. Consequently, ECEC programs deserve a place among the public policies that governments put in place to constitute a just society (Van der Gaag and Tan 2000).

From birth, children can receive early childhood development in formal and non-formal settings, in the home, in the community, or in schools. The purpose of an ECEC program can be to deliver services to young children themselves or to educate parents or community professionals in early childhood development techniques. These approaches are all designed to improve the growth of the young child.

The Need for More Early Childhood Development Programs

Canadian children live in a world that is often very different from the one their parents were raised in. There are more lone-parent families, and most families with two parents need two wage-earners. The typical Canadian mother works outside the home, usually at a full-time job. Often she returns to work soon after the birth of a child. Most lone parents are women, and women's wages are generally lower than men's. With ever more mothers working, many young children spend more of their waking hours with non-parental caregivers than they do with their families. Human Resources Development Canada found that young Canadian children receive, on average, nine hours a day of non-parental care for 250 days a year. Almost 74% of Canadian children under the age of five receive non-parental care while their parents work or attend school.

Some families choose to look after their children at home and require flexible work schedules to allow for this. For example, one parent may work part-time, or on a night shift, providing care for the child during the daytime hours when the other parent is working. Other families may prefer to make private child care arrangements but need access to information and referral services to accomplish this.

In reality, this range of services is not available in most communities across Canada. Families have been left to struggle on their own, balancing work demands with their children's needs. The supply of early childhood development programs is inadequate, especially for school-age children and infants; virtually no ECEC programs exist in some areas of the country, and where there is an adequate supply, quality is uneven. Increasing numbers of children between the ages of 5 and 12 are at home alone because working parents cannot establish a stable care arrangement. Parents may not be able to afford or find a regulated space. They may have difficulty making satisfactory arrangements in the unregulated sector. Children who care for themselves are at increased risk for injury, loneliness, and unhealthy eating habits (Canadian Institute of Child Health 2000).

There is little evening or weekend care for children of shift workers. There are no services for mildly ill children and, since family friendly policies are absent from so many work places, parents often face loss of income if they take time off from work. Children with special needs often find too few settings that are inclusive. Where a full range of quality ECEC services exists, many parents are barred by the high cost. The study *Working for Change: Canada's Childcare Workforce* (Beach et al. 2004) reported 4.5 million children from birth to 11 and only 593 430 regulated child care spaces in 2004.

A 1999 study by Canadian Policy Research Networks (Jensen and Mahon 2001) found that three-quarters of Canadians want a new child care system that provides economic supports for children in their first three years of life. Progress is needed to increase the total number of regulated child care spaces, but there cannot be a large-scale creation of spaces without general agreement on the **standards** that must be met. Standards identify what needs to be in place to support provision of a quality early childhood development program. Standards must be established that reflect the kind of high quality environment Canadian children need.

These figures clearly demonstrate a great unmet need for quality early childhood development programs and show why families, advocates, and women's groups have been pressing, over a number of years, for the creation of a national early childhood development policy. The federal government with all the provincial/territorial governments except Quebec (which had already put a universal program in place) is creating a national ECEC program, which incorporates four principles: quality, universal inclusion, accessibility, and early development.

What Should Comprise an Early Childhood Development System?

These principles correspond to the system proposed by Hertzman (2000) that a Canadian early childhood development strategy should be comprehensive, universally available and accessible, integrated, community-driven, accountable, and of high quality. He states that ECEC programs must incorporate three basic components: early childhood education, child care, and parenting/caregiving support. Comprehensive ECEC programs should meet the needs of parents who are at home as well as of those who participate in the paid labour force.

All families should have the opportunity to participate in ECEC programs in their community. These programs should be sustainable, well-resourced, and publicly supported. There would be parent fees, but they would be affordable and programs would be accessible to those who choose to use them. Attendance at early childhood development programs should be by choice rather than required.

Many experienced advocates note that there should be a public infrastructure (such as school boards or local governments) to operate programs rather than relying on parents or volunteers to initiate, fund, and operate programs. However programs would continue to be responsive to and involve parents and would be shaped and delivered at the local level. The Toronto First Duty Project, a research project with OISE and the City of Toronto, the Toronto District School Board, and partnering community agencies, is studying such a blend with an integration of child care, kindergarten, and family support programs.

We need continued leadership by governments to continue to move toward the long-term goal, estimated to take from 10 to 15 years, of a universal ECEC system

---

The Organisation for Economic Cooperation and Development identifies three groups who need additional supports to fully participate in ECEC programs:

- Children with special needs, including those with identified developmental and physical difficulties and who require adaptations to the social and/or physical environment.

- Children who live in families who face social and economic challenges related to poverty.

- Children and families who are newcomers to Canada or who live in distinct cultural communities and may face linguistic and other challenges that are barriers to their full participation.

Source: Organisation for Economic Cooperation and Development (OECD), *Starting Strong: Early Childhood Education and Care* (Paris: Education and Training Division, OECD, 2001).

To understand the place of such standards, we need to look at the question of what defines quality:

- What are the components of a high quality setting?

- How do these elements interact?

Answers to these questions will guide the efforts of practitioners and spur action to upgrade the quality of our nation's early childhood services.

What Is Quality Early Childhood Development?

The term "quality" refers to the extent to which something is desirable or meets more than the minimal standards. Quality has become a central topic of study among early childhood practitioners and developmental psychologists, and no single issue related to early childhood development is as complex or important. Over the past 25 years, the discussion has moved beyond debates about whether ECEC programs help or harm development or which types of ECEC services are best. The question today is, How can we make them better? Peter Moss, a European early childhood expert, cautions us about only looking at child care for working parents. He believes that every country should have a comprehensive early-years policy that provides flexible, coherent, and high quality services with equality of access for all children, whether or not their parents are employed.

Ecological Model of Early Childhood Environments

Children and families are affected by systems with which they interact. They are affected by the neighbourhoods where they live, their parents' workplaces, and the nature and scope of available support services such as schools and health care facilities. These aspects of family life in turn are affected by government social policies and ideologies. In assessing early childhood environments, researchers in the early childhood field take an ecological approach: To understand these settings, they look at the interactions among children, parents, and practitioners and the relationships of each with the environments in which they work, play, and live. They consider not only how to structure ECEC environments to foster children's growth but also how these environments interact with influences outside the setting. Often efforts to improve early childhood programs have seen each program as a self-contained unit and thus have concentrated on internal changes—such as buying new equipment or adjusting the curriculum. However, knowledgeable practitioners have come to understand that if a setting fails to consider the wider environment within which its programs take place, the impact of such changes will be limited.

Many writers incorporate the framework for looking at ECEC settings provided by Bronfenbrenner (1979, 1986) in his **ecological model** of human development. His model can be adapted to provide a framework for understanding the influence of contextual factors on a child's daily experience. Bronfenbrenner thinks in terms of four systems, each embed-

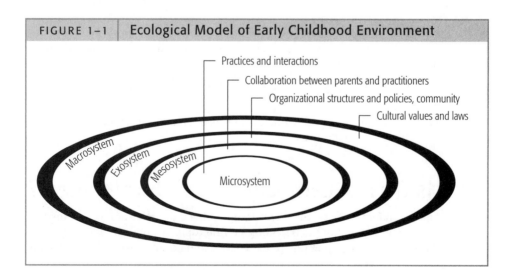

FIGURE 1-1   Ecological Model of Early Childhood Environment

Practices and interactions
Collaboration between parents and practitioners
Organizational structures and policies, community
Cultural values and laws

Macrosystem
Exosystem
Mesosystem
Microsystem

ded within the next (see Figure 1–1). His model provides a way of moving beyond the immediate setting to consider, in turn, the layers of influence acting on the developing child, along with the impact of the early childhood experience on the family, community, and society.

At the heart of this ecological model, the microsystem (*micro* = small) is centred on the developing child within his or her immediate settings—the family, the early childhood development environment or peer group. The microsystem is made up of the physical environment; the resources within it; the curriculum; the relationships between the parent, caregiver, and child; and the interactions among the children.

The second level is the mesosystem (*meso* = middle), where different microsystems are linked together through relationships—such as the caregiver–parent interaction—or through employment practices that affect the family—such as parental leave benefits. Here, for example, one would consider the relationship between the early childhood development environment and the home. These interactions will be influenced by how different adults perceive the child as well as by child rearing beliefs; a critical factor is the need for the environment to be welcoming to all those who use it—the child, the staff, and the parents. As a second instance, if an employer changes a parent's work schedule to one that does not conform to the hours of the early childhood setting, this impacts on the lives of the parent as well as the child. The parent may have to find and pay additional child care costs and the child may sense the impact of increased stress.

Outside the mesosystem is the exosystem (*exo* = outside), which represents the social structures, both formal and informal, that influence the settings the child experiences. In this dimension, one must consider the roles and influences of parents' jobs, various government agencies and policies for early childhood settings, and the family, the local economy, the mass media, the workplace, and the immediate community. Families are strongly affected by government policies regarding who will receive child care subsidy or whether practitioners receive wage enhancement grants that promote staff stability. As another example, to provide program quality, directors need to be aware of funding sources, how to access them, and where to refer families for support; it is also essential that they keep abreast of government philosophies that underlie policies.

All these sets of relationships are located in a macrosystem (*macro* = great) encompassing the ideologies and patterns of culture such as the economic, educational, legal, and political systems. Included here are attitudes toward the family and the role of mothers and community definitions of appropriate environments for young children. The macrosystem defines what is possible; for example, in a society that believes children belong to their parents, rather than to society at large, government involvement in early childhood development is greatly restricted. An example of a macrosystem issue is the public image of child care services—how the families who use the services are viewed and whether the staff is valued and respected or patronized and held in disdain.

The quality of services depends on the interactions of these four dynamic systems. The young child and her or his family are not isolated entities. The child brings the home to the early childhood setting and the ECEC program to the home.

Elements of Quality Environments

The quality of a program is critical in determining how developmentally beneficial it is to children. Research has identified a number of discrete elements of quality. Many of these indicators are interrelated, and their mutual impact ultimately affects the child's well-being.

Doherty has written extensively on elements of quality, synthesizing numerous studies conducted in Canada, the United States, Europe, and elsewhere—and identifying a common core of caregiver behaviours and program characteristics associated with positive outcomes for children in both the short and long term.

There are various ways of conceptualizing quality. Traditionally, when researchers focus on quality, they highlight three critical elements: the **adult:child ratio**, the number of children in a group, and the staff's professional education in child development. The experts have called this trio the "iron triangle" because these elements exert so much influence on quality, particularly when they are clustered together. For some time, they have been considered the foundations of quality ECEC programs.

In addition to the perspective of the experts in the field regarding quality, Katz (1992) encourages the point of view of children, parents, practitioners, and the community and society at large. The child's perspective derives from her or his actual experience. For example, does the child feel welcome and protected by adults and accepted by other children? Families may look at the extent to which the service meets their needs and priorities. Caregivers' definitions of quality may be influenced by their experiences and working conditions. Various communities have different perspectives. A quality early childhood development service may be one that reflects and supports the values, beliefs, and needs of the people served. Understanding and ensuring quality involves a continuous process of merging the perspectives of different stakeholders.

Researchers discuss the quality of early childhood settings in terms of structural quality and process quality. **Structural quality** generally refers to variables that can be regulated, including adult:child ratio, **group size**, and the education and training of the staff. Structural factors are concrete and relatively easy to assess objectively and accurately (this explains why structural components are typically found in provincial/territorial licensing regulations). Structural variables are so interconnected that to speak of them separately as unique contributors to overall development is difficult.

Process quality refers to relationships; the provision of **developmentally appropriate** activities; caregiver consistency; **parent involvement**; and warm, nurturing, sensitive caregiving. Process variables have a direct influence on children, but because they require interpretation by experts, these variables are more difficult to regulate. We may consider the example of caregiver consistency, which encourages the development of trust and provides an environment in which children feel free to explore; this approach supports learning. In this case, structural quality and process quality are related—and structural quality can be regulated. In another example, however, most people would agree that caregivers should be sensitive to the children in their care. But a process quality such as sensitivity is not easily measured: It is difficult to imagine how a director could, through either a hiring process or a performance appraisal, ascertain an individual's level of sensitivity. Research findings show, though, that practitioners with more years of formal education are more likely to offer high quality environments that provide better outcomes for children (Barnett 2003). Therefore, a requirement of more formal education is intended to ensure that practitioners are more likely to be sensitive.

While research has helped answer many questions, others remain unanswered. Those interested in the improvement of quality in early childhood development services must consider the setting's relationship with the external environment, and the exploration of this relationship needs to be placed on the research agenda.

Provincial/territorial licensing and regulatory systems that are well designed and effectively administered can help assure the provision of early childhood development programs that will nurture, protect, and educate young children. Regulation by itself does not ensure quality: it is designed to prevent programs from harming children rather than to promote programs that enhance development. Although regulation does not ensure quality, it is an important factor in safeguarding it.

The Child's Environment

ELEMENTS OF QUALITY ENVIRONMENTS FOR YOUNG CHILDREN

The Child's Environment

- adult:child ratio and group size
- curriculum
- physical environment
- relationships
- continuity of care
- cultural continuity

Adult:Child Ratio and Group Size   One of the strongest indicators of quality is the ratio of adults to children. Specifically the frequent supportive, individualized interactions between adult and child that are required to foster development in young children. An adult who is responsible for too many children can do little more than attend to their physical needs and safety. The caregiver is also likely to feel stressed in such situations, and this increases the probability of harshness and restrictiveness.

Optimal ratios vary with the age of the child and appear to be especially important for infants to children under the age of three. In this age group, ratios lower than one adult to four children have been observed to result in increases in child apathy and distress. For older children as well, the more children per adult, the more time staff must spend simply managing and controlling activities, and the less time they have to interact with the children.

In family child care environments, there is typically a range of ages and thus a wider range of developmental needs. The addition of two children of different ages can change the dynamics of the home. Howes and Norris (1997) found that when two school-age children were added to a family child care home, the providers had a more difficult time attending to the younger children.

Group size—the total number of children in a group—is typically considered in conjunction with adult:child ratios. For children older than the toddler stage but under age five, adult:child ratios may be less significant than group size (see Table 1–1). Where groups are smaller, caregivers spend more time interacting with the children and less time simply watching them. As well, because moderate-sized groups permit children to have a choice of playmates while protecting them from overstimulation, peer relationships may also be enhanced. In smaller groups, children are more verbal, more involved in activities, and less aggressive, and they make the greatest gains in standardized tests of learning and vocabulary.

Maximum group size should be determined by the distribution of ages within the group, the developmental needs of the children, the activity, and the **inclusion** of **children with special needs**. The group must be small enough to permit caregivers to facilitate both individual and group needs effectively. This will encourage the appropriate development of independence, self-assertion, problem-solving skills, co-operation, and friendliness. Health officials also recommend group-limiting strategies—that is, keeping small groups of children consistently together—to reduce the spread of infection.

TABLE 1–1   Staff:Child Ratios within Group Size

	Group Size									
	6	8	10	12	14	16	18	20	22	24
Age of children:*										
Infants (birth–12 months)	1:3	1:4								
Toddlers (12–24 months)	1:3	1:4	1:5	1:4						
Two-year-olds (24–36 months)		1:4	1:5	1:6**						
Two- and three-year-olds			1:5	1:6	1:7**					
Three-year-olds					1:7	1:8	1:9	1:10**		
Four-year-olds						1:8	1:9	1:10**		
Four- and five-year-olds						1:8	1:9	1:10**		
Five-year-olds						1:8	1:9	1:10		
Six- to eight-year-olds								1:10	1:11	1:12

* Multi-age grouping is both permissible and desirable. When no infants are included, the staff:child ratio and group size requirements shall be based on the age of the majority of the children in the group. When infants are included, ratios and group sizes for infants must be maintained.

** Smaller group sizes and higher staff:child ratios are optimal. Larger group sizes and lower staff:child ratios are acceptable only in cases where staff are highly qualified.

Source: Canadian Child Care Federation, *National Statement on Quality Child Care* (Ottawa: Canadian Child Care Federation, 1991).

Curriculum   In quality ECEC environments, caregivers with education in child development use their skills of observation and assessment to plan appropriate experiences to facilitate the development of the whole child. The term "curriculum" includes such items as program goals, planned activities, the daily schedule, and the availability of materials and equipment.

Children need choices and opportunities to explore their own interests. Practitioners who are guided by the principles of developmentally appropriate practice ensure that the curriculum enhances the development of the whole child in all developmental domains—including social, emotional, aesthetic, moral, language, cognitive, and physical—and that activities are individually, age-group, and culturally appropriate. Curriculum planning is based on a caregiver's observation of each child's special interests and developmental progress. Children need adequate amounts of uninterrupted time in which to pursue self-chosen tasks and activities.

Cultural relevancy must be an integral and continuous part of the program, which should reflect the diversity of the wider society in which the child lives. In an **anti-bias curriculum**, the early childhood practitioner models and conveys respect for differences and encourages children to recognize the many options open to them regardless of gender, age, ability, race, ethnicity, or culture. Children and their parents are encouraged to share aspects of their culture and lifestyle with the other children.

Different curriculum approaches emphasize different aspects of child development. In general, highly structured programs emphasizing cognitive and language development are particularly effective with children from disadvantaged backgrounds. In programs structured by adults, children show less independence and initiative, but do better on intelligence and achievement tests. In open, or **child-centred**, programs—which facilitate the selection of activities by the children themselves—children are observed to be more independent and persistent. Children in moderately structured programs appear to fare best overall, demonstrating gains in creativity and self-esteem as well as in cognition and achievement. Whatever the approach, a program's success is related to how clearly its philosophy is defined as discussed in chapter 4.

Physical Environment   Whether indoors or outdoors the environment needs to provide opportunities for exploration and learning. The nature of the physical environment affects both the level of involvement of children and the quality of interaction between adults and children. Children demonstrate more advanced cognitive skills and greater social competence in environments that are safe and orderly, contain a wide variety of stimulating material, and are organized into learning centres (Gestwicki 1999).

In examining the impact of the environment, practitioners must consider:

- indoor and outdoor space;
- overall size, design, and layout of space;
- availability of materials and equipment; and
- health and safety needs of the children.

Early childhood environments must ensure a minimum number of square metres per child. Studies have found that, as the number of children in a space increases, so do aggressiveness, destructiveness, and apathetic behaviour.

Equipment and materials are part of the environment. Equipment requirements are difficult to quantify, since many types of equipment contribute to the objectives of high quality programs. Equipment should be designed to develop skills in children of various ages. Materials should be available in sufficient quantities to allow choices by children and avoid unnecessary competition.

One of the most obvious environmental elements in quality ECEC programs is health and safety, including such factors as personal safety, the inclusion of nap/rest times, and nutritious meals and snacks. Health and safety are central aspects of government regulations, which specify such things as the number of fire exits, the presence of first aid kits, and staff health and safety training. Centre-based programs require regular fire and public health inspections as part of the licensing process. (See chapter 8, "Managing Safe and Healthy Learning Environments," for more information on this aspect of quality.)

Relationships   The most important factor in early childhood development programs is the relationships between the adults and the children. Keating and Mustard state, "The quality of the social environment in which children are brought up—especially through inter-

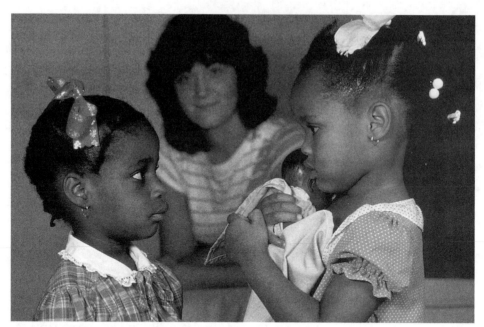

A stable relationship with the caregiver provides the child with a sense of security.

action with peers and adults—is a major influence in early life and therefore on competence and coping skills in later life" (Canada 1996b). Interactive forms of emotional communication are the key mechanisms of interpersonal relationships that help to shape the emotional and social development of the growing mind of a child (Siegel 1999).

Responsive care is the most important ingredient of healthy development and attachment. Adults who are sensitive and responsive excel at reading and understanding each child's verbal and behavioural cues and are able to anticipate children's needs. Optimal development is enhanced by relationships with adults who are positive, supportive, and individualized. Adults sustain developing independence by supporting children to do what they are capable of and want to do for themselves, helping only when needed.

Young children also develop through peer interaction. Here again, adult support and guidance are crucial. Caregivers support children's beginning friendships. The program should accommodate a variety of play levels where children play with and beside other children. Interactions between children and staff should provide opportunities for children to develop an understanding of self and others characterized by respect, affection, freedom from bias, and humour.

From a child's point of view, early childhood experiences are a joint enterprise of parents and caregivers. Studies that examine the joint effects of home and early childhood environments on child development have raised some concerns about caregiver/parent relations. For example, Galinsky (1988) found that some caregivers harbour negative attitudes about the families of children in their care, and that these attitudes vary with the caregiver's perceptions of the quality of parental child rearing, parents' education and marital status, and whether the family is using subsidized care. This research points to a need for further study in this area and indicates a need for additional caregiver education on how to accommodate a variety of parental needs.

Quality of interaction is affected by the ratio of adults to children, caregiver education, group and program size, and **continuity** of care (see below). In her summary of early childhood development research, Doherty suggests that ratio has a direct influence on the child's experience of caregiver responsiveness—or lack of it—and this ultimately affects the child's well-being and development. This aspect of a program can be assessed using an evaluation tool such as the Early Childhood Environment **Rating Scale** (Harms and Clifford 1998). (Caregiver characteristics that have an impact on the quality of interactions are discussed in chapter 7, "Promoting Professionalism.")

Continuity of Care   A secure attachment to a primary caregiver provides a child with the sense of security necessary to reach out and explore people and the environment. Such an attachment is based, in part, on the availability of a consistent caregiver who responds quickly, sensitively, and appropriately to the child's needs. It is recommended that the child remain with the same caregiver for the first 36 months of life. In a primary caregiving approach, babies interact with all adults in the environment but are assigned to a particular adult who meets most of their caregiving needs and serves as a primary contact for parents. In programs offering continuity of care, the caregiver moves up with the children, staying with the same group of children for two, and sometimes three, years. Lally (1995) advocates the development of policies and practices that keep children and caregivers together in familiar environments. This approach aids the child by providing a supportive emotional climate within which to work through the development of identity, rather than having to repeatedly form new relationships while at the same time trying to define self (Miller 1999). Job dissatisfaction stemming from low compensation and an undervaluing of work, which can lead to high staff turnover, is a deterrent to providing this continuity of care.

Cultural Continuity   Culture is a fundamental building block of identity, and a setting must be sensitive to the cultural backgrounds of families served. Early experiences should be in harmony with the culture of the home. Different cultures have unique ways of viewing the world, preferred ways of social organization, and unique language patterns, learning styles, and concepts of acceptable behaviour. To help make the program more familiar and meaningful to the child, whenever possible caregivers should incorporate practices from the child's home into the early childhood environment. Caregivers should represent as well as learn about the cultures of the families served, and the environment should include pictures and objects representing those cultures.

There are a number of resources designed to assist settings in developing culturally appropriate curricula. Bernhard et al. conducted research into practices, which is documented in *Paths to Equity: Cultural, Linguistic, and Racial Diversity in Canadian Early Childhood Education* (1995). Chud and Fahlman, in *Honouring Diversity with Child Care and Early Education* (1995), have collected materials for curricula in professional preparation programs.

The BC Aboriginal Child Care Society is developing standards for culturally responsive child care programs. Following is a selection from their draft standards, Elements of Quality Child Care from the Perspectives of Aboriginal Peoples in British Columbia:

> Keeping of Aboriginal Languages—These are key elements of our identity and heritage. The continuation and revival of Aboriginal languages are urgent priorities. Child care programs have a critical role to play in preventing further loss of Aboriginal languages.

Elder Involvement—A defining feature of Aboriginal cultures is the special respect given to elders. We look to our elders for guidance and we include them in important decision-making. We ask our elders to help us learn the traditional teachings of our cultures. Elders play valuable roles in our communities and we turn to them for their knowledge and wisdom. (BC Aboriginal Child Care Society 2004)

To create a program that is culturally and linguistically appropriate and incorporates the values and traditions of the Inuit community, the Avataq Cultural Institute in collaboration with Kativik Regional Government developed materials based in Inuit culture (Avataq Cultural Institute 2004). Wide consultation was held with the Inuit communities of Nunavik, and an elder leader was hired to provide elder guidance, expertise, and advice. Twenty-six story sets, including handcrafted dolls, videos, and materials, were created in order to promote Inuktitut language and Inuit culture through the use of timeless legends and stories of Inuit life. These materials support caregivers to provide geographically relevant and culturally and developmentally suitable curriculum in their work with young children in the Far North. These two aforementioned initiatives illustrate some of the work being done to support cultural continuity.

Caregiver Characteristics

ELEMENTS OF QUALITY ENVIRONMENTS FOR YOUNG CHILDREN
Caregiver Characteristics
* education and experience
* stability and job satisfaction

Education and Experience   The professional education of the staff is the factor that most positively affects the quality of early childhood development programs. Professional education includes pre-service and ongoing professional development, also called in-service training.

Research studies consistently report that caregivers with post-secondary education in early childhood development are more likely to be responsive, provide children with activities that are stimulating and developmentally appropriate, and support parents through the provision of child development information. These benefits of post-secondary education are found with family child care providers as well as centre staff (Kontos, Howes, and Galinsky 1996). Caregiver training in child development contributes to positive outcomes for children in areas such as social interaction with adults, the development of pro-social behaviours, and language and cognitive development. Appropriate education results in more social interaction between caregiver and children and, among children, more co-operation and task persistence and less apathetic, unengaged behaviour.

The amount of professional preparation, both pre-service and in-service, predicts program quality, which in turn is linked to positive child outcomes, especially in terms of language and representational skills—critical areas for later school success. Caregivers with more education have less authoritarian styles and more knowledge about child development. Access to good training is an important vehicle for creating a competent workforce.

In contrast, experience alone appears to bear little relationship to positive child outcomes. By itself, caregiver experience is not a predictor of effective caregiving, and in the absence of other factors, it has been linked to less cognitive and social stimulation among children and more apathy among infants.

Practitioners should have education in the requirements of children with special needs and an awareness of the social and political forces affecting ECEC programs. They must possess the knowledge, skill, and competency to interact sensitively and successfully not only with the children they care for, but also with families, co-workers, and community professionals.

Stability and Job Satisfaction   Highly qualified, competent practitioners are leaving the profession because they cannot afford to stay at their current wages. Staff who are paid better tend to stay longer in their jobs, forming consistent relationships with the children and fostering the emotional stability necessary for learning and growth. Caregiver continuity is particularly important for infants and toddlers, because they are in the process of forming attachment relationships. With caregiver turnover rates averaging 21.7% annually in Canada (Doherty 1999), with a high in Alberta of 44.8% and a low in Prince Edward Island of 15.5%, lack of caregiver continuity is a serious concern—and turnover is estimated to be even higher in family child care.

Stability is only one of several ways in which job satisfaction among caregivers results in better child behaviour and development. Studies indicate that salary is the best predictor of job satisfaction: higher salaries are associated with higher job commitment, and practitioners with higher salaries are more likely to view early childhood development as a viable career. Whitebrook, Howes, and Phillips (1990) also found that caregivers earning salaries at the higher end of the range worked in programs of better quality.

Caregivers who are satisfied with their jobs are more likely to provide encouragement and guidance to children. Caregivers who are dissatisfied tend to be harsher and more restrictive with children and less likely to provide activities that will support and encourage child development. Programs across Canada are struggling with staff recruitment and retention problems. In addition to low wages, a lack of opportunities for career growth is causing staff to leave the field to pursue opportunities outside child care (Doherty 2004). (Chapter 11, "Advocating for Canada's Children," discusses the need for concerted efforts by professional and advocacy groups to improve the salaries and working conditions as well as perceived public perception of caregivers.)

Contextual Factors

ELEMENTS OF QUALITY ENVIRONMENTS FOR YOUNG CHILDREN
Contextual Factors
- infrastructure
- director's administrative style
- wages
- working conditions
- auspice
- government regulation and funding
- relationships with the external environment
- family involvement

"Contextual factors" are variables outside the family child care home or early childhood development program that influence quality. The following contextual factors associated with quality have been researched: infrastructure, auspice, and government regulation and funding.

Canadian ECEC programs are heavily dependent on parent fees for revenue. Caring for young children is a labour-intensive service, with cost depending on the staff:child ratio and the wages and benefits paid to the staff. Research has demonstrated that caregiver salary levels influence the way caregivers behave with a child. Thus, quality requires favourable ratios and group sizes, adequate supplies of appropriate equipment and materials—and reasonable compensation. All of these require adequate funding. Government funding over and above fee subsidy assists programs by providing additional operating funds. Research findings indicate that funding over and above fee subsidization, such as salary grants, is a valuable means of encouraging quality.

Infrastructure   The infrastructure of an early childhood development program plays a key role in quality. There are three major infrastructure elements at work:

- *The director's administrative style and the **organizational climate** of the program, family child care agency, or home.* Directors who have higher education levels are better able to provide curriculum and pedagogical leadership to staff. Equally importantly, they need to provide good human resource practices to retain staff (Beach et al. 2004).

- *Wages.* Staff salary levels are the best predictor of the quality of the early childhood development program (Doherty 1999).

- *Working conditions.* When working conditions meet staff needs (such as paid preparation time, opportunities for professional development, and high adult:child ratios), staff are more likely to be satisfied with their jobs, their interactions with the children tend to be warmer and more supportive, and program quality is likely to be higher (Doherty 1999; Berk 1985).

Auspice   The term "**auspice**" is used to describe the sponsor of an early childhood development service, or the type of organizational structure under which a service is operated and/or licensed. In Canada, ECEC services operate under the auspices of non-profit or for-profit organizations and corporations, municipalities, or schools. A parent group, an organization such as the YMCA/YWCA, a voluntary board of directors, a municipal government, or a First Nations band may sponsor non-profit programs. The for-profit, or commercial, category includes unincorporated owner-operators of one or two programs and centres or homes that are part of a local system with two or more settings. The availability of each type of program varies widely across the country.

High quality ECEC programs are more likely to be found under non-profit than commercial auspices (Doherty 1999). Practitioners in non-profit centres generally have higher levels of formal education and more specialized training in child development, and non-profit settings usually have better staff:child ratios and caregiver consistency. This is not to deny the existence of high quality for-profit programs—or of poor-quality non-profit programs.

The differences between the for-profit and non-profit categories may, in part, be the result of the absence of direct government grants to commercial programs (Doherty 1999). Public funding for for-profit child care has been controversial in Canada for many years. However, the issue of auspice is more complex than has often been portrayed. The differences in the sectors suggests that various factors are at work and that quality depends upon more than a program's auspice.

Government Regulations and Funding   The establishment and enforcement of standards is part of the administration of an ECEC service. In Canada, provincial/territorial govern-ments regulate ECEC programs—both those delivered by voluntary organizations and those run by commercial operators—by establishing standards that must be met in order to obtain a licence to operate. **Family child care providers** can operate without a licence pro-vided they do not provide care to more children than the number specified in their province's legislation. The level of regulatory requirements exerts an influence on quality. Regulation can encourage quality by setting standards for structural elements, but it can only be effec-tive when there is both adequate monitoring for compliance and strict enforcement of the required standards. Licensing requirements are minimal and measurable. Programs can move to higher voluntary standards and gain professional recognition.

The level of a program's operating budget has an influence on quality. *You Bet I Care! A Canada-Wide Study on Wages, Working Conditions, and Practices in Child Care Centres* affirmed the substantial reliance by ECEC programs on parent fees for revenue (Doherty et al. 2000a). Yet fees must be kept affordable, so that enough parents can have the means to pay for them. When government funding over and above fee subsidization is available, programs can pay higher wages and thereby attract and keep staff with higher levels of education, and an increase is seen not only in structural quality but in process quality as well (Doherty 1999).

Community Relationships   Any effort to improve the quality of early childhood devel-opment programs needs to direct some attention to developing and maintaining good relationships with external parties. ECEC programs benefit from cultivating relationships with community members such as health care professionals, legislators, bankers, licensing officers, elected officials, community leaders, and others. Communities offer an array of resources to the programs and the families they serve.

WHEN ECEC PROGRAMS AND COMMUNITIES WORK TOGETHER

- Families can access community resources more easily.
- Programs can distribute information regarding cultural, recreational, academic, health, social, and other resources that serve families.
- Employers can be encouraged to adopt policies and practices that promote and support families.
- Programs can involve community members as volunteers.
- Programs can collaborate with community agencies to provide family support services.
- Staff members can be more informed about the resources available in the community and strategies for using these resources.
  Community interaction should include:
  - awareness and appropriate use of community resources;
  - communication and interaction with elementary schools;
  - sensitivity to changing community needs; and
  - co-operative projects within the community, such as multi-generational projects and public education endeavours.

Family Involvement   With significant numbers of children spending many hours each day in early childhood settings, caregivers and parents, more than ever before, are partners in many aspects of child rearing and socialization. Children benefit when parents and staff share a common commitment to acting in the best interests of children, communicate openly, and have mutual respect; in particular, open and regular communication between caregivers and families has a very significant impact on positive outcomes for children (Wilson 2005). For example, when parents and staff communicate about child rearing practices such as discipline and routines, potential conflicts and confusion for the children are minimized, and some cultural continuity can be achieved.

Family involvement in early childhood development programs can range from a simple newsletter for parents to active partnerships between parents and staff. Outcomes for children are optimized when the parent is observant and has become informed, perhaps by serving as a member of the program's board of directors or advisory group or by participating in the evaluation of the program. (Chapter 9, "Building the Partnership with Families," provides more examples of how to achieve family centred programs.)

Cost of Quality

Quality programs are minimally more expensive than poor ones. One American study, *Cost, Quality, and Child Outcomes in Child Care Centres* (Hepburn et al. 1995), found that, while only one in seven of the programs assessed provided care of a quality that promotes healthy

Children's experiences are enhanced by family involvement in early childhood development programs.

development and learning, better quality services cost, on average, just 10% more than mediocre care. States with less stringent regulations had more programs of poor quality. These findings suggest that modest investments, combined with reasonable regulation, could significantly improve the efficacy of early childhood intervention.

This study also confirmed that programs paying higher wages attract better quality staff. Variations in program quality corresponded to wage levels and the practitioners' level of education and specialized training. Parents were not generally found to be good judges of quality, tending to overestimate the quality of care their children were receiving.

Ongoing Program Evaluation and Change

If quality is to be attained, monitoring and assessment are required. Monitoring is the process of identifying what is really happening for children, parents, and staff. A systematic approach is needed. There are a number of ways to systematically monitor what is going on at a program, including observation and asking parents, staff, and children about their experiences. Directors will want to create a culture where there is ongoing monitoring of program outcomes experienced by children and parents. As well, there should be regular evaluation of the program's purpose, philosophy, goals, and objectives. (Program evaluation, including sample tools, is discussed further in chapter 4, "Planning and Evaluating the Program Goals.")

The mechanisms that can be used to maintain quality fall into three general categories:

- regulatory methods
- voluntary standards
- other non-regulatory methods

Any effort to assure quality in early childhood development programs must begin with an effective licensing and regulatory system. Licensing provides the necessary foundation upon which all other efforts can build. Provincial/territorial government licensing requirements tend to address solely structural indicators, such as staff:child ratios, even though process dimensions may be more indicative of quality. Nonetheless, research indicates that regulatory requirements increase the probability that all children in licensed settings will receive a higher quality of care (Doherty 1999).

Quality levels higher than the minimum licensing standards can be established by professional organizations or funding agencies. Professional bodies may require that individual staff members meet certain educational levels. Or such standards may be made a condition of funding. A funding agency can define the level of quality it is prepared to purchase. For example, a municipal government may require a program in which it is purchasing subsidy spaces to meet higher standards than those set by the provincial government. These additional standards will, in effect, raise the quality of the service. The Canadian Child Care Federation developed both program and Occupational Standards for Child Care Practitioners (Doherty 2003) identifying nine standards, accompanying skills and abilities, and the core knowledge needed for competent practice. Examples of these program and occupational standards (such as the Standards for Communications, below) are featured throughout this book.

COMMUNICATIONS—DIRECTORS

The director communicates positively and effectively with a broad range of stakeholders in a way that enables them to articulate their needs and furthers the objectives of the program and the quality of its services. The director is able to:

- understand and communicate the roles of the governing body and herself, and act accordingly;

- act as a liaison between the governing body, practitioners, and support staff;

- solicit input from families and the community about needs;

- clearly convey the governing body's philosophy, policies, and procedures to families, practitioners, and support staff;

- work with practitioners and support staff to develop and implement policies, procedures, and strategies that provide the families of the children with clear and timely information, help them express their needs, assist them in obtaining a fee subsidy, and enable them to have meaningful input into program and policy development;

- work with practitioners and support staff to develop and implement user-friendly communication mechanisms that provide information to families;

- provide accurate and timely information about the program to other organizations in the community and facilitate inter-organizational communication;

- develop and maintain ongoing communication and co-operative working relationships with other services for children and families;

- remain aware of the availability of the services of other organizations and access them as required;

- liaise with licensing officials and develop and implement procedures for reporting licensing-related issues promptly and appropriately;

- work co-operatively with early childhood training institutions and be involved with practicum placements; facilitate the learning opportunities provided to the students; and

- provide information to the general public in order to increase general awareness about the work of the program and the role of caregivers.

Source: Gillian Doherty, in Canadian Child Care Federation (CCCF), *Partners in Quality: Tools for Practitioners in Child Care Settings* (Ottawa: CCCF, 2000).

Accreditation of programs is a type of quality control by which a representative body, recognized by both service providers and the ECEC community in general establishes standards for service that are above the basic requirements of government. Unlike licensing, accreditation is owned and administered by the profession. Programs apply on a voluntary basis for evaluation against these standards and, if found to meet or surpass them, are granted accreditation status. An outside professional verifies, or validates, the accuracy and completeness of program documents submitted as part of the accreditation process. Although accreditation is usually a voluntary process, it can be required of a program by funding bodies. This trend is occurring in some US states, such as Oklahoma, which provides additional funding to those programs operating at higher standards than those outlined by the National Association for the Education of Young Children (NAEYC).

The second method used to improve program quality is credentialling, or **certification**, of qualified individuals. For an individual to become a competent practitioner, specialized training in early childhood development is essential. To gain certification, practitioners must complete specific training programs and demonstrate specific competencies in working with children. Certification of Early Childhood Education (ECE) program graduates can provide assurance that the individual is able to translate theory into good practice. Two provinces—Alberta and Newfoundland and Labrador—have mandatory certification under regulation and two others—Ontario and Nova Scotia—provide voluntary certification for members of professional organizations. Some certification programs require a certain amount of professional development to be completed in order to renew certification. For example in Newfoundland and Labrador, a practitioner must complete 30 hours of professional development in a three year period. (Accreditation and certification are elaborated on in chapter 7, "Promoting Professionalism.")

There are a variety of initiatives underway to improve the quality of programs through the work of professional organizations and increased government funding.

Summary

Children are not aware that early childhood settings vary in form, function, auspice, or regulatory environment. What makes a difference for them is the quality of their relationships with caregivers and peers. High quality early childhood development services for Canadian children and their families depend upon the co-operation and support of all segments of the community.

More and more, policy makers and the general public understand that the achievement of optimal overall development for all children is beneficial not only to children and their families but also to society as a whole. It should be gratifying to caregivers that many of the principles of developmentally appropriate practice have been confirmed in brain research studies, which are read and heard about with great interest by the general public.

Policy makers move only within the limits of what they believe public attitudes to be. Public perceptions are cultural patterns, part of the macrosystem that defines what is possible. In order to achieve quality in ECEC settings for all Canadian children and their families, continued changes in attitudes are needed. An increased valuation of women's work in the home and the work of stay-at-home parents, an increase in the wages of ECEC practitioners so that their pay is commensurate with their knowledge and skills, and a change in the common assumption that women (rather than both parents) should expect to be the primary caregivers of their children are all needed. Many beliefs about motherhood, women's roles, the nature of families, and caregiving need to be revisited, since they impede the process of redistributing the costs of quality early childhood education into the public realm.

Key Terms and Concepts

Accreditation,   p. 20

Adult:child ratio,   p. 8

Anti-bias curriculum,   p. 11

Auspice,   p. 16

Certification,   p. 21

Children with special needs,   p. 10

Continuity,   p. 13

Developmentally appropriate,   p. 8

Early childhood education and care, p. 1

Early childhood setting,   p. 2

Ecological model,   p. 6

Exosystem,   p. 7

Group size,   p. 8

Inclusion,   p. 10

Macrosystem,   p. 7

Mesosystem,   p. 7

Microsystem,   p. 7

Organizational climate,   p. 16

Parent,   p. 1

Parent involvement,   p. 8

Process quality,   p. 8

Rating scale,   p. 13

Standards,   p. 4

Structural quality,   p. 8

Activities

1. Identify barriers to providing quality early childhood development services.
2. In small groups, identify and discuss indicators of high quality early childhood settings from one of the following perspectives: families, staff, community professionals.
3. How would you describe the quality of Canada's child care? Cite sources to support your point of view.
4. Assess the quality of an early childhood setting using one of the following tools:
   - Early Childhood Environment Rating Scale (Harms and Clifford 1998)
   - Family Home Day Care Environment Rating Scale (Harms and Clifford 1989b)
   - Early Childhood Work Environment Survey (Jorde Bloom, Sheerer, and Britz 1991).
5. Choose an aspect of your field placement site where you think quality could be improved. Identify a strategy and, if possible, implement it.

Recommended Reading

Beach, J., Bertrand, J., Forer, B., Michal, D., and Tougas, J. *Working for Change: Canada's Child Care Workforce*. Labour Market Update Study, Child Care Human Resources Council, Ottawa, 2004.

Doherty, G. "Elements of Quality." In *Research Connections Canada*. Vol. 1. Ottawa: Canadian Child Care Federation, 1999.

National Association for the Education of Young Children. *Accreditation Criteria and Procedures of the National Academy of Early Childhood Programs.* Rev. ed. Washington, DC: National Association for the Education of Young Children, 1998.

Organisation for Economic Co-operation and Development (OECD). *Early Childhood Education and Care Policy: Canada, Country Note.* OECD Directorate for Education, 2004.

Penn, H. "How Do Children Learn: Early Childhood in a Global Context." In H. Penn, ed., *Early Childhood Services: Theory, Policy, and Practice.* Buckingham, UK: Open University Press, 2000.

Weblinks

www.triangle.co.uk/ciec
Contemporary Issues in Early Childhood
This site includes online opportunities for discussion of articles in *Contemporary Issues in Early Childhood,* an online, fully refereed journal that provides a forum for researchers and practitioners to explore innovative approaches in their work with families and young children.

www.zerotothree.org
Zero to Three
This site offers a rich array of resources for parents and professionals, including information on brain development, a glossary, and tips. *Zero to Three* promotes the healthy development of infants and toddlers by supporting and strengthening families, communities, and those who work on their behalf. It is dedicated to advancing current knowledge; promoting beneficial policies and practices and community resources; and providing training, technical assistance, and leadership development.

www.accel-capea.ca
Aboriginal Children's Circle of Early Learning
This is a new clearinghouse of information relating to Aboriginal ECEC. The site includes a bulletin board, a calendar of events, a database of research, best practices, and links to training and mentorship opportunities. This website is a partnership of First Nations Child and Family Caring Society of Canada and the Canadian Child Care Federation.

www.worldbank.org/children
The World Bank
This site has a section on early childhood development programs that provides synopses of programs around the world, publications, definitions, and links to regional chapters.

chapter 2

Roles of Government

Objectives

- **Examine the functions of the various levels of government.**
- **Review social policy for children and families.**
- **Outline the roles of provinces and territories in licensing and regulation.**
- **Describe policy milestones.**

It is important for practitioners to have an understanding of the foundations of social policy and its implications for Canadian children and families. As well, practitioners should be knowledgeable about the ever changing roles of government and familiar with licensing procedures and other regulations pertaining to the provision of services for young children. Regulations and program policies guide and facilitate the functioning of ECEC programs— and affect its children, families, staff, and operator (the owner or board of directors). Regulations pertain to many early childhood issues. And many of these issues bring us face to face with the basic problems of the lack of quality systems and the difficulty of getting the public support and funding necessary for attaining quality.

Demographics and Societal Trends in Canada

In Canada, government funding priorities and policy heavily affect the provision and quality of early childhood development programs. In the past decade Canada has undergone enormous social and economic transformation, and to meet the new challenges and needs of Canadian families, many social policies and programs have been adapted. Each level of government plays its own role in meeting the needs of children and families. Governments express their priorities through funding allocations, such as federal–provincial transfer payments, income tax deductions, direct operating grants, and family child care subsidies. Although our governments are required to respond to the needs of society within a constitutionally and legally defined framework, each administration acts on its own political objectives as it collects and spends tax revenue.

In Canada, the federal government influences the development of health, education, and social programs through the application of its spending powers; however health, education, social services, and the regulation and funding of services to young children are the direct responsibility of the provincial and territorial governments. There are specific populations that the federal government is directly responsible for, such as Aboriginal people, military families, and new immigrants and refugees. Municipal governments enforce local bylaws that set standards in areas such as zoning, building and fire codes, and public health regulations. A few municipalities, primarily in Ontario, have a role in the allocation of subsidized child care spaces, and some directly operate ECEC services or are involved in the supervision of programs.

Caring for Children—A National Issue

Early childhood development programs play a role in meeting a broad range of national policy objectives. These include promoting the optimal development of all children, reducing child poverty by enabling parents to enter the workforce, supporting the effectiveness of the current workforce, promoting women's economic and social equality, and promoting social cohesion.

Canada has always been divided by regional and cultural issues and finding consensus on social policies continues to be a challenge. Canadians worry that the implications of social changes such as family breakdown, lack of job security, and global competition—for the security of their families and their children's futures—have not yet been considered seriously enough.

Our economy has seen a shift away from predominantly full-time jobs lasting an entire working life toward more contract and part-time work, more self-employment, frequent job changes, and an increased demand for retraining. These changes have been particularly difficult for already vulnerable low-income families: the number of low-income families with full-time employment declined between 1984 and 1996 (Canada 1999a). In fact, Canada has one in four workers employed in low wage jobs, making less than ten dollars per hour! Overrepresented among those who are living on low incomes are lone parent families, First Nations families, recent immigrant families, and families led by persons with disabilities.

Non-familial child care has increasingly become the norm and an integral part of Canadian childhood. With women's increased participation in the paid labour market and the increased mobility of Canadians, women's unpaid care of children, by mothers or female relatives, has declined. In fact, in the last decade of the twentieth century, almost 77% of Canadian mothers with children under age six were in the paid labour force (Canada 2002). Early childhood development services are especially critical during the preschool years, when fundamental social, intellectual, and physical development takes place. The vast majority of mothers return to the labour force soon after childbirth. Two factors—economic class and the receipt of maternity benefits—were found to be strong predictors of a mother's early return to work after childbirth (Canada 2000b). For example, mothers who did not receive maternity benefits were six times more likely to return to work by the end of their child's first month than were those who received benefits.

Parents who are not studying or employed also use non-familial care services. For instance, 42% of children under age six with a stay-at-home parent spend some time each week in an early childhood development program other than kindergarten (Lero 1994).

ECEC programs are increasingly a central influence in the development of Canadian children and are likely to remain that way.

The past two decades have brought sharp growth in the employment rate of women with children. In 2001, 77% of all women with children less than 16 years old were part of the employed workforce, up from 39% in 1976 (Canada 2002). Increases in the employment levels of women with very young children have been particularly dramatic. By 2001, 62% of women with children less than three years old were employed, more than double the figure in 1976. Of the children who were not in care, almost 40% (1 million) had spent time in an early childhood setting at some point in the past (Canada 2002).

Consequently, government policy with respect to the early years has become a matter of increasing public concern. Over the past few years children and families have come to be a key focus of public policy and to occupy a prominent place in social policy deliberations. Ottawa and the provinces have actively sought to improve the circumstances of vulnerable children. Numerous programs have been established at both levels of government, and existing ones have been reformed. The 2003 Campaign 2000 Report Card found that government investments in child benefits are beginning to pay off (Campaign 2000 2003b).

Most Canadians want their children to have a strong start in life. The rate of child poverty in Canada is up for the first time since 1996 and one child in six continues to live in poverty (Campaign 2000 2004). Participation in high quality early childhood development experiences enhances children's language and social development and their chance of school success. The quality of a child's early childhood experiences is the strongest predictor of success when that child enters the school system. High quality programs have been shown to lower the rate of school drop out and school failure, reduce the need to admit children into special education programs, lower juvenile delinquency rates, and increase the detection and treatment of health problems. Recent research suggests that 75% of the brain's development occurs after birth (Ontario 1999). The early years set the foundation for a child's ability to trust, to learn, and to develop the abilities needed to continue learning for a lifetime. Quality early childhood development services have the potential to support all families by providing enriching child development while enabling parents to attend school, job training, and work. Yet progress on making these services more widely available and affordable has been quite limited.

Due to the enormous changes in family structure and the dramatic increase in the employment of mothers, families and children have a greater need for early childhood care and education programs than ever before.

According to the report *Preschool Children: Promises to Keep* (Canada 1999c), 71% of all Canadian mothers have paid jobs by the time their youngest child reaches the age of six. For women who are single parents—a social group whose numbers have greatly increased over the past 25 years—the availability of child care often makes the difference between independence and welfare. Canada lags far behind other industrialized nations in ensuring that all children have access to quality ECEC programs. Very little regulated care exists in Canada. In 2001, there were only 593 430 regulated child care spaces (including part- and full-time care) nationwide; the majority of these licensed spaces were in centres (506 096) (Friendly, Beach and Turiano 2002).

Regulated child care has been losing ground. Although the number of regulated spaces grew, most of this increase was in Quebec, which has 40% of regulated childcare and 23% of the total child population (Friendly, Beach and Turiano 2002). This situation will likely change with the new federal government initiative to expand regulated child care.

The unavailability and expense of child care causes stress among working parents. Many parents cannot afford the fees that regulated services must charge in order to survive.

The number of child care fee subsidies far from meets the need. The proportion of children in regulated child care who receive subsidy was 36% in 2001, suggesting that access to licensed services is limited for low-income families. Today, less than one in three of the children using the regulated system have a fee subsidy (Campaign 2000 2003a). Many parents who might prefer to use regulated services are left to make other arrangements.

Most parents rely on informal, unregulated, and frequently unreliable care by family members or neighbours. Exact figures for those in unregulated care are difficult to obtain. Friendly, Beach, and Turiano (2002) reported there are 3 309 000 children between newborn and 12 years with mothers in the paid labour force. Table 2–1 shows that the number of regulated child care spaces in Canada at the end of 2001 totalled just 593 430, suggesting that over 2 700 000 children are in unregulated care.

Policy research shows that the recognition of high quality ECEC for children and families is well entrenched in other countries. In Belgium and France, 95% of children aged three to school-age are enrolled in publicly financed programs (OECD 2001). European nations publicly fund blended early childhood development services. France, Denmark, Sweden, Italy, Spain, Belgium, Finland, and others provide services for all children over the age of two-and-a-half years plus fairly broad coverage for infants and toddlers. The services operate within the context of a family policy that includes well-paid maternity and paternity leaves, generous child benefits, and comprehensive children's health services (OECD 2001).

TABLE 2–1	Comparison of Regulated Child Care Spaces, Provinces and Territories, 2001
Province/Territory	**Number of Spaces**
Newfoundland	4 226
Prince Edward Island	4 270
Nova Scotia	11 464
New Brunswick	11 086
Quebec[1]	234 905
Ontario	173 135
Manitoba	23 022
Saskatchewan	7 166
Alberta[2]	47 693
British Columbia	72 949
Northwest Territories	1 234
Yukon	1 348
Nunavut	932
National Totals	**593 430**

[1] Quebec's figures include school-age spaces under the Ministry of Education.

[2] Regulation is not required for school-age care in Alberta and is not included.

Source: M. Friendly, J. Beach, and M. Turiano, *Early Childhood Education and Care in Canada: Provinces and Territories, 2001* (Toronto: Childcare Resource and Research Unit, Centre for Urban and Community Studies, University of Toronto, 2002). Statistics reprinted by permission.

Canada's Commitment to Children

Canada needs to embrace the overarching concept that informs much of the policy making in Europe—that children are citizens with rights and that, as citizens, they have a claim to a fair and equal share of society's resources. This premise implies that children are of value in the present, as well as for what they may become in later years (better students or better employees, or less likely to be involved in criminal behaviour).

When it ratified the **United Nations Convention on the Rights of the Child** in 1991, Canada accepted this principle. It recognized that children, by virtue of being human, have rights. These rights include civil and political rights as well as economic, social, and cultural ones. The specific rights are often summarized and grouped as the "three *p*s": provision, protection, and participation. *Provision* means children have the right to possess, receive, or have access to certain things and services, including life, early childhood development services, health care, an adequate standard of living, education to develop to their fullest potential, and rehabilitative care. Under *participation,* children have the right to participate in society and in decisions affecting their lives, including "the right to express their views in matters affecting themselves." Included in *protection* is the right of children to be shielded from harmful practices and acts—such as discrimination or separation from parents—and the right to special protection if they are without a family. In addition, by virtue of being young and vulnerable, children have some special rights—to protection from harm, to promotion of their growth and development, and to participation in decisions affecting them according to their age and maturity. The Convention acknowledges the central role of families in safeguarding these rights and reinforces the state's obligation to help families meet the basic needs of their children.

As a signatory to the Convention, Canada needs to do a much better job of fulfilling children's rights and assuring them "a standard of living adequate for physical, spiritual, moral, and social development." Many nations fare better than Canada in tackling child poverty and mitigating the negative impact of unemployment and poor wages through substantial investments in comprehensive family policies that include income security for families, affordable housing, ECEC programs, and other forms of assistance (Campaign 2000 2003a).

The UN report *The State of the World's Children 2000* called child care "a moral imperative" and "sound economic service." The report stated that the reason many countries have not yet invested in early childhood development is that it holds no short-term political gain (UNICEF 2000). In Canada, health, education, and social services—the areas in which policies and practices most strongly shape the conditions of childhood—all fall under provincial jurisdiction. However, some decisions made at the federal level, such as taxation and child benefits, have a direct impact on children.

The Canadian Child Care Federation devoted its seventh volume of *Research Connections Canada* to the United Nations Convention on the Rights of the Child, creating a valuable resource on this topic. For more information on the Convention, visit the Canadian Coalition on the Rights of Children website at www.rightsofchildren.ca.

Role of the Federal Government

Canada is governed by a federal system that is key to how responsibilities for ECEC are defined. The Canadian Constitution confers legislative and executive powers on two levels of government—the federal government and the provinces/territories. Each level is

There have been many improvements in caring for children since this 1903 program.
Photo: Courtesy of the Toronto Reference Library, Baldwin Room, T11849.

independent, or sovereign, in its respective areas of responsibility. The 1867 *British North America Act* defines the federal and provincial/territorial responsibilities.

Canada's Constitution specifies that the federal government does not have direct jurisdiction over education, health, or social welfare. These are the responsibilities of the provinces and territories. Consequently, the federal government does not have the power to enact an early childhood development program without the agreement of the provinces. The functions of the federal and provincial governments with respect to ECEC programs are complex and interrelated. Many issues relating to family policy fall under provincial jurisdiction. While divorce law is federal, marriage laws and the enforcement of child support are under provincial jurisdiction. ECEC programs fall under provincial jurisdiction, although they receive substantial funds from the federal government. The federal government provides maternity and parental leave benefits, but for most Canadian employees, leave from employment is governed by provincial legislation. There is no federal role in public education, including kindergarten. The federal government does not pay for education and there is no national department of education.

With respect to supporting children, the federal government traces its role to the introduction of a tax exemption in 1918 (Canada 1994a). The 1942 Dominion-Provincial Agreement for Wartime Day Nurseries initiated a fifty-fifty federal–provincial cost sharing arrangement. After the Second World War, with the introduction of the universal Family Allowance Program, federal involvement was expanded. Subsequently, the influence of the federal government became primarily financial, through cost sharing payments it made to provincial government budgets for child care and related services.

In 1966, with the Canada Assistance Plan (CAP), the federal government made provision to share the cost of child care for low-income families. This program was cancelled in 1995. Today, early childhood development services are funded through a patchwork approach combining parent fees and funding from various levels of government (for more details on parent fees, see chapter 10, "Financial Matters"). In 1994, the Liberal government in Ottawa began a process of reforming Canada's system of social security. Because it provided working parents with the assurance of care for their children and thus provided critical support for employment, child care was seen as part of this agenda. In 1999 the most important federal–provincial arrangement for ECEC was created: the Social Union Framework Agreement (SUFA). The National Children's Agenda (NCA) is SUFA's primary activity consisting of a broad vision statement. This was followed by the Early Childhood Development Agreement in 2000 and the Multi-Lateral Agreement in 2003.

A National Policy for Children and Families

Government policy defines a broad vision that provides a framework for operational decisions. Policy addresses key issues such as *who* is responsible for programs for children, *what* types of programs should be provided, and *how* these programs should be delivered. At the heart of these discussions is the question of whether early childhood education and care should be a public or a private, family responsibility. A recent poll released by the Canadian Child Care Federation and the Child Care Advocacy Association of Canada showed an overwhelming majority of Canadians believe that child care is too expensive and not accessible enough to all children. Over 90% of the public wants "government to do more to ensure that all Canadians have access to quality child care" (CCCF and CCAAC 2003). These attitudes toward early childhood development are becoming more consistent with beliefs about public education for children aged 6 to 18. Beginning in the nineteenth century, the policy of providing education for all Canadian children transformed attitudes about public education, which became recognized as a right of all children.

Today, Canadians are generally supportive of children and families. The welfare of children is consistently rated a strong priority relative to other major issues such as taxation, the federal debt, and economic competitiveness. It is generally acknowledged that the impact of childhood experiences lasts for a lifetime and that the government has a critical role to play in providing services and programs that support children and families. This public opinion shift is a critical factor in moving governments toward making significant investments in early childhood development programs.

Canada Health and Social Transfer

In the 1995 federal budget, the Minister of Finance announced that cost sharing with the provinces and territories for welfare and social services (including child care) under the Canada Assistance Plan (CAP), and for health and post-secondary education expenditures would be rolled into a single block fund called the Canada Health and Social Transfer (CHST). According to Finance Canada, this move continues "the evolution away from cost sharing in areas of provincial responsibility, which had been a source of entanglement and irritation in federal–provincial relations" (Canada 1995). In 2004, the CHST was replaced by two new funds—health and social. The Canada Social Transfer combines post-secondary education and social transfers, which includes ECEC programs. Some feel this split recognizes the distinct needs of these areas from health.

Social Union Framework Agreement (SUFA)

The Social Union Framework Agreement (1999) is the most important intergovernmental agreement for ECEC. SUFA sets out how joint social programs will be constructed or modified. One key principle is ensuring access for all Canadians to essential social programs and to services of reasonably comparable quality. SUFA commits both levels of government to working in collaboration and to accountability. The federal government agreed not to introduce new social programs in areas of provincial jurisdiction without the agreement of the majority of provinces. The National Children's Agenda (NCA) has been SUFA's primary activity.

SOCIAL UNION FRAMEWORK AGREEMENT

- Promoting equity, respect, and equality of opportunity.
- Guaranteeing access to reasonably comparable services for all Canadians.
- Helping those in need.
- Promoting the active participation of all Canadians in social and economic life.
- Respecting the five principles of medicare.
- Ensuring adequate, stable, and sustainable funding for social programs.
- Respecting Aboriginal treaty and other rights.
- Ensuring Canadians have meaningful input into social policies and programs.

The pan-Canadian legislation permitted under SUFA enables the federal government to establish national standards for ECEC programs, as these would be consistent with SUFA's statement that Canadians would have access to comparable programs wherever they live. In the document *From Patchwork to Framework: A Child Care Strategy for Canada* (2004) the Child Care Advocacy Association of Canada details a list of recommendations encouraging the federal government to develop and enact legislation and supporting agreements to provide a legislative definition of child care and to identify service entitlements and standards. For example, it addresses the issue of universal entitlement—that every child in Canada is entitled to high quality child care services regardless of their abilities; economic, cultural, or linguistic circumstances; geographic location; or parents' work status.

National Children's Agenda

In January 1997, the federal, provincial, and territorial governments agreed to work together to develop the National Children's Agenda (NCA), a comprehensive strategy to improve the well-being of Canada's children. The NCA is not only intergovernmental, but also cross-sectoral, involving health, social services, justice, and education representatives.

After several years of dialogue about a National Children's Agenda, the **First Ministers** of the provinces and territories agreed to work together to promote healthy pregnancy, birth, and infancy; improve parenting and family supports; strengthen early childhood development, learning, and care; and strengthen community supports. A number of federal

---

NATIONAL CHILDREN'S AGENDA (NCA)

Objectives for Canada's children:

- physical and emotional health
- safety and security
- success at learning
- social engagement and responsibility

---

programs have been initiated under the umbrella of the NCA, including the National Child Benefit, extended parental leave under Employment Insurance, expanded Aboriginal Head Start programs, and the Centres of Excellence for Children's Well-Being.

The Government of Quebec agreed with the objectives of the NCA; however, it did not participate, as it wishes to assume full control over programs aimed at children and families. Furthermore, Quebec did not sign the Social Union Framework Agreement (SUFA), the objective of which is to reform and renew Canada's system of social services through partnerships between the federal and provincial/territorial governments. Thus, any references made here to joint federal–provincial/territorial positions do not include Quebec.

Early Childhood Development Accord

In September 2001, the Government of Canada announced an investment of $2.2 billion in early childhood development (ECD) over five years through the Canada Health and Social Transfer agreement with the provinces. The First Ministers pledged that "every child should be valued and have opportunities to develop her or his unique physical, emotional, intellectual, spiritual and creative potential" (Canada 2001b). Under the ECD Accord, provincial and territorial governments, with the exception of Quebec, will carry out the four priority areas.

EARLY CHILDHOOD DEVELOPMENT ACCORD

Objectives

1. Promote healthy pregnancy, birth, and infancy.
2. Improve parenting and family supports.
3. Strengthen early childhood development, learning, and care.
4. Strengthen community supports.

Within this agreement, each provincial and territorial government will tailor its early childhood development services to meet the unique local needs of children and families. For Canadian families, these investments are meant to provide for improved access to services such as prenatal classes and screening, early childhood development programs (including child care), and parent information and family support. Governments are obliged to be accountable through annual public reports on results based on specific outcome indicators of child well-being. The federal government also has a special responsibility to Aboriginal children under its fiduciary responsibility for First Nations people. Consequently, it is committed to improving and expanding early childhood development programs and services for First Nations children.

The 2001 federal budget extended maternity and parental benefits under Employment Insurance from six months to one year. More action is still needed to raise the levels of the benefits (presently 55% of earnings) and to ensure that all parents, including the self-employed, can access leave with benefits.

The National Children's Alliance, an advocacy group that has spent many years on planning and policy development for children and families, sees the federal government's investment as progress on children's issues. It believes it is critical that communities work with governments to develop timelines, targets, and mechanisms for measuring implementation of ECD Accord initiatives. In the spring of 2001, the provinces and territories announced how they invested the funds from the ECD Accord. Although key advocacy groups such as Campaign 2000 and the National Children's Alliance agree with the objectives of the agreement, they think more attention must be paid to child care, housing, employment, and improved child benefits.

To give some perspective on progress to date, European Union guidelines recommend annual expenditures of 1% of total national expenditures for early childhood development, learning, and care. This amount is endorsed by the Child Care Advocacy Association of Canada in its document *From Patchwork to Framework: A Child Care Strategy for Canada* (2004). If Canada followed these guidelines, it would commit $10 billion annually to early childhood development services, compared to the $4 billion that it actually budgeted in 2001(Friendly 2004).

Multilateral Framework on Early Learning and Child Care

The Multilateral Framework on Early Learning and Child Care (March 2003), a federal/provincial/territorial arrangement to invest in ECEC for children under six, is the sole federal policy dedicated to child care. Its objective is to promote child development and support parental workforce participation or employment training. The Canadian government is providing additional funds over five years to support provincial and territorial government investments in regulated programs for children under six. The program began in 2003 and the funds provided will rise to $350 million in year five. The funds are primarily directed to services such as child care programs, licensed home child care, and preschool programs.

Principles and the initiatives that support them:

- available and accessible—increased spaces, flexible hours, information and referral services for families;

- affordable—fee subsidies and operational funding;

- improved quality—enhanced ratios and group size, training, compensation to support recruitment and retention of staff, funding to improve physical environment;

- inclusive services—supports to children with differing abilities and training for staff; and

- parental choice—services are available that respond to varying needs such as rural, seasonal, or shift work.

The Ministers acknowledged the importance of accountability and their commitment to clear public reporting by agreeing to provide annual reports based on indicators such as the number of children receiving subsidy and the number of new spaces available by age of child and type of setting. Unlike CAP, where the federal government could withhold funds for provinces who were not in compliance, this agreement contains no enforcement mechanisms. There is agreement from the child care community that the Multilateral Framework is an important milestone in making the difference in the lives of children and families. Advocates want inclusion of national goals, objectives and legislation targets, and implementation plans as well as clear plans for accountability and monitoring. The primary concern regarding the Multilateral Framework is that it is a statement of intent between political leaders and as such is unenforceable and vulnerable to political change.

Tax Measures Related to Children

The discussion of tax concessions in Canada is complicated. In 1988, Canada converted a number of tax deductions into credits. Although these changes were touted as distributing benefits in a more progressive manner, many families suffered a substantial loss in benefits. Tax deductions or tax credits do not contribute to creating more regulated services that would enable parents to have a greater choice of child care arrangements.

A national Child Tax Benefit, a cornerstone of income security and family policies, is not new to Canada. This approach was taken with Canada's universal Family Allowance program, which began in the mid-1940s and was eliminated in 1993.

THE CANADA CHILD TAX BENEFIT (CCTB)

Components

- CCTB base benefit for low- and middle-income families
- National Child Benefit (NCB) supplement

Objectives
Together, the federal and provincial/territorial governments will:

- Help prevent and reduce the depth of child poverty.

- Promote attachment to the workforce (resulting in fewer families having to rely on social assistance) by ensuring that families will always be made better off by working.

- Reduce overlap and duplication through close harmonization of program objectives and benefits and simplified administration.

The Canada Child Tax Benefit (CCTB) is the federal government's primary means for helping families with the costs of raising children.

The federal government increased its investment in the CCTB by $2 billion over three budgets and lowered the income threshold so that middle-income families could benefit.

In 2001, the CCTB provided families with benefits of up to $1805 for the first child and $1605 for each additional child. When the family's combined income reaches $21 000, these benefits are gradually reduced. Families with combined incomes above $67 000 generally receive no benefits. The government estimates that 3.2 million families receive the CCTB, including 80% of Canadian children (Canada 2001). This program is only a partial step toward a long-term plan to address child poverty. The National Child Benefit (NCB) supplement provides additional income support to low-income families with children.

Through the CCTB, the federal, provincial, and territorial governments are working in partnership to reduce child poverty and promote parents' attachment to the workforce. To achieve these objectives, the federal government increased its benefits to all low-income families with children. However, the provinces and territories were allowed to decrease, by a corresponding amount, payments made to families who were receiving social assistance. Consequently, any financial gain from the money received from the federal government was erased when some provinces penalized families on social assistance. Provinces and territories were allowed to use these savings to provide comprehensive programs that would improve work incentives and services to low-income families with children. Under the Social Union Framework Agreement, each province and territory can determine the best way to meet these goals by reinvesting these funds in complementary programs and services for low-income families in the following areas:

- child care
- child benefits and income supplements
- supplementary benefit
- dental benefits and preventative services.

A concern about this approach is that, in the absence of quality child care options, low-income mothers are impelled into the labour force. Due to the absence of coherent plans for early childhood care and development services, public funds are spent on fragmentary, poorly focused programs (Canada 1992a).

The Canadian Child Tax Benefit served as an important first step in preventing and reducing child poverty (Freiner and Cerner 1998). It is estimated that, by 2004, the total assistance provided through the CCTB to Canadian families with children will be over $9 billion a year.

Practitioners must speak out to obtain government support for early childhood development.

Future Role of the Federal Government

At a time when Canada is undergoing social and economic change, social policies and programs must respond to the changing needs of Canadian families. A society that is interested in the long-term social and economic security of its citizens and a healthy and prosperous future must be committed to the care and nurturing of children. Canada is one of the few major industrialized nations without a national child care policy. In many parts of Europe, child care is viewed as a citizenship right; early childhood development programs are seen as important for young children regardless of the employment status of the parents. Because child care is regarded as a societal responsibility, services are publicly funded. Policies that enhance child development contribute to the social and economic security of the country. The federal government's 2004 election commitment to a broader set of social responsibility goals and its recognition of the legitimacy and value of caring for children are critical steps.

Role of Provincial/Territorial Governments

Early childhood development programs have the common characteristics of education, health, and social services, all of which fall under provincial/territorial jurisdiction (except for the welfare of First Nations children on reserve programs, which is a federal responsibility). There are significant variations in the ECEC programs and services offered by provinces and territories across Canada.

PROVINCIAL/ TERRITORIAL RESPONSIBILITIES

- regulation of child care services
- funding arrangements
- child care standards, policies and procedures, and guidelines

---

By the late 1980s, all the provinces and territories had enacted child care legislation and established systems for monitoring compliance of legislated requirements. Government funding and regulations remain fluid and change in response to current politics, new research, and monetary restrictions. Provincial/territorial responsibilities can be divided into financial and regulatory ones. A number of provinces and territories have increased their child care budgets since 2001, initiating new programs and enhancing existing ones. Many have applied Early Childhood Development Accord funding to the area of early learning and care to supplement provincial/territorial expenditures.

Financial Responsibilities

Each province and territory has developed its own system of planning, regulating, and funding ECEC services. Even under fiscal constraints, total provincial and territorial expenditures for ECEC services have grown in recent years. The major means of supporting child care is through subsidies for low-income families. Many provinces and territories have also developed grants that provide assistance to ECEC programs for capital costs, equipment, staff salaries, or other program expenditures. These grants allow for improvements to program quality without an increase in parental fees, thus providing assistance to all families who use the service.

The three main sources of revenue for an ECEC program—parent fees, fee subsidies, and grants—strongly influence wage levels and the kind and quality of services a setting can offer. From province to province, there is wide variation in the monthly costs to parents of child care (see Table 2–2). *You Bet I Care!* found that, although nationally, centres obtained 49.2% of revenue from parent fees, there was heavier reliance in some provinces such as Newfoundland (82.1%) and Nova Scotia (72.7%). Manitoba has the lowest reliance on parent fees. The study found substantial fee increases—of around 62% for infants, 43% for toddlers, and 39% for preschoolers— occurring in Alberta between 1991 and 1998. The Alberta government has reduced its operating grants each year since 1990 (Doherty 2000a).

Among the concerns identified by Doherty et al. (1995) about provincial/territorial funding approaches are:

* Fee subsidies do not cover the actual cost of care.

* There is a lack of accountability for the use of public funds used by subsidy recipients to purchase unregulated care.

* Public money is used to support commercial care.

* Too many parents are on waiting lists for subsidized child care.

As chapter 1 makes clear, a significant barrier to high quality child care is staff dissatisfaction, usually expressed through high turnover. The most common cause of turnover is inadequate

TABLE 2–2	Total Provincial Allocation for Each Regulated Child Care Space, 2001	
Province/Territory	Allocation for each space[3]	Total allocation
Newfoundland	$1835	$7 753 000
Prince Edward Island	$1334	$4 229 708[4]
Nova Scotia	$1125	$12 892 278
New Brunswick	$1066	$11 823 000
Quebec	$4651	$1 092 427 651[5]
Ontario	$2608	$451 500 000
Manitoba	$2731	$62 876 400
Saskatchewan	$2279	$16 331 911
Alberta	$1206	$57 500 000
British Columbia	$2256	$164 563 000
Northwest Territories	$1298	$1 602 000

3 Estimates based on total provincial allocation for regulated child care and total regulated spaces.

4 For the purpose of comparison with other jurisdiction where kindergarten is in the public school system, this calculation did not include spaces in part-day kindergarten or its spending on kindergarten since PEI's kindergartens are in child care centres.

5 This figure includes expenditures on school-age care from the Ministry of Education.

Source: M. Friendly, J. Beach, and M. Turiano, *Early Childhood Education and Care in Canada: Provinces and Territories, 2001* (Toronto: Childcare Resource and Research Unit, Centre for Urban and Community Studies, University of Toronto, 2002). Statistics reprinted by permission.

salaries, and after that, poor working conditions, which are usually the result of underfunding in other areas. The national average for ECEs and assistants in 2000 was $16 167 and for those working full-time $19 000 (Beach et al. 2004). Many graduates did not receive an increase in salary from 1997 to 2000. Most are seeking careers outside their area of education. There appears to be little immediate prospect of improvement, and this is a major reason why every practitioner in the field needs to be aware of the routes to public advocacy (see chapter 11).

The gaps between Quebec and the rest of Canada in ECEC policy, funding, and services are dramatic. In 2001, 58% of total Canada-wide provincial and territorial spending on regulated child care was spent in Quebec! In 1997, Quebec implemented a broad family policy that gave concrete expression to the educational dimension of early childhood development services. Half-day programs for five-year-olds were extended to a full day. Four-year-olds had a supplemental half-day program provided at no cost to the parent. By 2001, an additional 85 000 spaces were to be created for children aged from newborn to four, and the new regulations require double the former number of trained staff. Quebec's policy was a bold move toward universality whether or not parents are employed and regardless of total family income. This progressive social policy is regarded as the desired goal by advocates across the country.

Regulation through Licensing

Whether related to early childhood development, banks, or broadcasting, regulation is designed to ensure specific levels of quality and accessibility for the entire population. Regulation takes place through legislation shaped by the policy priorities of a particular government. The Millward Brown Goldfarb survey found that 96% of Canadians believed the quality of child care could be improved by "regulating all child care services to meet quality standards" (CCCF and CCAAC 2003).

The primary benefit from government regulation of ECEC settings is its help in assuring children's rights to settings that protect them from harm and promote their healthy development. An effective **licensing** system minimizes the potential for harmful care.

Each regulation is attached to a piece of legislation and can be enforced by law. Consequently, regulations are powerful tools for establishing basic standards such as health and safety provisions in a physical setting. The term "**standards**" implies degrees of excellence along a continuum, with some regulations only setting baseline standards for acceptability below which quality is unacceptable (possibly leading to criminal sanctions) and other regulations indicating excellent quality when met.

Regulation to do with early childhood development is administered by the provinces and territories and takes the form of licensing of centre-based programs and family child care agencies and homes. All provinces and territories have licensing standards, although these standards vary widely in scope. **Regulations** include the rules, directives, statutes, and standards that prescribe, direct, limit, and govern early childhood development programs. When regulatory systems are well designed and effectively administered, they can help assure an acceptable level of care. Directors of **licensed programs** are responsible for understanding licensing and other regulations pertaining to provision of services for young children. Directors must ensure that all requirements are fulfilled in a timely manner.

Licensing agencies should be aware of current research findings and the needs of families. Licensing standards should result from careful consideration of their value and benefit to children and should positively affect both children and caregivers. Regulations need to be clear, so everyone can understand them. Programs need to know what is expected of and from them, and government officials need to interpret and enforce standards fairly and consistently. Rigid standards and hazy guidelines are difficult to interpret and enforce. A functioning system of regulation establishes standards of quality and applies those standards to programs across the board. It specifies penalties and procedures for programs that do not meet the standards.

Licensing standards provide a baseline for acceptable care of children. In programs operating below that level of service, a child is actually deemed to be in danger. Regulations deal with structural aspects of quality that are readily measurable (floor space, staff:child ratios, and group size) as outlined in chapter 1. Licensing standards set forth the public definition of acceptability: regulated programs must meet at least this level of quality in order to legally operate. While services need to meet regulations, these alone cannot ensure an adequate standard of service delivery. Process aspects of care, such as caregiver–child interactions, provide a truer indication of quality. A licence gives a program permission to operate; it does not guarantee quality.

Many parents feel more secure placing their child in a licensed facility. Some agencies provide parents with information about the standards of quality they should be looking for when placing their child.

Although licensing regulations vary greatly from province to territory, most provincial regulations cover most aspects of a program—administration, organization, facilities, personnel, funding, and services—as detailed in the examples below:

- *Staff:* qualifications; medical requirements.
- *Building safety:* minimum fire and building safety standards, procedures for evacuation, and procedures for storage of harmful materials.
- *Program:* regulations ensure that the daily schedule offers opportunities and activities that promote children's development.
- *Physical space:* the amount of space necessary both indoors and outside, levels of light, fencing, and provision of diaper-changing areas.
- *Equipment:* the amount appropriate to the ages and numbers served, and specifications for equipment, such as cribs meeting Health Canada's product safety standards.
- *Record keeping:* policies and procedures, financial statements, and health records for children and staff.
- *Nutrition:* the requirement that children's meals meet *Canada's Guide to Healthy Eating* recommendations and are prepared safely.
- *Behaviour guidance:* prohibition of certain kinds of discipline; encouragement of positive guidance strategies.
- *Ratios/group size:* the specific number of staff required for the number and age of children served, in order to protect the safety of the children.

An operation can be licensed when it meets the basic criteria in these areas. Licensing has traditionally looked after the safety and protection of children, though other important areas such as record keeping, staff qualifications, and personnel policies must also be assessed before a setting can be licensed. Obtaining a licence can be a long and complicated procedure. Delays are not uncommon, and coordination among agencies such as fire and health agencies is weak.

The licence must be posted in a conspicuous place. It identifies the name of the operator, the number of children permitted, and the period for which the licence is in effect. The granting of a licence to a facility means that the province or territory also assumes responsibility for monitoring the centre or home to check compliance with standards.

Monitoring is essential for accountability. Families and the public need to be assured that, once a program is given a licence, it must continue to meet or exceed licensing standards. Monitoring can vary from unannounced spot checks to scheduled visits.

Doherty-Derkowski (1995), among others, views a lack of adequate monitoring as a contributing factor to poor quality early childhood development programs. Adequate monitoring involves appropriately trained inspectors with a thorough background in early child development, assessing the quality of care in the ECEC program.

Enforcement practices range from the granting of conditional licenses and the removal of licenses to fines and prosecution. In extreme cases, such as child abuse, flagrant lack of safety precautions, or outright negligence, a centre or home may be closed immediately and its director, owner, or caregiver may face criminal charges. The effectiveness of regulations is tied to their enforceability through penalties for non-compliance.

In some programs, untrained or poorly trained staff may be unaware of how to meet particular regulations. Very few programs are actually ordered closed if they do not meet standards, since it is usually felt that parents and children are better served if licensing officials work in a consultative capacity to improve weak programs. In such a case, the program is usually given a provisional licence listing improvements that need to be made by a specific date. Up to this time, officials and/or consultants work closely with the director to bring the program up to minimum standards. If a condition is not met, then the operator may lose its licence.

No regulatory system can guarantee quality, and many child care facilities meet only the minimum standards required by their province or territory. Others operate at a higher level. The minimum set by regulation should be considered the beginning of high quality, not the end goal. In any case, it should not be forgotten that less than 13% of the total number of children in non-parental care receive care in a licensed or regulated setting (including regulated family child care) (Friendly, Beach and Turiano 2002).

McLean (1994) reported that provinces and territories vary in how they apply sanctions, how frequently a program is visited, and the number of programs for which each inspector is responsible. In some provinces, including Nova Scotia, Ontario, Manitoba, and British Columbia, centres and homes are re-licensed annually; in others, such as Prince Edward Island, they are re-licensed every three years. A current trend is for governments to reduce the frequency of licensing and monitoring visits to help cope with funding restraints. Since regulations are only as strong as the system of enforcement, this trend has generated some concern about the effectiveness of the licensing system.

There continues to be much change in provincial/territorial legislation concerning early childhood development programs. For current information, consult your provincial or territorial office. Addresses are provided in the appendix at the end of this book.

A director may be required to work simultaneously with municipal and provincial/territorial regulators. The regulations from the various bodies are not always totally compatible. It is the role of the operator to ensure that the program is in compliance. If the program is not in compliance, the operator runs the risk of having to delay the opening of a new program, pay fines, or in rare cases close down a program for failure to meet a licensing requirement.

Regulatory Requirements for Family Child Care Providers

Of the estimated 180 000 family child care providers in Canada, approximately 95% are not licensed or regulated (Goss Gilroy 1998). There are two models of regulated family child care in Canada. Some provinces and territories license, or contract, with agencies to provide regulated care. Others directly license individual family child care homes. While all provinces and territories currently have some system of regulated family child care, they also permit the provision of care outside the regulated child care system for a specified maximum number of children per home; a license is not required until enrolment exceeds a certain number. The ages and number of children permitted in family child care homes, regulated and unregulated, vary by region. All jurisdictions limit the number of children permitted at any one time. Some providers choose to be licensed in order to participate in family child care support programs or to be eligible for subsidies. This process differs from the licensing of group settings, where licensing is not optional. (Chapter 5, "Caring for Children in a Home Setting," describes both regulated and unregulated care.)

The following provinces/territories license individual caregivers: British Columbia, Manitoba, Saskatchewan, New Brunswick, Prince Edward Island, the Yukon, and the Northwest Territories. Providers in jurisdictions that use the individual licensing model receive home visits from government officials. The number of visits ranges from one to four annually. Ontario, Alberta, Quebec, and Nova Scotia license agencies that supervise homes. Agency staff known as "home visitors" make regular visits to observe the care being provided. The required frequency of these visits ranges from twice monthly in Nova Scotia to four times yearly in Ontario and Quebec (Doherty 2000b).

Provincial/territorial **legislation** concerning family child care may include standards covering the physical environment, safety, minimum age and training of the caregiver, health and criminal record checks, the program offered, and meals and snacks.

The advantages and supports available to family child care providers working within the regulated system include:

- *Financial incentives.* Some jurisdictions offer operating, equipment, and/or maintenance grants to licensed family child care homes; families that qualify for financial assistance can receive child care subsidies.

- *Administrative assistance.* Many ministries/departments and/or family child care agencies provide sample contracts and forms (e.g., for child's health information, emergency contacts, permission to go on an outing) and other administrative information and assistance to family child care providers.

- *Resources, training, and support.* Most jurisdictions have available a variety of resources that may include orientation sessions and start-up assistance, workshops, toy and equipment loans, mediation and assistance with problem solving, and playgroups for caregivers and children.

Funding for Family Child Care

Regulated family child care providers in all jurisdictions can obtain government fee subsidies for eligible children. Start-up grants are available in Saskatchewan, the Northwest Territories, and the Yukon. British Columbia and Ontario fund a network of child care resource and referral programs with a mandate to assist in recruitment, support, and training of both regulated and unregulated providers (Doherty 2000b).

Role of Municipal Governments

Across Canada, child care is emerging on urban agendas. Prentice (2004) summarizes the initiatives of eight Canadian cities. In Ontario, local governments have both a regulatory and financial role in early childhood settings. In some situations, municipalities and provincial governments work together to ensure provincial requirements are reflective of municipal fire, health, and zoning bylaws.

Regulation

As part of the licensing process, regulated programs must comply with some local ordinances. The local or municipal government generally sets requirements in the areas of fire, safety, health and sanitation, building codes, and zoning through bylaws. A program must meet all these standards before it can accept children. A different department of the local government may administer each ordinance, and visits from several inspectors may be required.

Building codes and requirements concerning fire, safety, and sanitation have their statutory basis in public safety and health laws. The local fire department will require that an early childhood development program have fire extinguishers, alarms, fire escapes, and a procedure in place for fire drills. Local health and sanitation authorities will inspect food handling, water, toilets, sewage disposal, handwashing and diapering procedures, and plans for meeting the needs of children who are ill. Local health departments may also set requirements for immunization and the monitoring of the health of both staff and children. Building codes cover such areas as the type of structure that can be used for a child care centre, and the local department of building safety will be concerned with plumbing, electrical wiring capacity, and other related factors. The local zoning agency will be aware of the building and safety requirements. Zoning requirements restrict the use of land. Each municipality can regulate the use of land and the erection and use of buildings.

Some municipalities have in place bylaws specifically governing family child care. In some communities, a business licence is required to provide family child care. In others, the number and ages of children permitted in family child care are restricted.

Anyone setting up an early childhood development program needs to be knowledgeable about these regulations and how to meet them. Often a program hires a consultant to assist them in this area.

Funding

In most provinces, municipal involvement in child care is discretionary. Similar to senior levels of government, the attitudes of local politicians and financial priorities determine families' access to child care. Few municipalities have the tax base or the commitment necessary to support social services such as regulated child care. In many cases, local governments do little more than ensure that facilities meet local bylaws. Municipalities may determine the rules for making subsidies available to individual families and administer payment of those subsidies. Needs assessments and eligibility will vary from one jurisdiction to the next. Even within the same province, different cities may not be using the same guidelines or income cut-off points in their needs assessments. Thus, a family receiving a subsidy in one part of a province may no longer qualify if it moves to another municipality.

Provincial fee subsidy funding may be directed to local governments through a transfer of payments for early childhood development services. In some parts of the country, provinces have cut funding significantly. In other regions, such as Newfoundland, regional budgets have been enhanced. Provincial and municipal social services budgets pay for welfare as well as child care, and with the downloading of other costs, the provision of subsidies for child care has often had to take a back seat. A number of local governments have reduced the amount allocated to child care. When municipalities and provinces cut their funding, expansion of child care services, however necessary, becomes impossible, and it becomes increasingly difficult to maintain existing programs.

Municipally Operated Early Childhood Development Programs

Some municipalities operate their own early childhood development services. Others enter into purchase-of-service agreements with existing community programs. Some local governments do one or the other, some do both, and a few offer no services at all. In Ontario, municipalities play a significant role in providing direct funds for child care.

When a municipality embarks upon purchase of services, it contracts with a community program or agency to provide subsidized spaces. This may mean that the local government enters into an individual contract with an organization, either non-profit or for-profit, to enable parents receiving subsidy to use a certain number of its spaces. Often a local government will purchase services in geographical areas where high parental needs exist. The contracting procedure is analogous to letting a tender for road repair, where the municipality shops around for the best price.

Sometimes local governments use a purchase-of-service agreement to raise the quality of services for children. **Fiscal monitoring** refers to standards associated with funding. When the government buys or creates a service through a grant or contract, it establishes certain conditions for quality. This can be done by imposing requirements additional to those required by the province, such as that a program must be on a clear licence and not a provisional one, or that all staff members must have particular qualifications. A purchase-of-service agreement may also be directed at specific groups of children, such as those needing infant/toddler care, school-age care, special needs care, or family child care. In Toronto, a community program that holds a purchase-of-service agreement must meet the standards set out in *Operating Criteria for Child Care Centres Providing Subsidized Care in Metropolitan Toronto* (Toronto 2001). There is a similar set of criteria for regulated family child care homes.

Milestones in Policy and Legislation

Since 1970, numerous commissions and task forces have studied ECEC services in Canada and made recommendations. Simply put, the proper care and education of young children affects national productivity in two ways: productivity goes down if parents are worried about the care of their children, and future productivity depends on future producers—today's children.

Pages 44 and 45 describe some milestones in the development of Canadian early childhood development programs. It is crucial that early childhood practitioners understand social policy, keep up with changes to legislation, and contribute to continuous improvement in early childhood development services in Canada. We must ask ourselves:

- What will societal and governmental priorities be for new early childhood development services?

- Will new services be funded privately, by government, or through a combination of both?

- Will these new services be accessible and affordable to all parents and children in need of them?
- How can I lobby for quality early childhood development services for children and their families?

Milestones in Policy and Legislation

1820s Infant schools are started in Halifax to increase the number of workers available as well as to provide care and education for children.

1850 The earliest crèches are established in Montreal; they are provided by charitable organizations.

1883 Kindergartens are established by the City of Toronto Board of Education as part of the public school system.

1885 Factory work by children under 12 becomes illegal in Quebec.

1887 Ontario becomes the first province to recognize kindergartens as part of the public school system.

1890 Ontario's first recorded child care centre, called The Crèche, opens in Toronto; it also functions as an employment agency for domestics.

1914 Jost Mission Day Care is founded in Halifax during World War I.

1916 British Columbia moves ahead of the other provinces in terms of government intervention and support for child care services when the Crèche, founded in 1910 and organized jointly by the Associated Charities and the City of Vancouver, is placed under the jurisdiction of the provincial Health Department.

1918 The first federal Child Tax Exemption introduced.

1920 The introduction of the *Mothers' Allowance Act* of Ontario provides welfare benefits to single mothers, enabling them to stay at home to care for their children.

1926 Dr. Hincks, a leading figure in the early mental health movement in Canada, and Dr. Blott, head of the psychiatry department at the University of Toronto, establish the St. George's School for Child Study (later the Institute of Child Study) headed by Dr. Blatz, the founder of Canada's early childhood education movement.

1930 A Mother's Allowance is given to two-parent families on relief.

1937 British Columbia licenses child care centres, becoming the first province in the country to do so.

1942 The Dominion-Provincial Agreement for Wartime Day Nurseries enables any provincial government interested in establishing child care facilities to cost share with the federal government. Ontario and Quebec are the only provinces to take advantage of this agreement. The other provinces maintain they have no need for child care.

1945 Quebec decides to close wartime centres. In Ontario, a substantial public campaign keeps the centres open. The surviving wartime programs primarily serve children in low-income disadvantaged families. The Institute of Child Study (Toronto) develops the *Day Nursery Act*, then administered by the Welfare Ministry. Family Allowances introduced.

1950s A dramatic rise in nursery schools, which serve as enrichment programs for children.

1960s An insufficient number of licensed child care spaces and the high cost of child care are issues for parents as more women begin to enter the Canadian workforce.

1966 The Canada Assistance Plan (CAP) is passed by Parliament. Child care is included among social services for which the federal government agrees to pay half the cost of provincial subsidies for low-income families.

(continued)

1970s	The Royal Commission on the Status of Women calls for government recognition and expansion of high quality child care services, stating that women will not achieve full equality without government involvement in child care.
1981	The census reports that mothers in the workforce outnumber those staying at home with their children. Fifty-two percent of mothers participate in the workforce, and women make up 42% of the total workforce.
1984	A federal election year. For the first time, all three major parties make child care a campaign issue.
1987	Statistics Canada reports that the participation rate in the workforce of mothers with children under the age of 16 has increased to 65%.
1988	A Non-refundable federal Child Tax Credit replaces the Child Tax Exemption.
1989	The re-elected federal Conservative government announces it will reduce child poverty before 2000.
1990	The federal government limits annual increases to 5% on Canada Assistance Plan payments to Alberta, British Columbia, and Ontario This signals a withdrawal from the notion of universality.
1991	The 1989 United Nations Convention on the Rights of the Child is ratified by Canada.
1993	The Federal Child Tax Benefit and Work Income Supplement replace Family Allowances.
1996	The federal government announces that the assent of a majority of provinces is necessary for the federal government to embark on any new social programs.
1997	The federal and provincial/territorial governments agree to develop the National Children's Agenda to improve the well-being of Canada's children. Quebec implements its $5 per day child care policy.
1998	The National Child Benefit is implemented to build a co-operative approach between the federal and provincial governments to address child poverty.
1999	The federal, provincial, and territorial governments (excluding Quebec) sign the Social Union Framework Agreement (SUFA). SUFA sets the parameters for Canadian social policy.
2000	In the Early Childhood Development (ECD) Accord, the First Ministers, with the exception of Quebec's, agree to commit $2.2 billion over five years to support early development of young children. Maternity and parental leave benefits are expanded.
2001	Parental leave benefits extended from six months to one year.
2003	Paul Martin states "We must never forget that an innovative society rests on strong social foundations. A learning society like Canada understands, for example, the fundamental importance of early childhood development and of lifelong learning, which starts in infancy and continues well after the final degree is granted" (Campaign 2000 2003b).
2003	The Multilateral Framework on Learning and Care, a federal/provincial/territorial arrangement to invest in children under six, is introduced. The Child Care Human Resources Sector Council established to address key human resource issues.
2004	The Federal government announces $5 billion to begin a national child care program.

Summary

Public investment in good quality early childhood development programs has been shown to be cost effective. As a service to children, quality ECEC programs pay for themselves.

Initiatives such as the National Children's Agenda, Multilateral Framework, and Social Union Framework Agreement demonstrate a more co-operative federal–provincial/territorial relationship. These milestones have created the potential for the kind of framework for integrated ECEC programs so long envisioned by the early childhood community. The challenge is how to join these initiatives together and expand their capacity, to create an early childhood development system involving all levels of government, local communities, businesses, and voluntary groups. The public, as the community, plays an important role as a supporter and monitor of early childhood development programs. The Millward Brown Goldfarb survey (CCCF and CCAAC 2003) confirmed that Canadians see the creation of a national child care plan as priority. In fact, over 90% agreed that "quality child care is essential to the prosperity of Canada."

Canada's 2003 report card from the conference board of Canada showed good economic performance but the ratings had slipped from the previous year in the areas of health and social services. As Canada enters the twenty-first century, it must make the necessary investments to promote the well-being of children.

An estimated 3.5 million children need care while their parents are employed or attend school. This fact reminds us of how essential our role as caregivers is. When parents entrust such an important portion of the child's life to us, we must be the best that we can be. The provision of good early childhood experiences is an investment in healthy children. It contributes to child development, reduces child poverty, supports parents, and contributes to economic growth. The challenge is to persuade our governments to muster the imagination and political will to move the vision to reality.

Key Terms and Concepts

Fee subsidy,   p. 33

First Ministers,   p. 31

Fiscal monitoring,   p. 43

Legislation,   p. 41

Licensed program,   p. 38

Licensing,   p. 38

Monitoring,   p. 40

Regulations,   p. 38

Standards,   p. 38

United Nations Convention on the Rights of the Child,   p. 28

Activities

1. Would you make any changes to your province's or territory's legislation for child care? If so, discuss what you would like to see changed and explain why.

2. Construct your own "milestones chart" for legislation and other relevant facts for the last 24 months. Show what has been happening nationally, provincially/territorially, and locally. What changes would you like to see for children during the next 24 months?

3. Log onto the Canadian Child Care Federation's Policy Knowledge and Response Network website and locate the report for your province or territory. Note the latest news article on government policy development: policy.cccf-fcsge.ca.

4. Outline who in your local government parents should contact to apply for child care subsidies or financial assistance. Where are these officials' offices located? Are they easily accessible to families?

5. Make a list of the steps you would take to license a child care centre in your province or territory.

6. What grants and subsidies does your province or territory offer?
7. Find out what commitments your province has made regarding the spending of funds from the Early Childhood Development Accord.

Recommended Reading

Canadian Child Care Federation. "Convention on the Rights of the Child." In *Research Connections Canada*. Vol. 7. Ottawa: Canadian Child Care Federation, 2001.

Child Care Advocacy Association of Canada. *From Patchwork to Framework: A Child Care Strategy for Canada*. Ottawa: Child Care Advocacy Association of Canada, 2004.

Cleveland, G. and M. Krashinsky. *Our Children's Future: Child Care Policy in Canada*. Toronto: University of Toronto Press, 2001.

Doherty, G. "Issues in Canadian Child Care: What Does the Research Tell Us?" Part 5, "Funding Child Care." In *Research Connections Canada*. Vol. 5. Ottawa: Canadian Child Care Federation, 2000.

Friendly, M., J. Beach, and M. Turiano. *Early Childhood Care and Education in Canada: Provinces and Territories 2001*. Toronto: Childcare Resource and Research Unit, Centre for Urban and Community Studies, University of Toronto, 2002.

Government of Canada, Public Works and Government Services Canada, National Council of Welfare. *Preschool Children: Promises to Keep*, Ottawa, 1999.

Organisation for Economic Co-operation and Development (OECD). *Starting Strong: Early Childhood Development and Care*. Paris: Education and Training Division, OECD, 2001.

Weblinks

www.rightsofchildren.ca
Canadian Coalition on the Rights of Children
This organization is devoted to ensuring a collective voice for Canadian organizations encouraging rights for children. Its website provides resources and an interactive quiz on the United Nations Convention on the Rights of the Child.

www.childcarecanada.org
Childcare Resource and Research Unit
Part of the Centre for Urban and Community Studies at the University of Toronto, the Childcare Resource and Research Unit focuses on early childhood education and care. Its mandate is to promote universally accessible and high quality settings in Canada. It provides public education and policy analysis and publishes papers and other resources on child care policy, many of which are available online.

www.ccsd.ca
Canadian Council on Social Development
This is an independent, national, non-profit research organization that publishes the annual *Progress of Canada's Children* report.

www.cprn.org
Canadian Policy Research Networks (CPRN)
CPRN leads public debate on social and economic issues important to the well-being of Canadians. It operates three different networks concentrating on family, work, and health. Its activities include focus groups, literature reviews, research, and consultations.

www.nationalchildrensalliance.com
National Children's Alliance
This group, composed of over 30 organizations that work directly with families in health, education, and social and community services, works with all levels of government and all parties to raise awareness of the need for strong family policy and quality child care. It also offers a range of other supports and services.

www.childcarepolicy.org
childcarepolicy.org
At this site, four University of Toronto economics professors provide information and a forum for discussion on the economics of child care policy. Information on software for a Child Care Policy Evaluation Model is included.

Leadership in Early Childhood Development Programs

chapter 3

Objectives

- Outline the roles and responsibilities of the director.
- Review director competencies.
- Discuss the evaluation of director effectiveness.
- Describe leadership styles.
- Describe ways in which programs are organized.
- Discuss the relationship of the director to the owner/board of directors.
- Outline the roles and responsibilities of the board of directors.
- Provide strategies for recruiting board members.

Roles and Responsibilities of the Director

Being an effective **director** of an early childhood development program means wearing many hats—from budget analyst to nurse to curriculum expert to mechanic. The list is long and varied. The legal authority in a private program resides with the owner/s; in a non-profit program, it rests with the board of directors. This authority is delegated to the individual holding the title of director, who is responsible for the total program and services.

In some small programs, the director functions as both director and educator, regularly spending up to half of every day with a group of children. A director of a small program usually handles all the administrative tasks, including record keeping and telephone answering. Other directors do not work directly with the children, and some are responsible for several programs—which can involve travelling between sites and being aware of two or more sets of circumstances, children, families, and staff, two or more physical plants, and so on.

Some directors function as business managers and have other staff, such as an assistant director, administrative assistant, and/or accountant, to whom they may delegate specific tasks. Some directors are responsible to a **board of directors** or owners, others report to a **corporation**, a municipality, or a college's board of governors.

Different terminology is used to describe various types of directors. The term "administrator" refers to individuals administering, supervising, and/or managing an early childhood development service, be it a private or **non-profit** child care program, a nursery school or university or college laboratory school, a family child care agency, a setting for children with special needs, or a family resource program. The most common job titles are "program director," "manager," "supervisor," "teacher-director," "executive director," and "educational coordinator." Because of the broad professional expertise needed to carry out the job, such individuals are more appropriately referred to as "directors" or "managers" rather than the commonly used "supervisors."

The program director, or manager, runs the day-to-day **operations** of a program. Some directors manage programs that are one part of a larger organization. Other directors, such as those who administer small independent centres, private or non-profit, have more autonomy and less support. Some directors manage more than one program (they are sometimes called "head supervisors"). Because program directors work on site and directly with staff, supervision is a major part of their job. Directors who have both teaching and administrative duties are sometimes referred to as "teacher-directors."

An "executive director" is the chief administrator of a large early childhood development agency that is comprised of several social service programs. These positions are a small minority, usually in urban settings. Reporting to the board of directors, the executive director supervises program directors and, indirectly, other employees within the organization. Administrative and financial responsibilities are a major part of the executive director's role.

A director of a family child care agency holds the responsibility for the overall program along with that of quality assurance of the individual providers. Such directors plan, manage, and supervise home visitors who carry a caseload of family child care providers.

Less commonly, "educational coordinators" are responsible for the children's component of the program. Working in the areas of supervision, staff development, and curriculum development, they strive toward the goal of ensuring that playrooms and staff function according to program philosophy and for the greatest benefit to the children in the program. In the study *You Bet I Care!*, 13.9% of respondents identified themselves as head supervisors, 43.6% as teacher-directors, and 42.5% as administrative directors (Doherty et al. 2000a).

A MORNING IN THE LIFE OF A DIRECTOR

The job of director encompasses all aspects of the program and human resource management. Even with a daily plan, the director responds spontaneously to the ebb and flow of the day. For example, as a director walks in the door, she may learn that one of the staff has called in sick and no substitute has been found. She must call the roofers to repair a leak. A parent approaches; he is impatient to speak with her before he heads off to work. The payroll must be completed in order for the cheques for the staff to be cut. There is a long list of "to do's" to get through before a board meeting this evening. There are often so many squeaky wheels and daily crises, it is easy for a director to lose sight of goals and dreams for the program.

To perform any of the above mentioned tasks, a director must have skills and knowledge. To perform them effectively requires exceptional interpersonal skills. This individual must be able to bring out the best in varied groups of people: children, parents, staff members, board members or owners, and the community. More typically in small agencies, a director who has worked her way up through the ranks from playroom practitioner can bring to the job a broader perspective on the functioning of the program. Similarly, it is easier to empathize with parenting pressures if one is a parent oneself. Experience in a variety of settings can help the director see alternative options.

Defining Director Competencies

Research indicates that, in general, directors who are able to carry out these multiple roles effectively and succeed in creating a quality early childhood development program and supportive, collegial environment have strong educational and experiential backgrounds. There are several areas in which a director must excel:

General Education

An individual's general level of education has been shown to be a strong predictor for high quality practices in both teaching and administration. The director sets the standards and expectations for the early childhood development staff to follow and creates the climate of the program, as a caring and educational environment for children. The role requires a solid understanding of child development and the resultant program implications. In addition, the director must possess the knowledge and skills to provide leadership, successfully manage a budget, and engage in strategic planning. A key role of the director is to create and maintain the organizational culture. She must be clear on what makes her setting unique and why staff choose to work there.

At a minimum, to be a director one must meet requirements set by the province or territory. Current provincial/territorial regulations fail to recognize the importance of the director position. Virtually none of the provinces or territories requires early childhood directors to have training in management, supervision, or administration. Recently, Manitoba stipulated that directors must have a post-diploma certificate (in either Child Care Management, Children with Special Needs, or Infants/Toddlers). In specifying training requirements, several jurisdictions simply combine directors in with front-line staff.

ECE training programs do not adequately prepare graduates for administrative and management duties related to the supervision of early childhood development programs. Most education and training in early childhood development prepares individuals for working with young children in a playroom setting. Their preparation rarely provides them with the management skills and knowledge they need to be successful directors. The study *Working for Change: Canada's Child Care Workforce* found that over half of ECE programs did not specify course content on legislation, financial management, or administration (Beach et al. 2004). Among those jurisdictions that stipulate specific training requirements for directors, Ontario requires a two-year diploma or equivalent and two years' experience—the longest period of experience required; Newfoundland and Labrador, Nova Scotia, Prince Edward Island, and Saskatchewan require only a one-year Early Childhood Care and Education (ECE) certificate. No jurisdiction requires directors to have formal education in administration. Expanded availability of and access to specialized training for program directors are needed. The Child Care Human Resources Sector Council is developing occupational standards for directors, which will be available in 2005/2006.

You Bet I Care! found that, although the general level of education of directors has improved since 1991, many directors lack adequate preparation for the job. The study reported that most directors were involved in continual learning, taking credit courses toward an advanced credential as well as participating in professional development activities. However, only 27.7% had any specific training in business administration or management of early childhood development programs. In 1998, 47.8% of directors in Quebec and 39.2% in New Brunswick lacked any ECEC training. On a Canada-wide basis, less than 27.7% had any formal training in program administration. There may, however, be specific requirements established by the employer for some positions (Doherty 2000a).

Being a director of an early childhood development program is akin to operating a business. More college and university ECEC management programs are needed, as is government recognition that directors need such training to operate a quality early childhood environment.

Early Childhood/School-Age Knowledge and Skills

Directors need a strong foundation in the fundamentals of child development and educational programming and in administrative practices that promote the inclusion of children with special needs. They need to understand:

- health, safety, and nutrition components necessary to optimize development;
- developmental patterns in early childhood and in school-age children and their implications for the program;

The director's job involves establishing relationships with stakeholders.

- environmental psychology and the arrangement of the environment to support development; and
- diverse types of family composition and background—cultural, socio-economic, and religious.

Working for Change (Beach et al. 2004) found a lack of pedagogical leadership—that is, where the director expects and supports staff members to provide an environment that deliberately educates young children. This requires a process of planning, implementing and reviewing what children do and how they are doing. Increased demands on directors for record keeping and documentation related to health and safety requirements and financial accountability diminish their ability to provide pedagogical leadership.

Management Knowledge and Skills

The effective administration of early childhood settings requires a strong understanding of business and management practice. Directors need to administer the organization in a way that is consistent with legislative requirements such as human rights, provincial regulations, employment standards, and the directions of the organization's **governing body**. Directors need to be knowledgeable about both provincial/territorial and local regulations as well as professional standards pertaining to the education, care, health, and safety of young children—and they need to be able to develop and implement **policies** and **procedures** that meet these regulations and standards.

Increasingly, directors are required to ensure that their programs are financially viable; consequently, they must understand bookkeeping methods and accounting terminology and have skills in budgeting and cash flow management. They need to set service rates, prepare financial reports, maintain insurance coverage, and know how to secure funding from a variety of sources, including government grants programs and donors. Directors need to develop yearly operating and capital budgets and policies and procedures for monitoring and controlling revenues and expenditures. In addition, directors need to implement procedures to maintain accountability for government funding. Directors must be able to use technology and, especially, have well-developed computer skills and the ability to use software such as Excel for budgets.

A central theme that emerged from *Working for Change* is the "weak culture" of human resource management that exists within the sector (Beach et al. 2004). The demands of balancing tight budgets and meeting program regulatory requirements occupy their time, leaving little attention for human resource issues. Staff supervision and performance appraisal and clear policies to guide practices in areas such as conflict resolution, team communication, and employment termination are often missing. These issues are explored in chapter 6, "Human Resources Management in an ECEC Environment." It is necessary to provide the human resource infrastructure to sustain an early childhood team.

Organization and Leadership Skills

Directors should be able to:

- assess program needs;
- assist the governing body with strategic planning and the development of the program philosophy and policy;

- implement program goals and evaluate program effectiveness;

- recruit, train, support, evaluate, and supervise staff;

- promote and support team building;

- utilize strategies of mediation and problem solving;

- translate program goals into well-written policies and procedures that adhere to legislative requirements;

- understand leadership styles and group behaviour; and

- be aware of changing demographics, social and economic trends, and developments in the field.

Board, Parent, and Community Relations Skills

Directors need to be able to communicate positively and effectively with a broad range of **stakeholders** in a way that enables representatives to articulate their needs, furthers the objectives of the program, and improves the quality of services. Specifically, directors need to be able to:

- articulate a rationale for program practices to the board of directors, owner, or sponsor;

- understand the dynamics and diversity of family life;

- interpret child development for parents and others in the community;

- respond to parents' questions and concerns;

- support practitioners in their work with families;

- be aware of community resources that can support families;

- regularly contact professional organizations, legislative representatives, elementary schools, the media, community organizations, and others; and

- provide information to members of the general public to increase their awareness of the field and the role of practitioners.

Working for Change (Beach et al. 2004) noted child care management must include outreach to recent immigrants and newcomers and reflect the cultural, ethnic, and linguistic diversity of the population.

Experience

Experience on the job provides a basis for evaluating both effective and ineffective practices. Experience with different ages of children and different program models can comprise a powerful laboratory for learning. *You Bet I Care!* found that most directors have substantial experience in the field: 64% had worked for 11 or more years. There were some regional differences, with the least experienced directors working in New Brunswick.

The scope and complexity of the administrative role, and the repertoire of skills and competencies needed to effectively carry out this role, depend on:

- the ages and backgrounds of the children served;

- the range of services provided by the program;

- the legal sponsorship of the program (see the section "Ways in Which Programs Are Organized" later in this chapter);

- the size of the program (in a smaller setting, there may be fewer administrative tasks, whereas in a large program with multiple sites, there could be multiple funding sources and a more diverse staff to coordinate); and

- the philosophical orientation of the program.

There have been some recent efforts to delineate the specific skills and knowledge needed by directors. Nova Scotia's Child Care Connection conducted a national survey of provincial/territorial organizations and training institutions with an ECEC program to determine standard components in the early childhood development director's role. Standards for the credentialling of practice in Canada were drawn from this data. A detailed job description and questionnaire were circulated for feedback. The study is reported on in the paper "Child Care Administration Credentialling" (Ferguson 1997). Proposed qualifications for directors include completion of post-secondary training in ECEC and professional development in administrative, supervisory, financial, and budgetary management and operations planning. A minimum of two years' experience in the role of caregiver is additionally proposed.

The Early Childhood Development department of George Brown College has developed **best practices** for directors in lab school environments. And, as part of the Partners in Quality project, the Canadian Child Care Federation developed Standards of Practice for Administrators/Directors based on discussions with many experienced directors representing an array of organizations across Canada (Doherty 2000b). In addition, Partners in Quality researchers conducted an extensive literature review. Examples of the Partners in Quality standards can be found throughout this text.

The roles and duties of directors are as varied as early childhood development programs. Clear job descriptions can reduce conflict and uncertainty and provide a baseline from which to assess performance. Job descriptions should also identify the type of preparation required for the position.

Stages of Director Development

As directors gain experience in their roles, they undergo a series of changes in how they view themselves and their jobs. They face similar problems and frustrations in each phase, but their ability to handle problems changes as they move toward maturity. Anthony (1998) identifies four developmental stages for directors and, for each stage, suggests possible professional-development strategies, modelled on the work of Lillian Katz (1972).

In the first stage, the director is working to understand her new role and job expectations. A strategy of trial and error is often employed. New early childhood directors must acquire new competencies while they are establishing their authority and leadership. It is important to appear in control and become comfortable exercising authority. Success as an ECEC practitioner does not guarantee administrative success. New directors must establish credibility by being highly visible to staff and parents. Among the developmental tasks at this stage are:

- mastering the basic organizational tasks of the job;

- learning to cope effectively with crises that arise;

- formulating a self-image as director;

- learning new skills while managing one's own level of stress;

- staying focused on what it takes to get the job done; and

- recognizing the importance of commitment to the job.

Sample

COMPREHENSIVE JOB DESCRIPTION—EARLY CHILDHOOD DIRECTOR

Reports to:
Board of Directors/Owner

General Responsibilities:

- To ensure the development and management of the procedures required for carrying out the policy decisions of the board of directors/owner for the fulfillment of goals and objectives of the program.
- To exhibit professional attitudes and behaviours.
- To act as a role model for staff, parents, and children.
- To ensure a physically safe environment that shows sensitivity to the individual needs of children in all aspects of their development and to the needs of staff and parents.

Work Procedures:

- Ensure the program meets all legal requirements.
- Provide the board of directors/owner with support to make informed decisions.
- Ensure the operational policies established by the board of directors/owner are implemented.
- Ensure that the curriculum meets the policies established by the board of directors/owner.
- Ensure ongoing supervision of staff.
- Ensure accurate financial information is available to board of directors/ owner.
- Promote the program in the community.

Job Responsibilities:

1. *To ensure that the health, welfare, and safety of the children remain the first priority of the program.*

   a. Works with practitioners to ensure that policies, procedures, and practices are developed and implemented regarding the following:
      - safeguarding the children's health, safety, and nutrition;
      - maintenance of updated medical and developmental progress records of all children; program kept up-to-date on children's allergies and other health/developmental needs;
      - behaviour management;
      - developmentally appropriate supervision of children;
      - handling sick or injured children and emergencies;
      - obtaining parental consent where applicable;
      - ensure that children are only released to authorized persons and accurate names are kept for the awareness of staff, permanent and supply; and
      - reporting protection concerns and complying with court orders.

(continued)

b. Works with practitioners to develop and implement plans for responding to allegations of misconduct or abuse.

c. Ensures the program's procedures for administering first aid are followed, all supplies are in good condition, and all staff have updated training.

d. Ensures all accidents, injuries, and illnesses are properly recorded and communicated to parents.

e. Maintains up-to-date emergency information cards for all children and ensures that this information accompanies any group leaving the premises for outings.

f. Arranges for daily inspection of the playground in accordance with approved checklist.

g. Inspects the entire premises daily for safety, cleanliness, and appropriate use and storage of materials.

h. Arranges promptly for repairs.

i. Supervises the cook with regard to development of appropriate menus, sanitary food handling, menu adherence, and economical ordering of supplies.

j. Works with practitioners and support staff to ensure physical environments are safe, clean, and organized.

k. Conducts and records monthly fire drills.

l. Carries out all recommendations and directions of the public health inspector and the fire department.

m. Works diligently with all government licensing staff to consider their recommendations.

2. *To ensure that the program meets the standards of all legislation and the expectations of the board of directors/owner.*

a. Knows and maintains the standards of the legislation pertaining to children and other government standards that apply to workplace settings.

b. Understands and implements directives from the board of directors/owner in accordance with the strategic plan.

c. Maintains accurate work-related human resource information for all staff as well as children's records.

d. Ensures that the children's daily arrivals and departures are accurately recorded.

e. Maintains a daily staff logbook.

f. Reviews and assists with updating the staff manual on an annual basis.

g. Submits complete and accurate weekly staff time sheets.

h. Ensures staff receive their paycheques as scheduled.

i. Collects parent fees as required.

j. Plans and conducts weekly meetings with groups of staff, according to program needs.

(continued)

k. Prepares and submits a concise and accurate monthly report to the board of directors/owner and assists with developing the budget.

l. Attends all meetings with the board of directors/owner and board committees as requested.

m. Accurately maintains petty cash account, keeping within allocated budget.

n. Works collaboratively with others.

o. Ensures the required training is provided in areas such as protocols and procedures for reporting protection concerns and complying with court orders and emergency evacuation.

3. *To provide a professional service to families.*

a. Answers all enquiries for service promptly and courteously.

b. Maintains an accurate, up-to-date waiting list.

c. Conducts parent interviews for admission, and makes all the necessary arrangements for subsidies and care for children with special needs.

d. Ensures that each family is carefully oriented to the program, the routines, the staff, health expectations, and financial obligations.

e. Facilitates the maintenance of accurate daily records and observations of every child in attendance.

f. Oversees the preparation of developmental records and individual program objectives for each child. These are discussed with parents upon request and at frequent intervals during the year.

g. Facilitates the preparation of an informative regular parent newsletter. Monitors all notices and requests to parents.

h. Ensures that parents have reliable, prompt telephone access to program staff.

i. Works with the program committee to foster parent participation through workshops and social and volunteer events.

j. Provides referrals to additional services as needed.

k. Communicates effectively to parents the program philosophy of understanding and respect for diverse cultural, socio-economic, and religious backgrounds, types of family composition, and special needs.

l. Maintains confidentiality at all times with regard to family situations.

m. Solicits input from families about their needs.

n. Helps staff to develop and implement a variety of user-friendly approaches that encourage and support parents to express their needs and preferences and have meaningful input into policy and program development.

o. Helps practitioners to implement a variety of methods to provide families with information about their children and the service.

4. *To develop and deliver an exemplary program.*

a. Ensures that daily schedules are workable, carried out, and evaluated seasonally.

(continued)

b. Reviews the program plans on a weekly basis to ensure that the children's developmental needs are met; see that the plans are carried out and amended as needed; and decide if plans are consistent with the program philosophy. Evaluates the plans quarterly with staff.

c. Supports the use of observational techniques to assist in:
- the identification of children's skills, abilities, interests, and needs;
- the evaluation of activities provided for children; and
- the program as a whole.

d. Maintains an ongoing system of supplies inventory, purchasing, storage, and maintenance.

e. Ensures that the program offers a variety of self-directed learning experiences that include art, music, movement, sensory activities, science, language, drama, and social interactions.

f. Provides leadership to practitioners in their development of the children's daily program to ensure that the activities and materials are developmentally appropriate.

g. Ensures that a regular rotation and cleaning of play materials is carried out.

h. Spends periods of time weekly observing or participating in various parts of the program.

i. Encourages true welcoming and inclusion of children with special needs.

5. *To hire, train, monitor, and develop a highly motivated staff.*

a. Participates in the recruitment, hiring, and termination of practitioners in accordance with program policy and legislation related to human rights and employment standards.

b. Provides a thorough orientation to all new staff (permanent or supply).

c. Ensures confidentiality regarding human resource issues.

d. Actively monitors and promotes staff respect and understanding for diverse cultural, socio-economic, and religious backgrounds, types of family composition, and special needs.

e. Encourages a collaborative, co-operative approach among all practitioners by providing opportunities for group discussion and problem solving and for meaningful input into policy and program development.

f. Provides effective levels and types of support by promoting an environment that meets the needs of staff.

g. Works with practitioners to develop clear, objective behavioural and job performance expectations and to undertake performance appraisals and provide constructive feedback.

h. Develops and implements individual professional development plans that have achievable, realistic goals and objectives and are regularly reviewed and revised.

i. Maintains staff:child ratios, always remembering the welfare of the staff and children.

(continued)

j.   Oversees the orientation, supervision, and evaluation of field-placement students.

k.   Appoints a reliable delegate in any absence.

l.   Rotates work schedules so that all aspects of the program can be observed monthly.

m.   Reviews job descriptions annually.

n.   Works with practitioners to ensure that job descriptions and human resource policies and procedures are understood, implemented, and monitored for ongoing relevance.

o.   Ensures that staff have adequate levels of human and other resources to enable them to provide quality care and education.

6.   *To present the program professionally.*

a.   Maintains regular attendance, punctuality, and professional appearance.

b.   Ensures that a positive working relationship exists with other colleagues and the board of directors/owner.

c.   Advocates in the community for the interests of child care through meetings, letters, and other vehicles as appropriate.

d.   Remains aware of the availability of other services from other organizations and accesses them as required.

e.   Liaises with licensing officials; develops and implements procedures for reporting licensing-related issues promptly and appropriately.

f.   Works co-operatively with early childhood preparation programs to facilitate learning opportunities with students.

g.   Provides accurate, timely information about the program to other organizations in the community.

h.   Demonstrates a respect for lifelong learning by working on a professional development plan.

i.   Performs additional tasks as assigned and discussed in advance.

Minimum Educational Qualifications:

•   ECE diploma or equivalent as approved by Ministry.

•   Two years' experience or more in the field of early childhood development.

•   Holder of a valid standard first aid certificate.

Source: Adapted from Gillian Doherty, "Standards of Practice for Administrators/Directors," in Canadian Child Care Federation (CCCF), *Partners in Quality: Tools for Administrators in Child Care Settings* (Ottawa: CCCF, 2000); the Pay Equity Kit developed by the Ontario Coalition for Better Child Care (OCBCC) (Toronto: OCBCC, 1993); and the supervisor's job description from the St. Lawrence Co-operative Day Care, Toronto.

The director's professional development needs at this stage include ongoing feedback on performance; learning how, when, and whom to ask for support; acquiring a lot of new information on business practices, budgeting, **organizational structure**, policies and procedures, and human resources management; and, finally, learning techniques for managing stress and promoting health.

In the second stage, the director is managing organizational tasks well, is more comfortable with authority, and has more realistic expectations of herself. During this stage, the focus is on:

- managing specific areas in depth (e.g., staff development, parent involvement, budgeting);
- developing broader areas of expertise;
- learning effective time-management skills, such as delegation and how to say no; and
- seeking support from outside the program.

Some strategies to help a director develop in these areas include visiting other programs, attending workshops and conferences on specific topics, and reading a variety of publications, such as *Child Care Information Exchange.*

By the time a director has reached stage 3, she is confident and secure in her role. Recognizing and respecting the strengths of staff members, she is willing to share authority. Problem solving is viewed as an ongoing task. The areas requiring further development are:

- balancing the needs of people and operational tasks;
- identifying one's own strengths and limitations; and
- developing an effective, forward-looking vision for the program.

Strategies the director might use to achieve these goals include acquiring information to strengthen her awareness of how differences in personality types and communication styles can affect working relationships with both staff and parents, learning about other programs' policies and procedures, and putting more effort into evaluating the program's effectiveness.

In the final stage, the director is mature and has dealt with a variety of problems and challenges. She possesses the characteristics of mature professionals: self-knowledge, self-confidence, an in-depth understanding of problems and issues associated with her work, and the skills necessary to do an effective job. She may be looking for new challenges. The focus will be on:

- mentoring others, such as staff or new directors, and sharing professional expertise;
- taking on a leadership role in advocacy and becoming active in professional organizations such as those listed in the appendix; and
- finding new challenges and refocusing her energy.

The professional development focus will be on sharing and giving rather than just taking in information, finding new projects and challenges through professional linkages, conducting workshops and writing, and expanding the existing program.

Growth through these stages is ongoing and frequently uneven. During their careers, directors may move back and forth from one phase to another when they work in new roles or unfamiliar settings. In some cases, directors may not move beyond the first two stages. Every director's approach to the job differs based on background and previous experience. Careful attention to professional development and support can enhance success, increase job satisfaction, and prevent burnout.

Leadership Attributes of a Good Director

As previously stated, most directors of early childhood development programs come to their positions with little experience or education to prepare them for the awesome task of trying to run a quality ECEC program, often with less-than-adequate facilities and resources.

However, whatever the external factors, one has the power to shape the environment. Leadership toward that end has the potential to contribute to social change. A leader affects everyone involved in the early childhood development program and influences the character of the facility. The leader has a major impact on the organizational climate—the attitudes, beliefs, and values of the individuals involved in the work setting. A strong leader helps others be better at their jobs and inspires them to meet new challenges. An effective director is a person who combines skills, knowledge, and caring. Not everyone excels in all of these ways at once. The following attributes are all characteristic of leadership.

Communicate a Vision

It is essential for a director to have a vision for the program that gives the work meaning. A vision can inspire one to act. When a director believes she is building an organization that will make a difference, she exudes an enthusiasm that energizes everyone in the program—children, parents, staff, board members/owner, and community. The raw material for the vision is the collective views of the families; the vision is defined and articulated by the board of directors/owner, using informa-

In the final stage, directors take on a leadership role in advocacy.

tion supplied by the director. Creating a vision expresses the organization's deepest values about children, family, work, and community. Organizations do not in themselves have values; the values that guide organizations come primarily from their leaders.

Next, the director must translate the vision into achievable goals and motivate people to achieve these goals. By clearly communicating an organizational goal, such as "encouraging co-operative behaviour" or "expanding the program to include a family resource centre," the director can focus the resources and efforts of the program toward achieving that goal. (Leadership and the program vision are discussed further in chapter 4, "Planning and Evaluating the Program Goals.")

Determine If the Program Is Meeting Its Goals

A director needs to keep her finger on the pulse of the program and continually assess the performance of the organization. The progress of the organization toward accomplishing its goals can be monitored using both informal and formal methods.

In addition to being aware of what goes on inside the centre, the director must keep up with changes outside the program. The director needs to follow relevant trends in research, technology, government funding, business, and society in general. She can then better assess whether the program's goals and policies, such as the programs offered and hours of operation, are meeting the needs of current and potential users of the service.

An effective director will determine how well the program is functioning by:

- spending time daily observing the program on an informal basis;
- regularly meeting with individual staff and the team;
- randomly conducting parent interviews that will assist in determining whether the program is meeting its goals for the children;
- using anonymous parent surveys on a regular basis; and
- obtaining feedback from the children themselves.

Select Priorities

As there are only so many hours in a day, it is essential for a director to focus her attention on areas where additional effort will have the most impact. Once the day starts and the myriad of telephone calls, visitors, and unexpected small crises compete for the attention of the director, it may seem impossible to stick to one's agenda. The director must select those tasks that will provide maximum benefit to the program. She must learn to use a variety of time-management strategies, such as grouping or delegating tasks and planning a time-line. Voice mail, e-mail, and other electronic communication approaches should be used to keep both in touch and in control of one's time.

Encourage Participative Management

A key leadership strategy is to develop an effective team. A director must recognize that she cannot accomplish everything by herself. Developing an effective team takes time and effort, but when caregivers are given the opportunity to participate in making decisions that affect them, they experience greater job satisfaction and higher morale. Once team members have been identified, they can be given greater responsibilities and provided with opportunities to develop more skills. Involving people in making decisions gives them a greater stake in carrying them out.

A director doesn't work to make people love her but rather to make people love working for her. Employees' willingness to work hard will ebb and flow depending on their current attitude toward their work and the director. Staff must be motivated to achieve the goals of the program. In part, this is achieved by involving staff in setting the program goals (Jorde Bloom 2000). To build commitment to the goal setting process, a director should encourage staff members to shape goals they personally care about. Then they will have an investment in the accomplishment of these objectives.

It is necessary to construct a stimulating and secure working environment for staff. To achieve this responsive environment, the director will have high expectations, respect the employees' autonomy (give them full responsibility for carrying out tasks), arrange opportunities for professional growth, provide feedback on performance, recognize achievements, encourage collaboration, foster creativity, and be there as a resource when needed. By delegating certain managerial responsibilities, the director can focus on specific tasks that only she can carry out. Participative management is based on the belief that when more people participate, a synergistic effect increases the possibility of better decisions. (These topics are elaborated on in chapter 6, "Human Resources Management in an ECEC Environment.")

Be an Effective Decision Maker

The skilled director recognizes that both logic and emotion are part of making decisions. She knows when to offer support, when to delegate to those who have the expertise to act on their own, and when to shoulder the responsibility. At times it is necessary to reverse a decision or insist on implementation in the face of opposition. To build credibility, it is important to be decisive. If a director takes forever to make routine decisions, fails to follow through on decisions previously made, or is inconsistent in decisions made about similar issues, then staff will doubt the director's ability and judgment. It is important to solicit staff input before making decisions. Occasionally, a director must admit that she is wrong and reverse a poor decision. Decisions must be made in a timely fashion and they must be announced clearly and without apology.

Finally, a director must keep her work life in perspective. A fully committed effort at work does not preclude a life outside of work. A successful director understands the relationship between health and professional performance. She exercises regularly, eats well, and has a sense of humour. It is useful to become involved in networking groups where directors can share with other directors the joys and frustrations of their jobs.

What Staff Expect of a Director

Establishing credibility as a director of an organization is not a one-time event; credibility must be built continuously—and occasionally rebuilt. Meeting mutual expectations and establishing trust achieve credibility. When a director endeavours to meet staff expectations, she can legitimately have certain expectations of the staff:

Staff expect a director to make good decisions. Many of the decisions a director makes involve financial, organizational, and tactical factors that few staff are aware of. Staff must trust that the director is balancing all these factors and making decisions that are in the best interests of the program. It is critical to keep staff in the loop about issues facing the program—both good and bad. However, there are times when the director has information that must be kept confidential.

Staff expect directors to listen. It is demotivating to believe that others do not respect your judgment. Employees need to believe the director values their opinions and takes their input seriously. Time needs to be set aside to discuss issues in a rational way.

Staff expect directors to have expertise. Staff respect directors who know their stuff and understand what is needed to deliver a quality ECEC program. They need to know that, if they have a problem, they can turn to the director and get the support and guidance they need. Directors should keep current with child development research and other aspects of knowledge listed in the director competencies outlined above. There is a link between this and the following point.

Staff expect directors to know what is going on. A concern occasionally expressed by staff is that the director is out of touch with what is happening on the floor. Directors must understand and care about the day-to-day issues that staff face. It is important to visit playrooms and get up to speed on issues faced by staff.

Staff expect directors to be fair. Staff must be convinced that they are treated fairly when it comes to scheduling, compensation, supervision, attention, and opportunities for advancement.

A key part of being an effective director is evaluating one's own performance on an ongoing basis.

Evaluating Director Effectiveness

There is usually an abundance of opinion about the director's performance—from board members, employees, parents, community members, and the director herself. The process used to evaluate a director's performance should provide a mutually supportive and professionally enhancing experience for all involved.

Performance evaluations are usually conducted annually. However, with a director who is new to the position or organization, it may be appropriate to schedule more frequent evaluation sessions—perhaps twice during the first year. More frequent evaluations can also be useful in situations where the board and the director want to enhance their communication. The next step is to determine which criteria will be used to assess performance. Ideally, the director and board of directors will determine together which evaluation tools will be used. Having a detailed job description, such as the one provided earlier in the chapter, provides a solid place to start. Generally, a committee of the board of directors is responsible for evaluating the director.

Enough time should be set aside for the process; a couple of meetings are usually required. Input about the director's performance can be sought from the following groups: parents, staff, **colleagues** of the director, funders, and other board members. After the feedback is compiled, a written report is prepared by the committee and reviewed with the director. The evaluation process can become a valuable tool for improving services to children and families.

Sample Evaluation Process

Following is a sample questionnaire a program could use to help evaluate a director's performance. To use this questionnaire, distribute the "My Director . . . " questionnaire and a blank envelope to each individual who works at the program more than 10 hours per week. (If the director is male, the wording of some of the questions will need to be altered to reflect this.) For more accurate results, it is advisable to distribute questionnaires to both program staff and support staff. Place a box labelled "Questionnaire Return Box" in the program's office or staff room and ask respondents to deposit their completed surveys in this box. Assure staff of the confidentiality of their responses.

It is suggested that the director should simultaneously complete a survey such as the Leadership Style questionnaire and the Supervisory Beliefs Inventory in *Blueprint for Action: Achieving Center-Based Change through Staff Development* (Jorde Bloom, Sheerer, and Britz 1991). The results of this self-assessment can then be compared to the collective perceptions of the staff, determined using the scoring tools given following the questionnaire.

Staff Questionnaire

"MY DIRECTOR . . . "

Dear Staff:

One of the hallmarks of an early childhood professional is the ability to reflect on one's performance. Your feedback about my leadership style is important in helping me improve and grow professionally. Please take a few minutes to complete this questionnaire. When you are finished, insert it in the attached plain envelope and put it in the "Questionnaire Return Box" in the office. There is no need for you to put your name on the questionnaire.

Thank you.

PART I

Place a check in front of the statement that most nearly reflects your director's leadership style in different situations. (Check only one response in each group.)

WITH RESPECT TO PLANNING, MY DIRECTOR . . .

1. _____ does most of the planning herself by setting goals, objectives, and work schedules for staff to follow. She then works out procedures and responsibilities for staff to follow.

2. _____ does very little planning, either by herself or with the staff. She tells the staff she has confidence in them to carry out their jobs in a responsible way.

3. _____ gets staff members together to assess centre-wide problems and discuss ideas and strategies for improvement. Together they set up goals and objectives and establish individual responsibilities.

WITH RESPECT TO WORK ASSIGNMENTS AND THE DAY-TO-DAY OPERATION OF THE CENTRE, MY DIRECTOR . . .

4. _____ checks with staff regularly to see if they are content and if they have the things they need. She does not see the necessity of precise job descriptions, preferring instead to let the staff determine the scope and nature of their jobs.

5. _____ is flexible in adapting job descriptions and changing work assignments as needed. Updates centre policies and procedures depending on the needs of the staff, parents, children, and board.

6. _____ tends to go by the book. Expects staff to adhere to written job descriptions. Follows policies and procedures precisely.

WITH RESPECT TO LEADERSHIP PHILOSOPHY, MY DIRECTOR . . .

7. _____ tends to emphasize people's well-being, believing that happy workers will be productive workers.

8. _____ tends to emphasize hard work and a job well done. We are a results-oriented program.

9. _____ tends to emphasize both what we do and what we need as people.

DURING MEETINGS, MY DIRECTOR . . .

10. _____ keeps focused on the agenda and the topics that need to be covered.

11. _____ focuses on each individual's feelings and helps people express their emotional reactions to an issue.

12. _____ focuses on differing positions people take and how they deal with each other.

THE PRIMARY GOAL OF MY DIRECTOR IS . . .

13. _____ to meet the needs of parents and children while providing a healthy work climate for staff.

14. _____ to keep the centre running efficiently.

15. _____ to help staff find fulfillment.

IN EVALUATING THE STAFF'S PERFORMANCE, MY DIRECTOR . . .

16. _____ attempts to assess how each individual's performance has contributed to centre-wide achievement of goals.

17. _____ makes an assessment of each person's performance and effectiveness according to prede-termined established criteria that are applied equally to all staff.

18. _____ allows people to set their own goals and determine performance standards.

MY DIRECTOR BELIEVES THE BEST WAY TO MOTIVATE SOMEONE WHO IS NOT PERFORMING UP TO HIS/HER ABILITY IS TO . . .

19. _____ point out to the individual the importance of the job to be done.

20. _____ try to get to know the individual better in an attempt to understand why the person is not realizing his/her potential.

21. _____ work with the individual to redefine job responsibilities to more effectively contribute to cen-tre-wide goals.

MY DIRECTOR BELIEVES IT IS HER ROLE TO . . .

22. _____ make sure that staff members have a solid foundation of knowledge and skill that will help them accomplish centre goals.

23. _____ help people learn to work effectively in groups to accomplish group goals.

24. _____ help individuals become responsible for their own education and effectiveness, and take the first step toward realizing their potential.

WHAT THREE WORDS OR PHRASES MOST ACCURATELY DESCRIBE THE LEADERSHIP STYLE OF YOUR DIRECTOR:

<table>
<tr><td align="center">PART II</td></tr>
</table>

Circle the numeral that most nearly represents your assessment of your director in each of the areas described.

My Director Is . . .	strongly disagree				strongly agree
...knowledgeable. She knows what is going on in the program for staff, children, parents, board, and administrators.	1	2	3	4	5
...in control. She has a handle on things and is actively and effectively in charge of the centre's programs and operations.	1	2	3	4	5
...dedicated. She demonstrates interest in learning more about her job from peers, professional groups, and reading material.	1	2	3	4	5
...confident. She has a sense of mission and a clear vision for the centre.	1	2	3	4	5
...enthusiastic. She has the energy to cope with the daily demands of her job.	1	2	3	4	5
...an effective communicator. She keeps us well informed about policies, procedures, activities, and schedules.	1	2	3	4	5
...responsive. When adults or children need her attention, she is able to focus on their needs.	1	2	3	4	5

My Director Is . . .	strongly disagree				strongly agree
...*available to parents.* She knows the families and encourages them to participate in the program.	1	2	3	4	5
...*open.* She encourages employees to participate in decision making and welcomes their suggestions.	1	2	3	4	5
...*fair.* She investigates all sides of an issue and distributes criticism and praise with grace and equity.	1	2	3	4	5
...*predictable.* Expectations are clearly defined, and policies are routinely followed.	1	2	3	4	5
...*a trainer.* She encourages my professional growth by providing opportunities for ongoing training and development.	1	2	3	4	5
...*a delegator.* She uses authority with fairness and according to the staff's talents and time.	1	2	3	4	5
...*prepared.* She has a sense of priority about the centre and the requirements of her role.	1	2	3	4	5
...*respectful.* She understands people as individuals and shapes her expectations of them accordingly.	1	2	3	4	5
...*understanding.* She realizes that each of us has different interests, abilities, attitudes, and personalities.	1	2	3	4	5
...*available.* I am comfortable bringing my concerns, criticisms, problems, and successes to her.	1	2	3	4	5
...*efficient.* She handles the day-to-day routines of the centre promptly and skillfully.	1	2	3	4	5
...*supportive.* She looks for opportunities to give feedback and offer praise.	1	2	3	4	5
...*a motivator.* She encourages each of us to give our best effort.	1	2	3	4	5
...*realistic.* She has a sense of humour and is able to keep things in perspective.	1	2	3	4	5
...*an influence in the community.* She is an advocate for children and quality care.	1	2	3	4	5
...*genuine.* She greets me warmly and demonstrates interest and concern. I know where I stand with her.	1	2	3	4	5
...*flexible.* She encourages creative problem solving, facilitates personal growth, and keeps things interesting.	1	2	3	4	5
...*resourceful.* She knows where to go and what to do to get things done. She makes good use of community resources.	1	2	3	4	5

SCORING

The composite results of Part I summarize the staff's perceptions of the director's dominant leadership style. The following scoring sheet includes a brief description of the three leadership styles assessed by this questionnaire.

SCORING—PART I

To score Part I, tally the responses by noting with a mark each time staff checked a particular response:

1. _____	9. _____	17. _____
2. _____	10. _____	18. _____
3. _____	11. _____	19. _____
4. _____	12. _____	20. _____
5. _____	13. _____	21. _____
6. _____	14. _____	22. _____
7. _____	15. _____	23. _____
8. _____	16. _____	24. _____

Now total the marks for the following responses:

Task-oriented: 1, 6, 8, 10, 14, 17, 19, 22   Total _____

Achieving centre goals is most important in this leadership style. Strong concern for high performance and accomplishing tasks. Emphasis is on planning, directing, following procedures, and applying uniform standards and expectations for all. This director may be viewed as too structured, bureaucratic, and inflexible.

People-oriented: 2, 4, 7, 11, 15, 18, 20, 24   Total _____

Achieving harmonious group relations is foremost in this leadership style. Strong emphasis on maintaining comfortable, friendly, and satisfying working conditions. Allows staff to exercise control and be self-directed with minimal intrusion of centre-wide policies and procedures. Staff working in centres with this style of leadership may complain about the lack of order and coordination.

Transactional: 3, 5, 9, 12, 13, 16, 21, 23   Total _____

Achieving both centre goals and maintaining high morale is important in this leadership style. This director is flexible and fair, recognizing that different situations may require a different emphasis on centre-wide needs or individual needs.

SCORING—PART II

For Part II, add up the total score for each respondent. (Scores will range from 25 to 125.) Add together all respondents' scores and divide by the number of individuals returning questionnaires. This will yield an average score regarding the staff's evaluation of the director's performance in a wide range of administrative and supervisory behaviours.

On any assessment such as this where perceptions may vary considerably, it is important to note the range of scores (the lowest score and the highest score). Also, it is helpful to do an item analysis to discern those two or three items that staff rated the director lowest on, and those two or three items where the director consistently scored highest. This will provide the director specific feedback about those perceived areas where staff may feel he or she has the greatest skill and those areas in need of improvement.

Ways in Which Programs Are Organized

In Canada, early childhood development programs may be operated by non-profit organizations, commercial or independent operators, or public organizations. It is essential for the director to understand the functioning of these various structures. With the exception of owner-operators, directors report to boards of directors or owners who have the ultimate responsibility for a program.

The term "**auspice**" refers to the legal status and ownership of programs. The issue of auspice has often been a contentious one in Canada. One side of the discussion holds that privately operated centres should not profit from caring for children and that child care should be a fully funded public service or a community-based non-profit service supported by government funding, as it is in British Columbia and Quebec. The adherents of this view further believe that private businesses should not benefit from government funding. Supporters of commercial child care argue that caring for children is the responsibility of individual families. Their position is that, even if governments assist individual families to pay for care, governments should not determine where parents choose to send their children.

Different provinces and territories have adopted different ideological and legislative stances with respect to auspice and the funding implications of auspice. Some provinces, such as Nova Scotia, provide funding, including subsidized fees, only to non-profit centres. Ontario allows subsidies to be used in both commercial and non-profit facilities; in Prince Edward Island, no distinction is made with respect to auspice. In Canada, programs are operated predominantly under non-profit or commercial auspices.

Most programs are non-profit and sponsored by social service agencies, parent-run organizations, municipalities, colleges and universities, or churches. Some non-profit programs are stand-alone organizations operated, according to legal bylaws, by a voluntary board of directors that may include parents, community representatives, and individuals with specific expertise. Or a non-profit program might be operated by an agency such as the YMCA, which operates over 75 programs. In a non-profit program, any budget surpluses must be poured back into the program or returned to the sponsoring agency.

Commercial programs, also referred to as "proprietary" or "**for-profit**" programs, are privately owned businesses. They are structured and operated to generate a profit for the owners. The director is responsible to the owner, who determines the organizational structure. About 25% of Canada's child care programs are commercial businesses, ranging from small owner-operated programs to larger chains. Most proprietary programs are found in Newfoundland and Alberta, while Manitoba has no commercial child care programs. These Canadian figures stand in sharp contrast to those for the United States, where about 60% of all child care programs are commercial operations. Presumably, government incentives for non-profit programs, or the lack of them, are reflected in these numbers. In Saskatchewan, until 1990, only non-profit programs were eligible for government funds. Ontario and Manitoba have at times given non-profit programs subsidies to enable them to increase caregiver salaries.

Some programs are run as a public service under the auspices of a municipal government. This type of program is most common in Ontario, and only a very small percentage of programs are of this kind. While these programs are operated under various types of ownership and management, all are operated as small businesses. All must generate sufficient income to pay salaries and expenses, recruit families, purchase supplies, and so on.

Some large Canadian companies have created ECEC programs to support their employees' child care needs. They believe that employees with young children may more often be late for work, need to leave work early, or need to deal with child-related issues while at work. To support their workers' child care needs, some employers join with other employers to operate a program run by a consortium of employers.

Each province and territory has legislation that governs for-profit and non-profit corporations. Commercial programs distribute their profits to owners or shareholders while non-profits are required to reinvest surpluses back into the organization. Non-profit organizations must have a board of directors that makes key decisions and manages the organization. In for-profits, owners may make decisions without any consultation with others. Families and community members may have input into non-profits; such input is less likely at commercial programs, although some centres have a parent **advisory board**.

These differences may influence to some extent the primary goals of the organization. Non-profit programs will aim for a balanced budget while for-profit programs will wish to turn some profit. Lyon and Canning (1999) note that these goals may influence the priorities of the organization (such as staff qualifications), and this in turn affects the quality of service offered.

Advantages and Disadvantages of For-Profit/ Non-Profit Status

In general, it is much easier and less expensive to set up a for-profit organization. The establishment of a non-profit program involves filing articles of incorporation. A corporation is a legal entity. The corporation protects individuals from certain liabilities by creating a decision-making and accountable board of directors. Corporations remain legal entities until dissolved by the board of directors or a court. Several documents, such as the bylaws of the organization, are required to incorporate. Non-profits typically have greater access to funding from public and philanthropic sources. As well, they are more likely to receive charitable donations from individuals and corporations. The average commercial program spends three times as much as the average non-profit in occupancy costs. Community organizations are more likely to contribute space at no or lower cost to non-profit programs.

Volunteers are more likely to work in a non-profit program, and training institutions in some parts of Canada are more likely to use non-profits for student placement experiences. Parents are often unaware of the legal status of the program they select for their children. They tend to choose based on cost, location, and caregiver warmth.

Decision making tends to be more complex in non-profit programs, where there are more players and procedures. Often, board members do not have sufficient time to invest in thoroughly understanding all the legal, financial, educational, political, and demographic issues involved in operating an early childhood development program. Consequently, they may delegate much of the decision making to the director or defer to her recommendations. Non-profits with boards of directors made up of diverse individuals may be more in tune with broader changes in the community and better at fundraising or finding new sources of revenue.

It is too simplistic to believe that individuals who operate for-profit programs are driven solely by a desire for economic gain. Most early childhood entrepreneurs believe strongly in the importance of early childhood development and see their business venture as making a difference for children and families.

Individuals who aspire to leadership in the non-profit sector clearly have a desire to contribute to society. They also become motivated to effectively run the business side of the organization.

Working with a Board

The board of directors and the program director share responsibility for the operation of the program. Effective communication between the two is essential. The working board is responsible for the overall operation of the program. Its members are elected at an **annual general meeting (AGM)**. Some boards are comprised primarily of parents, while others include representatives from the community. In practice, board involvement runs the gamut from ongoing involvement of the board in the program to leaving almost all the work to the director. Some directors cite as their biggest concern boards that get involved in the day-to-day running of the program, thereby undermining the director. Ideally, a board should function somewhere between these two extremes by carrying out clearly defined functions related to the organization's human resources, finances, facility, and program.

Most boards meet on a monthly basis. In addition, a designate of the board should keep in close contact with the director. The director serves as the liaison between the board and the parents and staff. She both uses the board's knowledge to improve the program and helps the board to understand the rationale for decisions made based on her specialized knowledge of child development. Individual board members may have expertise in financial management, fundraising, human resource issues, health, property, or lobbying for children and family rights. Board members are often new to community work and need a comprehensive orientation to their responsibilities and this responsibility often falls to the director.

Types of Boards

There are two kinds of boards, governing and advisory. A **governing board** makes and enforces policy, which is implemented by the program director. An advisory board has no power to enforce; instead, it suggests policies and procedures or provides information to those who administer the program. A parent advisory board may meet several times a year. Its members act as consultants to the director of the program; they offer advice and resources and raise any concerns about issues that may affect the program's quality. (Chapter 9, "Building the Partnership with Families," elaborates on parent involvement on boards.) The bylaws of an organization should state clearly the purpose and functions of the board of directors.

Recruiting Effective Board Members

The size of a board of directors can range from as few as three members to 10 or more. The bylaws of an organization prescribe the minimum and maximum board sizes, although, like other rules of governance, these bylaws can be amended. The board should be small enough to act as a deliberative body. Small boards can be cohesive. What a board may lack in size and formality, it can make up for with enthusiasm and directed energy. (It should be noted that some board members may be content to serve in name only.) Large boards provide an opportunity to diversify member representation, expertise, and responsibility. Early childhood organizations with a small staff can lack critical expertise and may rely on the community support that can be provided by a larger board. In order for a large board to function well, it needs an effective chairperson and rules of procedure and decision making.

It is important to determine the board's needs, skills, professional qualifications, and interests. With an existing board of directors, it is useful to inventory the skills and expertise of the members and identify gaps to be filled by new recruits. Most early childhood development programs include parents on the board of directors. Participation gives parents the opportunity to influence policies that govern the program and staff. Some boards have a chartered public accountant serve as treasurer or chair of the finance committee. A faculty member from a local college or university can bring to the board expertise in the developmental needs of children and may facilitate student placements. A lawyer can be helpful, particularly if the organization is in the process of incorporation. The board should include someone with a knowledge of health issues, such as a public health nurse or pediatrician. For a new organization, a director from another early childhood development program in the community can bring firsthand knowledge of the issues faced by the program, such as setting appropriate fees and developing schedules. A board member with expertise in human resource issues is essential. This is not an exhaustive list. At various times, members with particular skills—from fundraising and public relations to facilities construction—may be required.

Sample

JOB DESCRIPTION—BOARD MEMBER

Position:
Member, Board of Directors

Reports to:
President, Board of Directors

Term:
Two years

Duties:
1. Come to each meeting prepared to discuss the business before the board.
2. Read background information in advance of meetings and note any assigned responsibilities.
3. Attend all scheduled meetings and special meetings where board member representation is required.
4. Review and approve the organization's annual operating budget, interim financial reports, and annual independent audit.
5. Participate in the selection, support, and evaluation of the early childhood director.
6. Approve contracts and agreements for the early childhood development program.
7. Participate in the organization's strategic planning process and abide by the decisions made.

(continued)

8. Help ensure the financial solvency of the program by:
   - overseeing the financial management of the organization; and
   - actively participating in the fundraising process.
9. Promote the program among influential persons, donors, and the community at large.
10. Represent the interests of all children and parents when making decisions.
11. Participate in periodic self-assessment and evaluation of own contribution to the board.
12. Participate on one or more committees of the board.
13. Provide advice and consultation to other members and the director.

Qualifications:
- a commitment to the mission of the agency and the parents and children who benefit from its services.
- the ability to work collaboratively as a team member.
- having adequate time to devote to the organization (approximately 40+ hours per year).

Common Areas of Board Responsibility

In *Maximizing Child Care Services: The Role of Owners and Boards,* Ferguson and McCormick Ferguson (2001) provide a framework for getting the best out of early childhood development programs. Owners and boards play a key role in the provision of quality. In an early childhood operation, the role of the board (or owner) can be defined under six headings:

- *Direction.* The board sets the direction for the provision of quality services, defining what the service intends to achieve and the client base.
- *Guardianship.* The board hires, monitors, and evaluates the director and ensures that the resources necessary for the provision of a quality service are available so that the director can carry out her responsibilities in an efficient and effective manner.
- *Public Relations.* The board ensures that the operation is promoted. As well, board members represent the organization to the public. They speak out on the organization's behalf and contribute to public discussions on policy and societal trends that affect early childhood services.
- *Advocacy.* The board advocates to government, the general public, and the business community regarding the inherent value of early childhood development programs.
- *Legal Conduct.* The board ensures that all legal requirements of the organization— including employment and tax laws, licensing regulations, and business and incorporation laws—are being met.
- *Ethical conduct.* It is the board's responsibility to uphold prudent and ethical best practices—to ensure that all actions of the organization and its representatives are carried out in an ethical manner.

These areas of responsibility are all interrelated.

These are purposeful practical and legal reasons why the board of directors and staff share some program responsibilities. Following is a brief description of the generally accepted roles and responsibilities of each party.

Board Committees

The work of the board of directors is carried out by committees, although some small boards operate without them. Committee responsibilities are spelled out in the organization's bylaws. Some of the typical standing committees are executive, finance, human resource, program, and property. On occasion, ad hoc committees may be appointed by the board to perform specific short-term tasks and then report to the board. The board chairperson may appoint members to each committee on the basis of their interests and expertise.

The *executive committee* is composed, at a minimum, of the board's officers—the chairperson or president, treasurer, and secretary—with the program director serving as an ex officio member. This committee advises on actions to be taken and changes to be made. It conducts board business between meetings and, in an emergency, can act for the full board. The president or chairperson is the designated leader of the organization and often speaks for the program at public meetings. The chairperson and the director need to develop a close working relationship and have regular contact between board meetings. One or more officers usually sit on the executive committee and take on the responsibilities of the chairperson in her or his absence. The treasurer chairs the finance committee and works closely with the director to develop and monitor the budget. The secretary keeps minutes of all board meetings and the annual general meeting. Other duties involve updating bylaws and handling all correspondence specific to the board of directors.

The director assists the chairperson, helps volunteer committee members to implement action, and provides ongoing feedback on the impact of board decisions on the day-to-day operations. The director functions as a resource person, assists in the recruiting of board members, ensures the development of an agenda, and takes responsibility for implementing assigned tasks. The director may be required to arrange meeting times, make copies of minutes and reports, and arrange refreshments. Administrative services such as mailing, copying, cheque writing, and so on are usually carried out by the director. As well as the director, other staff may be invited to attend board meetings, but none have a vote. Minutes of board meetings are often posted so that families can monitor board proceedings

Financial oversight of the program is usually assigned to the *finance committee*, which is chaired by the treasurer. This committee reviews the organization's income and expenses, balance sheet, investments, and other matters related to the program's financial situation. It is responsible for submitting the annual operating budget to the board of directors for approval, comparing income and expenses to the approved operating budget, and arranging for the annual audit. Because they prepare the budget and appropriate the funds, finance committee members must have a good understanding of the overall operation and the program philosophy.

The *human resource (HR) committee* deals with the organization's most valuable resource—its employees. The cost of salaries, payroll deductions, and benefits exceeds 60% of an ECEC program's total operating budget. Staff are the means by which services are delivered. Their skill level, satisfaction with their jobs, and commitment to the program and children and families served all contribute to their effectiveness. It is the board's responsibility to establish the human resource policies that govern the employment of program staff. Human resource policies must reflect the legal requirements concerning employment—

such as employment standards or health and safety requirements—and the specific policies of the program—such as vacation and sick-day accrual, employee performance evaluations, and **grievance procedures**. (HR policies are elaborated on in chapter 6.) The board is also responsible for approving and revising job descriptions and setting salary levels. In essence, the board of directors provides the framework within which the staff, through the director, is managed. The director implements the HR policies. The HR committee is responsible for hiring the director, preparing her employment contract, evaluating her performance, and, if necessary, firing her.

The responsibility for finding and maintaining a facility rests with the *property committee*. The busiest time for the property committee is prior to the launch of a program, when the committee must decide whether to purchase, construct, or lease a facility, make decisions about renovations, and ensure that the program meets all zoning restrictions and bylaws. Once the program is established, the committee must ensure that the building and grounds are clean, safe, and attractive. This committee is also responsible for maintaining the program's equipment. For all major equipment purchases, the director must obtain the board's approval of both suitability and cost.

As well as the children's program and strategies for family involvement, the *program committee*'s responsibilities may include the professional development program for the staff. This committee recommends policies to the board on enrolment and grouping of children, the hours and days of operation, and health, safety, and nutrition.

RESPONSIBILITIES OF THE BOARD OF DIRECTORS

- Develop all long-range and strategic plans.
- Through the design, development, and monitoring of the program, ensure that the program meets the needs of the children, families, and community it serves.
- Ensure that the program meets all legal requirements.
- Develop the **mission statement**, bylaws, and policies that govern the program, and review them annually.
- Develop and set the annual budget; monitor the budget by reviewing the organization's financial status on at least a quarterly basis.
- Maintain accurate records of board meetings and operations.
- Define qualifications, authority, and responsibilities of the director along with outcomes expected.
- Hire the director; facilitate an annual written evaluation of the director's performance based on the job description and indicators of performance that have been previously established.
- Ensure that fair hiring and HR policies are established and implemented.
- Annually, negotiate staff salaries, benefits, and working conditions.
- Develop criteria for and regularly evaluate program effectiveness.
- Participate in promoting the program and advocating on its behalf; be involved in fundraising.

Other standing or ad hoc committees may include a fundraising, nominating, and/or grievance committee. The *fundraising committee* is charged with soliciting donations of cash, equipment, or services (such as printing or computer consulting). It may take on special-event planning, such as raffles, and other forms of community fundraising. The *nominating committee* screens potential new board members and prepares a slate for election by the board of directors. It may be responsible for orientation of new board members. A *grievance committee* may be formed to act as a mediator for parent or staff complaints. This committee must be careful not to undermine the authority of the director and cause even greater problems.

The board of directors sets the overall direction of the program and is legally responsible for what it does.

Summary

An effective director brings skills, knowledge, and caring to her job. Directors fill a variety of roles, but all must balance the management and operation of the program with the care of and communication with the people who are the essence of a quality environment. Programs are operated by non-profit boards of directors, owners, and public organizations.

A well-organized board operates through a group of committees whose functions relate to the major components of the program's operation. The principal responsibilities of a board of an established program include strategic planning, acquiring financial resources, and advocating for the program. Good communication between the board and director is necessary for a well-run organization. The board creates policies and the director implements them. The board of directors of an early childhood development program needs to develop policies and procedures that will serve as the guidelines for achieving program goals. The effective operation of the program depends upon the director's ability to interpret and carry out a mission by bringing individuals together and motivating them toward a common goal.

Key Terms and Concepts

Advisory board, p. 71

Annual General Meeting (AGM), p. 72

Auspice, p. 70

Board of directors, p. 50

Colleague, p. 65

Corporation, p. 50

Decision making, p. 71

Director, p. 49

For-profit, p. 70

Governing board, p. 72

Governing body, p. 53

Grievance procedure, p. 76

Mission statement, p. 76

Non-profit, p. 50

Operations, p. 50

Organizational structure, p. 60

Policies, p. 53

Procedures, p. 53

Stakeholders, p. 54

Activities

1. Visit the director of an early childhood setting. Discuss approximately how much time is spent on various aspects of the job, such as communicating with the parents, staff, children, owner/board of directors, community stakeholders, and funders; keeping financial records; responding to emergencies; and so on.

2. Arrange with the director to attend a board of directors or advisory committee meeting. What topics were discussed? How were decisions made? What are your perceptions of the functions of these bodies? Compare your findings with those of other class members.

3. For each statement that follows, indicate whether the primary responsibility rests with both the board of directors and the director (B) or only the early childhood development director and staff (S). If you feel that both are responsible, list them in order of level of shared responsibility:

   a) drafts the centre's annual budget for approval _____

   b) establishes HR policies _____

   c) plans fundraising events _____

   d) approves legal contracts and agreements _____

   e) analyzes unusual budget line-items (revenues and expenses) _____

   f) recommends new service directions for the program _____

   g) is legally responsible for the affairs of the centre _____

   h) writes grant proposals/applications to public/private sources _____

   i) prepares reports for funding agencies _____

   j) maintains the centre's financial records _____

   (Answers on next page.)

4. Arrange to talk with some members of the board of directors of your college. How did they become board members? What are their duties? How often do they meet? How many members are on this board?

Recommended Reading

Carter, M. and D. Curtis. *The Visionary Director: A Handbook for Dreaming, Organizing, and Improvising in Your Center.* St. Paul, MI: Redleaf Press, 1998.

Culkin, M., ed. *Managing Quality in Young Children's Programs: The Leader's Role.* New York: Teachers College Press, 2000.

Doherty, G. "Standards for Quality Child Care Programs"; "Standards of Practice for Administrators/Directors." In *Partners in Quality: Tools for Administrators in Child Care Settings.* Ottawa: Canadian Child Care Federation, 2000.

Ferguson, E. and T. McCormick Ferguson. *Maximizing Child Care Services: The Role of Owners and Boards.* Halifax: Child Care Connection NS, 2001.

Jorde Bloom, P. *Circle of Influence: Implementing Shared Decision-Making and Participative Management.* Lake Forest, IL: New Horizons, 2000.

Jorde Bloom, P. *Leadership in Action: How Effective Directors Get Things Done.* Lake Forest, IL: New Horizons, 2003.

Rood, J. *Leadership in Early Childhood.* 2d ed. New York: Teachers College Press, Columbia University, 1998.

Sciarra, D.J. and A.G. Dorsey. *Leaders and Supervisors in Child Care Programs.* Albany, NY: Delmar, 2002.

Weblinks

www.childcareexchange.com
Child Care Information Exchange

This is a publication for directors of early childhood development programs. The website has a comprehensive list of resources on program development, organizational management, planning and evaluation, and more.

www.ncnb.org
National Centre for Non-Profit Boards

This site provides many hard-to-find resources including books and videos on topics such as board ethics, bylaws, board basics, and strategic planning. Most helpful are comprehensive question-and-answer features, sample job descriptions for each member of the executive, and questions one should ask when considering joining a non-profit board of directors.

www.eccdc.org
Early Childhood Community Development Centre

The Child Care Resource Link for Owners and Boards on this site provides a listing of resources to help decision-makers maximize their operations. The Web page is organized around six key areas of responsibility: direction, guardianship, public relations, advocacy, legal conduct, and ethical conduct. Included are bibliographies and lists of contacts, links, and articles.

Answers to question 3 based on commonly applied organizational wisdom:
a) S, b) B, c) B/S, d) B, e) S, f) S/B, g) B, h) S/B, i) S, j) S.

Planning and Evaluating the Program Goals

chapter 4

Objectives

- **Define program philosophy.**
- **Describe a vision of an early childhood program.**
- **Examine the purpose and implications of a philosophy statement.**
- **Identify the steps in developing a philosophy statement.**
- **Identify who determines the program philosophy.**
- **Describe the role of leadership in actualizing the vision.**
- **Describe the characteristics of effective program evaluation tools.**
- **Identify tools for assessing program goals.**

Building a quality early childhood program requires creativity and energy. In order to respond to the full range of needs of the children and families, an ecological approach (described in chapter 1) is needed. Leadership by directors in the design and review of the program vision is crucial; it is they who will lead efforts to put this vision into practice.

Defining a Program Philosophy

The first step in planning a program is to set goals for serving the children and families attending the program. After determining the needs of children and families, key stakeholders (parents, staff, board of directors/owner, community representatives) must define the program **philosophy** and decide how to shape the program to meet it. Once program goals are chosen, decisions regarding the program—policies, human resources, physical facilities and equipment, the family program, and so on—should be consistent with them. The director's role is to act as the catalyst to facilitate the program goals. Directors must determine the process by which goals will be met, operationalize the strategies necessary to meet the goals, and evaluate the progress the program is making in fulfilling them.

What Is a Vision in Early Childhood Programs?

Quality in early childhood settings rests on the goals, values, assumptions, and principles that guide the program. A vision of quality extends beyond a concern for good care and education, health, and safety to encompass children's total development; the program is thought of as the total experience of the children in the setting, not just those activities that might be termed "educational." The vision includes the program's relationship with each child and family. It acknowledges that children and families live and grow within different cultures and that all cultural beliefs and values deserve respect.

A vision is a realistic, credible, attractive future for the organization and provides direction for what we wish to become. It is who we are, what we do, how we do it, and who we do it for. A vision for early childhood programs should be formed using a combination of information and knowledge and a concern for the well-being of the stakeholders of the program who will, in turn, benefit from the implementation of the vision. The vision can inspire stakeholders to focus on goals and energize them to work proactively to achieve them. It provides a dynamic concept for the future that motivates an organization to make changes, incorporate new ideas, and take new directions. It is through the process of working proactively to achieve a vision that a program achieves excellence. The vision first needs to be articulated, then owned by those who form it, and, finally, a strategic plan to achieve the vision needs to be outlined and followed. The philosophy is a statement of the values underlying the vision.

Program Philosophy

Every program needs its own vision of quality that becomes reflected in the daily activities, such as children's play, the interchanges between families and staff, and the way staff feel about themselves and others as they go about their work in the program. Everything about the program should be considered in light of this vision of quality: how the program looks, how it sounds, and what it expects from all involved—families, children, staff, and community.

The philosophy of an early childhood development program determines the characteristics of the program; it has a direct impact on the development of the curriculum, staff hiring, the extent of family involvement, and interaction with the community. A **mission statement** outlines the beliefs and goals that the stakeholders consider central to educating and nurturing young children and helps parents, the director, caregivers, support staff, and the community to accurately realize these goals. It is critical that this important declaration be established in a thoughtful, systematic manner.

DEVELOPING A MISSION STATEMENT

Consider the following:

- What are the needs, characteristics, and learning patterns of young children?
- What do families need in order to raise responsible, happy children?
- Do families feel recognized by the program as the most important people in their children's lives?
- What are the desired qualities of caregivers, and what kind of educational background should they possess?

A mission statement is a dynamic, living document that responds to the needs of the community and incorporates new research. Since the program philosophy is a culmination of beliefs and goals for early childhood development, it should be re-evaluated on an ongoing basis, and decision makers should be open to new ideas.

A philosophy is about goal orientation; it also serves as a yardstick to measure the performance of the program in meeting its goals. Program goals for children and families are statements of what really matters in a program—reference points for assessing whether the policies and practices are achieving what they were intended to achieve.

Although the words "goals" and "objectives" are often used interchangeably, there is a difference. "Goals" is used to indicate changes that take place over a longer period of time. When the goals of a program are broken down into smaller, more easily attainable targets, these are called "objectives"—changes that take place over a shorter period of time, such as a day or week. Objectives constitute the tasks individuals need to accomplish for the organization's goals to be met. The hallmark of any successful organization is a shared sense among key stakeholders of what they are trying to accomplish. Agreed-upon goals and ways to attain them provide the foundation for rational planning and action.

Who Determines the Philosophy?

A vision for an organization cannot be just one person's ideas. The responsibility for developing the philosophy depends to some extent how the program is structured. In a for-profit program, it is the owner who develops the philosophy, whereas in a non-profit program, it is the board of directors. Ideally, the development of the philosophy occurs through a collaborative process, one that often includes families, staff, and representatives from the community. The director is responsible for the implementation of this collective understanding and for meeting the goals articulated in the philosophy.

In the case of a newly created program, the individuals who are developing the program discuss and formulate the program philosophy. Planners often have very specific ideas about the program philosophy. Sometimes, the process is delayed until the director is hired, so that she can be involved in the development of the statement. In an established program, it is important to hire a director who can operate within an adopted philosophical framework.

Regardless of who has the initial inspiration for a program's purpose, if the philosophy is to grow, the interest and involvement of others must be cultivated. It is important to communicate the vision when hiring staff. Staff members must feel comfortable with the philosophy. Frustrations over incompatible philosophies can create unworkable situations for staff. The opportunity to participate in program decision making is a leading factor in the morale of caregivers. Involving staff in the revision of an existing philosophy statement gives them a critical stake in it.

Many early childhood directors lack experience in working with a vision. Resources exist that can aid in the development of this skill. *The Visionary Director: A Handbook for Dreaming, Organizing, and Improvising in Your Center* provides many specific examples to help directors develop and/or revise a philosophy statement (Carter and Curtis 1998). *Circle of Influence: Implementing Shared Decision Making and Participative Management* offers a balance of theory and practical tools for promoting change and increasing program effectiveness (Jorde Bloom 2000).

When a director meets with prospective families, she should discuss the philosophy statement with them to ensure that they understand it and that it is consistent with their goals and traditions. It is not enough to make grand statements about the philosophy— parents want to see this vision translated into action. They want to see the ways in which parents and caregivers work together to provide the best experience for the child.

Having a clear, jargon-free statement of intent based on a vision that has been formed inclusively greatly benefits families as well as staff. Early childhood development programs are relationship based, and for some families, their supportive relationships with the program staff help to fill the gap left by the absence of extended families. Encouraging the involvement of families in the visioning process builds their confidence in, awareness of, and desire to participate in their child's education—and families who feel ownership of the vision will feel more motivated to contribute. This can lead to real involvement in the program and a genuine parent–caregiver partnership. This inclusive approach has a positive influence on children's learning and development outcomes. (The creation of a **family-centred** program is explored further in chapter 9, "Building the Partnership with Families.")

Last but not least, the philosophy statement provides ground for understanding between the program and colleges and universities that educate future practitioners. When using a community program for field placement, post-secondary institutions need to be aware of the program's philosophy and be prepared to support it. During a student's orientation to the program, the director and co-operating staff must provide multiple opportunities for the student to discuss the philosophy and its application.

Standard

Program Philosophy, Goals, and Objectives

A statement of the program philosophy and a statement of goals and objectives serve as the basis for decision making, daily practice, and program evaluation.

1. A written statement of philosophy clearly articulates the principles and values followed in an early childhood development program.

2. There is a written statement of program goals and objectives, such as the ages of the children to be served and the types of services to be provided.

3. The statement of program philosophy is discussed with and given to and read by potential staff, family child care practitioners, assistants, and alternates (casual or temporary staff) before they begin to work in the program and copies of the statements are provided upon employment.

4. The statement of program philosophy is discussed with and given to parents/guardians before the child is enrolled.

5. The statement of program philosophy is readily accessible at all times to families/guardians and people working in the program.

6. The statement of philosophy and the statement of program goals and objectives are reviewed on an annual basis.

Source: Gillian Doherty, in Canadian Child Care Federation (CCCF), *Partners in Quality: Tools for Practitioners in Child Care Settings* (Ottawa: CCCF, 2000).

Steps to Develop the Program Philosophy

At some point, a program's decision makers need to make a public declaration of their vision for the program. This can occur when a new setting is being developed or whenever changes in the operation of an existing ECEC program are desired.

Be knowledgeable about theories of child development. Key stakeholders preparing a philosophy statement must have a clear understanding of the various theories of child development and learning. Some theorists emphasize one area of development over another; some espouse a holistic approach.

   Most of the curriculum models follow the whole child approach. A recent example of a comprehensive, inclusive approach to early childhood education is the Reggio Emila model, which involves an entire community in the development of a system of early childhood services. Two resources that summarize various theories are *Early Childhood Education and Care in Canada* (Mayfield 2001) and *Introduction to Early Childhood Education, third edition* (Essa and Young 2003). Stakeholders should research various theories and choose an approach that can be integrated with the key values and beliefs of the stakeholders.

Consult with stakeholders. Identify everyone involved in the ECEC program who will need to be consulted. This includes the board of directors/owner of the program, parents and children, staff and director, community representatives, and others who have a vested interest in the program. Once the **stakeholders** have been identified, invite interested representatives from each group to form a working committee to draft a philosophy state-

Include key stakeholders in the formation of the program philosophy.

ment. Ask participants to identify their values and what is important to them. Input can be solicited through a variety of formats including questionnaires, discussions at meetings, or interviews. Use open-ended questions that facilitate the participants' exploration of their beliefs about quality early childhood experiences. Another approach to forming a vision is to ask stakeholders to collectively brainstorm their goals and aspirations for the program; a facilitator may be helpful during this process.

Standard

Collaboration with Stakeholders—Family Child Care Home

Interact positively and effectively with a broad range of stakeholders including, but not limited to, families, colleagues, alternates, practitioner's family members, other community services, and regulatory and/or agency staff and officials, by:

- integrating the practitioner's own family into the family child care home while ensuring protection of family members' privacy and rights;

- establishing and maintaining a co-operative partnership with the family of each child receiving care;

- effectively communicating the practitioner's philosophy, policies, and procedures to families and other people working in the home;

- effectively soliciting input regarding the home's policies and program from families and community;

- working with colleagues and alternates to provide the families of the children being cared for with clear, timely information, assist families to express their needs and preferences, assist families in obtaining a fee subsidy if required, and enable families to have meaningful input in their child's care;

- working with colleagues and alternates to develop user-friendly ways of providing child care and other related information to families;

- providing support for colleagues and alternates and working co-operatively with them;

- developing and maintaining a positive relationship with representatives of regulatory bodies and/or the sponsoring family child care agency;

- providing accurate information about the home and program to other organizations in the community;

- developing and maintaining ongoing communication and collaborative working relationships with other community services from other community agencies; and

- providing information to the general public in order to increase general awareness about family child care and the role of family child care providers.

Source: Gillian Doherty, in Canadian Child Care Federation (CCCF), *Partners in Quality: Tools for Practitioners in Child Care Settings* (Ottawa: CCCF, 2000).

Identify key considerations.   Jorde Bloom, in *Circle of Influence: Implementing Shared Decision Making and Participative Management* (2000), identifies 50 decisions that may need to be made in defining the philosophy. Some examples include:

- deciding the content of the curriculum;
- identifying the criteria for hiring staff;
- determining the educational objectives for different age groups;
- setting the expectations for family involvement;
- determining the types of relationships with community agencies;
- establishing food-services procedures and contracts; and
- determining the guidelines for staff performance appraisals.

Identify priorities.   Once all the stakeholders' input has been gathered, identify key areas of agreement. Assess how strongly each stakeholder feels about specific concepts. State explicitly any key values that should be maintained, for example, "We want to ensure that staff have the appropriate educational background." Narrow down the possible wordings by using words and phrases from the respondents' comments. There are a number of methods that can be used to build consensus. Get people to work in small groups. Ask respondents to rank concepts from most to least important or put a dot on those areas they want to see included. Or, use a criteria matrix of key points. Common threads of agreement will appear as the priorities of individual stakeholders emerge. These key points can then be used to draft the philosophy statement.

Draft the philosophy statement.   It is wise not to focus on any particular statement too early in the process. The statement must be refined to reflect feedback. Once the draft is circulated, all stakeholders should be given time to reflect on its implications and a chance to express their views and concerns. This step may be repeated. The final statement needs to be acceptable to all participants.

Operationalize the statement.   Once the development process has been completed, the next step is to operationalize the beliefs and values contained in the philosophy statement—in other words, use them to guide practice. Remember, a philosophy statement is a living document, and it should be reviewed on a regular basis.

Developing a Personal Philosophy

It would be difficult to work with young children and families in an appropriate way without a belief system that gives direction in interactions with people. The concept of formulating a **personal philosophy**, or mission statement, may seem intimidating; however, it should not be. Organizations have a mission statement outlining both what the program believes and hopes to accomplish. Based on the organization's beliefs about its purpose, the mission statement represents a commitment by the organization, and it determines the way an organization conducts business. Similarly, a personal philosophy—one's beliefs and goals—determines an individual's actions. It commits the individual to certain intentions and implies a plan of action.

Many individuals are not highly aware of how their beliefs influence their day-to-day life and work. Some early childhood practitioners believe deeply in the value of strong social relations and networks among the families at the program. Others may think the program's primary purpose should be caring for the children and passing on information to families.

Employees should seek employment in a program whose philosophy is largely compatible with their own personal and professional beliefs. Accepting a job in a program whose philosophy conflicts with personal goals and values can lead to dissatisfaction, friction, and turmoil.

Sample

Philosophy Statements

Millbrook Children's Centre—A Learning Community for Children and Adults
Where children are valued for their ability to do meaningful work, their wonder and curiosity, their perspectives and ability to play.

Where families are valued for their bonds and traditions, their ability to play, their commitment to work, home and community, and their dreams for their children.

Where staff are valued for their vision, their delight in children, their skill, heart, and knowledge, their commitment to families, and their ability to play.

We cherish what we can learn from each other.

Fonthill Child Development Centre
At the Fonthill Child Development Centre, we believe that:

Children are entitled to environments and opportunities that foster positive emotional, social, cognitive, and physical development and that value inclusivity, multiculturalism, interdependence, and dignity.

Families are entitled to be involved in a meaningful way in the early childhood experience and deserve assurance of quality care for their children while they are involved in work commitments, educational or personal fulfillment or while early childhood development programs are part of a care plan for a family.

Staff are entitled to a working environment which recognizes and respects their education, skills, and commitment to early childhood development and which demonstrates this through respectful communication and personnel policies.

The program enhances the lives of children, their families, and the community by providing a caring, supportive, and vital community service.

Staff in a program do not always fully agree with the policies and practices of a program. The greater the diversity in staff backgrounds, the wider the range of beliefs and values. It is acceptable for staff to be different and to believe in dissimilar things. It is also important that the program have a clear, articulated point of view and goals that the staff understand and accept, in other words, that they agree to be guided by and follow. Thus, it may be necessary to define those areas where staff do not have to behave alike. In other areas, they must follow program guidelines for behaviour, even when this means that they may have to adapt their own caregiving practices.

In writing down a personal philosophy, one develops a guideline. This statement grows and is adapted as one's knowledge and experience deepen. For example, a student's philosophy statement will likely evolve as she or he completes additional course work. After graduation, an individual should pull her or his personal philosophy out periodically to reflect on it. Increasingly, graduates report on the ability to discuss their philosophy during job interviews. Evaluating one's day-to-day practice in light of one's statement of philosophy serves to keep ideals and realities aligned.

An individual's beliefs grow more comprehensive with experience and knowledge. This experience affects the development of one's philosophy. Examples of philosophical statements include common ideas and beliefs about children such as "All children have the right to inclusive education," "I believe children learn through play," and "Parental input and involvement are a critical extension of the family-centred environment."

Shimoni and Baxter (2005) encourage caregivers to examine their own beliefs in order to understand parents' values. They believe that through such **reflection**, caregivers can increase their understanding of differences in values and beliefs between caregivers and parents and that they must develop strategies to demonstrate respect and empathy to each family.

CAREGIVER REFLECTION

- What do you think are the qualities of a good parent?
- Being as honest as possible, define your attitude toward families. Do you judge them harshly or leniently?
- What is your attitude toward discipline and guidance within the family? Why do you think some parents still spank their children? Does your attitude toward parents change based on ethnicity, income, or marital status?

The Role of Leadership in Actualizing the Vision

Directors must demonstrate a capacity to organize ideas and ideals in addition to time, talent, and tasks. This aspect of leadership is exercised through participation in the development of the program vision, which is translated into the program's philosophy. The vision is the means by which directors capture the imaginations and engage the loyalty and support of staff and families. It is the philosophy that provides direction for and gives meaning to decisions, the search for new practices, and the policies to improve effectiveness of the service. The vision can boost morale and self-esteem and act as a buffer against stress during times of change. (The director's leadership role was elaborated on in chapter 3.)

Policies and procedures are critical to the delivery of quality ECEC programs and are typically founded on the philosophy of the program. Although most programs would state that they have a philosophy, it is not uncommon to find little time devoted to this topic. Many programs have something written on paper about their purpose. Often this is in the form of a philosophy statement outlining the program's intent to serve children in need of care, treat them respectfully, and meet their developmental needs. Directors hired into programs are seldom asked how they would like to see this statement brought to life. Philosophy statements are occasionally posted in programs, and they are usually found in parent handbooks or the organization's literature. Too often, these statements are not used as a guiding vision for program environments, policies and procedures, or daily decision making. The director and the owner/board of directors play key roles in inspiring others to participate in, actualize, and expand the vision of the program.

One of the characteristics of successful teams is that they have a set of achievable goals that are understood and accepted by all. Many ECEC staff teams have not had the opportunity to be involved in the development of goals, policies, and job descriptions. Some staff teams do not even consider this to be part of their responsibility. However, all programs have some form of program philosophy, mission statement, aims, objectives, and policies that determine the operation of the program. Given that the director or board of directors/owner may have imposed these, not all staff may agree with and accept such goals and policies. In situations such as these, directors need to encourage open problem solving to resolve this issue.

Because they are based on values, goals and policies can easily engender conflict. Individual beliefs, values, and perspectives that have a strong emotional component dominate the field of early childhood development. Understanding that not all people are likely to accept or agree with the goals and policies of a program is important. Providing opportunities for discussion, the sharing of perspectives, and regular review of goals and objectives is necessary to minimize conflict.

Rood (1998) identifies four steps that a director must take to get results in an organization:

1. *The definition of organizational and individual goals and/or objectives.* First, the director will provide a clarification of the service and its purpose, an outline for future directions, a description of procedures, an identification of resource requirements, and an explication of the roles and responsibilities of each parent and staff member.

2. *The setting of individual standards and expectations.* Delegated tasks will be outlined in terms of the functions specified in each staff job description, including standards of performance.

3. *The provision of support and feedback.* Assistance will be provided to individual team members to develop their expertise. Constructive feedback will be given to ensure that performance is maximized.

4. *The monitoring and evaluation of outcomes.* A process for regular review is essential to ensure that the program is meeting professional standards and achieving its objectives within the specified time frame.

Evaluating the Program

The program goals, and the program itself, are designed to meet the vision for the operation. Directors are accountable for the programs they administer, and the evaluation of how well the program is meeting its goals and objectives has become one of the director's most significant responsibilities. Directors may have a global impression that things are either going well or not so well at the program, but they often lack specific information. Information gleaned from an assessment of the program can help directors turn those vague feelings into precise data about what aspects of the program can be improved. They can then prioritize their time and resources to address these concerns.

How does a director define program quality? What methods are used to identify what is good in the program and what needs improvement? How is this information communicated to families, staff, funders, and other key stakeholders? To facilitate this communication and help all concerned to work together to improve program quality, a good program evaluation process is essential.

Some are concerned that the overall quality of early childhood programs is declining (Whitebrook, Howes, and Phillips 1990; Cryer and Phillipsen 1997; Doherty et al. 2000a). Major barriers to program quality include: financial instability and insufficient government funding; low levels of staff education and training in some jurisdictions; directors who are inadequately prepared for their jobs; and a lack of comprehensive community services and insufficient integration of new ones. As well, a poor quality of recruitment and retention is a factor in many provinces and territories. Quality is directly related to the development and fulfillment of program goals. When quality is lacking, programs are constrained from attaining goals for services for children and families.

Since the goals for the program are closely tied to the philosophy of the organization, they change slowly. Nevertheless, each year, directors should plan a method for evaluating the program. The annual evaluation and planning processes should complement each other, with the evaluation providing the information to guide strategic planning. As well, the data collected from evaluations can document how far toward its goals the program has come. The assessment process is essentially a self-renewal process. It is a means for developing teamwork and building collective action to bring about an understand-

Program philosophies should be reassessed regularly to ensure that they reflect current research on child development.

ing of changes necessary to reach program objectives and acceptance of responsibility for implementing those changes. The planning process can be used to set goals in areas needing improvement.

For example, the philosophy statement may state that the program serves children and families from a range of cultures and children of varying abilities and economic groups. However, it may be found that this is not the case. A goal may be set to diversify the population served. Some of the barriers to achieving this goal may include a homogeneous staff, an environment that only reflects one culture, and materials that are available only in English. To meet the goal of increasing the diversity of the population served, the program could set specific objectives, such as:

- hiring staff from a variety of ethnic backgrounds for the next available positions;
- providing professional development opportunities on a monthly basis for staff to learn more about culturally relevant programming; and
- targeting professional development events at conferences.

In addition, as one of the steps needed to achieve these objectives, the program will need to determine who will be responsible and when the actions should occur. To get broader feedback on the functioning of the program in meeting diversity, the director could ask two or three people representing the diverse community to review human resources, enrolment, health, and nutrition policies and procedures and forms.

Ongoing assessment is an integral tool for creating, designing, improving, and maintaining effective early childhood development programs. When staff have an active role in assessing the program and generating solutions, they feel a greater responsibility for implementing change and incorporating new practices.

Characteristics of Effective Program Quality Measures

When assessing program quality, it is important to select the right tool:

- First, staff need to use program tools that are consistent with the values and curriculum models being implemented in the program.
- Program assessment tools should define quality along a continuum. By using a continuum to rate quality, the assessment tool helps programs identify where they are on the path to achieving quality and the successive steps they must take to continue their progress.
- Program assessments are most helpful when they provide users with examples. To ensure that individuals use the assessment instrument fairly and objectively, it should be explicit about the practices and behaviours that define poor, acceptable, and excellent levels of quality. Instruments designed in this manner produce a higher level of agreement, or interrater reliability. (This means that instrument outcomes are similar despite having different evaluators—or raters.)
- Program assessments are most informative if they are comprehensive. Assessment tools should look at the process elements as well as the structural elements of quality (described in chapter 1). Most instruments do a detailed job of looking at structural elements, such as the safety of the physical features or the diversity of the materials

and equipment. However, many tools fail to pay equal attention to the most vital aspect of quality—the nature of the interactions between caregivers and children. These interpersonal characteristics are crucial to promoting child development. Additionally, complete program assessments will assess how caregivers interact with families and colleagues, the amount of support directors provide to staff, and how management secures adequate resources.

• It is important to choose program assessment tools that have been tested and validated to ensure interrater reliability.

• An effective program quality assessment tool can also serve as a staff development tool by helping staff and directors decide what areas they want to emphasize in professional development. An assessment of a program's quality should highlight its strengths and identify areas for improvement.

• Effective tools can enable directors to observe individual staff and provide them with constructive feedback. Following the observation, the director and staff member can review and discuss the ratings, acknowledge areas of strength, and identify specific strategies for professional growth.

Sample

Program Assessment Tool

Human Resources	1 Does not meet criteria.	2 Needs improvement.	3 Meets criteria.	4 Exceeds criteria in some areas.	5 Exceeds criteria in all areas.
Program Staff Criteria: There must be at least one trained staff on duty at all times. Infant ratios (one staff member for every three infants) must be maintained at all times.	*Requires Immediate Attention* Trained staff are not always on duty.	Trained staff are on duty except at day beginning or end.	Trained staff on duty at all times and the staff:child ratios always maintained.	More than one trained staff on duty at all times.	All staff on duty at all times are trained.

Source: Excerpted from Children's Services Division, *Operating Criteria for Child Care Centres Providing Subsidized Care in Toronto*, rev. ed. (Toronto: Community Services, Children's Services Division, City of Toronto, 2004). Used by permission.

Tools for Evaluating the Organization

The choice of evaluation method will depend upon how the results are to be used. The key is to use a variety of methods that involve key stakeholders in the process. As well as standardized instruments, questionnaires, interviews, observations, and records and documents are all possible sources of data. Global assessment tools evaluate multiple factors in early childhood settings.

EARLY CHILDHOOD DEVELOPMENT ASSESSMENT TOOLS

- Early Childhood Environment Rating Scale (ECERS)
- Family Day Care Rating Scale (FDCRS)
- Infant/Toddler Environment Rating Scale (ITERS)
- School-Age Environment Rating Scale (SAERS)
- High/Scope Program Quality Assessment Instrument (PQA)
- Early Childhood Work Environment Survey
- SpeciaLink Inclusion Practices Profile
- Partners in Quality: Tools for Practitioners in Child Care Settings

---

A widely-used global assessment tool is the Early Childhood Environment Rating Scale (ECERS). Developed by Harms and Clifford (1989a/2004), the ECERS approaches the early childhood development program from an ecological perspective. It has 43 items in seven separate subscales: personal care routines, space and furnishings for children, language and reasoning, activities, interactions, program structure, and parents and staff. These items are rated on a scale of 1 (inadequate) to 7 (excellent). The scores for each playroom may be compiled to get a quality score for the program. Versions of the scale have been developed for specific types of early childhood programs serving infants, preschoolers, school-age, and home child care environments (Harms and Clifford 1989a/2004; Harms, Cryer, and Clifford 1990; Harms, Jacobs, and White 1995).

The High/Scope Program Quality Assessment Instrument (PQA) was developed by a diverse team of researchers, training consultants, and caregivers. It was validated in a variety of early childhood settings, including settings following the High/Scope Educational Research Foundation philosophy and settings using other curriculum approaches. It uses a five-point rating scale (High/Scope Educational Research Foundation 1998).

The Early Childhood Work Environment Survey developed by Jorde Bloom (1989) can be used to assess the organizational climate and working conditions. Since the staff are the most critical component in achieving quality, this is a key area for evaluation. When staff are dissatisfied with their work, the results are turnover, stress, and burnout—and even departure from the profession. In such a situation, it is impossible to maintain a quality program. The areas surveyed by this tool include:

Collegiality: the extent to which staff are friendly, supportive, and trust one another.

Professional growth: opportunities for professional development.

Director support: perceived amount of support given to individual staff members.

Clarity: the extent to which policies, procedures, and responsibilities are defined and communicated.

Reward system: salaries and benefits, working conditions.

Decision making: the extent to which staff are involved in program decisions.

Goal consensus: the degree to which staff agree on the goals and objectives of the program.

Task orientation: the emphasis placed on good planning, efficiency, and getting the job done.

Physical setting: the extent to which the environment facilitates work and meets adult needs.

Innovativeness: the extent to which an organization adapts to change and encourages staff to find creative ways to solve problems.

This instrument measures staff's perceptions about a wide range of organizational practices. It can be administered annually to check the pulse of organizational functioning.

A number of strategies can be used to solicit families' viewpoints and suggestions about the program's communication network, the meeting of mutual goals for children, and the ambiance of the environment. Certainly the daily interchanges with parents provide critical and ongoing informal feedback. But on a regular basis, a formal approach should be used. There is a myriad of questionnaires and rating scales available. Each program should determine which tool best suits its needs. See an example in *Partnerships: Families and Communities in Canadian Early Childhood Education, second edition* (Wilson 2005).

Partners in Quality: Tools for Practitioners in Child Care Settings was developed by the Canadian Child Care Federation (CCCF 2000b). It includes standards of practice and self-reflection tools for practitioners, a **code of ethics**, and standards for settings and directors. The standards apply to family child care homes, group settings, and family resource programs. (Examples of various standards are featured in relevant chapters throughout this book.

Early Childhood Educators, directors, consultants, parents, and therapists often express concerns about how inclusion is working in their programs. They are committed to inclusion, but are searching for a framework, for a sense of direction about "what to do next." The SpeciaLink Inclusion Practices Profile is a tool for use with the SpeciaLink Inclusion Principles Scale to assess sustainable and evolving inclusion quality. As more children with special needs attend community-based programs this is a critical aspect of the program to evaluate. The creators recommend the tool be used along with ECERS as the terminology, procedures and description are compatible. The areas assessed include physical environment, equipment and materials, the director and governance committees, staff support and training, therapies available to the program, individual program plans, families, involvement of typical children, and transitions to school.

Sample

SpeciaLink Inclusion Principles Scale—Involvement of Typical Children

Note frequency and intensity of play that involves children with special needs and typically developing children.

Inadequate 1	Minimal 3	Good 5	Excellent 7
1.1 Typically developing children rarely interact with children with special needs. 1.2 Staff take no active role in encouraging inclusion.	3.1 Typically developing children sometimes interact with children with special needs, but mainly in a helping role. 3.2 Staff make ineffective comments or gestures to promote social inclusion.	5.1 Children with special needs are often included in group play, usually as "babies" or in other diminished status. 5.2 Staff suggest appropriate roles or dramatic situations that are inclusionary.	7.1 Children with special needs are included as valued participants in group social play. 7.2 Staff systematically use techniques of scripting, co-operative learning, and valued object sharing to promote social inclusion. 7.3 Staff receive specific training in promotion of inclusive social play.

Source: Sharon Hope Irwin, "The SpeciaLink Inclusion Principles Scale," Appendix B in S.H. Irwin, D.S. Lero, and K. Brophy, *Inclusion: The Next Generation in Child Care in Canada* (Wreck Cove, NS: Breton Books, 2001).

Summary

Each early childhood program has its own characteristics that are articulated in its philosophy and goals. One of the director's main tasks is to provide leadership in the development and implementation of the program philosophy and the evaluation of the program. A philosophy is a distillation of the ideas, beliefs, and values held by an individual, a group, or an organization. It has a direct bearing on curriculum development, staff hiring, the degree of family involvement, budget allocations, and the use of community resources. All key stakeholders—families, staff, the community, and other decision makers (board of directors or owner)—should be involved in the development of the philosophy statement. Everyone in the ECEC program should be informed of the philosophy statement. As well, each practitioner should continue to develop and reflect on her or his personal philosophy.

An inclusive vision for quality benefits all the stakeholders. An inclusive process encourages supportive relationships, open communication, and confidence in the program and is of benefit to both staff and management as well as families. The quality of a program is based on relationships: child–child, child–parent, caregiver–child, caregiver–parent, caregiver–caregiver, and so on. By creating a vision for quality that is owned by the stakeholders, a commitment to the pursuit of excellence is made, and a culture of self-reflection and continuous improvement is created. Forming a vision for quality is an important starting point for implementing quality processes in an early childhood development program.

Programs should evaluate the process and structural features of quality regularly and systematically. Only in this way can practitioners, researchers, and policy makers guarantee that the services delivered are of sufficient quality to promote the development of young children, encourage the involvement of families, and create supportive working environments for caregivers.

Key Terms and Concepts

Code of ethics, p. 94	Mission statement, p. 81
Clarity, p. 94	Personal philosophy, p. 86
Collegiality, p. 93	Philosophy, p. 80
Family-centred, p. 83	Reflection, p. 88
Goal consensus, p. 94	Stakeholders, p. 84
Innovativeness, p. 94	Task orientation, p. 94

Activities

1. In your field placement, request the philosophy statement. Determine the statement's implications for planning the program for children. Are the statements compatible with or contrary to your beliefs? Discuss your observations with your co-operating staff.

2. Collect three philosophy statements from a variety of community early childhood development programs. Compare these statements. Identify what you like about each statement. What else might be included? Draft an ideal personal philosophy statement.

3. Design a brochure, web page, or short video that explains the benefits of parent–staff partnerships for the children, families, and caregivers.

4. Brainstorm what you could do if your personal beliefs came into conflict with those of your co-operating teacher at your field placement. What are the pros and cons of each option?

5. Use one of the tools reviewed in the chapter to assess the functioning of a playroom. Discuss your findings with the staff.

Recommended Reading

Carter, M. and D. Curtis. *The Visionary Director: A Handbook for Dreaming, Organizing, and Improvising in Your Center.* St. Paul, MI: Redleaf Press, 1998.

Jorde Bloom, P., M. Sheerer, and J. Britz. *Blueprint for Action: Achieving Center-Based Change through Staff Development.* Lake Forest, IL: New Horizons, 1991.

Jorde Bloom, P. *Circle of Influence: Implementing Shared Decision-Making and Participative Management.* Lake Forest, IL: New Horizons, 2000.

Rood, J. *Leadership in Early Childhood.* 2d ed. New York: Teachers College Press, Columbia University, 1998.

Weblinks

www.eccdc.org
Early Childhood Community Development Centre
The Child Care Resource Link for Owners and Boards on this site provides a listing of resources to help decision-makers maximize their operations. The Web page is organized around six key areas of responsibility: direction, guardianship, public relations, advocacy, legal conduct, and ethical conduct. Included are bibliographies and lists of contacts, links, and articles.

www.specialinkcanada.org
SpeciaLink: The National Centre for Child Care Inclusion
A resource and research helpline, SpeciaLink provides personalized responses to specific questions, referrals to other organizations, and sources of help, information, and technical assistance. It also provides the SpeciaLink Newsletters, fact sheets, books, and videos, as well as a speakers bureau. It maintains an alert network of key mainstream child care advocates across the country, who can quickly identify and respond to opportunities and threats to mainstream quality and funding.

Caring for Children in a Home Setting

chapter 5

Objectives

- **Describe the nature of family child care.**
- **Describe models of family child care.**
- **Outline the roles, responsibilities, and characteristics of providers.**
- **Outline good business practices in operating a family child care program.**
- **Understand the importance of written agreements with families.**
- **Review the challenges faced by family child care providers.**

Quality early childhood development has been recognized as a crucial component in promoting many broad societal goals—including optimal development and school readiness of all children, reduced child poverty, labour-force attachment for parents, and social cohesion. The high number of families using—and choosing—**family child care** indicates how vital a part of the early childhood development system it is.

This chapter examines the nature of family child care, outlines characteristics of the **family child care provider**, and discusses practices in running a small business. It identifies the role of child care agencies and other supports to family child care providers and considers some of the challenges facing providers.

The Nature of Family Child Care

More Canadian families are sharing their child rearing responsibilities with alternative caregivers in a variety of settings. Most children are cared for by family child care providers. Family child care takes place in high-rise apartments, townhouses, and private homes, in urban centres, small towns, and rural settings.

Family child care environments are preferred by many families.

Little is known about these private arrangements or the quality of care provided. Historically, there has been a tendency to treat family child care as a modified version of centre-based care—as opposed to a unique service with its own distinctive characteristics. Given the large number of children cared for in family child care homes and the extent to which this service is relied on by parents on a daily basis, the quality of family child care exerts a profound effect on Canadian children. There are an estimated 180 000 family child care providers in Canada. Approximately 25 100 of these caregivers participate in a regulated system serving 104 828 children, while the remaining provide unregulated family child care (Beach et al. 2004).

Some family child care homes look like a group ECEC program with just one playroom. Some specialize in just one age group, whereas others care for a range of ages. Some excellent home programs create stimulating environments for children. Real quality, measured in terms of supportive relationships with families and sensitive, responsive interactions with children, can be found in family child care.

Many parents prefer family child care, for the following reasons:

- It offers a more intimate, homelike environment for infants and toddlers.
- The same caregiver cares for a child for the whole day, providing more continuity for the child.
- For families with several children, this type of arrangement may mean that they can drop off all of their children at one setting.
- Care in the family's own neighborhood is more convenient, especially for school-age children.
- A child may have less exposure to communicable illnesses in a home than in a centre.

- Families from minority cultures often want to find caregivers who will honour and reinforce the values upheld in the children's homes.

- Family child care is readily available in most communities and sometimes considerably less costly than centre-based care.

- It may accommodate extended work hours and may be located more conveniently.

- Some providers will provide evening or weekend care.

Family Child Care—The Most Common Child Care Arrangement

In Canada, most children are cared for in people's homes. Johnson, Lero, and Rooney (2001) found that 33% of children aged newborn to five who received care while their parents worked or studied were in unregulated family child care. Of the remaining children in this age group, 22% were cared for by a relative, either in the relative's or the child's home; 20% were cared for in a licensed early childhood development program; 14% were cared for in their home by an unrelated caregiver such as a nanny or au pair; 9% were in regulated family child care; and 2% were cared for through other arrangements.

Types of Family Child Care

Unregulated care in the provider's home   Much of the child care used by parents is unregulated. It is not externally monitored, nor is it publicly funded, except indirectly through income tax deductions or vouchers available to some parents. Caregivers working in the unregulated sector make up about 95% of family child care providers (Goss Gilroy 1998).

Unlicensed care is sometimes called "informal care," a term that usually indicates situations in which parents bring their child to a neighbour's, friend's, babysitter's, or relative's home. These caregivers are considered to be self-employed. Conditions of employment and care are negotiated directly between the parent and caregiver.

While the quality of care in unregulated homes can be excellent, the fact remains that unregulated programs are not accountable for meeting basic health and safety standards, and the responsibility for monitoring the care the child is receiving rests with the parents. Lower fees may be an incentive for some parents to use unregulated care.

Unregulated care in the child's home   In-home child care arrangements include care by nannies and others who provide care in the child's own home. The caregiver may live in the child's home or reside elsewhere and come to the child's home for designated work periods. In-home care can provide greater flexibility for parents who commute or work long hours. In some instances, children receiving in-home care also participate in community early childhood development programs such as family resource programs, nursery schools, or playgroups. Many live-in nannies come from outside Canada. Through a federal government immigration program, a family may sponsor a nanny to live in their home for a two-year period, at the end of which the nanny may apply for landed immigrant status. A nanny is considered to be an employee of the parents.

Regulated care in the provider's home   All jurisdictions have regulated family child care. The regulations covering family child care are less consistent from province to province than those for centre-based care. Many people are surprised to learn that there are regulations governing family child care—including private arrangements between parents and providers. By setting basic health and safety standards, limiting the number and age mix of children present at any one time, and providing monitoring by an outside person, regulation establishes a framework for quality. Regulation can serve as a vehicle for accessing training, consultative services, and other support services, through a **family child care agency** or indirectly through an individual licensing official. (Regulation is elaborated on in chapter 2.)

In most provinces, family child care providers must be individually licensed, or registered, and must satisfy minimum government standards. **Registration** is a process that requires providers to certify that they have complied with regulations and maintain records. The provider's home and equipment must meet specific health and safety guidelines set out by the province/territory. In these situations, regulated providers who work in their own homes are licensed directly by the provincial or territorial government and are monitored by a government consultant.

Regulated family child care providers are licensed individually by the provincial/territorial government in all jurisdictions except Alberta, Ontario, Quebec, and Nova Scotia. These four provinces license or contract with community agencies to register and supervise family child care providers. In Newfoundland and Labrador, family child care providers can choose to be either individually licensed or affiliated with an agency.

The agency is usually responsible for recruiting, screening, and monitoring family child care providers. In addition, agencies usually refer families to providers, collect service fees, and provide services such as toy lending programs or professional development opportunities for caregivers. The agency's home visitor inspects home settings to ensure that they meet specified standards. (This role is discussed later in this chapter in the section "Family Child Care Agency.")

All provincial and territorial child care regulations permit child care in the caregiver's home without a license provided that a specific number of children is not exceeded. These regulations vary widely from province to province (see chart on staffing requirements, p. 102). In most provinces, the provider must maintain certain adult:child ratios and pass a TB test and health exam. (For current information about the regulations in each province or territory, contact the ministries listed in the Appendix.)

Regulations set minimum standards to ensure that caregivers' homes are safe, appropriate health and sanitary practices are in place, meals and snacks are adequate and nutritious, the caregiver uses appropriate methods of child guidance, necessary records are maintained, and activities and routines meet the children's needs. The presence of such criteria does not guarantee quality, but legislation and regulation set a baseline for quality care. Licensing staff are eager to see unlicensed providers become licensed and can be very helpful in linking providers to resources that will assist them in making changes to meet standards.

Advantages/Disadvantages to Being Regulated

The study *You Bet I Care! Caring and Learning Environments: Quality in Regulated Family Child Care across Canada* (Doherty et al. 2000b) identified three possible incentives for becoming regulated:

- access to children whose parents are eligible for fee subsidy;

- being permitted to care for more children and the potential for higher income; and

- access to training and other support.

STAFFING REQUIREMENTS FOR REGULATED FAMILY CHILD CARE, 2003

Province or territory	Caregiver:child ratio	Caregiver training requirements
Newfoundland and Labrador	Up to six children, including the provider's own children not attending school on a full-time basis. Not more than three children may be under the age of 36 months; of these no more than two may be under the age of 24 months.	Orientation course of 30–60 hours, depending on the age group the provider is responsible for. A minimum of 30 hours of professional development every three years.
Prince Edward Island	Up to seven children, including provider's own children under the age of 12, with a maximum of three children under the age of 2.	A 30 hour training course.
Nova Scotia	Up to six children of mixed ages, including the provider's own preschool children, or up to eight school age children, including the provider's own school age children.	No early childhood training or experience is required.
New Brunswick	Up to six children in a mixed age group: no more than three infants or five children from 2 to 5 years. Up to nine children 6 years and over. Maximums include the provider's own children under 12 years.	No early childhood training or experience is required.
Quebec	Up to six children including the provider's own children; no more than two children may be under 18 months. If another adult assists the provider, nine children are permitted with no more than four children under 18 months.	Providers must be supervised by a **CPE** (Centre de la petit enfance) and must complete a 45 hour course.
Ontario	Up to five children from 0–12 years, including provider's children under the age of 6. No more than two children may be under age 2 and no more than three may be under age 3.	No early childhood training or experience is required.
Manitoba	Up to eight children under the age of 12, including the provider's own children under age 12. No more than five children may be under age 6, of whom no more than three may be under age 2. If there is a provider and an assistant, up to 12 children under age 12, including the provider's own children under age 12. No more than three children may be under age 2.	An approved 40 hour course within the first year of providing child care for new providers licensed after January 2003.

(continued)

Province or territory	Caregiver:child ratio	Caregiver training requirements
Saskatchewan	Up to eight children, including the provider's own children under the age of 13; of the eight, only five may be younger than age 6 and of these five, only two may be younger than age 30 months. If there is a provider and assistant, up to 12 children including the provider's own children under the age of 13. Of the 12 children, only 10 may be younger than age 6 and of these, five may be infants and toddlers with not more than three infants.	Providers working on their own must complete a 40 hour introductory ECE course within the first year of being licensed. The charge provider in a situation of two providers must complete a 120 hour ECE course within the first year of being licensed. All providers must engage in six hours of professional development annually.
Alberta	Up to six children under age 11, including the provider's own children under age 11, with a maximum of three children under age 3 and no more than two children under age 2.	No early childhood training is required.
British Columbia	Up to seven children under age 12, including the provider's own children under age 12. Of the seven children, no more than five may be preschoolers, no more than three may be under age 3 and no more than one under age 1.	A course on the care of young children (length not stated) or relevant work experience.
Northwest Territories	Maximum of eight children under age 12 including the provider's own children under age 12. No more than six children may be under age 5 or younger, no more than three children may be under age 3, and no more than two children may be under age 2.	No early childhood training is required.
Nunavut	Maximum of eight children under age 12 including the provider's own children under age 12. No more than six children may be under age 5 or younger, no more than three children may be under age 3, and no more than two children may be under age 2.	No early childhood training is required.
Yukon Territory	Up to eight children, including the provider's own children under age 6. Where infants are present, the license is for six rather than eight. If there is a provider and an assistant, four additional children may be cared for.	Completion of a 60 hour ECE course within the first year of being licensed.

Source: M. Friendly, J. Beach, and M. Turiano, *Early Childhood Education and Care in Canada 2001* (Toronto: Childcare Resource and Research Unit, Centre for Urban and Community Studies, University of Toronto, 2002).

Thirty-five percent of providers in the *You Bet I Care!* Study identified the ability to care for more children as the main reason they joined the regulated system.

In British Columbia and the Northwest Territories, fee subsidies are not an incentive because they are also permitted in unregulated homes. And in Ontario, the government permits subsidies to be used in unregulated homes by children whose parents are in job training programs.

The main disincentive to becoming regulated is the related costs. When providers apply for regulation, they usually incur costs connected with upgrading their home, in such ways as fencing in the yard or buying equipment in order to meet regulatory standards. *Caring and Learning Environments: Quality in Regulated Family Child Care across Canada* recommends " . . . all jurisdictions must examine their existing policies and practices to identify those that act as disincentives for family child care providers to join the regulated system . . . [and] work on the development and implementation of policies and practices to encourage providers to join and remain in the regulated system."

Staying unlicensed is a viable option for many home providers. Unfortunately, lack of affiliation with an agency means a lack of access to training, resources, and ongoing support.

Caregivers in regulated family child care have a complicated employment relationship that makes it difficult to determine who their employer is or if they are self-employed contractors. Some have contractual arrangements with families, whereas others are supervised through child care organizations and are considered independent contractors, Family child care providers usually receive no (or few) benefits and are not usually eligible for paid sick leave, paid vacation, or maternity or parental benefits. At times, the provider's self-employed status puts a family child care agency in a difficult position. For example, when the province wants the agency homes to document a daily schedule, the agency must then impose this requirement on their providers. Such requirements are at odds with the self-employed status of providers and can have an impact on their relationship with the agency. In Ontario, a group of providers at the McCaulay Child Development Centre were deemed independent contractors under the *Labour Relations Act*. They unionized and collectively bargained with the agency. In Quebec, home providers are awaiting court determinations whether they are self employed or have the right to unionize. Some providers want to be paid for caring for children but do not want to be involved in running a business. Sometimes new providers believe it is not better to get licensed—it may seem like a hassle or an invasion of privacy. They may not want to keep records. They may not understand that—whether licensed or unlicensed—they are legally required to annually file a tax return that reports all of their income, and thus they may fear that becoming licensed will mean paying more income tax, which will reduce their already low earnings. Unlike experienced providers, they may not be aware of the compensatory tax write-offs available to small businesses, including the self-employed. Experienced providers understand that getting a licence offers benefits to their small business and reflects the attitude that early childhood development is a profession. Additionally, regulation is a form of consumer protection for parents and can offer some personal protection for children.

Providers who work in the regulated sector are motivated to obtain support services, to increase their sense of **professionalism**, and to get assistance in finding families who need care for their children. Expanding the supply of high quality regulated family child care homes is a key policy tool for supporting children's development and allowing parents to work outside the home, thus increasing families' economic security and hence the quality of their children's lives.

Quality of Environments

In home programs, as in centre-based care, a wide range of quality can be found. Practices range from excellent to harmful. At their best, family child care homes are wonderful places for young children. The small scale, informality, and richness of a home environment allow for personalized care, experiential, active learning, and the formation of enduring relationships. The small number of children in a family child care setting provides more opportunities for the child to develop a close relationship with the caregiver. The stability and depth of this relationship contribute to the child's feelings of trust, self-confidence, and security. There may be children of other ages in the home. Children in **multi-** or **mixed-age groupings** can learn from one another.

Homes are often undervalued as learning environments for young children. A typical home offers different textures, sounds, sights, and objects to crawl over, under, and around—a rich environment for sensory motor-learning. Children can be involved in the life of the home—baking cookies, folding laundry, shopping—as well as in planned activities. The opportunities for language development and other developmentally appropriate activities abound.

At their worst, family child care homes can be dispiriting places subject to little or no outside regulation. They may offer infants and toddlers little except confinement and large doses of unsupervised television. When caregivers are disinterested, motivated primarily by income or obligations to family or friends, these situations have little to offer children.

The quality of the child care arrangement hinges on the quality of the interactions between the child and the caregiver. Recent studies on brain development confirm the importance for young children's optimal development of sensitive, responsive care and opportunities for exploration and play-based problem solving with other children (Shore 1997; Shonkoff and Phillips 2000; Keating and Hertzman 1999). Although *You Bet I Care!* found that physically and emotionally safe environments are the norm in Canada's family child care homes, in many cases children do not receive adequate opportunities to develop their language and cognitive skills (Doherty et al. 2000b). It is believed this is directly linked to a lack of training and professional development opportunities and other supports for family child care providers.

You Bet I Care! found the level of quality of a family child care home depended on whether the provider:

- had completed specialized training related to the provision of family child care; and
- networked regularly with other providers through an organized association or network.

Providers who were found to be more sensitive and responsive with children and obtained a higher score on an overall measure of quality were actively involved in an early childhood development organization.

Who Are the Providers?
Characteristics

Caregivers are diverse in terms of age, education, marital/family status, prior early childhood education, caregiving experience, and work experience outside the home. What is unique about family child care is that the provider is usually working in her own home, usually with a mixed-age group of children, and that the group often includes the provider's own children. Some providers, such as aunts or grandparents, are related to the child. Some sites care for one child while others care for up to five young children.

There is considerable diversity in the career paths of family child care providers. Some practitioners begin their career in family child care and move on to other roles. Some start caring for children in their homes after some years in the field of early childhood development. Some did not finish high school, while others have decades of experience and/or a graduate degree. Some providers choose family child care as a way to stay at home with their own children. Others chose this service because it is the best match for their own caregiving philosophy and style.

How family child care providers feel about their work directly influences both how they respond to children and the likelihood that they will continue to provide family child care. Providers who are more sensitive and responsive and offer overall better quality care have been found to be those who take a more professional approach to caregiving.

A PROFESSIONAL APPROACH FOR PROVIDERS

- Be committed to taking care of children and working with families.
- Seek out opportunities to learn about child development and good child care practices.
- Think ahead about what the children are going to do and plan for their involvement.
- Follow standard business practices such as having written policies and contracts and being insured.
- Seek out the company of others who provide child care.

Training

Virtually all the research has found a correlation between training and the quality of family child care (Pence and Goelman 1991; Taylor, Dunster, and Pollard 1999; Kontos, Howes, and Galinsky 1996). This has resulted in a call for more training for providers, regulations requiring training, and a discussion of professionalism as it relates to the status of providers. The training of family child care providers has been piecemeal, informal, and, on occasion, of questionable value. One of the reasons this sector's training has not been considered a serious issue is the commonly held view that the provision of family child care is only an extended application of the parenting skills of the provider (Chandler 1997). Some providers and their organizations see family child care as a professional service requiring training and providing a career path. Others view their services as an extension of their home duties and are opposed to the formalization of family child care. Some employers and parents are requesting more training of providers. As well, some providers are accommodating children with special needs or different cultural backgrounds, and this requires additional knowledge and skills.

The Canadian Child Care Federation and the Canadian Association of Family Resource Programs together with provincial family child care organizations developed the Family

Child Care Training Program (CCCF 2000a). The program is designed to be used in distance education, self-directed learning, small groups, workshops, or the classroom. It is available as a printed manual and on the CCCF website (see Weblinks at the end of the chapter). The introductory level of the program consists of 12 units for individuals working in the field, either in the regulated or unregulated sector. Topics include the family child care home; the program; health, safety, and nutrition; the business aspect; partnerships with parents; and connecting with the community. Level 3 has modules on financial planning, inclusion, child abuse awareness, and the ethics of caring.

As well, as part of the Partners in Quality project, the CCCF developed standards to help home providers identify the skills necessary to perform their tasks in a competent fashion. These standards can be used as a benchmark against which actual practice can be assessed, either by the provider or an outside professional.

PROVIDER SELF-EVALUATION

Many factors need to be considered before an individual decides to become a family child care provider. An individual must consider whether she is suited to and will enjoy being a caregiver, as well as the effects that caregiving will have on her family and home. The following rating scale can provoke some reflection on necessary qualities.

Directions:
Think about each trait and rate yourself.

1 = strongly agree; 2 = mildly agree; 3 = neutral; 4 = mildly disagree;
5 = strongly disagree.

1. I enjoy children very much and believe I could work well with them for long periods of time.

    1   2   3   4   5

2. I am a flexible person who can usually solve a problem.

    1   2   3   4   5

3. I have good common sense and handle emergencies well.

    1   2   3   4   5

4. I am generally warm and affectionate.

    1   2   3   4   5

5. I am fairly organized and able to keep financial records.

    1   2   3   4   5

6. I do not mind my home being messy sometimes. I can put the children's needs before my housework.

    1   2   3   4   5

7. I am willing to rearrange the furniture in some rooms of my home to accommodate toys and equipment.

    1   2   3   4   5

8. I am flexible and have a good sense of humour.

    1   2   3   4   5

(continued)

9. I usually appreciate my own accomplishments.

    1   2   3   4   5

10. I am in good health and have lots of energy.

    1   2   3   4   5

11. Providing home child care is acceptable to each member of my family.

    1   2   3   4   5

12. I would enjoy talking to parents about their child and our day together.

    1   2   3   4   5

13. I usually speak up when I have a problem.

    1   2   3   4   5

14. I accept children as they are and feel a deep commitment to them and their parents.

    1   2   3   4   5

15. I am able to guide and discipline children kindly and effectively.

    1   2   3   4   5

16. I expect to offer family child care for at least two years.

    1   2   3   4   5

17. I am able to arrange substitute/alternate care when needed.

    1   2   3   4   5

18. I have financial resources to fall back on for a few months while I get started.

    1   2   3   4   5

Evaluation:

A respondent who agrees with most of the statements above will likely find family child care a satisfying job. If there are a few statements that are disagreed with, special efforts to address these areas will need to be made. Some traits, such as the enjoyment of children and their parents and good health and vitality, are critical to success.

Source: K. Modigliani, M. Reiff, and S. Jones, *Opening Your Door to Children: How to Start a Family Day Care Program* (Washington: NAEYC, 1998).

Some practitioners define professionalism as choosing to pursue training and education, supporting and mentoring others, participating in and helping build professional organizations, and increasing mastery in direct work with children and families. Experienced leaders in the field value individual credentials, professional training programs, and referral offices and professional caregiver organizations that provide support to caregivers. As well as advocating for quality early childhood development services, professional caregivers provide a wealth of information and support.

In developing training for caregivers, organizers must remember that these practitioners have a variety of levels of education and experience in early childhood development. This influences the type of information needed. Providers identified seven areas where they would like to learn more (Pollard 1997):

•   communicating with parents

- child development
- business management skills
- behaviour management
- activity ideas
- children with unique or special needs
- caring for and empowering oneself

Caregivers want competent, qualified trainers with experience as family child care providers or a good knowledge of family child care issues. They want in-depth information that is clear, concise, well-organized, and stimulating.

Six provinces and Yukon Territory have training requirements for regulated family child care. For example, Saskatchewan requires providers to complete a 40 hour introductory ECE course and to engage in six hours of professional development annually. In Quebec, in addition to completing a 45 hour course, providers are supervised by a **CPE** (Beach et al. 2004).

The Family Child Care Training Project identified the following barriers to providers taking advantage of training/learning opportunities: lack of availability or accessibility, the provider's inability to obtain recognition for prior learning or experience, and a lack of materials in the provider's mother tongue. As well, many providers noted that professional training usually leads to no additional recognition in terms of wages or career advancement. Organizations providing professional development opportunities often lack financial resources to cover training costs; consequently, many post-secondary organizations only offer training opportunities on a cost-recovery basis. Other barriers to training include the cost of courses, transportation difficulties, and other demands on the provider's time and energy.

The Family Child Care Training Project took these factors into account when it developed the online Family Child Care Training Program. (The address of this website is provided at the end of the chapter.) Some agencies facilitate opportunities for experienced providers to act as mentors or trainers. This strategy can reduce the isolation endemic in the field and provide professional development for both experienced and novice providers.

A COMPETENT PROVIDER:

- establishes a safe, healthy learning environment
- advances physical and intellectual competence
- supports social and emotional development and provides positive guidance
- establishes positive and productive relationships with families
- ensures a well-run, purposeful program responsive to participants' needs
- maintains a commitment to professionalism with an additional emphasis on business practices

Source: K. Hollestelle, "At the Core: Entrepreneurial Skills for Family Child Care Providers," in J. Johnson and J.B. McCracken, eds., *The Early Childhood Career Lattice: Perspectives on Professional Development* (Washington: NAEYC, 1994).

Working Conditions

Job satisfaction is emerging as a key contributor to quality. Providing high quality care to children is physically and emotionally demanding work. Feelings of isolation and inadequacy are not uncommon in highly demanding service professions such as early childhood development. The provider needs to be able to recognize these feelings and make time to reflect upon them and find support. Good working conditions are related to job satisfaction; poor working conditions lead to provider turnover. Family child care providers generally work alone for up to ten hours a day with no breaks.

The study *You Bet I Care! Caring and Learning Environments: Quality in Regulated Family Child Care across Canada* (Doherty et al. 2000b) found that higher quality care was associated with providers who:

- took more vacation days;
- were compensated for extra time and/or were paid when children were absent for reasons such as a family holiday; and
- had higher remuneration rates.

Only 36% of the providers who participated in the study were satisfied with the respect accorded to their work by others. Remuneration levels may be part of the reason why providers do not feel their work is valued. Given the high reliance on parent fees for operating revenue, there is little opportunity to improve income. For example, Alberta providers reported a gross annual income of between $10 000 and $15 000, while most providers in Quebec and Ontario earned between $15 000 and $25 000 a year. In many cases, a significant portion of the family child care provider's income was used for child-related expenses. It is important that parents express appreciation for the work done by the provider and, where appropriate, show recognition of the provider's skill and expertise.

Caring for Children with Special Needs

Since the home is a natural environment for children, family child care can be beneficial for children with special needs. There is growing recognition that the small group size and continuity of care can provide a particularly appropriate setting for a child with special needs. However, providing personalized and appropriate care requires an understanding of the child's condition and, possibly, adaptations in the provider's way of communicating with the children and/or daily activities. Some children with special needs will require adaptations to the physical setting or special equipment. In order to respond to the unique needs of the child, providers need specialized training.

Caring for a child with special needs places additional responsibilities on the provider. It requires commitment. Community supports exist. An agency might offer visits by a **resource teacher** who can suggest specific ways to work with the child and set up the environment. As well, the agency can facilitate access to community services such as an infant stimulation program. Occasionally, the family child care provider may be offered respite care on a weekly basis.

Family Child Care as a Small Business

Family child care providers are first and foremost nurturers and caregivers, but they are also entrepreneurs. As operators of small businesses, they are unique in the early childhood development profession. Whether providing care through a family child care agency or independently, the service needs to be organized like a small business. It is necessary to define boundaries between emotions and the business of making a decent wage for important work.

Sample

Operation of a Family Child Care Home

Operate the family child care home as a small business consistent with legislative requirements, by:

- maintaining current information about regulatory requirements;
- meeting all applicable provincial and municipal regulations;
- developing and implementing a written contract with each family and written policies in areas such as program philosophy, discipline and guidance methods, authorization for pickup, children's personal care, fee schedules, and child illness;
- ensuring that written policies and procedures are understood by everyone concerned, implemented, reviewed for ongoing relevance and effectiveness, and changed as required;
- developing and implementing effective communication strategies to keep other staff aware of changes to policies or regulations;
- maintaining up-to-date records for each child, including health information and emergency numbers, and up-to-date business records in an organized manner;
- ensuring records and information are maintained in a way that protects confidentiality and meets legislative, regulatory, and contractual agreements;
- using resources in a way that maximizes their potential to foster the provision of quality care;
- developing and implementing methods to evaluate the extent to which the overall program is meeting the needs of children cared for and their families and taking corrective action as needed; and
- addressing all legal aspects pertaining to the operation of a family child care home.

Source: Gillian Doherty, in Canadian Child Care Federation (CCCF), *Partners in Quality: Tools for Practitioners in Child Care Settings* (Ottawa: CCCF, 2000).

A family child care provider/entrepreneur should have a well-thought-out program of activities and maintain a policies and procedures manual. Contracts with parents and a system for collecting fees are musts. The resource *Dollars and Sense: Planning for Profit in Your Child Care Business* (Bush 2000) provides some guidelines. To have a healthy and stable program, the provider must care for her own needs as well as those of the families to whom care is provided. Family child care providers need to become acquainted with what laws and regulations apply to their business and what advantages are available to the owners of a small business.

The benefits of managing the business aspect of care include:

- improved relationships with families through the clarification of each party's responsibilities;
- more time to focus on caring for the children and less time spent on administrative tasks;

- increased efficiency and reduced stress through the development, organization, and maintenance of an appropriate record-keeping system (for receipts, files, etc.);
- increased earnings through better financial management and, potentially, increased tax rebates; and
- enhancing the image of family child care by complying with all regulatory requirements and demonstrating a professional attitude.

Before setting up a family child care business, providers need to ensure that this type of care is permitted where they live and find out if there are any zoning restrictions. Some municipalities have bylaws that may limit the number of children cared for. Some apartment leases forbid operating a small business from the home.

Agreements with Parents

A written agreement serves as an understanding between the family and caregiver regarding the services that the parents are purchasing. Experienced caregivers have found that having a written agreement with parents minimizes misunderstandings. Parents usually appreciate this approach, because it indicates that the provider pays attention to details and will likely give similar attention to caring for their child. The agreement should detail the hours of care and the rate and time of payment. In a two-parent family, both parents should sign the **contract**. Contracts do not have to be written in legal language. However, they need to be clearly written. Be sure to review the agreement periodically to ensure that it reflects any changes in the program.

As well, parents and providers will want to reach agreement on the following key areas:

- names of the child and parents, addresses, phone numbers, work numbers, and emergency contacts;
- identify who is authorized to pick up the child;
- fee payment policy/rates (daily or hourly; for regular or for drop-in care; late or overtime fees; registration fee, if any; discount for second child, if offered; and weekly or monthly payment schedule);
- hours and days of the week that care is provided (note whether care is provided on statutory holidays);
- what food will be provided (this may include breakfast, two snacks, a hot lunch, food for special diets, etc.) and any food policies (e.g., that all meals conform to *Canada's Guide to Healthy Eating* (Canada 1992));
- behaviour management strategies while the child is in the provider's care;
- payment polices, including termination notice by either party, increases in child care fees, and vacation periods for the provider;
- permission to administer medication;
- conditions of mild illness under which care will be provided;
- emergency consent; and
- information that must be communicated, such as late arrival, sickness, planned absences from care, changes in address and phone number at home or work, change in emergency contact, or any other changes in circumstances that would affect the child's well-being.
- identifying the use of a substitute caregiver when the provider or her children are ill or on holiday.

Sample

Written Child Care Agreement

The following agreement is made between:

Parent's Name _____

Address _____

Phone #: Home _____

          Work _____

          Cell _____

Caregiver's Name _____

Address _____

Phone # _____

For the care of (child's/children's name/s) _____

Child care will be provided at (caregiver's address) _____

_____

It is agreed that child care will be provided from (e.g., 7:30 a.m.) to (5:00 p.m.) for the following days of the week: (e.g., Tuesday to Friday).

The weekly/daily fee for child care is $_____, due and payable on the (e.g., Friday of each week of care). The full fee is due and payable whether the child attends care on the agreed days or not.

Overtime fees will be charged at the rate of (e.g., $4) per (e.g., 30 minutes) or part thereof and are due and payable on the day of overtime.

The child care home will be closed on the following days, for which payment (will/will not) be required: New Year's Day, Good Friday, Victoria Day, Canada Day, Civic Holiday, Labour Day, Thanksgiving, Christmas, Boxing Day.

The caregiver and parent agree to provide (e.g., three weeks') notice if this agreement is to be terminated.

Caregiver's signature _____

Date _____

Parent's signature _____

Date _____

Policy Statements

Policies are statements of the provider's practices in providing quality child care. These policies should reflect individual needs, strengths, goals, and day-to-day operations of the program. This information needs to be discussed with parents and supplied in writing at the time of enrolment. Policies need to be well thought out and consistent. Caregivers should consider their child care philosophy carefully. (See chapter 4 for more information on developing a program philosophy.) Policies need to reflect the caregiver's needs as well as those of the children and their families. (In chapter 9, "Building the Partnership with Families," suggestions are given for indicating a family-centred approach.) Policies that reflect the family child care provider's own needs will result in a healthier, more stable program. Providers should check if the family child care agency or licensing office has regulations regarding child care policies that must be complied with. The following sections cover some of the areas in which policies may be needed.

Fees   Fees provide the financial basis for the business as well as the provider's income; for her business to succeed, the provider must generate a consistent income. Providers must set realistic rates from the beginning, as it is difficult to increase fees significantly after parents have experienced a lower rate. Explain fees clearly, then be firm about collecting all fees owing. Other policies, such as whether the provider charges for days the child is absent due to family holidays or illness (parent or child), and whether care will be provided and/or charged for on statutory holidays, can have an impact on earnings. (Additional information about fee policies is provided in chapter 10, "Financial Matters.")

Some parents may pay more if a provider cares for fewer children; for a high quality environment with developmentally appropriate toys and equipment; for a provider who has good training; or for a provider who takes the children on outings.

A number of factors may affect fee levels:

- Rates for part-time care tend to be higher than those for full-time care.

- Lower fees may be charged for additional children from a family.

- Fees may be higher for infants as they require more care.

- Higher rates may be charged for late pickup.

Fees can be amended upwards on an annual basis. Caregivers need to be sure to give parents advance notice of the change so there are no misunderstandings. Give clear information regarding fee payments, such as:

- when they are due;

- whether cheques or cash are accepted;

- whether or not fees will be charged when the child is away on a vacation; and

- how much notice parents must give when withdrawing their child.

This information is usually given to the parents in writing when they enroll their child. Parents need a receipt in order to claim their child care deduction on their income tax return. Sometimes providers do not give receipts and offer a lower fee to compensate for the parent's lost tax deduction. These providers are usually not reporting their full income for tax purposes, which is illegal.

Hours   In setting hours of operation, the provider should set her own schedule. There is usually a higher demand for infant care, part-time care, and before- and after-school care. Parents' child care needs vary greatly depending on their workday and the distance they must commute. Some parents work evenings, weekends, or on rotating shifts. Some providers can be flexible and provide evening or even overnight care. Others are able to provide care only during the regular workweek. The provider must consider her own family circumstances when setting hours for care. Parents are obliged to pay for all of the hours of care that they reserve, even if they do not use them.

Food   It is important to include the parents in planning good nutrition for their child. The provider should be aware of the nutrients that foods provide and the roles these nutrients play in growth and good health. Some parents need to be informed about what kinds of foods children need and in what quantities. The provider should specify to parents what foods will be provided. Much of the information needed to provide nutritionally appropriate meals and snacks is contained in *Canada's Guide to Healthy Eating* (Canada 1992). Some providers prepare a rotating four-week menu for each season. Posting the menus helps parents plan their meals at home. When caring for school-age children, food preferences should be discussed with the child. Inform parents of anything special about the nutritional program, such as offering a vegetarian diet.

Sometimes parents request special dietary restrictions for their child, such as no milk products. If the provider is unable to accommodate a request, the parents may need to supply special meals. Caregivers should provide children with adequate food, a variety of food, and food that is safe for the child to eat (see chapter 8). The environment should foster healthy attitudes toward food and eating, and the provider should model healthy eating habits. Mealtimes should be social and educational, contributing to the child's enjoyment of food. Many important nutritional aspects of a healthy program are detailed in Unit 4 in *Healthy Foundations in Child Care* (Pimento and Kernsted 2004).

Emergencies   It is imperative that the provider have accurate and up-to-date emergency information. The provider should collect the following: the names, addresses, and phone numbers of parents or legal guardians; the name and phone number of the child's health care provider; any allergies or continuing medication; the names and telephone numbers of two people who can pick up the child if the parent is not reachable; the names of others who are authorized to pick up the child; an out-of-area phone number to be used if there is a natural disaster such as an earthquake or flood. Cards containing emergency information for each child should be carried with the provider at all times.

The provider should have current training in first aid and CPR and be prepared to handle emergencies. There should be a detailed plan for fire evacuation plus weather emergency plans. Some providers arrange to have their home inspected by the fire department, to ensure there are clear fire routes, and by the police, for security. An up-to-date list of emergency phone numbers should be posted near the phone. As well, a fully stocked first-aid kit and functioning fire extinguishers must always be on hand. In case an injured or ill child must be taken to hospital, it is critical to have a backup caregiver who can come immediately to care for the other children. Good prevention practices—such as ensuring that the children are supervised at all times and that the equipment is in good repair and developmentally suitable—are the key to minimizing emergencies. Some providers ask a specialist to give suggestions for childproofing their home. Caregivers need to support children's learning of lifelong safety behaviour.

Vacations and holidays   The provider needs to discuss with parents when their vacations are likely to be scheduled and come to some agreement about payment. She should give parents ample notice about her own vacation plans so they can make other arrangements. Some providers arrange for a backup caregiver. Parents pay for a reserved space whether it is used or not.

Child guidance/discipline   Child guidance and discipline is discussed with parents before they enroll their child, as the potential for disagreements in this area is great. A good parent–provider match will feature similar approaches for disciplining the child. Guidance should be positive and geared to the individual child's developmental level and temperament. It is vital that the caregiver understand child development in order to have reasonable expectations. There should be clear limits on and expectations for children's actions. Children should be encouraged to take responsibility for their actions and learn from the consequences of their behaviour.

Program   What the provider and children do together each day is central to their enjoyment and the success of the program. Some providers like to follow a daily schedule while others prefer to take a more spontaneous approach, responding to everyone's moods and any opportunities that arise.

Quality programs for young children are orderly but also flexible. They offer variety in experience, levels of difficulty, and pacing. They are based on the principles that learning should be the result of actual experience and that play is a significant mode of learning. Experiences should provide joy for both the children and the family child care provider.

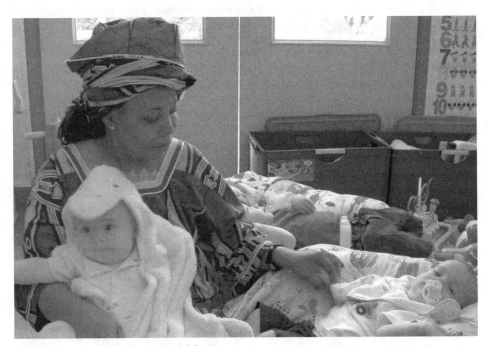

Provider informs parents about the child's day.

A good provider observes the children and builds on their interests. The choice of activities is influenced by the developmental levels of the children in care. One must observe their experiences and interests and consider their ages and unique needs. Both the home and play environment should accommodate activities that are suited to each child's stage of development; promote the development of motor, cognitive, language, and social skills; and appeal to the children's varied interests. There are many resources available—in print, over the Internet, and through workshops—to aid the family child care provider in planning developmentally appropriate and engaging activities for children.

Family child care providers inform parents of what has happened during the day. Some providers keep a written log of the day's events for parents.

Taxes and Record Keeping

A provider who cares for children in her own home on a regular basis is operating a small business. Her business records are vital to track income and expenses. They help the provider make decisions. The Canadian government considers the provider to be self-employed if she controls the number of hours she works, the premises where she works, and the way in which she performs her duties. All income earned by the provider is taxable and must be reported by law. Providers are required to file an income tax return whether their program is operating at a profit or loss. The better the records the provider keeps, the easier it will be to complete taxes.

When a provider cares for children in the parents' home and they specify the way in which the work is to be done and the number of hours worked, the caregiver is not considered to be self-employed; the parents, as the employers, are required to deduct and remit payroll taxes, including employer contributions, and provide an annual T4 slip.

Parents require receipts in order to claim the child care tax deductions to which they are entitled. If a provider fails to issue annual fee receipts early each year, parents may lose hundreds of dollars in tax deductions. It is essential to be organized and keep accurate, up-to-date records of income and expenditures. It is recommended that the provider set up a separate bank account for the business. This will simplify the bookkeeping. Some providers use the services of a freelance bookkeeper. There are many helpful small-business accounting software products available. Also, some child care organizations, such as the Manitoba Child Care Association, publish an annual Family Child Care Data Keeper calendar that includes a variety of forms and checklists to assist the provider in keeping records for tax and other purposes.

Records that must be kept for tax purposes fall into two categories.

- *Income.* The provider lists all fees received. She records the person who paid, the date of the payment/receipt, the period covered by the payment, and the amount.

- *Expenses.* This category includes all payments made for the child care program. Record the date, cheque number, total cost, and name of the item purchased. The following are eligible business-expense tax deductions:
    - toys, equipment, and arts and crafts supplies
    - food for the children
    - playground equipment
    - field trips

- substitute/alternate caregiver expenses
- home supplies such as paper towels and cleaning supplies
- a percentage of rent/mortgage payments and heating/utility costs
- a percentage of home repair and maintenance costs
- repair and maintenance of program equipment
- training and education expenses
- insurance related to the program
- office and record-keeping supplies
- accounting, bookkeeping, and legal fees
- bank charges

Current information about taxes is provided in Revenue Canada's publication *Using Your Home for Day Care* (Canada 2003), found online at www.cra-arc.gc.ca.

Insurance

As small-business operators, providers should ensure that they are adequately covered by liability insurance. Individual household insurance is not adequate when caring for other people's children in one's home. There are several types of insurance available to individuals providing family child care; liability and accident insurance are considered essential. Liability insurance will protect the provider and her family from financial hardship in the event of an injury to a child in her care.

Liability insurance can be quite expensive. Policies vary. Some providers put a rider on their homeowner's insurance policy to include coverage of the children in care. Separate child care coverage is more expensive, but it usually offers greater protection. A third alternative is group liability insurance, available through family child care agencies, child care resource and referral programs, and caregiver associations.

Most general liability policies cover:

- bodily or personal injury
- damage to others' property
- legal costs incurred during a lawsuit
- accidents happening to children while on field trips as well as at the home

If the provider transports the children in her car, she will require special motor vehicle insurance. Keep parents apprised of insurance coverage. If new or better coverage is added, this should be mentioned in the explanation of any increases in fees.

The provider is liable, and can be sued in court, if a parent alleges that an accident occurred because of negligence or failure to exercise reasonable care. "Negligence" is a legal term that means a person who was under legal obligation to act with reasonable care did not do so. Negligence might take the form of inadequate supervision at the time a child was injured, accidentally or by another child. It might involve equipment in poor condition or icy steps. A provider and/or her home or property can be found to be negligent.

Insurance brokers or agents can assist providers in obtaining the necessary coverage and can recommend an appropriate amount of coverage. To prevent misunderstandings, providers should ensure that all communication with agents or brokers regarding insurance coverage is in writing.

HOME SAFETY FOR PROVIDERS

- Childproof every room.
- Take first aid and CPR courses.
- Supervise the children at all times.
- Keep walkways, stairs, and sidewalks clear.
- Be aware of fire hazards.
- Develop clear policies and procedures about health and safety.
- Inform parents of policies.

Caregivers can get more information on the business aspects of care from the Family Child Care Training Program (CCCF 2000a).

Support Programs for Family Child Care

Most providers are aware of the value of regular networking with other providers, both to overcome the isolation associated with caregiving and as a learning opportunity. The level of quality in the home is affected by whether or not a family child care provider networks with other providers through some formal association.

In the past decade, more family child care provider organizations have been founded and supports for caregivers have increased. Most caregivers enjoy opportunities for sharing information and ideas, personal growth, and mutual support. Caregiver organizations work to inform the government, colleges, media, and the general public about family child care. They encourage the development of services for providers and families who use family child care.

SUPPORT PROGRAMS FOR FAMILY CHILD CARE PROVIDERS

- child care registries and referrals to parents
- home visiting
- drop-in programs for caregivers and children
- toy, book, equipment, and information libraries
- in-service programs, workshops, and courses on a variety of topics
- annual conferences
- relief services such as backup for illnesses, emergencies, and vacations
- technical assistance such as help preparing to meet licensing standards or with tax and business aspects of care
- support/education to help providers care for children with special needs

It is essential for the family child care provider to establish supports.

Community support programs include family child care agencies, family resource centres, provider networks, and associations. Community programs may offer a number of orientation and training programs and workshops. These tend to be more informal and limited in scope than training, credentialling, and accreditation programs offered by professional associations and community colleges (Beach et al. 2004).

You Bet I Care! Care and Learning Environments: Quality in Regulated Family Child Care across Canada found considerable variation in the extent of support available to providers (Doherty et al. 2000b). British Columbia is the only jurisdiction that not only licenses individual providers but also funds a network of caregiver **resource and referral programs**. Only Quebec provides consistent financial support to family child care associations. Family resource programs and other similar programs do exist in other provinces but, except in Ontario, there are relatively few in any jurisdiction and they depend on sources such as United Way for their operating funding. Few other jurisdictions have provider associations, and where they exist, they are struggling to survive on membership fees and fund raising activities.

Feelings of isolation no longer need to be a part of the daily agenda for family child care providers. These programs, which also advocate for quality child care services, provide a wealth of information and support.

Family Child Care Agency

Agencies are foremost a mechanism for regulating providers. This is most evident in Ontario, where a regulation attached to the *Day Nurseries Act* explicitly holds agencies accountable for ensuring that their affiliated providers and homes are in compliance with specific standards and practices set out in the Act. The regulatory role is also evident in other provinces. All provinces using the agency model require agency staff, known as home visitors, to make reg-

JOB DESCRIPTION—HOME VISITOR

General Responsibilities:

- Identifies and selects providers and facilities by conducting home assessments and evaluating suitability for provision of child care.
- Advertises for new providers; completes reference checks and necessary documentation.
- Arranges orientation and training sessions for providers. Provides information regarding requirements, resources, and backup provisions. Ensures provider establishes and maintains program standards.
- Arranges and conducts pre-placement interviews with families applying for child care and assesses child care needs. Arranges placement visits to ensure suitability with provider, completes contracts, and discusses/collects fees.
- Monitors and assesses children's care through regular visits to provider's homes.
- Inspects homes for safety, compliance with provincial licensing standards, and agency practices.
- Arranges backup care for emergencies, assists parents and providers in resolving emergency situations.
- Assists parents and providers in resolving conflicts.
- Prepares reports and maintains records/files as required by legislation and agency policy.
- Serves as a consultant on matters of child care/child development.
- Recommends placements for children with special needs based on interviews. Arranges for assessments/supports by resource teachers or other professionals as required.

Qualifications:

- Graduation from an approved Early Childhood Education program or Bachelor of Arts or Social Work or equivalent.
- Experience in licensed child care, education, or social service programs (minimum two years' experience).
- Knowledge of legislation related to family home child care.
- Possession of a valid driver's licence.

ular visits to observe the care being provided. The required frequency of visits ranges from twice monthly in Nova Scotia to four times annually in Ontario and Quebec (Doherty et al. 2000b).

In addition to monitoring the quality of care provided, family child care agencies provide professional development opportunities, resources, and support to families and caregivers. Agencies are operated by local governments, commercial businesses, or non-profit organizations.

The agency assists parents in identifying their child care needs. It will seek a suitable space for a child needing care. An agency staff member meets with the parents and caregiver for an initial placement interview and continues to monitor the arrangement on an ongoing basis. If the caregiver is not available for a period of time, the agency finds alternative care. Agencies may provide other services, such as assistance in applying for fee subsidy, information regarding child health, or guidance and mediation assistance with child care related problems. Through participating in regular evaluations of the service and/or on the board of directors or parent advisory group, parents are given a voice in decisions that affect their children.

The financial aspects of the arrangement are usually the responsibility of the agency. It sets the rates and reviews them annually. The caregiver submits time sheets and is reimbursed by the agency. The agency collects the fees from the parents and, in some cases, government sources if the family is subsidized.

The agency recruits caregivers interested in providing care in their own homes and inspects each home to ensure it is safe and provides information and resources to the provider. Agencies assist new providers with the set-up of their homes and businesses, provide sample contracts, and offer professional development activities. Providers appreciate getting ideas for activities with children as well as receiving supplies and resource materials from the agency.

The home visitor is an employee of the agency and the provider's main contact at the agency. The home visitor serves as the mentor/supervisor for a group of providers. Often she is responsible for recruiting and screening potential providers, giving orientation or training, deciding or participating in decisions on home placements, mediating misunderstandings between providers and parents, and communicating regularly with the parents.

Caregiver Support Networks

Caregivers need the support of people who understand their work. One effective way to find this is to participate in a caregiver support network. The groups tend to be small, and often caregivers meet in each others' homes. These groups are particularly needed in communities where family resource programs are inaccessible. Caregivers need adult contact, and they especially need contact with their peers. Many providers find it helpful to have a partner, someone they can call about a problem, for advice, or just to let off steam. Having a support group of providers to turn to encourages a feeling of professionalism and gives one confidence in making decisions. It protects caregivers from feeling isolated, which is one of the occupational hazards of this work. Some providers like having regular visitors who will appreciate and respond to what is happening in their child care group.

A caregiver network provides opportunities for caregivers to share ideas, information, problems, and solutions and to offer one another mutual support. A caregiver network can provide:

A sense of belonging and community. Belonging to a network can reduce isolation and provide opportunities for support.

An opportunity for professional growth. Caregivers can learn more about caring for children as well as the administration of their business, advocacy, and adult education.

Access to information. Caregivers can share information on community resources, ranging from neighbourhood parks to local businesses that welcome children to tour the premises.

Access to referrals through other caregivers. Caregivers may know of parents who are seeking care for their child.

Access to practical help. Caregivers can arrange exchanges of toys, equipment, and children's tapes, videos, and books.

Exchange of services. Caregivers may cover for one another during holidays, illnesses, or appointments.

Opportunities to give and receive support. Caregivers can plan playgroups together and go on joint outings with the children.

Some family child care providers use electronic mailing lists to access support and resources. Worotynec (2000) surveyed several e-mail lists and found requests for advice on coping with children's and parents' behaviour, handling taxes and receipts, and other business related issues. Providers who are at home all day, alone with children, long for adult conversation and stimulation. She concluded that, while e-mail lists have the potential to be a useful training and problem solving tool and an opportunity for providers to learn from one another, caution is needed in promoting the Internet as a resource for untrained home providers. She makes recommendations for healthy educational use.

The Challenges of Home-Based Family Child Care

As with other occupations, there are both advantages and disadvantages to being a family child care provider. Being one's own boss and having no travel time to get to work are clearly advantageous. Drawbacks include the loss of privacy and living space and feeling as though one never leaves the workplace.

The family child care provider plays multiple roles—paid provider for other people's children, business operator, and, often, parent to her own children. As well, she is responsible for practical tasks such as meal preparation and cleaning. A big challenge appears to be developing a sense of camaraderie without parents mistaking it as friendship and expecting special favours or waivers to contractual issues. From a parent's perspective, there appears to be a fine line between professional practices to support the child's development and friendship. Some parents may mistake one for the other. Providers walk a tightrope trying to remain professional and caring while not crossing the line into becoming friends with the parent.

Administrative requirements further expand the demands on a provider's time. Balancing the demands of their multiple and, at times, conflicting roles has been associated with stress among providers.

A disadvantage for family child care providers is the heavy load of responsibility and isolation. Caring for a number of children up to ten hours a day can be emotionally and physically exhausting. Working alone in their homes, family child care providers miss the informal sharing of observations, frustrations, and concerns enjoyed by caregivers in centres. They need to develop and maintain relationships with other home-based child care providers. Some providers meet in the park or at playgroups. These occasions provide adult company as well as an outing for the children.

Many family child care providers have encountered people who do not respect their work. Support for their career choice can be very important for a family child care provider.

This particularly applies to the provider's own family members. Some friction is to be expected when the provider first goes into business. The provider needs to sort out with her family what is expected and not expected of other family members regarding the children in care. This can be particularly difficult for the provider's children. Some children may find it difficult to share their toys and even "Mommy."

The provider has to balance the needs and demands for time and attention of the child care children and their families with those of her own family. Her work affects the family's control over its time and personal space. Private family living space and family belongings must be shared with unrelated children for extended periods of time. The physical arrangement of the house must be adjusted to accommodate toys and equipment used for the child care program. Non-family members, such as parents or, in some cases, home visitors, have the right to enter the home. These intrusions can feel inconvenient to family life.

Occasionally a provider's job can be very difficult. She may discover a case of child abuse among her families—or one of a child's family members may become very ill. A provider may feel she is losing control or become frustrated with an infant who won't stop crying. These are times when the caregiver should seek help in order to handle the situation in the best way possible.

Finally, as previously noted, there is considerable ambiguity in the employment status of family child care providers. Is an agency-affiliated family child care provider an employee or self-employed? Unlike employees, agency-affiliated providers do not get paid vacations or paid sick days and are not covered by workers' compensation programs. Canada Revenue Agency has historically recognized family child care providers as self-employed for income-tax purposes. However, some of the services provided by agencies, such as collection of fees and payment of the family child care provider with an income cheque, suggest employee status for the provider. Under current labour legislation, employees are entitled to minimum wage, breaks during the day, and benefits such as paid vacation and maternity leave. They are also prohibited from working more than a certain number of hours per week without their consent and overtime pay. This unresolved employment status is affecting the viability of the agency model, and this issue is being reviewed by agencies, unions, and governments.

Summary

Family child care may be more suitable for some children than a centre-based program because it can serve a broad range of needs, can be available for emergency care, and can provide evening and weekend care. Arrangements with family child care providers are usually made individually, although there is some regulation of the number of children for whom care can be provided in a given home. Most children in Canada are in unregulated care with no external monitoring. Providers have the challenge of running a responsive, caring service that is also a small business. Providers must learn to design effective business policies, customize contracts, set fees, keep financial and legal records, and market their business. Some providers join community groups to access information and support services.

Key Terms and Concepts

Contract,   p. 112

CPE,   p. 109

Family child care,   p. 98

Family child care agency,   p. 101

Family child care provider,   p. 98

Multi-age (mixed-age) groupings, p. 105

Professionalism,   p. 104

Registration,   p. 101

Resource and referral programs, p. 120

Resource teacher,   p. 110

Activities

1. Arrange a visit to a family resource centre and check out what services they offer. If there is a drop-in program, observe interactions between parents/children/caregivers/staff.

2. Identify what supports are available for caregivers in your community.

3. Interview any parents in your network of contacts who have a young child in family child care. Have them identify the benefits of and reasons for choosing family child care. List their concerns.

4. Arrange an interview with a family child care agency or licensed provider in your community. Learn about the training opportunities provided in the last year. Are there any areas they would like to see provided in future.

5. Meet with some family child care providers. Have them discuss the challenges they face in their work and what would be helpful to address these issues.

Recommended Reading

Bush, J. *Dollars and Sense: Planning for Profit in Your Child Care Business*. Albany, NY: Delmar, 2001.

Canadian Child Care Federation. *Family Child Care Training Program, Level 3*. Ottawa: Canadian Child Care Federation, 2003.

Doherty, G., D. Lero, J. Tougas, A. LaGrange, and H. Goelman. *You Bet I Care! Policies and Practices in Canadian Family Child Care Agencies*. Guelph, ON: Centre for Families, Work and Well-Being, University of Guelph, 2001.

Doherty G., D. Lero, H. Goelman, J. Tougas, and A. LaGrange. *You Bet I Care! Caring and Learning Environments: Quality in Regulated Family Child Care across Canada*. Guelph, ON: Centre for Families, Work and Well-Being, University of Guelph, 2000.

Dunster, L. *Home Child Care: A Caregiver's Guide*. Ottawa: Child Care Provider's Association, 2000.

Harms, T., and R.M. Clifford. *Family Day Care Rating Scale*. New York: Teachers College Press, Columbia University, 1989. (A revised edition is expected in 2005.)

Modigliani, K., M. Reiff, and S. Jones. *Opening Your Door to Children: How to Start a Family Day Care Program.* Washington, DC: National Association for the Education of Young Children, 1997.

Government of Canada, Canada Customs and Revenue Agency. *Using Your Home for Day Care,* 2000. Available online at: www.ccra-adrc.gc.ca/tax/business/topics/day-care/menu-e.html.

Weblinks

www.cfc-efc.ca/wcfcca
Western Canada Family Child Care Association of British Columbia
This site provides a wealth of information, including links to Child and Family Canada, current British Columbia legislation for operating a family child care home, and resources for parents and providers, both in print and through community groups.

www.nafcc.org
National Association for Family Child Care
This American organization has an accreditation program for providers. It has a national conference and provides resources.

www.childcare-ppin.com
Child Care Parent Provider Information Network
This site hosts forum discussion groups on topics such as "How often is it reasonable to increase rates?" and "Where to find training opportunities." There are links to other sites.

www.cccf-fcsge.ca
Canadian Child Care Federation
The Family Child Care page on the CCCF website showcases the Family Child Care Training Program. It also provides resource sheets, a community development section with strategies to reach out to unregulated providers, links to other sites, and a bulletin board with discussion forums and events.

chapter 6

Human Resources Management in an ECEC Environment

Objectives

- **Describe the director's role in creating a supportive, effective and professional work environment.**

- **Review effective human resource management policies and procedures.**

- **Identify considerations for effective recruitment, hiring, staff orientation, and developing effective teams.**

- **Outline strategies for performance management, personal and professional development, and career advancement.**

This chapter examines the director's roles and responsibilities in relation to people management, team building, and organizational development. The director's role is to lead the team so that the whole team, as well as each individual team member can fulfill their responsibilities; contribute to their full potential; and continuously demonstrate their professionalism, their commitment to the principles of healthy child development, and their dedication to a quality learning environment. To fulfill this role it is essential that the director ensure every team member understands the vision, mission, and values of the organization; its policies and procedures; its practices and protocols; and its program philosophy.

In *Quality Matters: Excellence in Early Childhood Programs* (1995), Doherty-Derkowski reviews research studies conducted over 15 years in a number of countries and confirms the critical role that committed and knowledgeable staff can play. A strong team, comprised of competent early childhood education professionals and practitioners, is critically important to achieve high quality programs.

In the ECEC field, lots of attention has been focused on how the physical environments of early childhood settings can be made responsive to children, but less attention has been given to the adult needs in the same setting. The general layout and design of space can help or hinder staff in carrying out their jobs and powerfully influence moods and attitudes. Staff must have the proper equipment, materials, and resources to do their work effectively. (This aspect of early childhood settings is discussed in detail in chapter 8, "Managing Safe and Healthy Learning Environments.")

The director must be on the alert for potential health hazards in the workplace. The Canadian Pædiatric Society (1996) cites the following health hazards in early childhood education: increased risk of illness; toxic substances in art supplies and cleaning agents; back problems from heavy lifting and frequent bending; physical strain from using furniture in an environment designed for children; poor lighting; high noise levels; and stress. Another major health hazard comes from the common tendency among caregivers to ignore their own health needs, because they lack extended health benefits and time off, and because they feel responsible for meeting children's needs first.

With the support of the board of directors/owner, the director is responsible for creating a program environment sensitive to the needs of adults as well as those of children.

In *Improving the Quality of Work Life*, Jorde Bloom (1997) identifies a number of factors affecting the quality of the work environment and, ultimately, the quality of care. These factors include the amount of support received from the director, opportunities for professional development, clarity of job expectations, an equitable reward system, and the physical **work environment**.

Core Competencies for Quality ECEC

The Early Years Study (Ontario 1999) notes that a competent early childhood staff is able to:

- Establish partnerships with families that support the program's responsibilities to the child.
- Plan play-based problem solving activities for the children that promote optimal brain development to establish coping and social skills and other competencies.
- Through the children's language and play experiences, promote the development of the crucial early cognitive base for literacy, numeracy, and science learning and the development of positive behaviour and social skills.
- Ensure that the environment and daily caregiving practices protect children's health, nutrition, safety, and well-being.
- Develop responsive relationships with individual children and the group; respect family and ethno-cultural diversity and appreciate the multitude of strengths of each child.
- Identify problems and difficulties early and provide appropriate interventions.
- Work with others in the community to support children's well-being.

Early childhood professionals and practitioners are committed to quality care and education of infants, toddlers, preschoolers, and children of elementary school age. The document *Occupational Standards for Child Care Practitioners* (Doherty 2003) is the baseline document for core ECEC competencies; it outlines skills and abilities and core knowledge in nine areas.

HR Management: The Director's Responsibilities

To create a competent staff, the director must make thoughtful decisions about hiring, training, and supporting the team; get to know the team—including knowing their individual strengths, areas for development, career aspirations, talents, and interests; and provide strong leadership through effective communication, mentoring and modelling professional behaviours, providing opportunities for continuous development, and providing positive feedback and direction for improvement.

Along with the program's governance body (board of directors or owner), the director has the following human resource management responsibilities:

- Create an effective, supportive, and professional work environment that meets the needs of the children and families, as well as the staff team, to maximize the program's success;

- Develop and implement effective human resource management policies that meet or exceed employment standards established by the provincial/territorial government, comply with a **collective agreement** where applicable, and fit with the program's philosophy and mission statement;

- Develop and implement effective recruitment, hiring, and orientation procedures;

- Develop and implement procedures and protocols to effectively and consistently manage performance, such as conducting regular performance reviews; and

- Provide formal and informal personal and professional development opportunities for team members.

Creating an Effective Work Environment

Before designing a job description for a new position or recruiting candidates to fill a vacancy, take time to review the program's mission statement and goals as outlined in Chapter 4 and carefully consider the program philosophy. Some questions to ask at this step are:

- How well does the program fulfill its mission and accomplish its goals?

- How committed are the staff to the mission and goals of the program? How do staff become engaged in the workplace and how long do they remain committed to helping the organization reach its goals?

- How do the children and families become connected to the program and what factors determine how long they stay involved?

- How does the organization measure its success and determine its need for development?

- How does the staff integrate the program philosophy in daily activities?

Through effective human resource management practices, including recruitment, interviewing, hiring, and leadership, the director can ensure she has a knowledgeable, caring, and competent team.

Building a Strong Team

A top-notch team is created by putting together the right combination of people with complimentary and compatible skills, competencies, interests, and values. Every day directors deal with the challenge of finding the right staff to work effectively with young children and families. Professional experience, educational credentials, and personal characteristics are important elements to consider.

A strong team works well together; they share a common philosophy; they support each other; and their skills and knowledge are compatible and complementary. A strong team provides not only a richer program for the children and families, but also provides opportunities for in-service training where staff can share their expertise and skills with one another.

For children, the quality of the program is determined by the attitudes, knowledge, and skills of the people who care for and educate them. To maximize program quality, directors need to create work environments that encourage employees to make a long-term commitment to the program and want to contribute to the program's long term success.

Given the importance of well-qualified staff, an employer must attract and keep skilled caregivers. A well planned and implemented recruitment strategy is a key first step.

Whether the goal is to build an entire staff team for a new program, fill a vacant position, or replace someone who is on a temporary leave, the overall approach to finding the most suitable candidate/s will be the same. A staff member's role will be defined by the specific job responsibilities, the objectives of the program, and the nature of the community in which the program is located.

Directors should involve members of the staff and parents in brainstorming desirable qualities and characteristics for each position in the program. Some questions to ask are:

- Describe a person who would complement and strengthen the current staff team.
- How much education does the candidate need to possess?
- How much and what kind of experience is necessary to meet the job requirements and meet the program objectives?
- What personal characteristics and attributes do you need to build a strong team?
- Which desirable characteristics are "must-have," which are behaviours that "can-be-taught," and which are "could-be-developed-on-the-job"?
- Which skills can be developed on the job with careful supervision, mentoring, and professional development?
- What capacity does the program have to provide the **professional development** and support needed for the development of the required skills?

Answering these questions will help programs focus the search process to maximize program quality.

Human Resources Policies and Procedures

The program's **human resources (HR) policies** (historically referred to as **personnel policies**) should reflect the philosophy of the overall program, convey the program's values, and express the management principles. Policies must comply with all federal and provincial/territorial employment legislation plus all provincial/territorial child care legislation and municipal regulations.

Effective HR policies balance the staff's need to feel secure and confident in their daily work with the director's need for effective program management. Clarity and consistency of HR information will provide the foundation for smooth operations.

HUMAN RESOURCES POLICIES

HR policies reflect organizational goals, clarify management expectations, and establish operational guidelines. HR policies should be supplemented with a set of procedures and management guidelines. HR polices should be accompanied by an effective orientation program, an ongoing professional development strategy, and a supportive management process. A set of well articulated HR policies is the cornerstone of an effective performance management process.

A Human Resources Policies and Procedures Manual is an important written document outlining details about the employment relationship, including hiring practices, termination procedures, and conditions of employment; management expectations and practices; and operating procedures related to the staff team.

The manual should also include details about organizational structure; roles, responsibilities, and accountability (reporting and supervision procedures); evaluation and disciplinary procedures; health and safety matters; and a description of the process to amend policies. This information is usually communicated to the employee at the time of hiring/orientation and made available for reference during the employment period.

By keeping all employment related information located in a single HR Policy and Procedure Manual, most HR questions can be handled by simply referring to one document. One source for the information makes it easier for staff to find answers than if it is scattered across various memos, minutes of meetings, and bulletin boards. It also reduces confusion and eliminates the possibility of contradictory statements.

Organizations will often develop an employee handbook that summarizes the key points in the HR Policy and Procedure Manual. A comprehensive, clear, and well-written employee handbook as well as informing employees about their rights and **benefits** also describes the types of behaviours that are encouraged and discouraged. It should serve as quick reference for staff to any questions that might arise regarding the organization as well as their employment.

Developing and Amending HR Policies

Generally, the board of directors/owner, directly or thorough an HR committee, develops HR policies; the director is responsible for implementing them as discussed in chapter 3. When organizations develop HR policies and procedures they must comply with applicable laws, such as the provincial/territorial employment standards or labour legislation, which includes regulations on leaves, minimum wages, and hours of work. In a unionized work environment, policies must also conform to union requirements, which are generally spelled out in a negotiated **collective agreement**.

The personnel policies should include a statement that details the procedure for amending the policies. On an ongoing basis, the board of directors, staff, and director should review the HR policies to determine whether any changes are necessary. The decision makers can then follow the amendment procedures. Once a change is adopted, the director needs to formally inform the staff of the changes.

Recruitment, Hiring, and Orientation

Designing Job Descriptions

Role clarity reduces uncertainty, minimizes conflict and decreases workplace stress. A well-written job description can motivate employees and be the foundation for an effective performance management program. Job descriptions should include the following key elements:

- *Job title*: a simple description of the nature of the job.

- *Accountability*: who the employee reports to (supervisor's full title), frequency of performance reviews, and length of **probationary period**, if applicable.

- *Job summary:* a brief description highlighting the general characteristics of the position. This summary is often use in recruitment activities.

- *Job requirements:* minimum education, experience, skills, and personal qualities. Basic qualifications are often determined by licensing standards and union contracts; however, each program has the right to require more than the basic requirements stipulated by the regulations.

- *Roles and responsibilities:* a more detailed statement of what duties the employee is expected to fulfill. This section generally outlines the tasks for which the employee will be held accountable.

- *Salary and benefits schedule:* the range of pay for the position and what benefits will be provided.

- *Work schedule:* hours of work, work schedule, vacation entitlement, and any other work arrangements available such as job sharing.

Job descriptions should be prepared prior to hiring a new employee. Job descriptions may be altered while someone is already in the position, however, employees must have ample notice for any changes.

On a regular basis (minimum annually), the director should meet with existing staff to review existing job descriptions and assess their individual and team strengths and needs for training and development. This gives everyone an opportunity to have input into the development of the team and the organization, facilitates the recruitment process, and contributes to the smooth operation of the program.

Identifying Potential Candidates

Given the relatively small pool of qualified personnel, early childhood development programs may well find themselves competing against each other for staff, and directors will be wise not to underestimate the challenge of recruiting enough suitable applicants from which to choose. This shortage, along with strategies to expand recruitment, are being addressed by the Child Care Human Resources Sector Council. Consider specific features of the organization's mission statement or work environment that are likely to attract the candidate wanted, then make sure to highlight these features in the advertisement for the job. Post the job internally to ensure that present staff know about it and have a chance to apply. They should not have to hear about a position from outside, and they may know of a good candidate to recommend. Often desirable candidates can be drawn from those who have completed student placements with the program or are currently working as casual staff.

After that, start looking for potential employees in logical places—community colleges, universities, and professional organizations. Consider advertising the position in diverse communities. Remember the many possible combinations of education, experience, and personal attributes that could characterize qualified applicants, and target recruitment strategies accordingly. Programs should establish and follow the same procedures for recruiting, interviewing, and filling vacancies each time the need arises.

Finally, consider the cost-effectiveness (in terms of both time and money) of potential recruitment strategies. Frequently recommended strategies include:

- actively encourage applications from current staff;
- generate word of mouth among colleagues;
- use networks of non-profit organizations and other professional associations;
- notify career-counselling offices at local colleges and universities and other programs that provide education in child development and related disciplines;
- notify faculties of human development, psychology, social work, education, and other disciplines within colleges and universities;
- advertise in low-cost professional and community newsletters; and
- post on websites for early childhood organizations, non-profits, or practitioners (e.g., the site for Child and Family Canada, Monster.ca, or Charity Village).

Hiring for Diversity Directors should actively recruit caregivers who reflect the ethnic, cultural, and linguistic diversity of the families served. A diverse staff is more likely to help families from all backgrounds feel welcome in the facility. In any group of families, there is likely to be diversity in ethnicity, faith, economic status, and interests. Parents may feel an affinity to a staff member with a similar background. The staff member who connects with a family can increase the overall quality of the family's experience with the program.

Staff must be able to meet the children's diverse developmental, cultural, linguistic, and educational needs. They should have an understanding of socio-cultural and economic issues pertaining to the communities in which the children live. This knowledge can be useful in supporting families on the use and development of the child's home language and in the acquisition of English and/or French. Staff that speak more than one language and are knowledgeable about more than one culture are an invaluable resource.

A second consideration in recruitment is gender. Our society is generally not supportive of men working with very young children. Some parents may want their children to have positive male role models; therefore, they may prefer programs that include a male staff members. Compared to the number of similarly qualified women, there are relatively few qualified males available to fill the positions.

Children need positive male role models.
Photo: Paul Chartrand. Reprinted with permission.

Canada has less than 4% male staff; whereas the European Economic Union is targetting 20% male staff in ECEC by 2015. This situation stems in part from societal beliefs that women have a natural, instinctive ability to nurture children and men do not. Male staff can fill a special role for young children, particularly those that who grow up in single-parent homes without a male role model. Yet men leave the early childhood field at a greater rate than women. Some male caregivers have reported that they were subject to subtle prejudicial attitudes from parents, female co-workers, and directors. They report underlying tensions based on the misconceptions and false assumptions that men who work in early childhood settings may get romantically involved with co-workers or parents or male caregivers are more likely than female caregivers to abuse children. Directors and staff need to examine individual attitudes and help increase parental awareness of the value of male staff members.

Like female staff, males report poor wages and working conditions as a pivotal factor affecting recruitment and retention. Economic factors often prevent men from entering or staying in the early childhood field.

Here are some ideas for bringing more men into the field and encouraging them to stay:

- Babysitting is one way that boys discover they like working with young children. In school-age programs, encourage boys to learn skills caring for children. Support older boys who would like to read to and mentor young children.

- Help male staff to be visible. At the program, display photos of males interacting with young children.

- Be recruiters for the profession. When directors find men who feel comfortable caring for young children, they should encourage them to pursue a career in early childhood education and care.

To build an effective team, directors and staff need to help male staff feel comfortable, connected, and valued. Consider what it is like to be in a minority. Imagine what it would be like to be the only woman working with dozens of men.

Gender and cultural diversity should be reflected in policies. Review documentation such as policy manuals, philosophy statements, parent handbooks, or other documents outlining program beliefs and guidelines. Most programs have a process for adding to or amending information in these documents. Consider adding statements like: "The presence of men is essential to the lives of young children—particularly in light of the changing dynamics of families" and "Preference will be given to candidates from the same cultural and linguistic backgrounds as the families served."

Interviewing Potential Candidates

The interview process provides an opportunity for both the program staff and applicant to ask questions, provide information, and get to know each other. A good match is critical. A good fit will increase the possibility of success and improve the likelihood of the staff person remaining at the centre. It will also ensure that the considerable time it takes for a new staff member to get to know the children, families, co-workers, and overall operation will not be wasted. Staff changes are very unsettling to children, families, and other staff. When a program hires someone who doesn't work out, it loses all of the time and energy it took recruiting, interviewing, hiring, and orienting the person—only to have to begin the process all over again.

Determine a hiring team before the recruitment process begins. In non-profit programs, the team generally involves representatives of the board of directors and/or one or two parents. Many programs use a standard five-step process for hiring: screening, interviewing, observing, selecting, and negotiating.

The first step involves the initial screening of resumés against the identified requirements. The director or hiring team identifies the applicants to be interviewed.

The second step involves the preliminary interviews, which narrow the field by determining how well the candidates' qualifications fit the program's needs.

In the third step, potential candidates are invited to participate individually in the playroom for a minimum of two hours, to allow the director and/or staff to observe their skills in interacting with children and other staff.

The fourth step involves the interviewing team selecting a candidate for the position following a thorough assessment of the candidate's resumé, the results of the interview, an assessment of the observation, discussion of the program's needs, and information gathered during the reference checks.

The fifth step involves the preparation of an offer of employment. The team prepares the offer, presents it to the candidate, and completes the negotiations.

Involving staff in the hiring process helps to build a strong team. Staff may be included in the process by reviewing resumés or applications, asking questions and/or taking notes during the interview, and observing a candidate's style of interaction in the playroom. A staff member who participates in selecting a candidate is likely to be more supportive in facilitating the new member's integration into the staff team.

Conducting an Interview

AREAS TO COVER WHEN INTERVIEWING A CANDIDATE

- education, skill, and experience related to the position
- knowledge and understanding of child development
- personal philosophy of early childhood development
- demonstrated ability to plan a learning program
- strategies used for guiding and supporting children's behaviour
- evidence of problem solving strategies and conflict resolution style
- methods used for involving families in the program
- commitment to personal and professional development
- attitude, talents, attributes, and characteristics
- interpersonal and communication skills
- salary/benefits expectations and availability (possible start date)

Use open-ended questions and scenarios to learn how a candidate thinks and responds. For example, "What do families need in order to raise responsible, happy children?" As well as providing information about the candidate's skills and knowledge, this type of question allows the team to learn more about how she or he thinks and explore how well her or his philosophical beliefs match those of the program. Decide on the questions before the interview, ask each candidate the same questions, and thoroughly document all responses. Some examples include:

- Why do you want to work with young children and families?

- Describe a technique you have used in the past to calm a child, redirect inappropriate behaviour, introduce a new activity, etc. Describe the situation, your technique and the results of your action.
- Describe your greatest strength in working with young children and families. What professional development opportunities are you interested in pursuing?
- Describe your personal philosophy.
- How might employers/colleagues describe you? If they had to name one quality that gets in the way of your success, what would it be? Do you agree with their perception?
- What new skills would you like to learn? How do you learn best?
- Describe your ideal work environment: the people, the interpersonal relationships, the program, the setting.
- Describe how you have managed in a situation when you were faced with people who had values that are different from your own.
- Describe how you have managed in stressful situations.

The interviewing team must be aware of human rights legislation and know which questions are legal and illegal to ask. Some programs have employment equity hiring practices, where preference is given to qualified candidates who are from a visible minority, are a member of a First Nation, or have a disability; in the field of early childhood, preference may also be given to male applicants.

Remember, while the candidate is being interviewed, she or he is also interviewing the program. Time invested in planning an effective hiring process will ensure that both the hiring team and candidate have many opportunities to exchange information and make well-informed decisions about the job match. Effective hiring procedures result in greater compatibility between employee and program, a higher level of job satisfaction, and, ultimately, a higher quality program.

Checking References

Prior to making an offer to a candidate, it is important to check references. References generally include character references from people who have known the candidate for a long time, professional references from people who have supervised or worked with the candidate, and criminal references from the local law enforcement authority.

Character and Professional References The director should tell the person giving the reference what position the candidate is applying for and give a brief overview of the most important qualifications for the job. Ask the referee to describe how the candidate's characteristics or experience demonstrate that they will be able to fulfill the job requirements. Ask about the referee's history and general experience with the candidate. Ask them to describe the areas in which the candidate needs to grow or requires support or professional development.

Criminal Reference Checks Many provinces have established background-check requirements. In addition to checking professional and personal references, the director must make a criminal and abuse registry check on each applicant who is a serious contender for the position. One must be very cautious when hiring individuals who will work directly with young children. Those in the decision making role need to develop policies for how to handle a **criminal reference check** that comes back showing a conviction. Criminal reference checks do infringe on the rights of individuals who have records. In the field of early childhood development, however, the rights of adults with criminal records are subordinate to the rights of the children, who need to trust and depend on the staff members.

Making an Offer/Signing a Contract

Once the hiring team selects a candidate, an offer is presented stating the salary, details of the benefits package, and terms of employment. Once the offer is accepted, an employment **contract** is prepared. A contract is a binding legal agreement between an individual staff member and the board of directors/owner specifying the services the staff member will provide and the sum of money to be paid for those services. Other details documented in a written contract include the date of hiring; probationary period, if appropriate; evaluation process; pay for the period covered by the contract; benefits; conditions for termination; and, where appropriate, the termination date.

New Employee Orientation

Integrating new staff members takes commitment, determination, and patience. A well-planned, individualized orientation program sets the stage for open communication and is an opportunity to model good practice. An effective recruiting and hiring process introduces new staff members to general aspects of the program such as philosophy, objectives, curriculum, program design, and level of family involvement.

During orientation employees should be provided with information about the history and mission of the organization, the human resource policies, and operational practices. Many programs provide an employee handbook to help new employees become familiar with the organization. Employee handbooks generally provide information including but not limited to:

- *Organizational structure:* board of directors, staff reporting.
- *Terms of employment:* job descriptions, hiring procedures, compensation, discipline, termination, conflict resolutions/problem solving, resignation/termination.
- ***Performance-appraisal** process and probationary period*, if appropriate.
- *Benefits for employees:* holidays, sick days, health benefits, insurance, staff development.
- *Expectations of employees:* behaviour guidance, reporting requirements, health and safety, family/staff/child relations, attendance.
- *Policies, procedures, and protocols:* Confidentiality, documentation, and record keeping.

Formal orientation should be at least two to three days long and may be up to a few weeks long. Allow time for on-the-job orientation when the new staff member can review the staff manual and learn the specific responsibilities of the position.

Existing staff can help integrate new staff by serving as mentors. **Mentors** can help provide a basic orientation. More important, mentors can introduce the new staff member to all employees and families. Mentors can also be safe people for new employees to come to with lots of questions that they may not feel comfortable asking the director.

In the end, time spent orienting the new employee, introducing them to the children and families, and familiarizing them with the overall operation is time well spent. Strategies to assist parents in welcoming a new member of the staff may include a profile in a newsletter and/or on a bulletin board and a welcoming introduction at a parent meeting. Such measures will help to build a successful long-term relationship with staff members, and they will feel respected and valued as a member of the team.

Managing Performance
Goal Setting and Performance Appraisals

Some directors view performance management as one of their most difficult, time-consuming, and emotionally challenging tasks. Although directors have overall responsibility for performance management, sometimes board members/owners are involved.

Regular one-on-one performance management meetings with individual staff and their immediate supervisor provide an opportunity to identify strengths and areas for improvement and respond to problems as they arise. These meetings should be more frequent for new hires: weekly for the first two months, every two weeks for the next two months, and once a month for the next two months; then, if the person is performing as expected, once or twice a year thereafter.

Every performance management meeting should include a review of the staff member's performance since the last meeting, a review of the goals set at previous meetings, and plans for the next period. All performance meetings should be documented, and the documentation of the discussions should be initialled by both the employee and their supervisor. This documentation provides a foundation for personal and professional development but can also provide the basis for a decision to terminate employment or for a decision to offer a promotion or salary increase or bonus.

Sample

Job Description—Early Childhood Practitioner

Job Summary
Under the direction of the program director and in co-operation with early childhood colleagues, plans, implements, monitors, and evaluates the program in accordance with provincial regulations and program philosophy.

Job Responsibilities
1. To ensure that the health, welfare, and safety of the children remain the first priority of the program:
   - Monitors all areas used by children, including washrooms and playground, for safety.
   - Checks toys and equipment used in activities to ensure safe functioning.
   - Sets up and tidies activity areas.
   - Observes and assesses the development of individual children.

(continued)

- Prepares accident reports as necessary.
- Participates with other staff to ensure the safety of children in care.
- Reports unusual situations, such as allergies, accidents, parental requests and concerns, or behavioural irregularities, to the director.
- Provides/arranges for first aid in case of emergencies and creates records as required.
- Administers medication as authorized by physician and maintains records of all medication administered.
- Conducts a daily health check of children.
- Records illness and contacts parents regarding illnesses.
- Ensures that any special dietary requirements are met.
- Feeds children, ensuring adequate nourishment.
- Provides an emotionally supportive environment and shows sensitivity to the individual needs of children in all aspects of their development.
- Uses fair and consistent methods of behaviour guidance in accordance with the program's policies.

2. To provide environments that are carefully planned to meet individual needs and facilitate children's progress in all areas of development:
   - Works with the program director and other staff to provide age-, individual-, and developmentally-appropriate activities to enhance cognitive, physical, emotional, and social development.
   - Uses a variety of teaching techniques including modelling, observing, questioning, demonstrating, and reinforcing.
   - Provides a daily balance of quiet/active, indoor/outdoor, and individual/ group activities.
   - Implements a schedule that incorporates child-directed activities, care routines, and transition times.
   - Develops, implements, and evaluates programs to promote and enhance creativity in all areas: arts and crafts, drama, sensory domain, cognition, emotional awareness, music appreciation, science and nature, and fine- and gross-motor activities.
   - Provides social experiences that foster sharing, co-operation, respect for others, and self-sufficiency.
   - Plans and implements opportunities that facilitate understanding of a variety of cultures and value systems.
   - Provides experiences and play materials that actively promote anti-racist and non-sexist attitudes.
   - Plans and carries out activities that encourage problem solving.
   - Incorporates intervention programs, such as speech therapy and physiotherapy, to meet the individual needs of children.

(continued)

- Maintains files on each child consisting of samples of the child's work.
- Observes children's progress and behaviour to ensure that the program meets individual and group needs.
- Recommends referral of children to community agencies as required.
- Participates in educational assessment conferences with outside agencies.
- Attends and participates in staff meetings in order to discuss the implementation of the overall program, share information, and discuss work with individual children and their families.
- Participates in evaluation of programs and recommends modifications to improve effectiveness in meeting developmental needs.

3. To provide a highly professional service to families:
- Develops responsive relationships with parents of children in care.
- Responds to all inquiries from parents regarding their child's progress and behaviour.
- Maintains confidentiality at all times.
- Encourages and provides opportunities for families to participate actively in all aspects of planning and decision making for their children.
- Completes intake interviews, initiates the sharing of information with families on a regular basis, plans and attends parent interviews and parent evenings, and acts as a resource to families in situations requiring problem solving.

4. To ensure that the program meets standards set by legislation and the expectations of the board of directors/owner:
- Assigns tasks to early childhood assistants, students, and volunteers as necessary.
- Demonstrates proper procedures to early childhood students and others.
- Keeps aware of policy changes.
- Adheres to staff and family policies.
- Attends professional development events.
- Attends staff meetings, contributes to the agenda, and takes minutes on a rotating basis.
- Attends board meetings and other functions, such as fundraising events, as required.
- Participates in the annual performance review process.
- Actively takes responsibility for own personal and professional growth and development.

Source: This job description was compiled from materials from St. Lawrence Co-operative Centre; Conestoga College's Child Care programs; and Gillian Doherty, in Canadian Child Care Federation (CCCF), *Partners in Quality: Tools for Practitioners in Child Care Settings* (Ottawa: CCCF, 2000).

In a supportive climate, the review process is motivating, builds competence, and increases commitment to the organization. An effective staff development program can go a long way toward influencing and increasing the staff's professional skills and self-esteem.

All staff members need to know that they are valued and respected for their work. It is a major challenge for directors to create an atmosphere that encourages all staff to enhance their skills and participate in self-assessment—and one that values and encourages planning to create a high quality program. A director plays a vital role by providing ongoing support for staff and giving them open, honest, and regular feedback. While it is up to the individual to make the decision to change her or his behaviour, this feedback on performance provides direction for change. It makes individuals aware of what they do well and may help them improve their performance in areas that need attention. Such feedback need not be directive. The best evaluation model is one where director and staff work together to identify challenges, generate solutions, and explore alternatives.

Such an appraisal model concentrates on the staff member's performance, rather than on her or his character. The evaluation focuses on how a person acts rather than judging who they are. It is specific rather than global and focuses on the future rather than dwelling on the past. Regular, open communication will have a more enduring impact on an individual's self-esteem and overall performance than any specific resources that are provided to the individual. Both Caruso and Fawcett (1999) and Sciarra and Dorsey (2002) provide a comprehensive look at supervision practices from a perspective that acknowledges the stages of employee development.

Standard

Early Childhood Staff Performance Appraisal

Employee: _____   Date: _____

Director: _____

Type of Review: _____ Three-month   _____ Six-month   _____ Annual

The purpose of the appraisal is to provide employees with some measure of how well they are performing in their current job, and to identify any training/development requirements. Comments should include whether they meet or exceed expectations, or need improvement. Please give specific examples to support your ratings.

Review position description form and revise if necessary. Identify status.

Key Job Areas	Performance Indicators	Comments
Demonstrates positive human qualities with children	• provides warm, nurturing environment • values and respects children • fosters child's self-esteem, sense of security, and trust • encourages choice making and independence	

(continued)

Key Job Areas	Performance Indicators	Comments
Plans, prepares, and implements a developmentally appropriate curriculum	• plans and posts curriculum for the specific ages of the children • has resources readily available • carries out planned curriculum for fine and gross motor, receptive and expressive language, social, emotional, cognitive, and self-help skills both indoors and outdoors • supervises and educates children in nourishment routines, rest periods, and all transitions	
Reports unusual situations to program director	• reports unusual situations, such as allergies, accidents, parent requests or concerns, and behavioural irregularities to program director • provides or arranges for first aid in case of emergencies	
Functions as team member	• respects colleagues • resolves conflicts with children, parents, and co-workers • shares resources, skills, and materials	
Supports parental involvement	• initiates the sharing of information with parents on a regular basis • acts as a resource to parents in problem solving situations • supports and maintains rights of parents as able • carries out intake interview and contributes to parent evening	
Performs professionally	• is punctual • ensures confidentiality • fulfills responsibilities • seeks and obtains directions and assistance when needed • acts on previously established objectives • maintains requirements of legislation	

The relationship between the director and staff is the most critical element in producing improved performance. The quality of the director's skills combined with the degree of trust between the director and the staff, determines the success of the evaluation process. Effective directors use the performance management process as an opportunity to build trust and foster commitment in the program's most valued resource—its staff.

Performance reviews can acknowledge superior performance, give the employer feedback on the results of the selection process, and provide a basis for career planning and professional development. Feedback that clarifies the expectations of the program can be especially helpful to new staff. The performance management system used must fit the professional skills, maturity, and experience of the staff. A comprehensive approach to assessing staff performance will use a variety of formats to meet the needs of individual practitioners at each stage of their development. (The four stages of professional growth are discussed in chapter 7, "Promoting Professionalism.")

Supporting Staff Development—The Director's Role

Directors will want to create an environment that enhances the professional life of the staff and contributes to the development of relationships within the program. Such an enabling environment will flow from the program philosophy. To grow professionally, staff need to share ideas and problems with each other and receive appropriate **in-service training**.

Directors can explore different ways of creating opportunities for staff to increase their knowledge base, develop new skills, and enhance their competencies. One way is to provide release time for staff to visit other early childhood or children's programs. Formal education, professional conferences, and workshops also provide opportunities for staff to acquire new information and discuss practice-based issues with colleagues. Such activities not only rejuvenate individual staff members, their benefits often have a ripple effect when new ideas and resources are shared with other staff members.

Directors need to ensure that resources—time and money—are available for staff development. Staff opportunities for continuous growth not only bolster morale, they enhance the program's ability to foster children's healthy growth and development. Some programs provide money for staff to take relevant courses through colleges or universities and/or give staff members time off to complete their field placements and daytime courses. Increasingly, e-learning programs are providing new opportunities for professional growth and development. Examples of online opportunities include attaining credentials, collaboration, policy discussions, and access to guidelines for appropriate practice.

To keep staff well informed, there should be a resource area in the staff room stocked with videos, professional magazines, journals, and books.

Investing in a professional library is a cost-effective way of enhancing program quality. Noteworthy resources should be circulated among staff, students, and families.

Managing for Wellness   Directors provide leadership and need to manage in a manner that promotes and enriches both organizational health and individual well-being. The program can model work–life balance. As workforce diversity increases, managers need to remain aware of ways to support employee's health and wellness and work–life balance. A survey of employers revealed that eldercare resource and referral has nearly doubled since 1998 and paid leave for adoptive parents is up 30%. Two-thirds of the companies surveyed

---

IN THE STAFF RESOURCE AREA

• Reference materials on early childhood development, parenting skills, and community resources.

• Information posted about upcoming conferences and workshops on a variety of topics.

• A computer with Internet access to facilitate staff use of online resources (staff may wish to bookmark websites of interest or subscribe to regular updates such as those sent by the Child Care Resource and Research Unit).

• Catalogues and brochures from distributors of equipment and materials.

• Newsletters and information on current legislation.

• Journals and publications of professional organizations.

• Textbooks and audiovisual resources concerned with various aspects of child development, administration, child guidance, curriculum, etc.

---

offer the option of working part-time; 50% offer a compressed workweek; 45% flex-time; and 40% job-sharing (Child Care Information Exchange 2001).

Documentation and Record Keeping

Employee Records   HR management involves maintaining up-to-date **employee records** on each individual employee in accordance with provincial/territorial regulations and the program's policies and procedures. Employee records must be kept current and confidential. They should be kept in a secure place and access should be restricted to the individual employee, the director/immediate supervisor, and the HR committee chair.

Items often contained in an employee record include:

• *Personal information,* including employee's name, address, and telephone number; social insurance number; names, addresses, and telephone numbers of those persons to be contacted in the case of an emergency; physician's name and telephone number.

• *Application material,* including transcripts, references, and resumé.

• *Health records that meet licensing requirements,* including a physical assessment stating that the individual is free from communicable diseases; a negative tuberculin test or follow-up on a positive one; and an immunization record. These should be updated in accordance with your local regulations or at least every two years. Any on-the-job injuries should be documented, along with the treatment given. Records of frequent absences due to illness should also be included.

• *Employment record,* including start date, leaves, salary levels, history of salary increases, vacation accruals, benefits documents, termination.

• *Professional development history,* including transcripts from any courses completed after hiring, certificates documenting participation in professional development activities, etc.

- *Performance appraisal records*, including goals set at previous meetings and plans for the next period.

- *Record of any disciplinary action taken,* documented as per HR policies. These records should not be kept after they have fulfilled the purpose for which they were intended.

Emergency information for each employee should be easily accessible and always current. It should include information on any allergies or conditions that may be critical in an emergency. Employment records can be kept on a computer and kept confidential by restricting access through the use of password protection. Individuals have a legal right to privacy, and directors must keep abreast of the privacy laws pertaining to record keeping, security, and confidentiality. As of 2004, Canada's *Personal Information Protection and Electronic Documents Act* came into effect. The Manitoba Child Care Association (MCCA) has developed resources to aid ECEC programs in developing a privacy policy. Employment records must be stored in accordance with regulations even after employment is terminated.

Conflict Resolution and Problem Solving

Ideally, the director has created a working environment that promotes self-discipline. However, from time to time, situations arise or things occur that need to be addressed. These tend to cluster around a few issues: concerns about co-workers who make the job difficult or are perceived to negatively impact the program quality; problems with staff or volunteers who are unprofessional; or staff concern that the director does not manage people effectively.

Solving these problems can be challenging. Rarely does one quick, easy answer suffice. Often the problem is complex and multi-faceted. The more complex the problem, the more time-consuming and difficult it can be to find a solution. In most cases, the director will have to provide leadership and make tough decisions.

Requesting an individual meeting with the person involved to discuss concerns and problems is often the first step. However, the best way to handle problems is prevention. The director can minimize conflicts by creating supportive work environments that facilitate the establishment of positive working relationships among co-workers, building strong and effective teams based on an atmosphere of mutual trust, respect, and honesty. In Saifer's *Practical Solutions to Practically Every Problem: The Early Childhood Teacher's Manual* (1990), there are some very helpful suggestions to aid staff in resolving concerns.

Close contact with each employee, periodic performance appraisals, and immediate feedback can prevent or quickly resolve any conflict or solve problems. Dealing with situations early can mean easier and quicker resolution. An astute director will recognize signs of dissatisfaction and immediately set out to identify its cause.

At the heart of every **conflict resolution** procedure is the fundamental question of the rights and responsibilities of employment. A conflict resolution procedure is a written statement informing employees that they have the right to express complaints and that the employer will review and respond to their complaints. One area of concern is the interpretation of HR policies. No matter how clearly policies are written, there are always situations that do not fit the existing policies and will require a judgment call. Second, there may be an employee–supervisor conflict. A conflict resolution procedure will include an explanation of how an employee can appeal to a higher level in the organization a decision or action made by a supervisor or director. For example, if an employee is not satisfied with a director's decision, the employee may appeal to the board of directors/owner.

The first step for a staff member to address an issue or resolve a situation should be to speak directly to the person involved. Most situations can be solved this way. If that fails, the next step is to involve the director. Everyone involved has the right to see that conflict resolutions reach a logical conclusion. The conflict resolution policy should be discussed with staff and acted upon, so that individuals realize it is not just there for show. The director needs to establish themselves as a person who will listen to concerns, takes complaints seriously, address issues quickly and consistently, solves problems competently, and resolves conflicts fairly.

Effective Communication

Early childhood educators cite a work environment where their opinions are valued and where they can work co-operatively with others as a source of job satisfaction. Effective communication is a key element in a supportive work environment. Staff meetings are one of the most critical forums for ensuring effective communication. Meetings are essential for the smooth functioning of any organization, yet few people speak favourably about having to attend. Staff often view meetings as a burden and waste of time.

In early childhood programs, meetings are the primary vehicle for decision making and problem solving. Most programs have a series of meetings at various levels to gather individuals together to talk about the program and/or to share concerns or discuss mutual interests. Most programs schedule regular parent conferences—one-on-one meetings of staff and parents to discuss a child's progress and identify and resolve any problems

Most programs have regular team meetings. Team meetings should be held as often as is productive. It is essential to plan each meeting carefully and involve staff in the creation of an agenda. Determine, in advance, what is to be accomplished (solve problems, receive reports, plan strategies, give direction to staff, provide an opportunity to develop staff skills, clarify issues, or share information). Circulate the agenda to the staff ahead of time so they can make a meaningful contribution to the meeting.

There are no ideal meeting times that meet the needs of every setting. The time and frequency of meetings will vary depending on the amount of business to be carried out. It may be better to schedule weekly or biweekly meetings that are brief and productive than to make meetings longer and less frequent. Meetings should start and end on schedule. Good time management will allow more to be accomplished.

Productive meetings not only contribute to a sense of accomplishment, they can also serve to promote co-operation and feelings of **collegiality**. Follow up the meeting with brief notes on topics discussed, decisions made, and action items to be completed. These notes provide clarification, are helpful for future reference, and inform those who were absent. They are also a tool used to assess the effectiveness of staff meetings (Jorde Bloom 2002).

If staff are expected to attend meetings outside of regular work hours it should be made clear in advance that their attendance is required and it should be clarified whether there will be any reimbursement or comp time for attending meetings.

Leave Policies

A program's leave policy is intended to fulfill the employees' need for time off in a way that maintains program quality, effective program management, and consistent staffing.

Leaves may be with or without pay. Minimum leave policies are based on provincial/territorial employment legislation or collective agreements. Paid leaves include vacation time, sick days, and personal leave. Unpaid leaves include parental leave, leave without pay, bereavement leave, disability leave, and leave for jury duty.

Leaves can be confusing because they involve workplace policies, provincial and territorial labour standards, and sometimes federal employment insurance benefits programs such as maternity leave, parental leave, compassionate leave, etc. They may also include benefits from your insurance program such as a short-term or long-term disability benefit.

Leaves, program closures, or staff holidays will vary depending on the community, religion, and culture of the staff and families using the program. Each of these policies should be clearly documented in the HR Policies and Procedures Manual and all employee and parent handbooks. Documentation should include details such as eligibility requirements, what is paid/unpaid, what can be accumulated, what happens to unused days, and what is the process for applying for time off (notice period, start dates, return dates, approval process, appeal process).

Programs may choose to offer leaves above the minimum requirements, for example offering three weeks vacation instead of the two weeks required by law. However, any additional provisions must be documented in the HR Policy and Procedures Manual and applied fairly and consistently.

In designing leave policies the program should consider legislative requirements (ratios, employment legislation); program quality; staffing continuity; team effectiveness; costs for replacements (recruiting, hiring, orienting, managing replacement staff); and return-to-work plans following long periods of absence such as maternity, parental, or disability leave.

Termination of Employment

Employment can be terminated by the employee (quitting) or employer (firing) or employment agreement (contract ends, program closes). Termination of employment for any reason can be disruptive and unsettling for the children, staff, and families.

When employment is terminated the physical, emotional, and mental well-being of children must be considered. Since a relationship is established between the children, their family, and the staff, any termination of employment should be communicated to everyone involved.

If an employee leaves a program, they should have the opportunity to say goodbye to the children and the families as well as the staff team. The length of a typical notice period should be documented in the HR Policy and Procedures Manual.

If the employer decides to terminate the employment based on a performance issue, inappropriate behaviours, an unacceptable situation, or a legal matter, the employer will determine how to communicated the news to the staff, children, and families. Any communication should be immediate, clear, and concise. The program will need to ensure it is protecting employer/employee confidentiality and the employee's right to privacy. Swift communication from the director minimizes the spread of rumors, conveys decisive management, and demonstrates a commitment to quality.

A decision to terminate someone's employment is never easy. However, when a staff member is not performing at an expected level and support and training opportunities have not been successful, the decision to terminate is inevitable. Termination must be for a just cause and due process must be followed. Conditions for termination should be clearly defined in the HR Policy and Procedures Manual.

Performance Related Termination   If an employee is not performing as expected, the employee and supervisor should discuss the issue immediately. If necessary, the director or supervisor may need to take disciplinary action. Should an employee fail to meet the minimum performance standards, fail to comply with the policies and procedures of the program, or violate any program rules, the issue should be discussed with the employee and followed up in writing.

If the employee fails to correct their actions or change their behaviour or continues to break the rules, they should be given a written warning including the consequences of continued behaviour or unsatisfactory performance. For example, an employee is repeatedly late for work without explanation—the memo or letter may include the following "*As part of your employment agreement you agreed to arrive on time. However, you have been consistently late without notice, including arriving for your scheduled shift 15 minutes late on the 15th of July, 25 minutes late on the 28th of July, and 40 minutes late on the 30th of July. As we discussed during our meeting of August 1, for the safety of the children and the integrity of the program and out of respect for your team members, you are expected to arrive ready to work at the time indicated on the shift schedule posted on the staff bulletin board. As per our HR policies, if you are unable to work the scheduled shift, you must notify the director at least one week in advance. Continued failure to arrive on time will result in your termination of employment.*"

The policy should be clear. The director should implement the policy consistently. Evidence of any performance issue should be documented (time sheets, staff schedules, meetings held to discuss the issue, etc). After careful consideration, documentation, attempts to resolve the issue, and assessment of the consequences for the program, the staff, and the children, the director may need to follow through and terminate the employment.

The director should inform the board or directors/owner of the intent to terminate the employee if the policy/procedure requires notification. The director may need to inform or consult with an attorney to ensure the interests of the organization are protected.

A thoughtful director will not underestimate the impact of a termination on the rest of the staff, the children, and their families. Sciarra and Dorsey (2002) outline strategies to heal a staff after a dismissal.

Other HR Considerations: The Role of Unions

As early childhood professionals and practitioners experience the frustration of fighting individually for improved wages and working conditions, questions often arise about representation of the field by unions, federations, or professional associations. The key question emerging is that of who should represent the interests of early childhood educators, professionals, and practitioners?

While wages, benefits, and hours are the items most frequently associated with collective agreements, such agreements also cover many other significant issues such as personnel policies, grievance and hiring procedures, performance appraisals and promotion systems, provision for professional development, breaks, and input into program decision making.

Hadley (2001) found that Canadian women in unionized workplaces have more opportunities to rise through the ranks because of the benefits of job security, wage protection, and child care for their own child on-site or financial support for child care in a community setting. As well, there are positive impacts on income levels, benefits offered, and pension plans. In fact, the study found women were sticking with traditionally female jobs because of the pay levels achieved by unions.

Non-salary benefits frequently contribute as much to job satisfaction as salary benefits do. They can be critical in helping staff provide better services. For example, input into a program's decision making process can be an attractive guarantee in a contract. Members of Services Employees International Union (SEIU) Local 299 in Moose Jaw, Saskatchewan, negotiated a provision guaranteeing that their employer would meet with them once a month to hear concerns on matters affecting the quality of the program. Examples of other innovative contract provisions include a staff room "for the use and enjoyment of employees" and reimbursement for the cost of dry cleaning or shampoo occasioned by an outbreak of lice at the program.

Staff recognize the union or professional association as a long-term political ally that can assist early childhood practitioners in advocating for better funding and expanded services. The strength and unity of representation can be used to influence government funding for quality early childhood development programs.

Unions have been quick to identify large commercial child care organizations that operate with large profit margins and are then able to negotiate increases in staff wages without raising parent fees.

Only a small percentage of the early childhood workforce is unionized. According to *You Bet I Care!*, unionization is most prevalent in Quebec (19.2%), Ontario (18%), and Saskatchewan (15.5%). No staff reported being in a union in Newfoundland, Prince Edward Island, or the Territories. The caregiving staff in unionized programs earned an average of over three dollars per hour more than did their colleagues in non-unionized programs (Doherty et al. 2000a).

The diverse and isolated nature of the early childhood delivery system, coupled with an unusually high turnover rate, has worked against the development of successful organizing campaigns. *Taking Matters into Our Own Hands*, by the Child Care Employee Project (1990), provides some insightful information on the role of unions. (The role of unions and professional organizations is discussed further in the next chapter.)

Summary

To most people, a job is more than a means to earn money. Their work is an important part of their lives. It gives them a sense of accomplishment; helps them feel valued, trusted, and respected; and makes them feel safe and secure. Early childhood education is physically and emotionally demanding. The director is responsible for making sure policies, practices, work environment, and organizational values are responsive to staff needs and contribute to their job satisfaction.

Children need environments where they feel secure and free from anxiety. Minimal staff turnover and stable staff–child groupings build security for the children and allow for consistent application of the program philosophy. High staff turnover adversely affects both the children and staff morale, which in turn decreases program quality.

Numerous surveys, such as *Who Cares?* (Whitebrook, Howes, and Phillips 1990), *You Bet I Care!* (Doherty et al. 2000a), and *Working for Change: Canada's Child Care Workforce* (Beach et al. 2004) show that caregivers stay in the field longest when they have appropriate training, wages commensurate with their training, and good working conditions.

Employees in early childhood environments have the same legal rights as other workers. Both federal and provincial laws protect workers with respect to minimum wage, overtime pay, and a variety of working conditions. Directors, owners, and boards of directors must be aware of these laws and ensure their HR policies and procedures reflect current legislation.

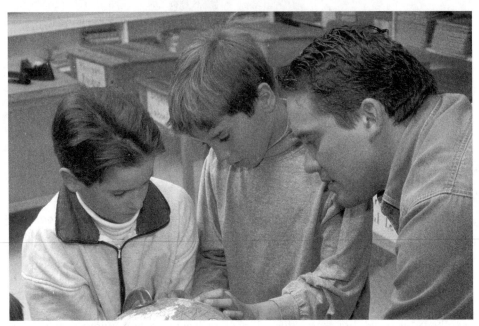

Directors need knowledgeable, skillful, and caring staff to provide responsive care to children.

Over the past decade, considerable energy has been devoted to the improvement of wages and working conditions in early childhood settings. Many caregivers are underpaid and feel they are undervalued by society. However, while recognizing this general inequity, caregivers can feel that their own program's policies are equitable and just. It is essential for directors to have systems in place to ensure that pay, job security, opportunities for professional development, and opportunities for career advancement are fairly administered and clearly communicated to all staff.

Recognizing the significant expansion taking place in the field of ECEC, attention to strengthening the labour force is important. The factors that impact the effectiveness of early childhood development programs are multi-faceted and complex. Numerous studies support the contention that caregivers have a significant impact on a program's quality. Directors need knowledgeable, skillful, and caring staff to provide responsive care to young children and families. It is critical to develop and follow thoughtful, systematic procedures when seeking new staff members. A well-planned and carefully executed orientation program provides a sound base for new staff. Key factors to consider are education, personal characteristics, skills, knowledge, and a cultural match with the population served.

Once the staff is hired, the director must manage the program and implement HR policies fairly and consistently. Directors have key roles and responsibilities in facilitating each staff member's growth as a professional. This requires fair and effective opportunities for professional development, supervision, and performance appraisal. It is essential to establish a relationship with each employee based on trust and mutual respect. Some HR practices and records are required by various regulatory agencies. HR policies serve to make working conditions better for staff, which aids job satisfaction and, in turn, program quality.

Key Terms and Concepts

Benefits, p. 131

Collective agreement, p. 131

Collegiality, p. 146

Conflict resolution, p. 145

Contract, p. 137

Criminal reference check, p. 137

Employee records, p. 144

HR policies, p. 130

In-service training, p. 143

Mentor, p. 137

Performance appraisal, p. 137

Probationary period, p. 132

Professional development, p. 130

Staff development, p. 143

Work environment, p. 128

Activities

1. Collect job applications from three different employers. Note the different kinds of information requested.

2. Arrange meetings with several directors to discuss salaries, benefits, and their orientation procedures.

3. On a scale of 1 to 5 (1 = weak, 5 = strong), rate yourself on the following traits:
    - team player
    - participator
    - flexibility
    - problem solving skills
    - creativity
    - energy
    - communication skills
    - resourcefulness

4. Contact the director of your field placement and request permission to attend a staff meeting. Assess how the staff are involved in decision making. What went well at the meeting? What could have been handled differently? To gain a deeper understanding, arrange to share your observations with the director.

Recommended Reading

J. Beach, J. Bertrand, B. Forer, D. Michal, and J. Tougas. *Working for Change: Canada's Child Care Workforce*, Labour Market Update Study. Ottawa: Child Care Human Resources Council, 2004.

Caruso, J. and M. Fawcett. *Supervision in Early Childhood Education: A Developmental Perspective.* 2d ed. New York: Teachers College Press, Columbia University, 1999.

Canadian Child Care Federation. *Partners in Quality: Tools for Practitioners in Child Care Settings*. Ottawa: Canadian Child Care Federation, 2000.

Doherty G., D. Lero, H. Goelman, A. LaGrange, and J. Tougas. *You Bet I Care! A Canada-Wide Study on Wages, Working Conditions, and Practices in Child Care Centres*. Guelph, ON: Centre for Families, Work and Well-Being, University of Guelph, 2000.

Jorde Bloom, P., M. Sheerer, and J. Britz. *Blueprint for Action: Achieving Center-Based Change through Staff Development*. Lake Forest, IL: New Horizons, 1991.

Jorde Bloom, *Making the Most of Meetings: A Practical Guide*. Lake Forest, IL: New Horizons, 2002.

Sciarra, D.J. and A.G. Dorsey. *Leaders and Supervisors in Child Care Programs*. Albany, NY: Delmar, 2002.

Weblinks

www.ccw.org
Centre for the Child Care Workforce
This non-profit research, education, and advocacy organization is committed to improving child care by upgrading compensation and working conditions and reducing turnover of child care centre staff and family child care providers. The site lists research papers, publications, and information about training events.

www.hrsdc.gc.ca
Human Resources and Skills Development Canada
This government website provides information for individuals and employers. For HR management follow the links to Business. You will find information and resources on hiring, labour standards, occupational heath and safety, and work–life balance. It also provides details about maternity, parental, adoption, and compassionate care leave benefits. You can also access all provincial labour legislation by following the appropriate path.

www.monster.ca and www.workopolis.com
Online Employment Sites
These are two of Canada's largest online recruitment sites, listing jobs in all sectors including early childhood education.

www.charityvillage.com
Charity Village, Online Employment in the Non-Profit Sector
This employment website is dedicated to the non-profit sector, providing news, information, and resources for executives and staff. Charity Village lists thousands of jobs in the Career Centre and many HR management resources in the Resource Centre.

www.ccsc-cssge.ca
Child Care Human Resources Sector Council
The Sector Council is mandated to develop a skilled child care workforce and commissioned the study *Working for Change: Canada's Child Care Workforce*. Priorities include increasing the respect for and recognition of the child care sector, improving work conditions, and stimulating research. Available resources include topics related to unionization, recruitment and retention, and training and development.

Promoting Professionalism

chapter 7

Objectives

- **Develop an understanding of professionalism.**
- **Introduce professional terminology.**
- **Introduce occupational standards.**
- **Describe ethical and professional standards of performance.**
- **Understand a code of ethics as a part of professionalism and consider its implications.**
- **Outline the role of reflective thinking as a method to improve practice.**
- **Identify the role of unions and professional groups.**

Defining a Competent Early Childhood Professional

Providing high quality early childhood education and care for a group of young children requires patience, energy, commitment, and knowledge of children's developmental levels and needs. A range of skills and competencies is also necessary. When asked what qualities, personality traits, values, beliefs, knowledge, and skills are most valuable in working with children, most would identify warmth, sensitivity, energy, knowledge of children, and patience, to name a few. Others would add knowledge, values, beliefs, ethics, a commitment to children, an ability to work with families as partners in their child's development, and practice based on well-founded pedagogy. An early childhood professional is one who has learned the skills and strategies of reflective practice and continually strives to be knowledgeable about theoretical foundations of early education and care.

The Need for Specialized Education

Numerous research studies and policy documents report consistent and significant associations between higher staff education levels and quality programs and better outcomes for children. Adults who have post-secondary education tend to be more responsive to children and provide them with stimulating activities that are appropriate to their developmental level. Early childhood practitioners and family child care providers who have ECE or related credentials are more likely to be responsive and emotionally available and provide a stimulating environment that promotes language and cognitive development and skill acquisition. They more likely use the kinds of questioning, listening, and reflecting strategies that facilitate children's expressive and receptive language development. Knowledgeable professionals understand children's emotional, social, and cognitive development and are able to recognize and use "teachable moments" (Doherty 2000a)

In a high quality early childhood environment, qualified staff will use specialized skills to meet the needs of the group as a whole while remaining focused on the needs of each individual child and family. The kind of specialized knowledge gained through caregiver preparation includes a foundation in theory and research. This foundation supports the development of appropriate individualized, concrete, and experiential programs for young children. The value of such programs is seen in the children's developmental outcomes, such as increased social interaction with adults, development of pro-social behaviours, and improved language and cognitive development.

CHARACTERISTICS OF A GOOD CAREGIVER

Characteristic	Behaviours, attitudes, abilities, skills
Articulate	Communicates so children and families understand
Available	Interacts responsively with children and families
Caring	Demonstrates compassion and empathy
Committed	Devoted to caring for children
Creative	Uses a variety of teaching strategies
Fair	Responds to each child equitably
Flexible	Demonstrates ability to adapt to situations
Fun	Has a sense of humour
Individualizes	Adapts program to individual child's needs and interests
Knowledgeable	Knows current teaching strategies and materials and matches them to children's interests, needs, and developmental levels
Motivating	Promotes active involvement; makes learning fun
Open	Sees things from other's perspectives
Organized	Arranges environment, materials, time and curriculum plans
Patient and pleasant	Even tempered, uses effective voice tone and gestures
Professional	Conscientious about carrying out responsibilities; uses strategies to keep personal pressures from interfering
Reflective	Reflects upon performance and accepts constructive feedback

Source: Adapted from Kay Albrecht, *The Right Fit: Recruiting, Selecting and Orienting Staff* (Lake Forest, IL: New Horizons, 2002).

A competent practitioner should have a thorough background in developmental psychology, the equivalent of a college graduate's general knowledge, and access to current research. While formal training alone does not guarantee high quality programs, the standard of care improves when the staff has this education in early childhood development.

As noted previously, there is a strong correlation between overall levels of education and ECEC-specific education. Beach et al., in *Working for Change: Canada's Child Care Workforce* (2004) found 60% of early childhood practitioners and assistants had a post-secondary credential compared with 53% in all occupations.

Staff should have specialized education for the age group they work with. The span of the ages of children served in early childhood development programs will affect the length, content, and structure of professional education programs. Some experts in the field hold the view that early childhood education extends to age eight or even 12, whereas others concentrate on the period from birth to age six.

Competent caregivers need a theoretical grounding in order to develop a conceptual framework in which to observe and respond appropriately to children. As well, it is important for the early childhood practitioner to receive broad-based professional education in such areas as human growth and development, program planning, working with adults, interacting with families, interpersonal communication, and behaviour guidance (Spodek, Saracho, and Peters 1998). A field placement experience is a critical factor that enables the application of theory to practice. In this experience, a student has the opportunity to practice and develop skills with the guidance of a co-operating staff. Field placements provide the opportunity to learn to interact effectively with young children and families, as well as to work as part of a team.

More specialized knowledge and skills may be added around the core curriculum, as required. For example, many educators are increasingly aware of the need to address the areas of employee rights on the job and working with children who require extra supports.

Another key area is appreciation of diversity of families. Many college and university programs are infused with the philosophy of diversity, enabling students to graduate with an understanding of the breadth of human culture, an appreciation of issues such as bilingualism and second-language development, and an ability to respond proactively to bias and prejudice. Some provinces, such as Ontario and British Columbia, have firmly addressed this area of need. In *Early Childhood Education Program Standards,* the College Standards and Accreditation Council mandated that all early childhood graduates must demonstrate the ability "to act in a manner consistent with principles of fairness, equity, and diversity to support the development and learning of individual children within the context of family, culture, and society" (Ontario 1996). In order to keep pace with changes in the families served, caregivers must be prepared to participate in professional development throughout their careers.

One proposal for professional education suggests a three-year diploma, with all students participating in a common, core program for the first two years. In a separately streamed third year, students could choose an area of specialization such as working with children with special needs or administration of early childhood settings, or could specialize in a specific age group such as toddlers or school-age children. A different model offers the year of specialization as a post-diploma program following graduation. Many provinces have developed articulation agreements between two-year college and four-year university programs in order to provide a continuum of professional preparation opportunities and facilitate professional growth. Mechanisms that transform diverse training and learning experiences into academic credit are critical to retaining an experienced workforce.

Range of Roles/Career Paths

Many roles exist within the field of early childhood development, in a variety of settings. Positions vary in the specific knowledge, competencies, and levels of education that are required. Among the possible roles are family child care provider, director, family resource program staff, resource practitioner, and early childhood practitioner. As the field of early childhood development expands and diversifies, the specific educational needs for each position are being re-examined. Beach et al. (2004) note that several American studies are recommending increased qualifications and that some of the staff in centre-based programs should have university degrees focused on early childhood studies.

The diversity of roles within the field of early childhood development reflects its roots in both social welfare and education. Despite that fact that child care and early education services are generally funded and regulated by different sources, the essential nature of the service varies little when carried out in the appropriate manner for the individual child. Although historically, settings have focused on either a child's need for a program that promotes her or his development or the parents' need for child care while working or going to school, there is increasing recognition that this is a false dichotomy. Quality early childhood programs meet both the children's and families' needs.

A **career ladder** for professional growth can serve as an organizational framework to support staff development. A career ladder is a way to describe a continuum of professional development. Each rung represents predetermined criteria for advancement to a new step, objective, or opportunity for practitioners to take on new roles.

By clearly setting the standards and rewards for advancement, a career ladder helps individuals make decisions based on personal needs and goals. In essence, the individual is helped to take control of her or his own professional development. This model can serve as a supportive framework to energize employees to achieve higher levels of performance and fulfillment. The **career lattice** concept (Willer 1994) recognizes that professional growth is multi-dimensional—more like a climbing frame than a single ladder of qualification. An early childhood career lattice incorporates multiple, interlocking career ladders providing for the multiple roles and settings within the profession. Each step of greater preparation is tied to increased responsibility and compensation. There are several entry points and it is possible to move to new positions laterally as well as vertically. For example, when an individual begins working in an early childhood program while taking her or his diploma, she or he would move vertically up the lattice when the diploma is successfully completed. Sometime later, this same individual may change rooms to work with another age group. This move would constitute a horizontal—or lateral—movement. The lattice framework recognizes that continued professional growth can lead to movement around the lattice, into diverse roles and positions.

The need for career ladders and lattices in early childhood development to retain experienced caregivers has been frequently identified. Lateral moves recognize and reward experience and knowledge by providing new and meaningful challenges for people who have been in the field for a number of years. Whitebrook and Bellm (1996) found that involvement as a mentor reduced by almost a third the incidence of leaving the field among experienced early childhood practitioners. Orientation programs that include high quality mentoring, common planning time, ongoing professional development, an external network, and a performance appraisal process are critical to improving staff retention. Many of these strategies were reviewed in chapter 6. This information suggests that more attention needs to be given to strategies that support professional advancement within the field.

The next sections focus on some distinct roles and related skills and knowledge within the field of early childhood development.

Licensed family child care   In this type of setting children may be cared for in a private home by a non-relative. Provinces/territories allow care for up to 12 children. Differences in the roles of the ECEC practitioner and the family child care provider relate more to the focus on particular skills than on fundamental differences in knowledge, skills, and abilities (Read 2000). Since care is often provided in their own home, family child care providers must simultaneously meet the needs of children and families and determine the boundaries necessary to ensure that they meet their own as well as their family's needs. Family child care providers often work with a multi-age grouping; consequently, caregivers must provide environments and experiences that are safe, healthy, and developmentally appropriate for several different age groups. Family child care providers need to work with families to establish schedules and routines that are developmentally appropriate, culturally sensitive, and meet individual needs. Family child care providers must demonstrate the effective organizational and administrative skills needed for running a small business. (For a detailed description of the responsibilities of the family child care provider, see chapter 5.)

Infant/toddler care   The educational needs of those working with children of up to three years of age are specific. Because infant/toddler caregivers must learn about and be sensitive to the differences between the developmental needs of infants, toddlers, and preschool youngsters in terms of nurturing, activities, and the design of the physical environment, they require specialized education. Course content on how to meet the individual physical and emotional needs of each child and the importance of forming secure, trusting relationships is critical. And since infants and toddlers are not able to express their needs verbally, communication between staff and parents about a child's day and how the child is developing is crucial.

There are fundamental philosophical principles that need to be embodied in any comprehensive professional development program related to infants and toddlers. Practitioners' underlying philosophical beliefs about what children need for healthy emotional and physical growth and development will affect all practical aspects of early childhood education and care settings, including group size, the quality of the environment, the disposition of primary caregiving assignments, the continuity of care, how caregivers relate to the child's family and cultural contexts, and choices about how individual needs are met within a group context.

Before- and after-school programs   These programs are offered in schools by a variety of agencies, as well as in family child care homes, before- and after-school programs, and full-day holiday and summer care. School-age child care is designed for children between 5 and 12 years old. The intent of these programs is to strike a balance between the functions of providing educational, social, and emotional support and encouraging the children's pursuit of their individual interests and talents.

Musson (1999) reports that working effectively with school-age children requires a special set of skills and qualities, although he acknowledges that there is a fair amount of overlap between that and the skills required by those working with younger children. In addition, preparation should include a focus on the development of children aged 5 to 13, program planning that gives increased responsibility and independence to this age group, and more developmentally appropriate behaviour management strategies that keep pace with the child's moral development.

Some staff of school-age programs may align more closely with a variety of fields that include child and youth work, parks and recreation, social work, and/or elementary education.

Multi-age groups

Multi- or **mixed-age groups** are another model of child care that includes children who are at least a year apart in age. Special skills and knowledge are needed to work with multi-age groups. Multi-age groups predominate in family child care homes and parent-child resource centres, although staff in centre-based care may be required to work with more than one age group for part of each day. Children from families with more than one child are accustomed to dealing with children of different ages. However, given the small families of many Canadians today, a lot of children have not had the experience of living with a sibling. For these children, daily interactions with children of different ages can be beneficial. Care for multi-age groups is even more common in rural settings.

Essa, Young, and Lehne (2003) note that both younger and older children benefit in multi-age groupings. Positive social behaviours such as sharing, taking turns, and helpfulness are encouraged. Older children have more opportunity to practice leadership skills, and young children become involved in more complex forms of pretend play. There appear to be cognitive benefits for the children from this type of grouping as well as practitioner satisfaction. The Multi-Age Operating Criteria (Children's Services Division 1998) may be used to assess the program's structure, activities and experiences, physical environment, materials and routines.

Children with special needs

Increasingly, early childhood practitioners work with children who have a wide range of physical and emotional needs, whether the practitioner works with the children exclusively or encounters them as mainstreamed, often unidentified. All children ought to be welcomed in early childhood settings regardless of their ability, cultural background, family income, or whether their parents work. Inclusion or integration with "typical" peers provides children with special needs with irreplaceable opportunities to develop and enhance social and adaptive behaviours. As well, young children benefit from getting to know children who have special needs.

The range of issues addressed by the special needs category has also broadened, to include children who are born addicted to drugs, with fetal alcohol syndrome/effect, who have been abused or neglected, or who are considered "medically fragile." Deiner, Dyck, and Hardacre (1999) recommend that practitioner skills should encompass programming for children both with and without disabilities in one classroom, communicating with parents including parent/practitioner conferences, working with other professionals, writing and implementing Individualized Education Plans (IEPs), evaluation to determine the effectiveness of programs, and knowledge of applicable legislation. Only in British Columbia and Ontario do regulations stipulate some specialized education for staff working with children with special needs.

Some communities have a **resource teacher** to assist early childhood practitioners with the inclusion in settings of children with special needs. The resource teacher's role is to support all individuals who share in the success of the inclusion—the early childhood practitioners, parents, cook, custodian, other children, and volunteers. This career choice may serve as an alternate path on the lattice.

Another role in working with children with health issues is that of a child life specialist. This group uses play to aid children in being more comfortable during a hospital stay. They work with all the members of the child's health care team such as nurses, doctors, and social workers. They are experts in child development and have a solid understanding of how to support children during medical procedures and treatments. They provide support for families who are key members of the healing process.

Cultural, linguistic, and racial diversity   Adults provide learning environments that are rich in anti-bias materials and curriculum that promotes self-esteem and important social skills in young children. Practitioners must be prepared to work with a broad spectrum of children, families, and other practitioners. The ECEC curriculum needs to expand beyond mainstream cultural values and practices to recognize and integrate other values, knowledge, and practices.

CULTURAL, LINGUISTIC, AND RACIAL DIVERSITY

To meet the needs of children and families, all practitioners should understand and appreciate:

- The diversity of human culture.
- The history of oppression and inequities based on race, ethnicity, class, and gender.
- How to respond proactively to bias, prejudice, discrimination, and racist behaviour by children or adults.
- The importance of social advocacy.
- Patterns of child rearing in other cultures.
- Cross-cultural communication styles.
- Issues relating to bilingualism and second-language development; how to promote family language maintenance; and the value of caregivers learning/having a second language.
- The importance of family-centred, culturally responsive caregiving.

Whether early childhood programs are provided on- or off-reserve, cultural integrity is a major consideration for First Nations families. Early childhood education development programs that include First Nations children must have programming consistent with Aboriginal cultural values. First Nations families will feel more inclined to enroll their children in programs that clearly value family involvement.

Kindergarten to grade three   Early childhood services encompass services for children attending kindergarten through grade three. Developmentally appropriate practice for this age group involves an integrated approach acknowledging all aspects of human development—social, emotional, physical, cognitive, language, and creative. Educational content for professionals working with this age group should include child development between birth and age seven, individuality within a group setting, the impact of a variety of social and family contexts, child abuse, children with exceptionalities, family and school relations, and program design and development.

The growing integration of early childhood development programs within elementary schools has created a need for professional education to assist teachers and caregivers to communicate and collaborate. The Ottawa Board of Education employed ECEs with a two-year diploma in junior kindergartens. It was thought that the children taught by ECEs might be less prepared than children taught by certified teachers. In fact, there was no evidence to suggest much variation. In fact many early childhood graduates are continuing their education and being employed in the education system. This trend will continue, given the policy directions of provincial governments such as Ontario.

Administration/management   Some early childhood graduates become directors of early childhood development programs. The education and training of directors influences the quality of the program. As noted in chapter 3, directors need additional education to prepare them to handle budgets, work with a board of directors, and provide good human resource practices to aid in managing and retaining staff. Doherty (2000a) and Ferguson (1997) indicate that the qualifications for directors should include completion of post-secondary education in ECE and professional development in leadership responsibility, HR, supervisory skills, knowledge of regulations, financial and budgetary management, and operations planning.

Family resource settings   One career path for experienced ECEs is work with children and families through family resource centres. Among the goals of these services is prevention through providing family support and information about child development and community resources. Family resource centres often include a drop-in program where families and caregivers have the opportunity to meet with other adults, thereby decreasing feelings of isolation, and where children can interact with other children in a stimulating play environment. Services vary greatly depending on the client group, community, and available resources. They may include playgroups, toy lending libraries, child care registries, discussion groups, food banks, services for families with special needs, respite and emergency care, workshops, and information.

Among the additional competencies required are programming for mixed ages (infants to children of school age); working with adults; working with families with a wide range of needs, from typical parenting concerns to "at risk" communities; supporting groups with distinct perspectives—both parents and caregivers; administration and program management, including fundraising and staff and volunteer education and supervision; outreach skills; knowledge of community resources; and collaboration with other professionals. There are no provincial/territorial regulations stipulating family-resource centre staff qualifications.

Various roles within the field require that practitioners have specific skills and knowledge in addition to ECEC. All practitioners should be engaged in ongoing **professional development** to be aware of emerging research findings. Professional groups and post-secondary institutions need to offer an array of professional development opportunities in order for practitioners to meet the diverse needs of children and families in a variety of settings. As well, the profession must develop a framework for professional development that conceptualizes the coming together of regulation, education, and financing. The Child Care Human Resources Sector Council is doing significant work addressing many of these issues. (See the Weblinks section at the end of the chapter for information on their website.)

Personal Attributes

The competent early childhood practitioner must have the appropriate personal characteristics for working with young children—a high energy level, patience, warmth, a nurturing disposition, openness to new ideas, a tolerance for ambiguity, flexible thinking, and maturity.

Cartwright (1998) notes the difficulty in assessing the important quality of emotional maturity. Caregivers need to be people so secure within themselves that they can function with principles rather than prescriptions, exert authority without requiring submission, and admit mistakes without feeling humiliated. Also needed is an ability to put one's own needs on hold while meeting the needs of others. This must be balanced with taking care of one's own physical, emotional, and spiritual wellness, as detailed by Pimento and Kernsted (2004).

Bernhard et al. (1995) note that staff must demonstrate the ability to have respectful interactions with families whose backgrounds differ from their own. One discerns these qualities neither by resumé nor interview, but by observing practitioners work with children and families. Clear, consistent evidence of a caregiver's personal integration and inner sense of security is vital for her or his success with children and families.

We know intuitively that these are important qualities. But although attempts have been made to clearly and systematically determine what qualities make a competent practitioner, it is difficult to demonstrate concretely the impact of these qualities on the quality of children's experience. Individual staff members can be evaluated through observing their interactions with children, families, and staff and monitoring their implementation of curriculum.

However, desirable personal attributes alone are not enough to guide professional practice. Even the most dedicated caregivers sometimes encounter challenging situations. Practices such as mentoring or obtaining peer support provide opportunities for professional growth.

Early Childhood Education as a Profession

Early childhood practitioners understand that what they do is important. Many believe the level of professionalism in the field of early childhood development influences the quality of early childhood environments. The term "professional" tends to imply dedicated, knowledgeable, specialized, educated, well-paid, and ethical individuals. Early childhood practitioners seek recognition of their professional role. Increased recognition of educational qualifications, better salaries, and improved working conditions usually accompany professional status, and these are clearly warranted and appropriate goals for which to strive. They are also crucial conditions to ensure that the profession attracts and keeps good and experienced caregivers.

Professionalism is defined as the dynamic process whereby an occupation can be observed to change certain characteristics in the direction of a profession. It is a complex and intriguing issue to explore. As a concept, professionalism has been studied from a variety of perspectives and has long been thought to be the answer to many of the dilemmas within the field of early childhood education and care. Yet the field of early childhood development faces many barriers to being recognized as a profession—from both families and practitioners themselves. As well, it suffers from a lack of conceptual clarity and standardized terminology. Another dilemma is whether to be exclusive (keep out untrained persons) or inclusive (ensure individuals from diverse backgrounds access to the field).

What Could Be Negative about Professionalizing?

Some are concerned that increased professionalism will cause a rift between caregivers and families. As well, there is a legitimate concern about potential increased costs. To raise the level of professionalism will necessitate increasing compensation levels, which will mean increasing the costs of services. In Canada, in most provinces, this would entail increasing parent fees and/or government support. Some parents often don't equate education of early childhood staff with positive child–staff interactions. Some may associate education and professionalizing with institutional, uncaring settings for their child. Another argument against professionalism is that setting strict standards for entry and advancement will inevitably exclude some individuals.

Some of the aforementioned barriers are interrelated. Traditional routes to professionalism have tended to establish exclusionary, hierarchical systems of credentials; result in increased costs; and create greater distances between professionals and those they serve without necessarily improving the quality of the service. These results would not be compatible with the field's ultimate goal of improving the quality of care and education provided for all young children by ensuring a highly qualified workforce.

To avoid these pitfalls, the **early childhood profession** must face these challenges. Early childhood development is a professional field, and while open access is encouraged, everyone who enters the field must make a commitment to upgrade credentials and participate in ongoing professional development. Leaders in the field must ensure that meeting the increased costs of professionalizing does not result in higher quality programs being available to only a select few children. As well, the field must be willing to exclude those individuals who behave unethically or incompetently in their work.

Elements of Professionalizing

Professionalism refers to a combination of competence in a particular field of knowledge and identification with a group of colleagues that can collectively define and support quality practices. The Canadian Child Care Federation has facilitative work towards creating a supportive infrastructure for the field. Whitebook et al. (2001) identify the following benchmarks in professionalization:

- defining a distinct and exclusive body of knowledge
- establishing training and certification processes
- increasing political influence
- increasing the economic well-being of its members

The Canadian Child Care Federation has stimulated consensus building on defining a specialized body of knowledge; it also researched training and certification processes. A **code of ethics**, **ethics** training, occupational standards, and standards of practice have been developed and are becoming accepted within the occupation. CCCF is working for increasing economic well-being through relationships with governments and key organizations such as the Child Care Human Resources Sector Council. A number of organizations such as the Child Care Advocacy Association of Canada have increased political influence.

Elements to include in considering the professional nature of early childhood development are discussed in the next section:

Specialized knowledge: What is the body of knowledge and theory, relevant and specific to this field, that every practitioner is expected to master?

Standards of practice: What are standard procedures and practices?

Entry to practice and continuing competence: How much formal, specialized education is required? How much continued professional development?

A code of ethics and accountability: Is there a specific code of ethics that is accepted by the practitioners? Is unethical behaviour dealt with by a professional body?

Specialized Knowledge

A profession bases its work on a specialized body of knowledge and expertise that is applied to situations in the workplace. It is necessary to lay to rest the all-too-common assumption that working with children is something that anyone can do, something that requires no specialized skills or knowledge. This assumption is the root cause of the unsatisfactory compensation that characterizes the early education and care field in Canada.

One of the primary attributes of professionalism is having mastery over a formal body of knowledge not accessible to the public. This knowledge gives the professional the competence to carry out a certain type of work.

Specialized knowledge in early childhood development is derived from developmental psychology and other fields. A great deal of knowledge exists about how to care for and educate young children from birth through age 12, and those who have and apply this knowledge can provide better care and education for young children than those who do not have it. Developmentally appropriate practice bases decisions about best practices for young children on child development research and current knowledge of learning. This offers a body of specialized knowledge to caregivers.

There are a number of related professions that share some common or overlapping knowledge bases. Some examples of these would include elementary teachers, pediatric nurses, child and youth workers, and pediatricians.

Professional judgment involves assessing events, weighing alternatives, and estimating the potential long-term consequences of decisions and actions based on that knowledge. Consequently, the choice of courses of action is based on specific expertise acquired through professional preparation and ongoing professional development. Practitioners must continually challenge and evaluate professional judgments and practices to ensure that they are based on the best available information. As the body of knowledge changes so do the concepts of best practice. Professional development activities such as discussions with co-workers and/or mentors and reading professional journals enable individuals to gain new knowledge and keep skills and abilities current.

The Canadian Child Care Federation consulted widely with the field to determine what novice practitioners really need to know upon graduating and used this in the development of occupational standards. Recognizing the differences in provincial and territorial regulations, there is still considerable variation across the country in the length of professional preparation programs.

Standards of Practice

Professional standards, based on the best available knowledge and practice, are the profession's own benchmarks of quality beyond the requirements of legislation, and they contribute to the quality of early childhood settings. Professional organizations adopt standards of practice to ensure that members apply uniform procedures and principles in response to typical situations using their best professional judgment.

Occupational Standards for child care practitioners outline the skills, ability, and the core knowledge required for competent practice. The standards developed by the Canadian Child Care Federation in partnership with provincial/territorial affiliate groups apply to practitioners working in family child care homes, child care centres, and family resource programs. They are based on a review of the literature and broad consultation in the field—on what practitioners do and the skills and abilities required to facilitate a child's well-being and development while at the same time supporting families. These standards are part of the National Framework for Quality Assurance that is intended to move the field to higher professional practices (Doherty 2000b). Examples of occupational standards are included throughout the text. Similar standards for directors are being developed by the Child Care Human Resources Sector Council. These standards are developed by analyzing what a job entails and determining what a person must be able to do to be competent at that job. Occupational standards also protect the public interest by ensuring that all practicing professionals are working safely and ethically within a minimum set of guidelines. Standards of practice represent a starting point for increased credit transferability between post-secondary institutions, distance education, and prior learning assessment and recognition. Practicing professionals are committed to performing consistently at high standards, without allowing personal matters or moods to affect their work or relations with children, colleagues, or employers. Regardless of the environment, young children deserve to be cared for and educated by adults who possess the appropriate knowledge and skills. The process of professionalizing creates greater consensus among practitioners on the meaning of critical terms and concepts. Greater consensus supports work toward shared goals.

Standard

Caring for Children

Protect and promote the psychological and physical safety, health, and well-being of each child being cared for.

The practitioner is able to maintain a sanitary environment that minimizes the risk of infection or food contamination through:

- developing and implementing effective procedures to maintain the required level of cleanliness and sanitation;
- encouraging an awareness among children of good health and hygiene practices through modelling and a variety of learning experiences; and
- being able to recognize symptoms of common childhood diseases and take appropriate action.

The practitioner is able to maintain a hazard-free environment that minimizes the risk of accidents or injury through:

- developing and implementing effective methods of ensuing that, at all times, the building, the outdoor play area, the furniture, the toys, and the equipment are in good repair and safe for use by the children;
- ensuring the safe storage of medications and all potentially dangerous materials;
- providing supervision that is appropriate for the children's developmental levels;
- developing and implementing effective procedures for emergency situations; and
- assisting the children to develop safety awareness through instruction, modelling, and reinforcing safety concepts.

(continued)

The practitioner is able to promote children's health through:

- ensuring that snacks and meals are nutritious and balanced, taking into account cultural preferences within the parameters of *Canada's Guide to Healthy Eating,* or, in situations where families are responsible for snacks, encouraging and assisting parents to follow *Canada's Guide to Healthy Eating;*

- monitoring children's physical status on a daily basis and reporting concerns about possible abuse or neglect as required by and outlined in current provincial or territorial legislation;

- developing and implementing procedures to identify and monitor children who have allergies or chronic medical conditions that require special precautions or care and ensuring that such precautions are taken and/or the requisite care is provided; and

- developing and implementing a specific procedure for administering medications.

The practitioner is able to protect and promote children's psychological health and well-being by:

- providing an environment that conveys a sense of order, routine, consistency, and continuity;

- setting realistic expectations and clear limits and using positive and developmentally appropriate approaches to guiding children's behaviour;

- providing experiences that are appropriate for the child's developmental level and responding to each child's efforts to grow and acquire skills in a positive manner;

- noting, accepting, and respecting children's expression of their feelings, whether positive or negative, and the underlying message that is conveyed through body movement or facial expression;

- supporting children in openly expressing their positive and negative feelings through a range of verbal, non-verbal, and culturally-based communication strategies; and

- providing activities that respect each child's individual ethnic and cultural heritage and encouraging each child to feel proud of his or her heritage.

Source: Gillian Doherty, in Canadian Child Care Federation (CCCF), *Partners in Quality: Tools for Practitioners in Child Care Settings* (Ottawa: CCCF, 2000).

Entry to Practice and Continuing Competence

A major characteristic of a profession is that all practicing professionals have a minimum level of knowledge, experience, and qualifications prior to entering the profession. Provincial and territorial governments outline requirements for entry to the field. No province or territory requires all practitioners in early childhood development programs to have related post-secondary credentials. Since in most parts of the country it is not mandatory to undergo an accrediting process by a professional organization, many practitioners choose to forgo this option. These attitudes limit professionalization of the field. While some provincial early childhood organizations have a certification process in place, this process may be viewed as duplicating the role of the licensing authority, may appear to be optional, or has varying levels of commitment from the field. In Newfoundland and Labrador it is mandatory to become certified in order to work in a licensed child care setting. Certification is carried out by the Association of Early Childhood Educators, Newfoundland and Labrador (AECENL), which is funded through the provincial government.

Prolonged formal education ensures that early childhood practitioners learn the knowledge and techniques necessary for informed and effective performance before they begin work and that they continue to learn throughout their career. A variety of instructional formats—internships, field work, in-service workshops, professional literature, and conferences—can be used for training.

Working for Change: Canada's Child Care Workforce (Beach et al. 2004) examines human resources issues associated with employment in the early childhood development field in Canada. It specifically details some of the challenges in defining skills required by early childhood caregivers, gaps in skills, and issues in post-secondary education and professional development opportunities. The report provides recommendations for addressing these concerns.

The purpose of continuing competence is to ensure that practicing professionals are made aware of and educated about new knowledge in both their own and other disciplines. In many professions, the individual must fulfill a specified number of professional development hours each year in order to maintain registration in the professional body. For example, a certified social worker is required to fulfill 75 hours of professional development over a five-year period. Government regulations also influence staff participation in professional development. Regulations in Prince Edward Island and Newfoundland and Labrador require that individual practitioners in licensed settings are required to document 30 hours of in-service professional development in every three-year period. British Columbia grants a licence to practice to individual caregivers. Renewal of this licence requires the caregiver to have participated in at least 12 hours of professional development within the previous five years (Beach et al. 2004).

An additional process used to improve performance is early childhood practitioner self-reflection. Professionals consider their assumptions about how children learn. They then step back periodically and think about activities they have planned and how they can be improved. This process is termed "**reflection**." It can be defined as a natural process that facilitates the development of future action by the contemplation of past and current behaviour. It is like a conversation in one's mind. Reflection is a characteristic of professionals that helps them gain better perspective on, insight into, and understanding of their work. It is critical to the developing of professional judgment. A useful resource in exploring this concept further is *When Teachers Reflect: Journeys Toward Effective, Inclusive Practice* (Tertell, Klein, and Jewett 1998).

Code of Ethics and Accountability

Caregivers work with one of society's most vulnerable groups—young children. The quality of interactions between young children and their caregivers has an enduring impact on children's lives. The intimacy of the relationship and the potential to do harm demand a commitment on the part of early childhood professionals to adhere to the standards of ethical practice.

Standard

Canadian Child Care Federation Code of Ethics

The Principles of the Code

- Child care practitioners promote the health and well-being of all children.

- Child care practitioners enable children to participate to their full potential in environments carefully planned to serve individual needs and to facilitate the child's progress in social, emotional, physical, and cognitive areas of development.

- Child care practitioners demonstrate their caring for all children in all aspects of their practice.

- Child care practitioners work in partnership with parents, recognizing that parents have primary responsibility for the care of their children, valuing their commitment to the children, and supporting them in meeting their responsibilities to their children.

- Child care practitioners work in partnership with colleagues and other service providers in the community to support the well-being of children and their families.

- Child care practitioners work in ways that enhance human dignity in trusting, caring, and co-operative relationships that respect the worth and uniqueness of the individual.

- Child care practitioners pursue, on an ongoing basis, the knowledge, skills, and self-awareness needed to be professionally competent.

- Child care practitioners demonstrate integrity in all of their professional relationships.

Source: Gillian Doherty, in Canadian Child Care Federation (CCCF), *Partners in Quality: Tools for Practitioners in Child Care Settings* (Ottawa: CCCF, 2000).

To claim to be a professional is to declare publicly that one adheres to goals and values that go beyond immediate interests. Ethics is the study of right and wrong, duty and obligation. It involves using knowledge and skills to make responsible professional decisions—a fundamental skill of a competent early childhood educator. **Professional ethics** concern the kinds of actions that are right and wrong in the workplace. Personal attributes, values, and morals form the necessary foundation for an individual's professional practice. They need to be complemented with professional values and standards of ethical behaviour that apply to all members of the profession.

In order to attain true professional status, caregivers must adopt a common code of ethics. One of the hallmarks of professionalism is its recognition of and adherence to a code of ethical conduct. Such a code embodies guidelines for behaviour and facilitates decision making when a caregiver faces an **ethical dilemma**—when he or she must determine appropriate conduct in the face of conflicting professional values and responsibilities. Clearly stated standards in a code of ethics provide a common ground for caregivers who strive to do the right thing for children, families, and colleagues.

A code of ethics differs from the policies, regulations, and legal obligations that govern the field of early childhood development. A code provides guidance for individuals, not the regulation of programs. Members of the profession create its code of ethics, whereas they are rarely the ones to write regulations and licensing requirements. Regulations and laws are necessary to govern the field and provide basic protections for children and families; nevertheless, a professional code represents a higher standard.

A code of professional ethics provides common principles for dealing with dilemmas—principles based on a belief in the value of childhood as a unique stage of life, knowledge of child development, a valuing of family and cultural ties, and a desire to help individuals reach their potential through supportive relationships. Such a code is created through discussions with colleagues who reflect on challenges that occur regularly within the profession.

The process of developing a code of professional ethics may begin with the standard predicaments that caregivers confront in the course of their day-to-day work. All early childhood practitioners are faced daily with dilemmas. Many of these situations do not have easy solutions but can be resolved using defined professional ethics to guide decision making. Ethics may be defined as the way associates in a group specify their responsibility to their clients, one another, and the community in which they work. Statements found in a code of ethics guide practitioners in collectively expressing their commitment to children, families, colleagues, and community. This statement represents what is right rather than what might be expedient. What is best is not always easy to determine, and a code of ethics is an essential tool to guide staff in their daily decision making.

Ethics and the Early Childhood Educator provides a thoughtful framework for exploration of ethical challenges facing early childhood practitioners (Feeney and Freeman 1999). The authors provide examples of issues and the caregiver's obligations to children, families, colleagues, and community. For example, caregivers may occasionally be forced to choose between a parent's and a child's needs. Often, programs need to make the decision that a mildly ill child would be better cared for at home than if he or she remained at the program.

It is important for the public to have confidence that the profession will meet its obligations and serve the public good. The protection of vulnerable children demands that all individuals working with children conform to the highest standards of ethical conduct. Professionals not only agree to operate according to a high standard of behaviour, they also agree to monitor the conduct of others in the field. Penalties (fines or suspension/termination of one's right to practice) may be levied against members of the profession who are incompetent or fail to act in accordance with standards of ethical practice.

The national code of ethics developed by the Canadian Child Care Federation in consultation with provincial/territorial affiliate organizations is included in this chapter. The principles found in the code were developed for use by adults who work with children and families in a variety of early childhood settings. They are intended to guide practitioners and protect the children with whom they work. Professionalism creates additional ethical obligations to colleagues and the profession.

A final component of professional ethics is **altruism**—when work is service-oriented and client focused. Ideally, members are expected to perform their services with unselfish dedication and an emphasis on social goals. From its beginning, the practice of early childhood development has been grounded on the principle of improving the lives of young children and families. On this criterion, early childhood practitioners rank highly, since their concern is with children and families. Given that the field is dealing with human lives, practitioners must be accountable—and care about what they do and how they do it. Chapter 2 expands on the UN's Convention on the Rights of Children.

The application of all these criteria to the field of early childhood development suggests it is endeavouring to develop into a profession.

Stages of Professional Growth

The idea of developmental stages is commonly understood and used by caregivers of young children, however, the notion of steps of development among adults is not as readily considered. In fact, the discussion of practitioner development has been in the literature for some time. Individuals vary greatly in the length of time they spend in each stage:

* Stage I—Survival
* Stage II—Consolidation
* Stage III—Renewal
* Stage IV—Maturity

The authors describe an early childhood practitioner's typical behaviour at each of these stages and identify the specialized training and professional development appropriate to each level. (The supervisory style and its effectiveness with staff is discussed in chapter 6.)

In the initial years of working, the novice practitioner moves through a number of developmental stages. An experienced colleague serving as mentor can identify the stage of development and provide appropriate strategies to stimulate reflective thinking and professional growth.

STAGES OF DEVELOPMENT—EARLY CHILDHOOD PRACTITIONERS

Developmental stages	Training needs
I. Survival	On-site support and feedback
II. Consolidation	On-site assistance, mentorship, access to specialists
III. Renewal	Seminars, conferences, further education, membership in professional organizations
IV. Maturity	Leadership in professional organizations, conferences

Stage I—Survival

Mentoring is particularly helpful for new graduates feeling the full responsibility for a group of young children. Novice caregivers are often exhilarated and terrified. The practitioner's primary role is to provide hands-on care, assist with activities, manage behaviour, and contribute to facility maintenance. This experience is often jarring and anxiety filled; the individual typically experiences self-doubt and feelings of insecurity. At this stage, the novice caregiver's main need is for support, guided reading, encouragement, and guidance. Staff in the survival stage should not be expected to supervise students who are on field practicum. Mentoring is valuable in supporting new graduates through this period of self-doubt.

Mentors can provide encouragement, insight into the reasons for children's behaviour, and instruction in specific skills. On-site support and mentoring from experienced caregivers are the most appropriate strategies to support staff in the survival stage of development.

Stage II—Consolidation

On-site support from a mentor is an effective strategy for professional development.

As they pass the survival stage, practitioners begin to exhibit some degree of comfort and confidence in their skills and start to focus on specific tasks. The second stage of development is consolidation. They have experienced success in planning for children. Practitioners begin interpreting what is happening in their classroom and are eager to seek alternative approaches. During this step, they may move their attention to aiding challenging children or to situations that deviate from the norm. They learn by observing, modelling, and doing and thrive in a supportive environment that encourages problem solving and sharing. They learn to structure physical environments and activities in a way that reduces the need for external controls. At this stage, practitioners benefit from more focused observations and feedback that identify challenges, problems, and new curriculum approaches. A director or mentor can provide encouragement to develop resources and form a support network.

As they develop further and master fundamentals, practitioners are ready to develop more advanced skills. To stay motivated and avoid burnout, they require exposure to new ideas. In the later stages of the consolidation phase, individuals are ready for performance appraisal systems that facilitate introspection and personal goal setting. Possible methods include self-administered checklists, video analysis, or use of a mentor—most often the director or a lead caregiver—along with regular opportunities to formally review issues that have arisen in the course of daily practice.

Stage III—Renewal

Early childhood practitioners in this stage have reached a professional plateau. The practitioner is comfortable with the established program and routines. After several years of implementing the same curriculum to children at the same age level, she or he may no longer feel challenged. The practitioner may search for stimulation, asking, "What's new in the field? Are there new areas of curriculum I haven't considered before?"

When this occurs, the early childhood practitioner has reached the renewal stage. Practitioners at this stage are interested in learning about new developments in the field. They often enjoy meeting with caregivers from other programs. Professional development opportunities that are particularly beneficial at this stage include attending conferences and workshops, continued education, and active involvement in a self-assessment process.

Stage IV—Maturity

Mature practitioners view themselves as committed professionals. This final stage is reached by individuals at different points in their careers and represents a coming to terms with themselves and their profession. They have developed a philosophy of education and care and recognize the critical nature of early learning. Mature practitioners acknowledge the need for continual professional growth and self-renewal. They are committed to improving the early childhood profession and see sharing information as an essential part of this goal. They are often searching for the meaning of social, economic, historical, and political influences on society. Mature practitioners need opportunities to interact with others searching for similar insights and participate in events where their questions are addressed.

These four stages can be viewed as ever-widening circles, as the early childhood practitioner matures and develops. All practitioners can benefit from support and opportunities to expand their knowledge and skills throughout their careers.

Methods of Enhancing Professionalism

Although early childhood development is not yet a profession in the formal sense, competent practitioners seek out opportunities to improve their skills and knowledge.

Self-assessment is an indispensable route to professionalism. It helps one to be accountable to others; even more important, it makes one accountable to oneself. This process of validating accomplishments and identifying where work is still needed can lead the practitioner to feel more confident about her or his role. Directors and peers can assist, by providing feedback on strengths and support in the areas needing improvement.

Certification and accreditation were mentioned in chapter 1 as means of improving quality in early childhood settings. Both methods incorporate self-assessment as part of the process. These programs can improve standards of practice and promote the professional image of early childhood education. **Certification** is the awarding of a credential that identifies persons who possess the competencies needed to be a competent early childhood practitioner. Voluntary certification recognizes the educational qualifications of practitioners in a variety of early childhood settings. Individual employment policies may require that staff be certified. The qualifications required for certification stipulate that certified practitioners possess specified levels of professional competence or, in the case of Newfoundland and Labrador, a level of educational qualification.

There are no national certification standards for early childhood practitioners equivalent to those for kindergarten and primary school teachers. The roots of this discrepancy are probably as much economic as academic. Early childhood practitioners are generally paid more poorly than school teachers, and some decision makers fear that raising educational requirements would further increase the pressures for higher pay, thus increasing the cost of services.

Three provinces' provincial professional organizations offer voluntary certification: Alberta, Nova Scotia, and Ontario. However, only a small number of practitioners in each of these provinces are certified. The certification process needs to be better promoted, recognized, and valued by the early childhood field as a step toward becoming a profession. The process of certification varies among the different provincial organizations. Among the methods used to assess candidates are peer evaluation, self-assessment, a set exam, and development of a portfolio. Newfoundland and Labrador's regulations require certification of the staff of all licensed child care services.

Another route is **Prior Learning Assessment and Recognition (PLAR)**, which allows experiential learning to be identified, evaluated, and equated with an amount of post-secondary credit. There is growing interest in PLAR as a mechanism for granting advanced standing to candidates with related work experience. This process is not a replacement for academic credit, but a mechanism for recognizing prior learning. Among the assessment measures used are the presentation of a portfolio, transcripts from other institutions, challenge examinations, and performance evaluations. Early childhood practitioners with the appropriate background will find that assessment of their experience will enable them to complete a diploma or degree more quickly.

Professional bodies having the authority to regulate their members and their practice carry out the self-governance of a profession. The recognition of these groups is usually embedded in legislation. Some provinces are pursuing legislative recognition of early childhood practitioners. This process is intended to provide public accountability and a more respected status for practitioners. Part of the process is to develop a clear definition of an early childhood practitioner. The work done by the Canadian Child Care Federation and the Child Care Human Resources Sector Council in defining occupational standards are important steps.

Accreditation is a process of self-regulation and another way that the public and other professionals can recognize high quality early childhood development programs. While "licensing" implies meeting minimum standards, "accreditation" means performing to a high degree of excellence and meeting model standards. Accreditation is a process whereby a representative body, recognized by both the service community and the community in general, establishes standards for service. It is founded on the beliefs that for change to be real and lasting, it must be initiated by the early childhood organization, and that program improvement results from a collaborative problem solving approach involving directors, staff, and families in a systematic review of the program's strengths and weaknesses. In some models, excellence in settings is verified by visits and assessment by the body granting accreditation. A study of programs accredited by the National Association for the Education of Young Children (NAEYC) confirmed the positive impact of accreditation and also indicated that the process facilitated improvements to the program, which led to even higher quality (Herr, Johnson, and Zimmerman 1993). There is a growing trend in the United States to offer government funding only to accredited programs.

Some of the benefits of accreditation include:

- improvements in staff development, communication, and morale;
- measurable program improvements; and
- increased confidence on the part of families that they have made a good decision in choosing an accredited program for their children.

Both Alberta and Manitoba governments are studying accreditation models. The Alberta Accreditation Project is identifying child care centres and family child care agencies that meet or exceed standards and are eligible to receive additional funds. Accreditation programs are standard in the delivery systems of other services such as hospitals and post-secondary institutions. As the profession evolves, practitioners are becoming more knowledgeable about theories of development and learning and more skillful in applying these in their daily work with children and families. Organizations such as the Canadian Child Care Federation are addressing professional issues including ethics and standards of practice. As professionals, we must continually strive to do our best for young children and families through informed, ethical practice. Further, we must be willing to share this perspective with others. (Chapter 11, "Advocating for Canada's Children," provides a variety of strategies for public education.)

As early childhood education comes of age, the field is more aware of the importance of specialized expertise and education. But there is still some distance to go in developing a professional image. As practitioners work together on common goals, they invest part of themselves in the process, and this investment contributes to our shared professionalism. This enhanced sense of collective purpose is what makes practitioners willing to become involved in voluntary efforts toward the improvement of early childhood development programs.

In the words of one practitioner, "It is in this subtle area of private endeavour that a profession, in its totality, achieves greatness. Sometimes it is called professional spirit. It is the result of the association of men and women of a superior type, with a common ideal of service above gain, excellence above quality, self-expression beyond motive, and loyalty to a professional code beyond human advantage" (Pat Dickenson, personal communication, 1989). This is the commitment needed to realize quality early childhood experiences for every Canadian child.

Unions and Professional Groups

Advocating for the quality early childhood development services that every child should have access to is part of the practitioner's professional and ethical responsibility. Effective advocacy depends on numerous groups joining together to improve practice and influence policy and public opinion. There are parents, professional organizations, coalitions, and local networks that advocate for early childhood issues.

There is a need for early childhood practitioners to establish and reinforce ties with health care professionals, educators, and other groups concerned with families, children, and issues related to poverty. There are a number of roles that can be played in these organizations. Each role is important, whether it be testifying at a hearing, serving on a committee, or helping to get out an important mailing.

Join an organization that is working for quality early childhood development in your province or territory. Every member's name adds weight to these organizations' efforts to affect change. An organization will help make each voice heard through coordinated campaigns for action. Although legislators may not listen to an individual's recommendations, they may be persuaded by broad based support. Organizations can also provide information about issues and options. One sign of a profession is the existence of organizations to which members belong. Such organizations provide members with support and a common sense of interest and purpose.

In addition, membership can facilitate contacts that may be personally and professionally helpful and can provide access to research data or information about legislation and funding and assist with the development of skills. Through contacts at meetings, individuals may learn of employment opportunities, or directors may meet potential staff members. Professional organizations provide forums for expressing ideas, opportunities to discuss concerns with other professionals, and a place to speak before a group.

Unions are allies of the ECEC field in advocating for funding and services.

In Canada, early childhood practitioners have several pertinent organizations at the national level, with many more available at the provincial and territorial levels. The Canadian Child Care Federation has many provincial/territorial affiliate members in each province. See the Canadian Child Care Directory published by the Canadian Child Care Federation through their website www.cfc-efc.ca/child_care/directory.htm. It is important to join an organization and add your voice. In fact, *You Bet I Care!* reported that family child care providers involved with networks or family child care organizations were more sensitive and responsive than those without such affiliation (Doherty 2000a).

Unions have long served as political allies of the field, advocating for better funding and expanded services for children and families. *Working for Change: Canada's Child Care Workforce* (Beach et al. 2004) identified that union membership was held by over 15 000 child care staff. Unions across Canada advocate for public policy for universal child care, have bargained for improved family and child care benefits for their members and have worked to improve members' wages and working conditions. *You Bet I Care!* also found that collective bargaining had led to improved benefits in one-third of the programs (Doherty 2000a).

Lowe (2001b) writes about the Canadian Union of Postal Workers (CUPW) and their support for members who both work and care for children. The organization established a fund to pay for additional staff, add safety items to child care programs, and purchase equipment and toys to enable programs to meet the needs of a more diverse age group; as well, CUPW offers a 35% to 45% fee subsidy to enable workers' children to attend child care programs. CUPW supports 11 projects across Canada including a family resource centre that offers training and supports to caregivers, a toy lending library, and community referrals. As well, it runs a summer camp program and short-term emergency care service.

CUPW worked with SpeciaLink to develop a program to support families of children with special needs. The union became more aware of the high levels of stress and exhaustion, the limited child care services, the greater transportation needs, and the great deal of time needed to attend medical appointments confronted by these families. The union developed an education program for their members to assist them in becoming effective advocates for improved services. This one example illustrates the many ways unions work in partnership with the early childhood community to support families in their search for quality environments and to pressure governments to provide both the leadership and funding to achieve these goals.

Summary

Characteristics of a professional include a commitment to ongoing professional development. Early childhood practitioners share the responsibility to identify ways to continually improve their practice with children and families. This chapter outlines the stages in an individual's growth as a professional and how to accommodate the individual characteristics of each developmental stage. When directors understand the developmental levels of staff, they are better able to individualize supervision strategies. They can provide a forum for questioning, problem solving, and clarifying expectations. Engagement in ongoing professional development can move an individual to the next level of competence and may provide entry into a higher position, moving through and across the career lattice. Professionals in early childhood development programs believe in and support a code of ethics as well as the importance of being accountable for their actions. Unions and professional organizations make significant contributions to the growth of the field of early childhood development.

Key Terms and Concepts

Accreditation,   p. 172

Career ladder,   p. 156

Career lattice,   p. 156

Certification,   p. 171

Code of ethics,   p. 162

Early childhood profession,   p. 162

Ethical dilemma,   p. 167

Ethics,   p. 162

Multi-age (mixed-age) groupings, p. 158

Occupational standards,   p. 163

Prior Learning Assessment and Recognition (PLAR),   p. 172

Professional development,   p. 160

Professional ethics,   p. 167

Professional judgment,   p. 163

Professionalism,   p. 161

Reflection,   p. 166

Resource teacher,   p. 158

Activities

1. Download a copy of the Child Care Connections Canadian Child Care Directory published by the Canadian Child Care Federation through the website www.cfc-efc.ca. Review the list of groups in your area, and identify which organizations you want to learn more about. Contact them and arrange to attend a meeting and/or subscribe to their newsletter.

2. Invite a guest speaker from a union to talk with the class. In small groups identify how unionization aids in the retention of staff.

3. Review the Canadian Child Care Federation code of ethics (included in this chapter) and discuss how to apply the items to your work with children and families.

4. In the occupation of working with young children, the distinction between "care" and "education" is blurred. Identify a name for the field you would prefer (e.g., early childhood education, child care, educare, or early learning and care). What are the strengths and weaknesses of the name? What opportunities/barriers would this name present?

Recommended Reading

Beach, Jane, Jane Bertrand, Barry Forer, Donna Michal, and Jocelyne Tougas. *Working for Change: Canada's Child Care Workforce. Labour Market Update Study.* Ottawa: Child Care Human Resources Sector Council, 2004.

Feeney, S., and N.K. Freeman. *Ethics and the Early Childhood Educator: Using the NAEYC Code.* Washington, DC: National Association for the Education of Young Children, 1999.

Tertell, E., S. Klein, and J. Jewett, eds. *When Teachers Reflect: Journeys Toward Effective, Inclusive Practice.* Washington, DC: National Association for the Education of Young Children, 1998.

Doherty, G. *Occupational Standards for Child Care Practitioners.* Ottawa: Canadian Child Care Federation, 2003.

Weblinks

www.ccsc-cssge.ca
Child Care Human Resources Sector Council
This group identifies and works to improve workforce skills and learning challenges faced by the child care field. They have completed a labour market study and are developing occupational standards for directors.

pages.istar.ca/~cccns/index.html
Child Care Connection NS
Follow the link to the Retention & Recruitment Challenges page for resources on attracting and keeping qualified staff. Among the resources are discussion papers, reflection exercises, and a scan process.

www.partnersinpractice.org
Partners in Practice
The Partners in Practice mentoring website offers information on the mentoring model, resources on mentoring in practice, publications, events, and Canadian mentoring initiatives. Most important, it offers members an opportunity to talk with other practitioners about their work.

www.cwla.org
The Child Welfare League of America
This is the oldest and largest organization devoted entirely to the well-being of vulnerable children and their families. Its website provides links to information about issues related to morality and values in education.

www.bringingyourselftowork.com
Bringing Yourself to Work
This is a unique approach to training and supporting after-school program staff. It is based on the premise that having healthier, better relationships with others starts with understanding yourself. The site includes a discussion area where visitors can post and read comments and has links to other related sites and resources.

Managing Safe and Healthy Learning Environments

Objectives

- Outline the components of early childhood environments.
- Identify key players in providing safe, healthy learning environments.
- Provide guidelines for making effective equipment purchasing decisions.
- Overview maintenance of safe environments for children.
- Describe considerations for healthy environments.
- Discuss the principles of health policies and practices.
- Identify considerations in planning food services for young children.

Director's Role in Providing Safe, Healthy Environments

Good programs exist in all sorts of spaces, from basements or storefronts to environments specifically designed for children. Although the space does not determine the program, the environment regulates the experience. The physical facilities, the arrangement of space, and the equipment available can make quality easier or more difficult to achieve. Facilities can be made physically and psychologically more comfortable by applying an understanding of how children develop as well as structuring the environment to facilitate interactions.

Directors are ultimately responsible for their program's health, safety, and nutrition programs. They work closely with families, health professionals, and staff to create a safe, healthy learning environment. Since directors often have full responsibility for the planning, implementation, and monitoring of these key areas, it is necessary to be informed about the elements involved and the importance of these components to the children, families, and staff in the program. The director's responsibilities regarding the environment include the efficient use of space—indoor and outdoor environments, playrooms, administrative space, storage, and support areas such as the kitchen. Some areas are used mostly by children, some only by adults, and some are shared. The selection, variety, and maintenance of learning materials and equipment are vital parts of planning. The purchase of equipment is generally based on philosophical, practical, financial, and developmental considerations. The director, collaborating with staff, acquires, arranges, distributes, maintains, evaluates, and remodels the space.

Regulations

Directors need to be aware of licensing requirements or regulations in their province/territory that affect plans for the environment, both inside and on playgrounds. Directors have responsibilities to staff as well as to the children. For example, there will likely be regulations regarding the amount of space required for each child, the number of toilets/change tables, space for ill children, and areas for adults. Programs will be required to fence outdoor areas and possibly put in specific kinds of surfacing. Wallach and Afthinos (1990) found that licensing regulations for outdoor areas lag behind those for indoor environments. In addition to checking provincial/territorial regulations, directors must work within municipal guidelines. Building codes may specify the kinds of changes that can be made to space. Public health departments have strict requirements for the storage of food and cleaning supplies. The fire department has specific concerns such as fire walls and doors. Provincial health and safety legislation establishes rules and responsibilities for government, employers, and staff and sets minimum health and safety standards for the workplace.

Regulations relate to the following areas:

- requirements of health, fire, and zoning authorities;
- group sizes and room capacities: square metres per child, both indoors and outdoors;
- health and safety regulations;
- occupational health and safety standards for employees;
- playground requirements; and
- regulations regarding physical plant.

Regulations typically refer to minimal requirements—not what is needed to provide a program that promotes each child's optimal development. It can take time to incorporate regulatory requirements into overall planning. (The licensing bodies listed in the appendix will be able to provide helpful information to assist in the development of a program.)

Quality programs work closely with community professionals to ensure the optimal development of each child.

Quality Standards

Partners in Quality: Tools for Practitioners in Child Care Settings (CCCF 2000b) identifies standards of excellence for program environments (a sample appears below). A similar standard was developed for family child care providers. To ensure the environment meets the needs of all children, it is important to use universal design principles so that hallways are wide enough to accommodate wheelchairs and counters are at a reachable height. See SpeciaLink Inclusion Practices Profile for more specifics.

Standard

Environments in Early Childhood Development Programs

The director should ensure a safe, healthy, well-organized environment and a planned curriculum that meets the needs of the children and their families by:

- defining and explaining program goals and objectives to practitioners, support staff, and families;
- working with practitioners and support staff to ensure that policies, procedures, and practices are developed, implemented, and reviewed annually regarding such issues as:
  - safeguarding children's health, safety, and nutrition;
  - maintaining updated medical and developmental progress records on all children;
  - implementing behaviour guidance policies and procedures;
  - providing appropriate supervision of children both indoors and outdoors;
  - handling sick or injured children and emergencies;
  - obtaining parental consent where applicable;
  - release of children at the end of the program period;
  - reporting protection concerns and complying with court orders.
- working with practitioners and support staff to plan and ensure that required training is provided in areas such as protocols and procedures for reporting protection concerns and complying with court orders and emergency evacuations;
- working with practitioners and support staff to develop and implement plans for responding to allegations of misconduct by practitioners, volunteers, support staff, or others working within the early childhood setting;
- working with practitioners and support staff to ensure physical environments that are safe, clean, and organized to provide for quiet and active activities and that have materials and equipment that are appropriate in size and function and to provide access to safe outdoor play space;
- providing leadership and support for practitioners in the development of the children's daily program so that activities and materials are developmentally appropriate;

(continued)

- using and promoting the use of a variety of observational techniques to assist in:
  - the identification of children's skills, interests, and needs
  - the evaluation of activities provided for children
  - the program as a whole;
- ensuring, to the extent possible, that practitioners have an adequate level of human and other resources to enable them to provide quality care and education;
- working with practitioners and support staff to develop and implement a variety of communication techniques for providing families with information about the service and their children;
- working with practitioners and support staff to develop a variety of user-friendly approaches that encourage and support children and parents to express their needs and preferences and to have meaningful input into policy and program development; and
- encouraging inclusion of children with special needs, and children and their families from all cultural and ethnic backgrounds.

Source: Gillian Doherty, in Canadian Child Care Federation (CCCF), *Partners in Quality: Tools for Practitioners in Child Care Settings* (Ottawa: CCCF, 2000).

Guidelines for Selecting and Maintaining Equipment

Equipment is likely to be the early childhood program's largest non-staff expenditure. Therefore, it is important to make wise choices. Equipment selection is based on many factors, including personal preferences and curriculum. Whether purchasing a single shelf for the book centre or equipping an entire facility, the process of selecting learning materials and equipment requires research, planning, and organization to ensure that selections are safe, versatile, durable, appropriate, and affordable. Full enjoyment by all of the new equipment will only result if staff preferences, curriculum, quality of construction, ease of **maintenance**, safety, and budget are all considered. Here are some questions to ask:

- *Durability:* How long will it hold up? Group use is at least 10 times as hard on equipment as home use.
- *Safety:* Sharp edges or corners? Parts to swallow? Toxic finishes? Will the item be pulled or tipped over? Will it wear or break in a manner that will make it dangerous?
- *Health:* Does it allow for easy cleaning and disinfecting?
- *Size and scale:* Is it the right size and scale for projected and unanticipated use by all the adults and children—including those with special needs?
- Is it consistent with the program goals? Will it offer developmentally appropriate experiences and autonomy?
- Will it facilitate the caregiver's task? Equipment should also be selected with a view to preventing injury due to repetitive strain.
- Will it add to the children's and parents' sense of security?

- *Aesthetics:* Is the design attractive? Do the colour, size, and shape add to or detract from the overall aesthetic (e.g., will there be too much bright plastic equipment)?

It is advisable to establish a budget before the selection process begins. If the budget is limited, a master plan should be created to purchase the basics first and add items as additional funds become available. (See chapter 10, "Financial Matters," for a review of considerations in the budgeting process.) When purchasing playground equipment and furniture for a new facility, use a formula based on the cost per child as a guideline. The cost per child will be higher for younger children in rooms with higher staff:child ratios. Directors may wish to consider a range of costs, from base to medium to high. Costs may vary regionally. Considerable savings can be realized depending on the type of material selected.

Equipment

Selection of all equipment should be based on a set of pre-established criteria as well as the Canadian Standards Association (CSA) guidelines found in *Children's Play Spaces and Equipment* (2003).Whether adding a new piece to an existing playroom or creating a full equipment list for a new program, the process of selecting the right equipment and furniture requires careful planning. The first criterion is to buy something that will be enjoyed by both the children and staff, meaningful for the curriculum, and functional.

When possible, take design preferences into account; staff may look through catalogues and websites to find items that appeal to them and fit the program's requirements. Many early childhood vendors provide online catalogues and purchasing options. Attendance at conferences to tour exhibits for ideas and pick up catalogues is worthwhile. Another essential strategy is to visit other programs and talk to staff about the furniture and equipment they prefer. If the director is working with architects or interior designers, they may have access to manufacturers of unique designs. Today's selections primarily include furniture made of natural woods, colourful laminates, and plastic. Thorough research at this stage of the process will help ensure that the investment made will be a good one.

The type of curriculum used at the program influences the selection of equipment. A program with a special focus on cognitive development may, for instance, purchase a wide variety of materials that offer children math and science experiences. Programs with a curriculum that uses learning centres can break down needs by learning centre, such as the art or block area. More programs are being influenced by the Reggio Emila approach, which emphasizes the use of natural products and real objects rather than plastic replicas. There are

Selection of equipment should be based on established criteria such as Canadian Standards Association guidelines.

many excellent resources that explore this issue, including Greenman's *Caring Spaces, Learning Places: Children's Environments That Work* (1988).

It is a good idea to take measurements of the site to determine available space. One approach is to draw an accurate floor plan on graph paper, cut out to-scale versions of the equipment, and move them about the floor plan. In the planning process, consider how many children will use each room, as well as the functions that will occur in it. If the children eat in the same space, make sure there is enough space available for small, manageable groups and that all children and staff will be able to sit together at one time.

Always keep in mind the number and ages of children in the program. If mixed-age groups use the playroom, purchase equipment that fits more than one group, or choose equipment that fits the smaller children, so that the room will accommodate everyone. Provide for flexibility and versatility. Equipment that can be assembled in different ways will be more interesting to children and provide creative learning opportunities. Avoid thematic furniture pieces that tend to inhibit a child's imagination and may be left unused once the "newness" wears off. Some equipment can be used both indoors and outside; this is not only economical but provides a wider variety of learning experiences for children.

In determining the suitability of equipment, children with special needs must be considered. A child who cannot walk, for example, may need a table or easel that can be used by the child while sitting in a chair or wheelchair. When children who do not have special needs use these same materials, they may develop greater insights into the experience of children who do. *Resources for Educating Young Children with Diverse Abilities* provides further advice on selecting suitable equipment (Deiner, Dyck, and Hardacre 1999).

Another consideration is the back care of caregivers; back injuries are the most common type of injury for early childhood practitioners. These injuries are usually caused by inappropriate lifting and carrying and poor design and layout of the furniture. Adult chairs with shorter legs can be used to provide adequate back support for staff; to avoid back strain, sinks and counters should be built to suit an adult's height. The change table should have walk-up steps, particularly for toddlers. These types of adjustments can decrease the incidence of muscular skeletal injuries by reducing the amount of lifting required. Other strategies are detailed in *Healthy Foundations in Child Care* (Pimento and Kernsted 2004).

Quality and safety are key concerns when selecting equipment. All equipment and furnishings must be maintained in a safe condition and replaced when necessary. Safety is maintained when staff are alert to the condition and arrangement of the equipment in the learning environment. All-wood construction will ensure the greatest strength and durability. Look for furniture that has curved or bevelled edges—they are important safety features. Sharp corners are dangerous for children. All equipment used by children must be made of non-toxic materials. As infants and toddlers are likely to explore every nook and cranny, staff must consider safety features such as child-proof locks and hinges that prevent pinching and do not close too rapidly.

Ease of maintenance is always a key factor in choosing equipment. For example, sinks, toilets, and change areas must be cleaned frequently. The surfaces should be smooth, and all areas should be easy to reach. Some plastic surfaces are slightly roughened, and although the surface feels relatively smooth, there are actually shallow indentations that can attract and hold bacteria. Plastic furniture may be less expensive than other furniture, but maintenance problems usually outweigh the possible savings.

Durability and economy often go hand in hand. For example, a piece of equipment that costs three times as much as another product will be worth the original investment if it is safer, sturdier, requires less frequent maintenance, and will last three times as long.

Outdoor Space

The outdoors provides a great place for sensory motor exploration, experiencing the environment, and interacting with children and adults. Many of the principles for indoor environments can be applied to outdoor space.

Programs vary in their ability to provide outdoor play areas, particularly in urban settings. Make the best use of what is available, remembering that even small spaces can be sites for quality outdoor experiences. Experiences can change with the addition of "loose parts"—materials that can be stacked, sorted, separated, lined up, dumped, and so on. Natural materials include rocks, stones, leaves, sand, wood, and water. Changes in the seasons offer new sensory opportunities. Some key considerations include:

- *Sufficient square footage:* A space that is too small results in crowding and too few play experiences. As well, with active children, when crowding occurs, accidents are more likely.

- *Drainage:* Good drainage is essential. Decks and platforms should offer a flat surface that drains easily and can be used for water play or when the ground is wet.

- *Non-toxic landscape:* All vegetation should be checked to make sure there are no poisonous plants.

- *Good layout and zoning:* Defined play areas, clear pathways, and challenging equipment placed on the perimeter are best. Location of areas such as swings and bike paths must be well thought out.

- *Provide shade:* Roofs, canopies, and umbrella mounts are good alternatives if there is not adequate shading from trees.

- Consider ways to *increase the adults' convenience and comfort,* for example, with the addition of pillows, hammocks, and, if possible, portable changing areas to increase outdoor time.

Ideally, outdoor spaces offer a variety of stimuli. Programs with less-than-adequate outdoor space should find alternatives such as community parks and going for walks.

Playground Equipment

The purchase of playground equipment is one of the biggest decisions made by programs. Not only does it involve committing a large amount of the program's resources, it also impacts on the children's outdoor experiences for a number of years. Directors should interview other practitioners about their experiences with various products and vendors.

CONSIDERATIONS IN SELECTING EQUIPMENT

- appropriateness and activity capabilities
- safety
- type of construction material
- installation
- maintenance
- warranty

Start by considering the goals of the program. What are the goals of the outdoor program? What sorts of experiences are desired for the children? Once a director has clarified the objectives with staff, they must then evaluate how well different pieces of equipment will help accomplish these objectives. In comparing pieces of playground equipment, a primary consideration is the quantity and quality of activity made possible by each piece. Generally, the equipment selected should encourage children to engage in a wide range of social, motor, and imaginative-play experiences. Equipment should provide opportunities for upper- and lower-body development. It should be appropriately scaled and equipped for the children who will use it—and it must be fun for the children.

Young children's physical safety is the prime concern in evaluating any piece of playground equipment. The most serious injuries that occur in early childhood settings happen on the playground. According to the Canadian Institute of Child Health (2000), the leading cause of injury that requires hospitalization is falls. All equipment is required to meet the standards set by the Canadian Standards Association in 2003. These standards also indicate

Sample

Policy for Supervision of School-Age Children

The board of directors and staff of Challenge the Children Child Care are committed to providing a safe, healthy, quality child care program for all children by:

- ensuring that the minimum staff:child ratio as outlined in the Provincial Licensing Regulation is maintained at all times;
- appropriately enhancing the staff:child ratio to accommodate the needs of children who require additional support;
- for field trips and challenging activities, enhancing the adult:child ratio to one adult to four to six children by utilizing practicum students and volunteers;
- orienting and training all staff in supervision procedures/techniques; and
- ensuring that the children are supervised at all times.

Sample procedures

- Daily written sign-in/out forms will be completed by the parent/legal guardian and authorized pickup persons verified by the director.
- Head counts will be done every five minutes and after any transition.
- If children are divided into small groups, each staff will have a list of the names of children in their group.
- Developmentally appropriate activities will be provided that meet/challenge the needs of all children.
- A minimum of two staff will be present at all times when a child who requires additional supports is attending the program.
- Enrolment and attendance tracking will be done on an ongoing basis to ensure staffing ratios meet the program policies for typical and enhanced ratios.

Source: Adapted from the Policies and Procedures for Child Care Programs, *Tough and Sensitive Issues, Part II,* developed by Westcoast Child Care INFORM, Vancouver, BC, September 2000.

modifications that should be made to equipment to make it accessible to children with a wide range of special needs. Some things to look for: Are there any sharp edges, bars, or supports where children could easily hit their heads? Are there any aspects of the equipment that might tempt the children into dangerous behaviour? Are there any entrapment areas? Prior to using the playground, the first staff to arrive in the morning should carry out a safety check looking for items that need immediate attention, such as removing animal feces from the sandbox or picking up sharp items. Some provincial regulations require the completion of daily written checklists. Most playground injuries can be prevented with proper supervision. Directors should ensure that staff understand this, and that when over-seeing children, they ensure play equipment is being used safely. Assess how easy it will be for the staff to supervise the children. Can staff see every part of the equipment and playground? Can they quickly reach a child anywhere on the playground?

The safety of the area underneath the structure is a key consideration. A perfectly safe piece of equipment can become hazardous if it is erected over the wrong surface. Installation can be as expensive as the purchase of the equipment itself. Considerations include the suitability of the site, drainage and soil conditions, and underground utilities. Falls to the surface account for nearly 70% of all playground injuries. CSA standards specify the types of materials that can be used beneath a piece of equipment and how deep the materials must be. As for installation, there are choices: the seller can be paid to install the equipment, it can be installed under the supervision of the manufacturer's representative, or parent volunteers may be recruited. Paying the experts to install the equipment is clearly the safest, quickest, and easiest approach, although it can add 25% to 40% to the cost. Using a parent group will not only save money, the satisfaction of a job well done may be a team builder. However, this course of action may result in voiding the manufacturer's warranty, and the program may liable for any accidents that occur. Some companies will perform a post-construction inspection to verify that everything was done appropriately, thus maintaining the warranty and the manufacturer's liability. Annually thereafter, it is the program's responsibility to have the playground re-certified.

A key element of safety is maintenance. Accidents on playground equipment are often the result of poor maintenance. No matter what type of equipment is purchased, directors must establish and adhere to a strict schedule of inspection and maintenance. A safety audit is an essential first step. Safe Kids Canada, in consultation with the Canadian Standards Association, produced a video and booklet entitled *Child's Play: A Playground Safety Guide for Daycares, Schools and Communities* (*Child's Play* 1997) that help staff identify and correct potential safety hazards. Playground hazards come in many forms and are hard to spot without knowing what to check. A safety audit rates the seriousness of hazards from class A to C. A class A hazard can cause a major injury or death and needs to be corrected immediately. A class C hazard may cause minor injuries, such as scrapes or splinters, and may need to be dealt with in long-term planning and budgeting.

Most vendors suggest that if a playground structure is well maintained, not vandalized, and not exposed frequently to extreme weather conditions, it should last from 10 to 20 years. Be sure to ask questions about what is included in the warranty and whether there are conditions that will void the warranty. As a final step, staff should visit programs using the equipment the program intends to purchase. In this way, they can evaluate the quality of the installation as well as the durability of the product. Most important, they can observe how children are using the equipment. Are the children taking full advantage of all its features? Do the children using it exhibit enjoyment? What is the injury record for that particular piece of equipment?

Learning Materials

While learning materials constitute a small portion of the budget, they are critically important in shaping the experiences the children have while in the program. As well as assuring
that toys do not represent a threat to the health and safety of children, purchasers want to
ensure that toys have sound educational value.

CONSIDERATIONS IN SELECTING LEARNING MATERIALS

- appeal and stimulation
- developmental appropriateness
- flexibility/play value
- open-endedness
- diversity
- construction
- maintenance
- safety
- anti-bias

Learning materials should capture the child's interest and inspire further exploration
through actions or questioning. They should engage the children's active involvement.
Playthings should place realistic demands on children's dexterity, skills, and cognition.
They should be simple enough that children understand how to produce the desired effect,
yet provide a challenge. Well chosen learning materials can be used for years in many different ways. The very young child will use the learning material to discover textures and
explore and manipulate various parts. An older child may use the same learning material
for pretend play or to try on roles, imitate adult behaviours, refine motor skills, develop
symbolic thought, or enhance language skills.

Toys and materials should be open-ended, enabling the children to use them in different
ways. Children notice differences at very young ages. Ensure that learning materials represent
the diversity of human beings through realistic, non-stereotypical details. To select learning materials that promote maximum brain development, Schiller (2001) recommends:

Offer learning materials and equipment that are multi-sensory. The more senses
involved in a learning situation, the more likely the child is to process the information.

Pay attention to what has been learned about colours. Bright colours make the individual more alert. Infants notice red, blue, and green first. These are the colours that
should predominate in the infant room.

Rotate toys and offer homemade games. Novelty causes the brain to be more alert. The
playroom should be rearranged every three to four months. However, use novelty in
moderation. Too many changes at one time may be disconcerting to young children.

A program filled with bright plastic objects and pictures of animals and fairy-tale
characters is a limited and artificial world and should be avoided. Quality early childhood

programs emphasize natural materials and experiences. Provide materials and experiences that have meaning, such as materials for cleaning, food preparation, or laundry, and experiences of caring for people, animals, and plants. As with outdoor experiences, provide loose items such as pillows, blankets, tubs, woks, appliance boxes, wood pieces, stones, and so on.

In a group setting, toys and materials are used a great deal by children and they must be durable. How learning materials are put together is a factor in their durability and ongoing safety. As with other pieces of equipment, evaluate how much maintenance will be required to preserve the appearance and structural integrity of a learning material. Determine how materials can be cleaned and choose the appropriate solutions. The learning material will last longer and be healthier for children if bacteria and dirt can be easily washed off.

Inspect learning materials for potential hazards such as choking or poisoning. Look for small parts that could fit in a child's mouth or long cords that could ensnare a child. Toxicity or poisoning is an important safety issue. Ensure that there were no toxic paints or dyes used to produce the learning material. These considerations are much more thoroughly explored in *Healthy Foundations in Child Care* (Pimento and Kernsted 2004).

Managing, Securing, and Storing Equipment

Since considerable program resources are spent on equipment, it must be kept secure. Prior to the delivery of new equipment, a director should consider how equipment will be managed. Once received, all equipment should be checked and inventoried. A maintenance plan should be developed to minimize repairs and the need to replace parts.

Early childhood programs typically do not leave out items of high interest to burglars—cash, high-tech equipment, or medication. Few programs report incidents of vandalism, and those that do occur are usually minor. Some strategies to improve program security include:

- Keep expensive, portable equipment locked up when not in use. Desktop computers should be bolted down. Provide a secure place for staff to store their personal effects while at work.

- Ensure all entrances and gates are secured with high quality locks. Some programs have their buildings linked to local security companies.

- Establish and enforce financial procedures that provide for strict control of funds at all times. Enforce policies and procedures that limit exposure. Require fees to be paid by cheque or credit card, keep payments in a locked box, and deposit them in the bank quickly.

Providing adequate storage at early childhood programs is always a challenge. Both short-term and long-term storage should be considered. Items needing short-range storage include learning materials used daily and materials that will be consumed quickly. Most early childhood development programs have problems storing materials when they are not being used or organizing closets without having everything fall out. Good organization and labelling and adequate storage space help to create an environment that supports practitioners and support staff. Storage designed so that children can easily retrieve and replace materials will support their developing independence. The director's job is to supply the best storage system possible and establish routines that lead to easy accessibility of equipment for everyone. It is also the director's responsibility to ensure the staff's safety. Ideally, to be ergonomically correct, storage shelves should be at eye level. If storage is overhead, lighter objects should be placed highest and sturdy adult-sized stools or stepladders should be available to aid access. These routines make putting things away less burdensome for all.

Evaluating the Environment

As the children mature, or whenever the composition of the group changes, the arrangement of the space will need to be reassessed. There may be spaces that are not used or are underused, areas that are constantly messy and disorganized, and places where play is not as constructive as it could be. How the children and adults use the space needs to be observed. If a caregiver is constantly walking through play areas and disrupting the activities, there may be a need to look at the pathways. Look at space from a young child's point of view. What does the child see and feel? Periodically it can be helpful to have someone who works outside the room come in to observe. An outside observer can point out both areas that need attention and areas that are working well. (Some of the program evaluation tools described in chapter 4 can be used to assess the physical environment.)

A familiar space offers a feeling of security. Change should be thoughtful. Involving the children makes alterations in space less stressful. It takes time to tell whether a change in the environment will have the desired results. For most changes, children, families, and staff will need a few weeks to adjust and determine whether the change was helpful or not.

Space for Adults

Working in early childhood programs can be demanding both physically and psychologically. Programs should provide a comfortable space for the staff, parents, and visitors. Staff rooms should facilitate interactions as well as be a relatively quiet place for reflection and breaks. Staff need access to a preparation-and-planning space with a desk or table and chairs, cabinets in which to store resources and materials, and a computer, photocopier, laminator, etc. Staff require a secure place to store personal belongings.

Space is required in which to hold meetings with parents and with students on field placement. The program needs to consider the environment where parents exchange informal information with caregivers on a daily basis. It should include a resource area with a bulletin board to encourage parents to browse materials. Often programs ensure that the children's environment is wonderful, yet neglect to make sure the environment also meets adult needs.

Operating the Health and Safety Program

A coherent approach to health and safety in group settings for young children is always a work in progress. New information and research come forward from health professionals, and changes in public perceptions change the attitudes and opinions of families and early childhood practitioners. Directors must develop health policies for children and staff in keeping with current information. The right balance of challenge, safety, and strict health policies is critical. The key is to create a safe and healthy environment where families and children feel secure. Practitioners need to ask themselves how they can improve sanitation and reduce the spread of disease, eliminate injuries, and be prepared for emergencies.

Establishing safe policies includes hiring qualified and caring staff members; providing ongoing development for staff (for example, training in the duties and responsibilities of employers and workers regarding hazardous workplace materials); purchasing non-toxic art and play materials; maintaining adequate fresh air, ventilation, and heating in classrooms; monitoring the use of chemicals, including pesticides; frequently assessing the environment for potential hazards (through workplace inspections by health and safety representatives); and reducing the risk of harm or accident. In addition to establishing safe policies, the director recognizes that children will get sick, injured, or have difficulties because of their immature immune systems. Infants and toddlers frequently handle and mouth objects. A child's breathing zone is closer to the ground, where heavier pollutants are more concentrated.

Health Policies and Practices

Early childhood environments should protect the health and safety of children and adults. The director needs to work with staff to ensure that policies, procedures, and practices are developed and implemented to safeguard everyone's health and safety. Well considered health policies and procedures are critical to optimal early childhood development programs. Policies must be consistent with provincial/territorial regulations. Regular review of policies with staff assures their familiarity with the information and that enforcement will be more consistent. When practitioners are more aware of their responsibilities, they become more conscious of their actions. Policies must be practical and they must be used. They must not sit on a shelf or just be brought out during a licensing visit.

HEALTH AND WELLNESS POLICY AREAS

- daily admission and exclusion procedures
- children's health records
- administering medication
- care of a sick child
- notification of parents in the event of illness/injury
- staff health records
- staff illness
- training in first aid
- occupational health and safety policy for staff
- management of infectious disease
- reporting of suspected child abuse and neglect
- sanitation policies and practices (handwashing, diapering/toileting routines)
- food handling and mealtimes
- food preparation and storage

The benefits of incorporating healthy and safe practices are numerous for providers, children and families. For example, appropriate handwashing reduces the frequency of respiratory illnesses and diarrhea. This means fewer absences for children, fewer sick children at the program, and a reduction in staff illness that lowers the cost of care and the challenge of finding qualified replacement staff. As well, there can be fewer ear infections, which means the prevention of pain and potential hearing loss.

Secondly, programs need to increase the amount of physical activity in which the child engages daily and reduce the occurrence of childhood obesity. Cumulatively these practices can reduce visits to health care professionals and reduce health care costs as well as contributing to child and staff health.

Healthy settings depend on:

- thoughtful, strictly followed sanitary routines that are regularly monitored and evaluated. Careful diapering and toileting procedures, regular handwashing, and proper food handling are key;

- policies regarding staff and child illness and contagious conditions that minimize the likelihood of infection;

- careful attention to stress and adaptation of the environment and routines to reduce stress; and

- ensuring that staff follow universal precautions to prevent transmission of blood-borne diseases (Kaiser and Rasminsky 1995).

A checklist of sanitation practices should be developed and signed off with date and time by the staff member who is fulfilling the requirement.

The Canadian Pædiatric Society's *Well Beings: A Guide to Promote the Physical Health, Safety and Emotional Well-Being of Children in Child Care Centres and Family Day Care Homes* (1996) is an excellent reference on developing comprehensive health and safety policies. Included are sample health forms, detailed guidelines for admission and exclusion, and monitoring forms for health and sanitation. This resource was developed by the Canadian Pædiatric Society in consultation with early childhood development specialists.

Healthy Environments

Healthy children enjoy daily activities and have the energy and enthusiasm they need to grow and develop. Families feel increased confidence when a practitioner practices healthy habits and provides a healthy environment. In a healthy environment, children are sick less often and usually less severely.

Children in early childhood settings are highly vulnerable because of:

- close contact among children and adults, through feeding, diapering and toileting, and sharing objects, particularly moist sensory materials and items used in water play;

- children's underdeveloped immune systems;

- features of children's small body structures, such as the distance between the nose and throat and the middle ear;

- bumps and scrapes on the skin that can afford infectious agents entry into the body; and

- children's lack of understanding of how to protect themselves from infectious agents.

The incidence of infectious disease can be substantially reduced with good practices and education of caregivers in personal hygiene and environment sanitation. Pimento and Kernsted detail excellent practices in *Healthy Foundations in Child Care* (2004).

A key consideration in any early childhood facility is environmental control, including lighting, heating, cooling, and acoustics. Attention to these aspects can positively affect both child and adult behaviour as well as save money through energy saving practices.

Pediatric experts from government environmental health agencies and the American Academy of Pediatrics wrote the *Handbook of Pediatric Environmental Health* (1999), which summarizes concerns and offers practical remedies. There is a chapter dedicated to early childhood settings.

ENVIRONMENTAL HEALTH FACTORS

- good ventilation and lots of fresh air
- environment kept at an appropriate temperature (18–20° C) and free of drafts
- adequate humidity (30%–70%)
- a smoke-free environment
- clean air and water free from toxins and allergens
- a setting free of vermin
- pets that are free of disease and kept in clean cages

Protecting Staff Members' Health

Caregivers are exposed to infectious illnesses while working with young children. A staff member's illness can become a health hazard to children and co-workers, necessitate the costly replacement of the caregiver with a substitute, and cause a lack of consistency for the children.

Directors need to advocate for proactive employee health policies. Policies to protect the staff's health may include:

- pre-employment health assessment, tuberculin test, and updated immunizations;
- practicing good handwashing;
- professional development opportunities to learn techniques that reduce the physical hazards of work, methods for handling potentially hazardous products, and ways to deal with bodily fluids safely (visit www.ccohs.ca/oshanswers/information/govt.html to find the legislative and training requirements for each province);
- exclusion criteria for practitioners with infectious disease; and
- adequate paid sick leave.

Staff health records should include results of pre-employment physicals, updates at regular intervals, records of work injuries, and emergency instructions including information on the staff member's special health needs, such as allergies, physician, and contact instructions.

Building a Health Care Partnership with Families

Families appreciate knowing that the program is interested in their child's well-being. Early childhood practices play an important role in aiding children's health. Developing enlightened policies around health lets parents know that the program takes their child's well-being seriously. Programs should think through policies and practices regarding health and share them with parents at the pre-enrolment interview. Staff serve as liaisons in maintaining children's complete and up-to-date health records and aiding parents in identifying health resources. Parents should be required to provide a medical history for the child and an emergency contact form, which should be updated at least annually.

Young children often get sick. Preschoolers, on average, get between six and eight upper-respiratory infections per year. This makes life difficult for the child—who doesn't feel well—and the parents—who must find substitute care or take time off work. To make this situation easier on everyone:

Set clear guidelines when creating or reviewing health care policies;

Talk to a health care professional and the local licensing agency to ensure the program is up-to-date regarding health regulations.

Take into account the staffing and space available when setting program policies about children's illness and the administration of medication. For example, how ill is too ill to come to the program? What kind of attention can be provided for a child who is mildly ill without risking the health and safety of other children and caregivers?

Communicate policies to families. It is very helpful to put health policies in writing for families. When families know policies and the reasons behind them from the start, they can make plans and adhere to them.

Keep accurate records. The Canadian Pædiatric Society's *Well Beings* (1996) provides samples of forms to aid in keeping complete health records for every child, including: immunization history; medications the child is taking; any known **allergies**; and up-to-date information on the child's doctor, parents' or guardians' work phone numbers, and a contact to call in the event parents can't be reached. Check emergency information regularly with parents to keep it current.

Share observations. Since caregivers see the children every day, they are in a good position to spot any health concern that may be present. Let family members know if the child complains of any aches or pains or if a change in the child's behaviour has been observed—for example, a usually active child who seems listless, or a good eater who does not seem to be hungry.

Encourage families to exchange information. If a child is absent, ask the family for a reason. This way, caregivers can alert other families when a child in the group has a contagious illness, such as strep throat, that requires medical attention. Set up a bulletin board where health related information can be posted. Ask families to bring in articles they have found helpful or a copy of the pharmacists' prescription information sheet.

Strategies for communication with families are looked at in the next chapter.

Early Childhood Nutrition Programs

The director's role in planning the **nutrition** program is wide ranging. Ensuring adequate nutrition and sensible food policies and practices is important for healthy development due to the severe effects of hunger and malnutrition on the young child. Adequate nutrition is essential for growth and development as well as maintenance of the body. Brain research data indicate that including or not including certain food can affect brain development, from both physical and emotional perspectives. Dietitians of Canada have many useful resources on their website www.dietitians.ca. Another useful document is *Best Practices for Child Care Cooks* (George Brown College 2000).

The program's nutrition objectives may include planning the food services, providing and serving nutritious meals and snacks, helping parents to meet children's nutritional needs, identifying children's nutritional issues, and implementing nutrition education for children through daily activities.

The director generally oversees the menu planning. In an all-day program, this may involve breakfast, lunch, and two snacks daily. She can start by checking provincial/territorial regulations. Foods may be prepared at either an early childhood facility that complies with health standards or at another facility and transported to the program using appropriate sanitary containers and maintaining safe temperatures. A drawback to catered meals is that they are not under the control of the program. Some larger programs have a cook on staff and/or assistant to carry out this function. These employees should have appropriate qualifications and experience planning meals for young children. Programs are beginning to recognize the professional development needs of cooks.

Cooks need opportunities for professional development.

Source: Photo courtesy of Glenn Brown

Programs should access a nutritionist who is familiar with the unique nutritional needs and preferences of young children and can give advice on menu plans. Currently, no province or territory specifies any credentials for food service personnel, although in some regions, the public health department requires the completion of a food handler course. As part of a program's conditions for licence, public health inspectors will review the food preparation, equipment, and storage and serving facilities annually. In a smaller program or in a family child care home where the caregiver does all the cooking, meals must be ones that can be easily prepared. Regardless of how the food is provided at the program, the early child-hood practitioners are responsible for ensuring that the children have access to adequate nutrition each day. Generally, food consumed at the program constitutes a large portion of the child's daily intake, so meals must include the daily requirements as outlined in *Canada's Guide to Healthy Eating* (Canada 1992b).

Breastfeeding is necessary for optimal brain development, as outlined in the Nourish, Nurture, Neurodevelopment Resource Kit (CCCF and CICH 2001). Quality programs support the continuation of breastfeeding by providing a comfortable space for a mother to be with her child.

In some programs, financial constraints or limited kitchen facilities mean that parents must bring some or all of the food. Programs need a refrigerator in which to store food and some appliance with which to heat food (stove, microwave, or hot plate). Parents of infants often supply meals along with formula or breast milk. All food must be properly stored and labelled.

Both families and caregivers have an impact on children's nutritional habits. Although children decide on how much or whether to eat, adults are responsible for the foods offered. Some strategies programs employ to promote their partnership with families include:

Post weekly menus in an easily seen location so parents know what is served each day. This can aid parents in supplementing at home whatever the child had to eat at the program.

Provide parents with information about appropriate food choices. Share information through newsletters, bulletin boards, or handouts. If the child brings food from home for lunches or celebrations, suggest nutritious foods.

Keep parents informed about their child's food intake. Some programs have caregivers complete daily charts indicating how much the child ate. This written approach is particularly helpful with infant and toddler groups.

Develop a partnership with parents to plan food choices. The diets of very young children need to be carefully considered to avoid food allergies, digestive upsets, and poor nutrition.

A large number of young children are susceptible to food allergies and intolerances because their immune systems are immature. Ensure that parents inform staff of all food allergies and sensitivities. Common allergens include nuts, chocolate, dairy products, wheat, seafood, and eggs. When menus include these foods, be sure there is a substitute, preferably something similar in appearance that can be served to the child with the food allergy. Some programs have become nut free due to the severity of nut allergies for some children. To ensure that no allergens are served, staff should double-check all food before giving it to the child.

Be aware of families' food practices. Many families are practicing vegetarians, and programs should endeavour to accommodate these values.

Provide parents with recipes for foods the child particularly likes. Many children talk about a popular menu item, and the parent may want to prepare it at home.

Consider the child's ethnic background and incorporate foods using familiar ingredients. Some families may participate in new food experiences with the children.

Be sensitive to the family's financial resources. Some families do not have an adequate budget to buy a consistent amount of food throughout the month. Programs should have enough food available to provide extra servings to hungry children. Programs may work with food banks to supplement the food supply for families.

Early childhood programs should include nutritional education for young children. Children need opportunities to develop socially acceptable eating behaviours. Nutrition should be an integral part of the total curriculum, which should include opportunities to learn about food, good diets, and the preparation, storage, and origins of food.

STRATEGIES FOR DEALING WITH FOOD ALLERGIES

Develop written policies – Have parents request a doctor's statement outlining the specifics of the condition and what to do if the child is exposed. Post a list of children and their reactive foods in the food preparation and serving areas. Provide adequate training to administer emergency allergy medication. Have families provide additional medication to bring along on field trips.

Establish written procedures – Each person's role (caregiver and parent) is outlined. Staff should receive training from medical professionals on how to administer emergency medications.

Plan menus that consider allergies and intolerances – Children with allergies should eat food similar to other children to reduce feelings of difference or isolation. Allergy-specific cookbooks are useful for special diets such as wheat-free diets or diets for children who are lactose intolerant. Cooks must have professional development in planning special diets and label reading.

Ensure snack and mealtimes are safe – Staff must provide close supervision so the child does not have contact with offending foods or drinks or touch utensils that may contain traces of the allergens.

Plan and monitor food experiences thoroughly – Avoid using offending ingredients. Review recipes and labels for contents. Ensure food containers such as egg cartons or yogurt cups are cleaned thoroughly.

Communicate with families, children and other staff (including substitutes) – Successful management of food intolerances and allergies requires a co-operative, team approach.

Source: Mama Holland, "'That Food Makes Me Sick!' Managing Food Allergies and Intolerances in Early Childhood Settings," *Young Children* (NAEYC, Washington, DC) (March 2004), 42–46.

An important part of the curriculum is nutritional education for young children.

Summary

A comprehensive approach to high quality child health, safety, and nutrition services requires the co-operative involvement of directors, health professionals, families, and staff members. Menu planning and supervision of nutritional staff are an important part of a director's responsibilities. Nutrition at the program is highly important for young children, since program meals often provide up to 80% of the young child's nutritional requirements. As well, children develop lifelong eating habits as a result of early eating experiences. Staff members need to know the nutritional requirements of young children, how to provide a nutritious diet, and how to create an appropriate meal and snack environment by sitting with children and modelling appropriate nutritional habits.

Health affects every area of an individual's development. The health goals in an early childhood development program are to provide health care, prevent health problems, and coordinate health plans with families and children's health care professionals. Programs should also develop policies that promote the health of early childhood practitioners.

Key Terms and Concepts

Allergies,   p. 193

Nutrition,   p194

Maintenance,   p. 181

Activities

1.   Develop a health care policy. Your policy should include:

  •   practices you will put in place to protect children's health (diet, exercise, hygienic practices, fresh air, etc.)

  •   immunization schedule that assures all staff are up-to-date

  •   policies and practices concerning what to do when a child becomes ill

  •   responsibilities of parents and program regarding children who are ill (e.g., reporting child's exposure to contagious disease/keeping child at home)

  •   health information parents must provide to the program (immunizations documentation, child's health record)

  •   procedures for reporting workplace injuries

  •   opportunities for professional development to reduce the potential hazards of work (proper lifting techniques, safe handling of potentially hazardous products, procedures for cleaning up of bodily fluids)

  •   other policies

2.   Observe two meals in an early childhood development program. Evaluate the meals according to the following factors, rating each *excellent, good, fair,* or *poor*:

  •   attractiveness of location

  •   cleanliness of setting

  •   comfort of seating

  •   use of developmentally appropriate utensils

  •   appearance of food

  •   encouragement of child's independence

  •   food served considers ethnicity of children

  •   caregiver interaction with children

  •   general atmosphere

3.   Investigate the services for mildly ill children available in your community. For each service, outline the benefits and drawbacks, costs to the families, who operates the service, and the population using the service.

4.   Develop a plan for a field trip. Consider the following:

  •   age group for which the activity is developmentally suitable

  •   adult:child ratio required

  •   length of time the group will be away from the program

  •   form of transportation

  •   what staff will need to bring with them (e.g., food, beverages, diapers, first aid kit, emergency contacts, cellphone).

5.   Using a safety checklist, go through your home, including each room and any outdoor areas, and assess its suitability to be a family child care home. If applicable, be sure

to include both front yard and backyard, garage, shed, carport, and basement space. Note changes that could be made to your home to make it a safer place for a family with young children (your own family, if applicable) or for children in care. Examples include replacing/repairing loose tiles or installing a light fixture in a stairwell or a padlock on a shed.

Recommended Reading

American Academy of Pediatrics & American Public Health Association. *Caring for Our Children: National Health and Safety Standards - Guidelines for Out of Home Programs.* 2d ed. Washington, DC: American Academy of Pediatrics & American Public Health Association, 2002.

Canadian Institute of Child Health. *The Health of Canada's Children: A CICH Profile.* Ottawa: Canadian Institute of Child Health, 2000.

Canadian Pædiatric Society. *Well Beings: A Guide to Promote the Physical Health, Safety and Emotional Well-Being of Children in Child Care Centres and Family Day Care Homes.* Toronto: Creative Premises Ltd., 1996.

Pimento, B. and D. Kernsted. *Healthy Foundations in Child Care.* 3d ed. Toronto: Nelson, 2004.

Safe Kids Canada. *Child's Play: A Playground Safety Guide for Daycares, Schools and Communities.* Toronto: Safe Kids Canada, 1997.

Weblinks

www.cich.ca
Canadian Institute for Child Health (CICH)
This organization acts as a voice for children and is dedicated to improving children's health and well-being. The site lists many publications and resources for parents and health professionals. CICH works with governments to encourage appropriate policies and conducts research. One of its very useful publications is *The Health of Canada's Children: A CICH Profile* (Canadian Institute of Child Health 2000).

www.healthyenvironmentforkids.ca
Canadian Partnership for Children's Health and Environment
This website provides a variety of resources, such as guides to less toxic products, information on the impact of the environment on children's health, and a section with answers to frequently asked questions about children's environmental health in Canada.

www.canadian-health-network.ca
Canadian Health Network
Through a network of health information providers across Canada, this site provides easy access to a wide range of health information about how to lead a healthier life, take care of yourself and others, and help prevent illness and disease. There is specific information about children, people with special needs, and women.

www.ccohs.ca/oshanswers/information/govt.html
Canadian Centre for Occupational Health and Safety
This site provides resources on many issues such as injuries, work-related diseases, and ergonomics (the study of the relationship between people and their working environment, especially as it affects safety), as well as research on health and safety and lists of government contacts—including regional offices for occupational health and safety.

www.dietitians.ca
Dietitians of Canada
The Healthy Start for Life Environment Scan available in the Resource Centre of this site is designed to promote the development of healthy eating and activity patterns for toddlers and preschoolers. Parents and practitioners will find a plethora of resources at this site to aid with fussy eaters and to stimulate increased physical activity.

Building the Partnership with Families

Objectives

- **Emphasize the importance of family-centred practice.**

- **Heighten awareness of the role of the practitioner in supporting families.**

- **Increase awareness of the importance of program policies regarding diversity of values, beliefs, lifestyles, cultures, and the socio-economic status of families.**

- **Identify ways that families may participate.**

- **Discuss the purpose and identify the content of a family handbook.**

- **Increase awareness of a variety of strategies for achieving effective communication with families.**

- **Identify strategies for establishing relationships with families using home-based care.**

The jobs of the early childhood director and staff are ones that call for enormous skill in working with families. Families are at the core of an early childhood setting: practitioners share with families the responsibility for caring for young children. Some practitioners believe that working with families is the hardest part of their job—yet families are the people most connected with the children in the program, and strengthening relationships with families is an important way to improve interactions with children. With ever increasing numbers of young children being away from home for many hours a day, an important role for early childhood practitioners in their relations with families is as a facilitator of the transition children face between the two environments. Ongoing communication between families and program staff results in greater consistency for the children and is a key strategy for bridging the gaps between home and program. The younger the child, the more vital this consistency is. When caregivers work closely with families, fostering their sense of belonging and gaining their confidence, they strengthen each family's capacity to support their children for a lifetime.

The Changing Roles of Families

The family is and always will be the most important component in a child's life. The family is where children experience most deeply and closely the emotional and physical care vital to their well-being. **Parents** share this task of child rearing with early childhood practitioners. These days, mothers in the workforce are the norm. In 1997, almost two-thirds of women with children under age three and almost three-quarters of mothers with preschoolers worked outside the home. Mothers (and fathers) work at jobs other than parenting because they want and need to. For families with children under the age of 12, single parent families have tripled over the past two decades. These developments are creating a time crunch and parents have a shrinking amount of time to spend with the family. This merging of responsibilities for caring for and educating the child has prompted many parents and caregivers to reflect on their shared responsibilities.

Canadian families come in more sizes and shapes and represent more cultures than ever before. Each year, Canada welcomes about 150 000 immigrants, many belonging to visible minorities. It is important to gain an understanding of families as they exist in Canada today; as caregivers learn more about the diversity of families, they will become more competent.

The tug-of-war between work and home is becoming more challenging. A study conducted by the Conference Board of Canada (Bachmann and MacBride-King 1999) found that raising children, new and greater demands at work, and aging parents add to the challenges faced by working parents. Work lives are becoming more demanding and technology has brought with it the need for 24-7 support and availability. Half of the Canadians surveyed said they were experiencing high or moderate levels of stress. Among the reasons cited for this pervasive stress were fear of unemployment, low or frozen wages, heavy debt loads, or working fewer hours than needed. A child's early years were identified as the most demanding period in the lives of parents. Lack of family support plays a role, too. Increasing mobility means that family members often do not have anyone around to help out when children, parents, or elderly relatives are sick. Immigrant families often experience isolation and loneliness when they come to Canada.

Lone parents, carrying all the family responsibility with fewer resources, are the most stretched and stressed. Two-parent families are stressed, too. When parents work at low-paying, repetitive jobs or suffer from discrimination or lack of respect, all these effects are multiplied.

In the study *Ask the Children* (1999), Galinsky found that children worry when their parents are tired and stressed. She provides techniques that early childhood practitioners can use to help parents reduce stress:

- encouraging parents to think through the aspects of their jobs that cause them stress. This could be a focus of discussion at a parent meeting;

- helping parents to learn techniques for managing stress. Parents need to find ways to "turn off work," including activities such as meditating before leaving work, listening to music, or changing clothing;

- sharing with parents techniques for creating a homecoming ritual to smooth the transition from work to home; and

- encouraging parents to set realistic expectations about what they can accomplish at home. Being successful at two or three things is better than trying to achieve too many.

ARRANGING BACKUP CARE CHILD CARE

What are the alternative arrangements for caring for children of working parents? Backup child care is needed for stressed-out families. Nannies quit, the woman next door's children get sick so she can't look after the children, and the other parent who works from home and cares for the children may need to go out of town. The demands of jobs are often so intense that when child care arrangements break down, the parent may not be able to take the day off.

Addressing this problem, ChildrenFirst is a business that provides backup child care. It has over 30 centres serving more than 250 companies and 35 000 children. CIBC opened a ChildrenFirst facility in Toronto to be used exclusively by its employees when their regular caregiver is not available. The bank views the investment as strengthening their supports to their employees. The company found it more equitable to provide backup support for more employees than to run a regular child care program that would only serve a few families. This service is viewed as paying for itself because it supports employees to come to work.

Studies show that children worry when their parents are tired and stressed.

Family Involvement

Young children need their families and caregivers to work together. In a collaborative relationship, parties are mutually respectful; each person has ongoing input regarding the care of the child. A full partnership between a family and an ECEC setting means the family will have significant influence over their child's experience at the program. A full partnership with families means that parents, as a group, can have significant influence on the program's operations that determine the experience the children have at the program, including curriculum issues, allocation of resources, and family policies (such as drop off/pickup procedures).

Research shows that **family involvement** in the program is essential for the optimal development of the child. Follow-up studies of children who attended preschool programs show lasting gains through the children's school years into adulthood. One of the crucial factors was the involvement of families (Schweinhart, Barnes and Weikart 1993).

When families and early childhood practitioners respect the knowledge and strengths of each other and emphasize their common goals, these relationships empower both. Allred, Briem, and Black (1998) found that parents who feel ownership of their child's goals are more likely to consider these goals as top priorities in the family routine. Building relationships isn't always easy. Families may have very different expectations and styles from those of the practitioner. Parents may also bring negative attitudes and feelings about school and teachers based on their own childhood experiences. Communicating effectively and working together successfully may require a lot of effort, but the rewards can be great.

Each community has its own unique characteristics, and so do the programs within it. In order to be effective, family involvement must be tailored to fit the situation. Factors to be considered include the number of working parents, the stability of the community, and the values of the community. It is important to recognize the demands on working parents and not to interpret a reluctance to be involved as disinterest. Some families see home and the early childhood setting as separate entities and the program as the domain of the professionals. If the population in a community is largely transient, involvement will take a long time to develop, if it develops at all.

Families must feel welcome—that the program is their own, and not off limits. Early childhood development programs must revise the old perception of parents as merely guests at social occasions or helpers on field trips. A positive attitude toward parents and what they can contribute to the program should be modelled by the director and staff. Parents may feel threatened by the idea that the caregiver is very knowledgeable about children and fearful that their child rearing practices will be criticized. Some parents may feel inhibited due to their own unsuccessful experiences with school.

There are a number of strategies that can communicate feelings of acceptance and trust to families. Key are the parents' first impressions of the program—how they feel about both the physical environment and their initial interactions with staff. A less tangible thing that helps a parent feel welcome is the manner in which staff members handle telephone calls. It is very difficult to perceive what has the most impact on the parents' reactions to the program; directors need to be alert to any number of subtle factors that may be influencing parental attitudes and feelings.

Establishing the Connection

The director plays a critical role in facilitating the entrance of new families into the program. Families expect a great deal from programs that care for their children. These expectations vary and sometimes depend on the age of the child. Directors need to convey to families that they appreciate the parents' desire to make a good choice for their child. Every effort should be made to reassure parents that they will receive the information they need to make the right decision for their family, even if it means choosing another program.

A family's first impression of a program can be powerful. Many families who are searching for ECEC programs for the first time are unsure of how to make the right choice. Generally a visit is scheduled after an initial phone call. While the director plays the key role, staff should be integrally involved in developing family-friendly policies and implementing these on a daily basis.

The enrolment interview is the first opportunity to build rapport with a family. As well as going over the necessary forms and procedures, the interviewer should ask about the child's personality, how he or she likes to be held and comforted, and the child's preferred activities. Reassure the parents that they should never hesitate to ask a question or tell the caregiver how she or he can make things easier for the parents and child. Sometimes families also need reassurance that no caregiver will ever replace the parent in the child's heart. Seeing posted photographs of children and their families conveys a link between the program and the family home that can be reassuring.

It is helpful to provide families with a list of questions they may want to ask about the program and the staff working directly with the children. Another strategy is to personalize the visit to meet the family's needs.

Some questions that staff might pose to assess the messages sent to parents include:

- Did the parents receive the information they needed when they first telephoned the program?

- Does the program literature celebrate the uniqueness of each family and communicate the staff's willingness to meet individual needs?

- Do staff handle incoming calls in a manner that communicates that families are important?

- Were the parents encouraged to bring their child with them on their first visit to the program?

- Was the visit scheduled at a time when playroom staff were available to speak with the parents about the children's program?

Some programs encourage families to visit the program several times, with the child, before the child's actual start date. As well as making the child feel comfortable in the new setting, this enables the parent to see the staff in action and sense the loving care given to each child.

Building community in early childhood development programs is all about building relationships. When a new family joins the program, there is a unique opportunity to initiate a relationship that will last through the years that the child attends the program and beyond. The people in an ECEC program can become a new extended family for the child and parents—the equivalent of a whole new set of aunts, uncles, and cousins. In order to support a child's physical, social, emotional, and intellectual well-being and development, quality ECEC programs need to support the whole family.

Variety of Family Structures

The structures of families in ECEC programs vary widely from the traditional family of two married parents who live together with their biological offspring. Today's families include lone-parent families, teen parents, blended families, grandparents raising grandchildren, foster families, and same-sex parents. The Vanier Institute of the Family defines family as "a group of two or more people, children, siblings, foster parents, grandparents, uncles, aunts, cousins, friends, and any others who consider themselves a family" (2000). Family lifestyles differ due to such factors as cultural practices, religious beliefs, the home and community in which the family resides, and the responsibilities children have for their own care or the care of younger siblings. Other lifestyle factors include dual-career couples, special needs, employment/unemployment, and income levels.

Within each culture, there are many variations. Educational level, socio-economic status, occupation, temperament, and personal experience all influence values and beliefs. So do all the other cultures we belong to—race, language, ethnicity, religion, gender, workplace, age, sexual orientation, political orientation, time, and place. Each family has a unique culture all its own. When children and families have different cultural, racial, and linguistic backgrounds from their caregivers, practitioners are challenged to establish positive and appropriate adult–child interactions and learning situations. To work effectively with all types of families, many staff need to increase their understanding of ethnic, cultural, and socio-economic backgrounds different from their own.

The structure and lifestyle of a family are known to influence its ability to participate in, and its feelings of comfort about, program-related activities. Therefore, early childhood practitioners must know the families of the children they are working with in order to plan and provide flexible family-involvement opportunities that are suited to a variety of circumstances.

As practitioners accept the responsibility for becoming more aware of the diversity of lifestyles of children and their families, they will want to modify traditional involvement strategies. When planning an event or activity, practitioners need to be aware of the barriers that make family involvement difficult. A fuller understanding of individual families helps practitioners become more culturally competent and culturally responsive and assists them in creating strategies for involving all the families with children in the program.

Family-Centred Approach

"**Family-centred** care" means respectful collaboration between families and early childhood practitioners. Some of the basic premises are:

PREMISES OF FAMILY-CENTRED CARE

- The family is central to the child's life.
- Each family has its own strengths, competencies, resources, and ways of coping.
- Every family is respected and accepted on its own terms, without judgments or preconceptions.
- Each family's race, culture, ethnicity, religion, language, and socio-economic status is respected.
- Services and programs are effective to the degree they support the family in meeting the needs it has identified itself.

When practitioners and parents regard each other as equals, recognize each other's expertise, and acknowledge that differences in opinions are normal, they can use their combined strengths to develop trust, set goals, make plans, and solve problems. The child, the family, and the program all benefit.

Family-centred practice is based upon beliefs and values that:

• acknowledge the importance of the family in child development;

• respect the families as decision makers for their children and themselves; and

• support families in their role of raising and educating their children.

This family-centred perspective is radically different from the once-traditional model, in which professionals considered themselves experts who determined and implemented interventions for children without family input or participation. Family-centred practice is not defined by a particular set of forms or procedures; rather, it requires a willingness to embrace values that are respectful of and lead to collaboration with families.

The first step is to establish the families and children as the focus of the service. The needs of all family members must be recognized. Focus on the family as the constant in the child's life and acknowledge the influential role of the family in the child's development.

Second, support and respect family decision making by regarding family members as essential members of the team and primary decision makers about their child's education and care. Lastly, provide flexible, responsive, and comprehensive services designed to strengthen child and family functioning. This principle incorporates the need to respect family culture and diversity and help families to mobilize their informal resources, including friends and neighbourhoods. All families can benefit from information related to community resources. Some will need to access these services for their child and family. Early childhood settings that incorporate family resource centres and work closely with community services promote caring communities for children and their families.

A key feature of a family-centred collaboration is that it is a constantly evolving relationship. It creates an environment in which children and parents feel free to ask questions. There is a continual process of evaluation and rethinking approaches. No one is passive or complacent. The relationship changes and grows.

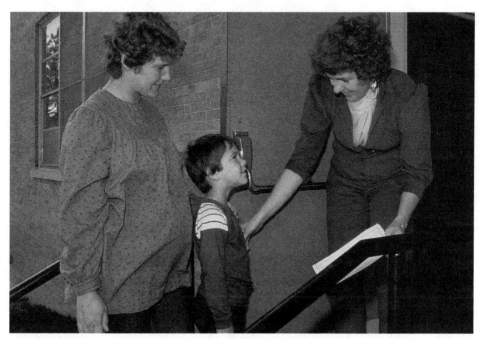

Ongoing communication between families and program staff provides greater consistency for children.

Communicating with Families

Communication is the foundation of a solid partnership. When families and early childhood staff communicate effectively, positive relationships develop, problems are more easily solved, and child outcomes improve. Too often, program communication is one way without the chance to exchange ideas and share perceptions. The two-way sharing of information that characterizes effective communication between the home and early childhood setting is vital to improved child outcomes. Partnering requires give-and-take conversation, goal setting for the future, and follow-up.

Contacts with families range from informal interactions during arrivals and departures to more structured **parent conferences**. Through these interactions, practitioners and families communicate whatever information they feel is important or of mutual interest. Interchanges occur most commonly and frequently each morning and at the end of the day. Pick up and drop-off times are often hurried or even stressful. There may be language and/or cultural differences that may present challenges. These are critical obstacles to overcome. It is key that early childhood practitioners maximize the opportunities presented by this interchange and make it an important part of their daily routine. These informal contacts and exchanges are the single most productive aspect of family involvement.

During these transition times, a good rule of thumb in exchanging information with families is to provide information they can use or do something about—such as about the child's day at the program (or time at home), behaviour, or health concerns. This kind of discussion will often lead to decision making. In general, parents of younger children communicate more frequently than those who have older children.

Staff should monitor their contacts with families and make sure that they connect with every parent on a daily basis. This can involve a chat or, simply, eye contact and a smile or wave. Directors need to ensure that staffing is sufficient to allow caregivers to feel

SUCCESSFUL PROGRAMS

- Use a variety of communication tools on a regular basis, seeking to facilitate two-way interactions.
- Disseminate information and compensate for any language barriers (e.g., translate communications to assist non-English-speaking families).
- Schedule opportunities for family participation, keeping in mind the varied schedules of working, studying, and stay-at-home parents and the need to provide care for the children while families participate.
- Communicate with families regarding positive child outcomes, behaviour, and achievement as well as concerns.
- Facilitate opportunities for families to communicate with other community professionals, such as resource teachers and elementary school staff, and provide space for meetings.
- Provide ongoing staff development regarding effective communication techniques and the importance of two-way communication between the program and the family.

confident that the children are well supervised while a caregiver is speaking with a parent. Often, many parents arrive to pick up their children at the same time, which can be challenging for the staff. Rotating shifts can mean that the child's primary caregiver is not available for discussion at pickup time. Since these interactions are so vital, there need to be safeguards to ensure that such communication occurs regularly. When staff determine that no regular contact is occurring, some other mode of communication should be devised.

Multiple information vehicles should be employed that include notes, journals, documentation panels, web wages, and meetings. Telephone calls are both convenient and effective ways to communicate. Some parents have work situations that allow them to receive telephone calls freely and they may welcome the caregiver keeping in touch. Others may wish to be called only when there is a specific concern or in an emergency.

The increase in the use of technology has opened up new possibilities for communicating with families using tools such as e-mail and pagers. Although technology will never replace direct contact with families, it can be extremely effective when families and teachers do not have opportunities for casual contact as in rural areas. Technology can enable staff to provide quick updates on the child's progress. E-mail can be a good way to remind families of events and requests for signed permission forms. Some parents may feel more secure with a program that enables them to link to video cameras in the playroom. Families may log on at a convenient time to observe their child at play. However, such approaches are not substitutes for face-to-face communication.

Communicating Policies

Families need to have a clear understanding of program policies and expectations. Policies that are ambiguous are a potential source of conflict between families and staff. Most programs provide families with information during the initial orientation and on a daily basis. During an orientation meeting, the director reviews the program's philosophy, purpose, and mandate, in addition to its policies and procedures. Families should understand their rights, how the program functions, and that they have access to minutes of board meetings. Families ought to become aware of the policies as well as the rationale for them. For example, when parents enroll their child, they should be informed that the program cannot operate with stability unless all fees are paid on time. Second, a policy manual should be provided for the parents' own reference. When changes occur, parents should be kept up-to-date; ideally, parents will be involved in the development of policies. Providing parents with a policy handbook serves to reduce the potential for conflict. A handbook can help parents to better understand the rationale for policies concerning food or transitional objects from home or why they need to inform the program if they will be arriving late for pickup.

However, conflicts can still arise when a parent claims she or he was not informed. On occasion, parents may be given information during transitions times when they have other things on their minds. The transition from home to the program can be a stressful time for families; it is rarely the best time to ask parents to remember details about program policies. Phrase policies in clear language and communicate them to families in a way they can understand. Providing opportunities for families to have input into the development, evaluation, and revision of policies enhances the likelihood that families will comply with the policies.

Early childhood practitioners identify the challenge of ill children as one of the most difficult they encounter. For parents, trying to continue to meet the demands of work or school while managing the care of their ill child can be extremely stressful. When a parent receives a call from the ECEC program to pick up a child who is ill, in addition to worrying about the child, the parent is faced with rescheduling his or her work, making a doctor's appointment, and returning to the program in the middle of the day. Few employees have a family responsibility benefit. Consequently, some parents may have to use their own sick leave benefits, if eligible, or take time off work without pay. These factors help to explain why some parents bring their child to the program even when the child is not feeling well.

Early childhood development practitioners are responsible for establishing with families—at the time of enrolment—a clear understanding of the program's exclusion policy. Staff:child ratios make it impossible to give the required individual attention to a child who is sick, and most children would prefer to be at home when they are ill. When considering an informed health policy, directors should refer to *Well Beings*, in which the Canadian Paediatric Society (1996) recommends exclusion criteria for ECEC programs.

Another potential point of conflict that policy should deal with is safety precautions, such as who is authorized to pick up the child. Families must feel confident that caregivers will not permit an unauthorized person to take their child from the program. However, occasionally a parent is unable to get to the program and he or she may arrange for someone who is not listed as authorized to pick up their child without communicating this to the program. It is necessary to clearly communicate the program procedures and rationales to families.

Understanding the potential sources of conflict and developing strategies to prevent and overcome them will ultimately enhance the relationship between early childhood development practitioners and families and benefit the children in care.

SUCCESSFUL PROGRAMS 2

- Communicate the importance of positive relationships between parents and their children.
- Establish policies that support and accept family responsibilities and recognize the variety of parenting traditions and practices within the community's cultural and religious diversity.
- Ensure that staff members demonstrate respect for families and the family's primary role in the rearing of children.

Family Handbook

A well-organized, effectively written, and attractively designed family handbook communicates basic program information and is given to parents during the enrolment process. It should outline the obligations and responsibilities of families and staff. Caring for children is a co-operative effort shared by staff and parents, and the development of the parent handbook is an example of putting this commitment into action. Ultimately, the director determines what information families need and the most effective way to convey it to them.

Information included in the handbook needs to be tailored to fit the program and the family population. The choice of wording should suit the families' level of understanding; the handbook should use language that is readily understandable. It should convey a sense of respect and acceptance of families. Whenever possible, provide written information in the family's primary language. Arrange the information in a logical and attractive manner that makes information easy to locate. Policy manuals should be living documents that evolve with the changing needs of the individual program. The director needs to consider how often the information will be revised and how changes will be communicated to families. In writing, reviewing, and revising the policy manual, the director should draw on the expertise of families, staff, and professionals in the community.

The handbook serves as a valuable orientation tool for families who are new to the program, as well as a handy reference for currently enrolled families. Parents need to know to keep emergency information current. The list of suggested items that follows is not exhaustive, but provides a useful starting point for content:

- *Philosophy:* a brief statement of centre philosophy and a description of the services of the program.

- *Policies:* information about program policies that directly affect families, such as the hours of operation, fees and arrangements for payment (including policies with regard to absences), and pre-admission requirements such as immunization records and completion of emergency information and health history forms.

- *Health and safety:* a description of health and safety precautions to be taken by the family and staff, including the program policy on administration of medication during the program, when an ill child would be excluded from the program, the procedures used by the staff if a child becomes ill while at the program, expected arrival and drop-off times and procedures, and so forth.

- *Program:* an outline of the daily program along with an explanation of how it fits the program philosophy.

- *Food:* details about meals and snacks and any adjustments to the posted menus; procedures for accommodating special diets or restrictions; an explanation of the program's policy regarding celebrations such as birthdays and holidays.

- *Guidance:* an outline the program's philosophy and policies regarding behaviour guidance.

- *Legal:* a description of the legal obligations of the staff to report any evidence of suspected child abuse; staff responsibilities to do with parental custody and access.

- *Family resources:* the philosophy of the program regarding participation and resources available to families; services available, such as parent conferences to discuss the individual child, group meetings, referrals, and so on.

- *Items from home:* guidelines for the child's use of transitional objects; bringing toys and food from home.

The handbook is a convenient tool for acquainting families with the program and helping them to understand their responsibilities and what to expect. However, it must be supplemented with other written and verbal communications to keep parents informed of program events and the progress of their child.

POLICY FOR CUSTODY AND ACCESS ARRANGEMENTS

Early childhood facilities should have clear and consistent policies regarding the status of children when family arrangements are governed by custody and related court orders. The most common type of custody arrangements are:

- Informal arrangements—usually emerging from a situation of abandonment by one parent or an agreement within a family.

- Written agreements—developed by a family, court-appointed family advocate, or mediator determining custody or access arrangements.

- Court orders—including temporary, continuing, and permanent custody orders, supervision orders, interim orders, and restraining orders.

Guidelines

- Enrolment or registration forms should request information about the existence and details of a family's custody arrangement and separation agreement.

- It should be made clear to enrolling families that copies of written custody arrangements, either legal or informal, should be submitted to the program to be placed in the child's file. Without information on custody and court orders, programs will not be able to honour legal and informal agreements.

- The policy should include reference to who has access to a child's files and information about the child's progress.

- In circumstances where an enrolling parent informs the staff that the other parent is not permitted to pick up the child, the staff should inform the enrolling parent that, without a legal custody document or court order, it is difficult to deny any parent access to their child.

- Some programs develop a policy regarding the visitation of parents on-site when there are custody arrangements.

Policy statement

If the parents have agreed to live separately, the program will assume that the information from the enrolling parent will be followed. However, without a custody or court order on file at the program, staff cannot deny access to the non-enrolling parent.

If custody has not been legally determined and conflict between the parents/guardians is evident, the program may not be able to care for the child unless both parents and/or other family members sign a written agreement confirming details regarding authorization for pickup and access to information about the child.

If the family has a custody or court order, a copy must be placed in the child's file and details about all arrangements contained in the legal documents will be followed at all times.

Staff will call the police if assistance is required to enforce a custody or court order.

Verbal and written information about the child will be shared with the enrolling parents/guardians unless otherwise agreed upon. Permission to share information with others will reflect the policy on confidentiality.

Source: Adapted from the Policies and Procedures for Child Care Programs, *Tough and Sensitive Issues, Part I*, developed by Westcoast Child Care INFORM, Vancouver, BC, September 2000.

Parent Participation

Family members can bring tremendous skills and knowledge that benefit the program. The concept of family participation in an ECEC program is multi-faceted, embracing a range of options and levels. Parent participation will vary according to each family's ability to contribute and according to their needs. Some families will invest a great deal of their time and energy in the program. Others need all their resources to cope with the stresses they face. Early childhood practitioners must be flexible, able to recognize each family's capabilities and needs and set expectations or provide support accordingly. Parents may sit on policy-making committees, participate in fundraising, volunteer in the playroom, or act as resources. Parents may be involved in operational aspects such as hiring or helping to evaluate staff.

When parents volunteer, both families and programs reap benefits. Parents express greater confidence in programs when they have opportunities to participate regularly. They feel more welcome and appreciated. In addition, when a parent assists in program events or activities, it communicates to the child, "I care about what you do here." At its best, volunteer work is valuable to the program and meaningful to the parent. Capitalizing on the expertise and skills of parents and family members can provide much-needed support to program staff in meeting children's needs.

One of the main rationales for involving families is that people feel a commitment to decisions in which they have a part. And, through volunteering, parents may develop decision making and other skills that can help them in other aspects of their lives. McBride (1999) identifies the following strategies to promote family choices and decision making:

- Help families to summarize what they want for their children and themselves by coming up with a list of goals written in the parents' own words.

- Acknowledge families as the true experts on their child.

- Work with parents to generate options for intervention strategies, and let parents determine which options best suit their needs and resources.

- Seek parents' opinions about changes in the program or playroom practices.

- Provide families with choices about when and where they will be involved in their child's education and care.

- Include family members on committees and advisory boards that make decisions about the program.

- Ask all parents regularly about how well the program is doing and what changes they might like to see.

Effective decision-making boards can promote a true partnership between families and the early childhood development program that provides support for the program, empowerment for the families, and increased mutual understanding. Parents can help to set policy by serving as members of an advisory committee or as family representatives on the board of directors (or a board committee such as finance or personnel).

Studies have shown that programs where families are involved in decision making and advocacy bode well for child outcomes and have greater public support. Effective partnerships develop when each partner is respected and empowered to fully participate in the decision making process. Programs that actively enlist parent participation and input communicate that families are valued as full partners in the care and education of their children.

Parents as Members of Advisory Boards

Advisory boards give families influence in the programs their children attend and may contribute to other goals. Many ECEC programs include parents as members of planning and advisory groups that work with the director and other staff, often as a think-tank or sounding board for program issues. Advisory boards may meet several times a year to be consulted by the management of the program. They offer advice and resources as well as raise concerns about current and future issues that affect the quality of the program for their children. They may suggest topics for parent meetings. In some programs, parents serve as playroom representatives who keep other families abreast of new activities in the program. As well, advisory board members may be available to respond to parents' questions and concerns. Parent representatives may attend staff or board of directors meetings. Generally, advisory boards have less power than boards of directors.

Standard

Working with Families

Establish and maintain an open, co-operative partnership with each child's family that supports the family in meeting their responsibilities for the child, by:

- demonstrating to families respect and consideration for differences in child rearing values and practices for individual, cultural, and community values and traditions;

- demonstrating to families a respect for their position as the child's primary caregiver and creating opportunities for families to feel comfortable in expressing their wishes and needs;

- providing families with information about service philosophy, policies, approaches, and procedures before the child begins attending the program;

- using a variety of approaches to encourage families to share information about the child on a regular basis, including the child's likes, dislikes, and schedule and familial preferences regarding child rearing practices, diet, and dress;

- assisting family members to feel welcome at any time that the child is present;

- using a variety of approaches, including interpretation and the translation of materials as required, to communicate with families about the child on a regular basis, including the results of observations about the child's daily experiences and development;

- providing a variety of user-friendly ways for families to be involved in program activities to the extent they wish;

- providing a variety of user-friendly ways for families to participate in program decision making;

- working co-operatively with families to develop and implement program activities and caregiving routines that reflect the children's cultural and religious backgrounds and the lifestyles of the children's families;

(continued)

- using negotiation and positive problem-solving strategies to find solutions to differences of opinion or difficulties; and

- keeping family enquiries, conversations with families, and children's records confidential.

Strengthen and empower the adults in their roles as parents, nurturers, and home child care providers and empower them to act on their own behalf, by:

- including them in a meaningful and active fashion in defining and determining their wishes, needs, and goals for their child;

- assisting them to identify and use their own strengths to address needs and concerns;

- being responsive to family requests for information and assistance;

- providing families with information about child development and suggestions to assist them in their parenting role in a way that respects cultural differences in child rearing practices and the family's right to transmit their values, beliefs, and cultural heritage to their children, encouraging them to use their home language with their children and to teach the practitioner about their culture;

- providing accurate and up-to-date information about other community agencies, programs, and supports; and

- assisting families to develop and maintain social support networks.

Source: Gillian Doherty, in Canadian Child Care Federation (CCCF), *Partners in Quality: Tools for Practitioners in Child Care Settings* (Ottawa: CCCF, 2000).

Members of a Board of Directors

Non-profit early childhood development programs are operated by a volunteer **board of directors**. As discussed in chapter 3, the director of the program is accountable to the board of directors. She reports regularly to the board on all aspects of the program, including finances, personnel issues, and programs. Often the board includes members of the community with specific knowledge and talents. Participation on a board of directors gives parents an opportunity to influence the policies that govern the program and the staff. When considering issues, board members need adequate information on which to base their decisions. Parents in these roles may need training to help them identify problems, generate solutions, understand regulations, and effectively communicate recommendations to a power structure.

There are challenges to involving families on boards. Some parents of young children have a limited understanding of issues facing early childhood development programs. Often they have many other demands on their time, and their awareness of routines, activities, and interactions are incomplete. As well, some parents may have trouble separating their personal agenda from their role as parent representatives. Occasionally, they may face a conflict of interest—if they vote to raise staff salaries, then their own program fees will increase. The director plays an important role in helping parents understand links between working conditions for the staff and the quality of service provided. (The need for ongoing public education is elaborated on in chapter 11, "Advocating for Canada's Children.")

Occasionally, it is challenging for caregivers to accept that they are accountable to people who have no formal education in the discipline. Caregivers who are comfortable

Standard

Relationships with Children's Families

The ability to maintain an open, co-operative relationship with each child's family requires . . .

Required skills and abilities	Required core knowledge
Child care practitioners are able to:	Child care practitioners know:
a) Use a variety of methods to encourage each family to share information regularly, including information about the child's likes and dislikes and the family's preferences regarding child rearing practices, diet, and dress.	1) The philosophy and policies of the child care setting in which they work.
b) Use a variety of approaches to communicate on a regular basis with families about the child's daily experiences, progress, and development in a way that assists families to set goals for the child and provide feedback on the child care program.	2) The major challenges facing families in Canada today, balancing work and family responsibilities, working non-standard hours or shifts, and how they may affect how children develop and what their parents need or want from child care.
c) Listen and respond to each family's views in a manner that supports and respects the individual family and encourages families to express their needs, desires, and preferences.	3) Some of the challenges facing newcomers to Canada, for example, adjusting to a different culture with different behavioural expectations, and how they may affect both how children develop and what their parents need or want from child care.
d) Use a variety of approaches to help families to express their opinions about the experiences their child is having or has had in the child care program and the experiences they would like their child to have.	4) Effective listening strategies with children and with adults.
e) Approach a family to discuss a problem that their child has or a problem with the child in the child care setting.	5) Effective communication strategies with children and with adults.
f) Effectively address differences of approach or opinion.	6) Effective strategies for addressing differences in child rearing approaches or opinion.

Source: Gillian Doherty, *Occupational Standards for Child Care Practitioners* (Ottawa: Canadian Child Care Federation, 2003).

with parental influence and control tend to be those who are experienced and knowledgeable in their field and confident in their ability to resolve different perspectives.

Home Child Care and Families

In deciding to become a family child care provider, the provider invites families as well as their children into her home. Developing and maintaining a good working relationship with parents is crucial to the healthy development of the children served. The child's life is shared by the parents and family child care provider as partners. Parents want to know about their child's day. In order to smooth transitions and provide consistency, the family child care provider needs to know what occurred in the child's life and how the child felt and acted since leaving care the previous day. Families are keen to hear the joys and achievements of the child's time in care as well as any concerns.

As trust develops, problems are more easily resolved. To achieve this openness, family child care providers can:

- Support parents by trying to understand their situation and perspective.
- Try to share something with each parent every day.
- Appreciate each child and talk with the parent about observations.

Often new caregivers are eager to meet everyone's needs. It is important for caregivers to recognize that they cannot please all of the parents all of the time. They may overcommit themselves, working too many hours or taking on too many children. It is necessary to set realistic expectations.

Family child care providers have to determine how to handle the unique needs of each individual family. Flexibility is desirable within a framework of policies and expectations and the plans for the day. Working families need consistent child care and young children need consistent caregivers. The family child care provider should arrange for reliable substitutes who know the children and can fill in when the provider is ill, on vacation, or unable to provide care for other reasons.

The family child care provider should communicate her expectations and preferences to families in writing (this is discussed in chapter 5). Use of contracts, newsletters, daily notes, or bulletin boards saves time, avoids misunderstandings, and allows the provider to focus conversations on less routine matters. Sometimes listening to a parent supportively, without making judgments or recommendations, makes a big difference. Time spent in this way may be time gained in the long run.

Many families feel guilty about entrusting their child to another caregiver. Family child care providers must come to terms with this reality so that they can act in ways that are best for children, parents, and themselves. While caring for children, the family child care provider usually becomes very close to their families. Setting a professional tone includes respecting confidentiality, which is critical to building trusting relationships with families. Some providers develop friendships with families. This can be rewarding for all, but it is important that the caregiver not try to be a social worker or therapist for the parent. When families need special help, the family child care provider needs to refer them to the appropriate community service.

Resources for Families

All families, at some time or another, need or want more support than their network of family and friends can provide. Often families have adequate support networks and can access services without the assistance of the program. But for those families who do require help, the rapport established with staff through daily interactions can be crucial. Often these interchanges can be instrumental in aiding families to get the help they need. It is necessary to respect the parents' ability to make choices on their own. Up-to-date information and other resources can help families to make good choices and decisions affecting their children and themselves. Early childhood practitioners, particularly the director, should make themselves aware of the different resources available in their community.

There are many services that can provide support for a wide range of family concerns. Practitioners need to keep current and be aware of subsidy waiting lists, costs, admission criteria, and so on. Families may benefit from knowing about food banks, where to get inexpensive children's clothing, or criteria for accessing bursaries for program costs. This is where the staff's well-developed networks with other professionals are critical; often, the program staff can smooth the way for families seeking service. Once the information has been researched, staff must discern what will be the most effective way to encourage families to utilize resources. For some, a display of pamphlets from different organizations—in the parent resource centre or on a bulletin board—is all they need.

A must-have resource for early childhood development programs is *Towards Partnership: Multi-Language Resources for Families in Child Care* (2001), developed by Westcoast Child Care Resource Centre in British Columbia. Topics include welcome, registration, gradual entry, language learning, guidance, play, and evaluation. Translations include Mandarin, French, Punjabi, Serbo-Croatian, Spanish, and Vietnamese. The handouts in this collection can be copied and reproduced without permission. Another way to provide information is by including brief descriptions of services in the program newsletter. And remember, many families will appreciate receiving the information through a discussion with the early childhood practitioner.

Community programs are used to strengthen programs and families and improve child outcomes. Every early childhood development program is part of a community and fulfills important community goals. Similarly, communities offer a wide array of resources valuable to ECEC programs and the families they serve. When a program and its community work together, both are strengthened and both make greater gains than either could accomplish on its own.

Quality ECEC programs provide information and support for families. The old conception of professionals as good-willed experts dispensing knowledge and advice has given way to a collaborative approach in which families and professionals are seen as partners. A key to this approach is to know when and how to call upon other professionals and resources in the community. The concept of parent support recognizes that all families have strengths and that most families are doing a good job. The primary role of families is recognized and respected: families know their child in ways no one else can. And there is acknowledgment, without blame, that families have limits to their knowledge, skills, and resources. For many families, parent education and support can provide additional knowledge and reassurance. It can be a powerful prevention tool. This support can directly combat many of the parental factors that can be harmful for children: isolation, stress, unrealistically high expectations, and a lack of knowledge about non-damaging discipline methods (Bennett 1989).

The journal *Zero to Three* polled 3000 families about their knowledge of child development. It found there are major gaps between what families believe are effective parenting practices and what child development specialists know to be appropriate expectations for young children. The report, *What Grown-Ups Understand about Child Development: A National Benchmark Survey* (Yankelovich 2000a), suggests that these misunderstandings can have a serious impact on the mental health of young children. Some of the findings:

- More than 50% of the respondents thought using flash cards with young children would increase their intellectual ability. Child development specialists, on the other hand, stress that using flash cards does little to help children develop important concepts about their world.

- More than 60% of grandparents surveyed said that repeatedly picking up a three-month-old crying infant would spoil the baby. In contrast, child development experts encourage this type of empathic response to a baby's crying as a means of building trust and a secure attachment to caregivers.

- More than 60% of families of children under the age of seven think spanking is an appropriate regular form of discipline and 25% expect a three-year-old to sit still for an hour or more. Child development specialists know that such unrealistic expectations can result in abusive families.

Families do not raise their children in a vacuum. Policies and programs have a direct impact on the ability of families to support their child's healthy growth and development. The results of this study underscore the importance of providing accurate information about child development and practices to families. (For more information, visit the *Zero to Three* website at www.zerotothree.org).

Summary

Today's rapidly changing world holds many social and economic challenges, and virtually all families with young children need some support. Supports given to families will have the most impact in the first years of a child's life. Early childhood development programs must adapt to accommodate changes in society and provide much-needed support to families facing considerable challenges. The director is responsible for setting the tone of the program. A major aspect of her role is to support staff members in establishing effective relationships with families and gaining an appreciation of the many family structures they will encounter. Parent participation in early childhood development programs benefits the program, the child, and the parent. There are many ways parents can be involved in the program. At the same time, the program must be realistic about what parents can do and help individual families to participate in a way that is both meaningful and manageable for them. A collaborative approach that recognizes parents as partners is key. Directors should review policies and procedures to reduce obstacles to participation and ensure a family-centred approach. Staff need to be aware of community organizations that can be helpful to families.

Key Terms and Concepts

Advisory board,   p. 214

Board of directors,   p. 215

Family-centred,   p. 206

Family involvement,   p. 204

Parent,   p. 202

Parent conferences,   p. 208

Activities

1. Determine if there is a directory of social service agencies available for your community. If not, survey your community and identify potential resources and support systems for families of young children.

2. Visit an ECEC program. What evidence of communication with parents do you see? Look at bulletin boards, pictures on display, and other written material. What kind of interaction do you notice between parents and caregivers?

3. Interview several directors of early childhood development programs about their goals for parent participation. How do their goals differ?

4. In groups of three, role play that a parent is inquiring about the program, with the possibility of enrolling his child. Give him a brief explanation of the program.

Recommended Reading

Canadian Child Care Federation. *Canadian Institute of Child Health Nourish, Nurture, Neurodevelopment Resource Kit.* Ottawa: Canadian Child Care Federation, 2001.

Newman, R. *Building Relationships with Parents and Families in School-Age Programs.* Nashville, TN: School-Age Notes, 2000.

Shimoni, R. and J. Baxter. *Working with Families: Perspectives for Early Childhood Professionals.* 3d ed. Don Mills, ON: Pearson Addison-Wesley, 2005.

Wilson, L. *Partnerships: Families and Communities in Canadian Early Childhood Education.* 3d ed. Toronto: Nelson, 2005.

Westcoast Child Care Resource Centre. *Towards Partnership/Vers un Partariat: Multi-Language Resources for Families in Child Care/Ressources multilingues pour les familles ayant un enfant en garderie.* Ottawa: Westcoast Child Care Resource Centre, 2001.

Weblinks

www.wft-ifb.ca
Canadian Child Care Federation
At this forum administered by the Canadian Child Care Federation, families help other families endeavouring to balance work and family life by sharing strategies that work. Categories include chores, child care, food, children with special needs, working at home, and workplace support.

www.investinkids.ca
Invest in Kids
Invest in Kids is a national charitable organization whose goal is to help families make the most of their children's first five years. This website provides parents with a wealth of expert information, including what to expect as your child grows and develops, child development and parenting tips, and a variety of resources and links to other websites.

www.chatdanger.com
Chatdanger, Childnet International
This site is administered by Childnet International, an organization dedicated to making the Internet a great place for children. Its goal is to alert parents to the dangers of chat rooms and provide safety advice.

Financial Matters

chapter 10

Objectives

- **Outline the items in an operating budget.**

- **Discuss the director's role.**

- **Identify types of budgets.**

- **Review major categories of expenses.**

- **Describe the budget process.**

- **Discuss sources of income.**

- **Review the family child care business budget.**

- **Identify accounting procedures.**

- **Discuss the value of using a computer for administrative financial tasks.**

- **Discuss small-business practices and marketing in relation to the field.**

The nature of a child's experience in an early childhood development program depends in large measure on whether the full costs of providing a quality service can be sustained. The factors that promote quality have a price. Better quality programs spend more per child on staff wages and benefits, including administrative salaries, than programs providing lower quality. When families alone are responsible for the costs of early childhood development, the need to keep programs affordable constrains quality. (Chapter 10, on advocacy, proposes that when all Canadians have a stake in the quality of services provided to young children more potential resources will be available to pay for quality.) The nature of a child's early childhood experience is determined by a program's ability to:

- Foster meaningful relationships between children and adults by limiting group size and the number of children per adult, promoting continuity for children, and enhancing staff–parent relationships.

- Ensure that staff have the specialized educational background and knowledge of early childhood development needed to work effectively with young children and their families.

- Provide adequate compensation (salaries and benefits) and good working conditions to attract and retain qualified staff.

- Establish a safe and stimulating environment that enhances children's ability to learn.

The crisis facing Canadian ECEC programs is rooted in the failure to recognize the conflict between three basic needs—the children's need for quality programs, the staff's need for adequate compensation, and the families' need for affordable programs. These needs are difficult to fulfill simultaneously. This chapter will explain some of the basic tools of financial management that any director should be able to use and that board members/owners should understand.

The Director's Role in Financial Planning

A basic component of a director's job is to ensure that there are sufficient funds to establish and operate a quality program. Most early childhood directors come to the profession because they want to work with people. Few receive adequate training in financial management. The ability to understand, plan, and control an organization's finances is a central and critical skill. As most programs operate painfully close to the red on a daily basis, directors must manage money effectively. If income and expenses are not carefully planned and controlled, a program can go out of business in a remarkably short period of time.

Those lacking financial skills may view the budget process as time consuming and intimidating. Directors may see budgeting, bookkeeping, and financial calculations as unwelcome tasks that can more easily be performed by a financial professional isolated from the program. Some directors without training or experience in financial management may believe they can simply turn the financial aspect of the program over to someone else, while retaining control of the program's policy. Such a belief is totally wrong! All hopes, dreams, and aspirations for what the program will accomplish for children, families, and staff are expressed in the language of money. Every line in the budget is a policy decision that directly determines what a program will be. There is no way to influence policy without controlling the budget process.

Financial planning affects all major aspects of the program. Consequently, it should involve input from all those involved in the program—the board of directors, staff, and parents. Advice solicited from parents, financial experts, and staff can supplement the director's skills, contribute to team building, and strengthen the program. By considering everyone's ideas, a more accurate conception of budgeting priorities, appropriate expenditure level, and revenue sources can be derived.

In the area of financial planning, directors must produce a well-reasoned budget that takes into account the various sources of **revenue**, including parent fees, government subsidies, and fundraising, and the projected range of expenditures. Directors must ensure that policies, procedures, and practices are in place to support the management of **cash flow**. Additionally, directors need the skills, abilities, and attitudes that will enable them to work both independently and with others to carry out their financial responsibilities.

Who Makes the Budget?

In a non-profit organization, the director, often in co-operation with the treasurer of the board, usually draws up the budget. The board of directors then approves it. In a commercial organization, the owner usually develops the budget with input from the director. A budget should reflect sensitive planning that responds to input from the staff. In the case of a new ECEC program, the group of people or individual responsible for getting the program up and running will develop a budget early in the planning stage to ensure that the program is viable.

Types of Budgets

When a centre is beginning **operations**, the director prepares two budgets: the **start-up budget** and the **operating budget**.

*   *Start-up budget.* This budget consists of all the one-time expenses incurred in starting a program, including initial building expenses (the down payment on the purchase of the building, the cost of renovations, or rent deposit), the purchase of major equipment, the director's salary for a period of time prior to opening the program, the cost of publicizing the program, and utility charges during this period. The equipment—for the activity and care areas, office, and kitchen—is a major part of the start-up budget. All equipment should not be purchased at the beginning. Add in rental equipment such as a photocopier. Total start-up costs vary widely. A capital funding grant will be needed.

*   *Operating budgets.* These budgets are used when programs become operational and annually thereafter. Programs that receive funding from government or other agencies will find it helpful to adopt the same fiscal year as the funding body. Before any financial transactions are made, the budget must be approved by the board of directors/owner and funding source. Once approval has been given, the director must follow the approved financial plan.

Step-by-Step Guide to Preparing a Budget

A **budget** is a statement of goals for one year, stated in financial terms. It is an important financial planning tool that can help an organization control expenditures and identify potential problems. A budget calendar should be established with deadlines identified to meet each step. For programs receiving funds from government agencies, this timetable is generally predetermined.

In planning a budget, there are two main considerations. First, the budget should be related to the overall planning of the ECEC program. Money must be allocated strategically to achieve program goals. Second, the key decision makers of the program should be involved at each step of the budgeting process. These leaders must set long-term goals for the organization, decide upon program priorities, and, ultimately, assume financial responsibility. They must be involved in the forecasting as well as the monitoring stages. The decision makers must also determine on an annual basis whether the program should:

a)   run at a break-even level (neither make a profit nor occur a loss);

b) operate with a small surplus; or

c) operate at a deficit (this is not generally an option).

The following steps are part of the successful budgeting cycle:

1. Make a Wish List

This step involves reviewing what the program wants to accomplish in the coming year. The decision makers determine objectives for the upcoming year; the director's job is to provide the route. A question to ask is, What would we do if cost was not an issue? This process forces people to think systematically about the program's mission, programs, activities, and long-range goals. Because it does not require close monitoring of costs, making a wish list can be fun. The program may have conducted a self-evaluation process or had feedback from an external consultant and/or licensing officer to suggest goals such as improving the outdoor playground or increasing opportunities for staff development. In these examples, allocating money for professional development or construction of a new playground would be included on the wish list.

2. Projecting Expenditures

After what to include in the budget has been determined, each item on the list must be costed out. The task of estimating expenses can be daunting at first. To make the task more manageable, focus effort on the most important items. Items of less significance, such as office supplies, do not need to be estimated individually; merely write down a reasonable figure for the category.

The basic costs of keeping the program operating must be included. In addition, the costs of new items will have to be estimated. Costing is not always an easy process. One approach involves **incremental budgeting**, which means relying on information contained in the budget for the prior year. To the figures in the previous year's budget, the director may add a percentage increment to cover inflation and other factors. A second technique requires that each line be newly calculated. This approach is called **zero-based budgeting**.

The previous year's figures are immensely helpful in estimating the coming year's budget. It is important to review the current year's figures to see how accurate projections were. It is better to estimate costs on the high side. If new programs are added, they are likely to increase administrative costs. Thus, it is unwise to calculate only how much would be spent specifically on the new program.

It is critical to understand the relationships between revenues, fixed costs, and variable costs. **Fixed costs** are those that tend to stay constant at least in the short term. Fixed costs are incurred regardless of the size of the program. Rent/mortgage, property taxes, and the director's salary are examples of fixed costs. These costs are the same in a given facility whether the program serves ten or a hundred children. **Variable costs** are those that increase as the number of children served increases. Practitioner's salaries are the largest variable cost in an ECEC program. The more children served, the more caregivers must be hired. The age of the children served is another example of variable costs—the younger the children, the greater the number of staff required. Other variable expenses include curriculum supplies, maintenance, food, and equipment. These expenses all increase and decrease as the number of children in the program changes. Programs receiving subsidy are generally required to use guidelines for their budget submissions. These types of guidelines may not allow for some aspects of quality, such as enhanced ratios, or for program enrichments, such as a music teacher. Whatever the budget format, the following expense categories would be included.

Salaries   This is the largest expense budget category, a program can expect to pay up to 80% for wages. Salaries play a critical role in the quality of the program. This line should include salaries for all full-time and part-time staff including the director, caregiving staff (including assistants and substitutes), cook, maintenance person, and administrative personnel. An error in this section can throw off the whole budget. In determining the budget for salaries, the director must consider several factors. First, the HR policies (discussed in chapter 6) would be consulted in regard to pay rates and benefits. Hiring policies that specify a certain education level or amount of previous experience will affect salary levels. The director must comply with minimum-wage laws and any other employment regulations. Union membership is another factor that will influence salaries.

A competent director recognizes the complexities of cost-effectiveness in the provision of high quality programs. She considers such factors as the ages of the children in each group, the physical setting, and the existing responsibilities of each staff member before deciding to enhance the staff:child ratio. She is also aware of the relation between salary levels and employees' self-esteem. It is essential that wages and salaries be paid on time.

Licensing regulations set minimum standards for staff:child ratios. The program may decide to exceed those ratios and hire additional staff to ensure a better program. Quality ECEC programs may also stipulate qualifications for their caregiving staff that exceed the requirements of the province or territory. The rate of pay is usually determined by the local

Providing for competent staffing is the largest expense category of the budget.

job market, the type of program, and job qualifications. Programs that want to recruit and retain qualified staff must provide an attractive salary-and-benefits package. The amount is determined by the number of staff, their rate of pay, and the hours they work. Some centres control costs by closely monitoring the number of children attending each day and altering the number of staff accordingly. *You Bet I Care!* found that, nationally, centres used 75.3% of their budget for wages, with the most being spent in Manitoba (82.4%) and the least in New Brunswick (66.3%) (Doherty et al. 2000a).

Benefits   There are two kinds of benefits: those that are offered by the program and included in the contract with the employee and those that are mandatory, or required by law. Mandatory benefits include taxes the program is required to pay to the government, such as the health tax and required employer contributions to Employment Insurance and the Canada Pension Plan. In some jurisdictions, payments to Worker's Compensation are mandatory, and in other areas, they are highly recommended. These costs should be estimated at approximately 9% of salaries although they can run as high as 21%.

The program incurs costs involved in maintaining accurate records for each employee and filing reports with various government agencies. Other benefits, which may include extended health coverage, dental coverage, financial assistance for professional development, and retirement or pension plans, comprise about 4% of gross salary costs. *You Bet I Care!* found two-thirds of teaching staff received paid coffee breaks, but only one-third received paid lunch breaks (this would contravene employment standards in some provinces). The 1998 study found some improvement over the 1991 *Caring for a Living* survey in terms of the percentage of caregivers who received compensation for overtime, including attending parent meetings and staff meetings after hours (Doherty et al. 2000a).

Benefits that augment the individual's salary or provide a measure of longer-term security are particularly important in an occupation with low wages. Most of the staff are female, with the majority under the age of 40. Consequently, job-protected maternity leave and reduced child care fees for employees' children are valuable benefits. Disability insurance and a pension plan are important when the wage level makes saving very difficult. Having paid sick days and being permitted to carry them over from one year to another provides some protection should an individual experience a prolonged illness. These provisions, necessary to establish a humane environment, do add considerable additional costs to the budget. **Personnel policies** also affect expenses indirectly through the cost of supply staff replacing regular staff off on sick leave, professional development days, or vacation.

Professional fees and contract services   In this last category to do with personnel, include all services provided by individuals not on the payroll. These may include an accountant, a lawyer, curriculum specialists, and—unless the program pays benefits for them—casual staff brought in when the regular staff are sick or on vacation. Casual staff are usually budgeted at 8 to 10% of gross salary. This amount would be determined by reviewing the program's HR policies. If the program uses consultants, they are usually paid on a per diem basis plus expenses.

Facilities   The largest cost in the physical plant category is the rent or mortgage payments for the facility. Also included in this category are utilities (heat, electricity, water, property tax, and insurance). Building insurance covers all the items associated with fire, weather, burglary, and liability insurance. Approximately 10% of the budget is used for rent or mortgage and 5 to 6% for utilities. In *You Bet I Care!*, 34.5% of non-profit centres and 3.4% of commercial programs reported subsidized or free rent (Doherty et al. 2000a). Similar numbers of programs reported subsidized or free utilities. Programs that do not have to pay the full costs of their facility can redirect these funds to other areas of the program, thereby enhancing quality. The costs for **maintenance** and repairs to the facility and grounds are part of this budget item. Regular maintenance cuts costs in this area in the long term. It is impossible to predict these costs, so an amount must be allocated.

Supplies and equipment   The large number of consumable supplies used in ECEC programs can be a source of either economy or extravagance. To save money, the director needs to be aware of how supplies are used. All the art materials, office supplies, cleaning supplies, and paper products used in the program should be listed, then the minimum amount of each item needed should be determined. Whenever possible, supplies should be ordered in volume from the least expensive source. Although making an inventory of supplies is time consuming, it is well worth the effort. Before buying items in bulk, consider the amount of storage space available, the shelf life of the item, and any additional costs of shipping or delivery. It is recommended that a program have an inventory level to carry it through two months of operation. Some programs buy co-operatively with other programs. This part of the budget covers all equipment that costs less than $250.

Transportation   This category may include the lease or purchase of vehicles used to transport the children to the program, to school, and/or on field trips. Include insurance, fuel, maintenance, and licence fees. Some programs contract with a company to provide transportation or rent a vehicle for specific occasions. Because of financial, safety, and liability concerns, many parents provide their child's transportation to the program. Costs for staff members to travel to professional development meetings or other programs may be included in this category.

Food   These costs vary between 5 and 10% of total expenditures. Many programs provide a nutritious meal and two snacks per day, with food either prepared on the premises or catered. For programs preparing food in-house, costs range from $2.00 to $2.50 per child per day excluding staff time, whereas catered foods cost from $3.00 to $3.60 per child per day. Consideration should be given to providing sufficient food for the staff to eat with the children. Food expenses are small in comparison to salary expenses. Even if estimates are off by 20% in this category, it will result in a variance of only 2% in the total budget, whereas if a similar error occurred in the salary category, it would result in a variance of 18% in total costs.

Miscellaneous   Other items include telephones (how many, cellphones for field trips), advertising (usually higher during start-up and when there are vacancies to fill), and annual audits, which are needed to assure board members and government agencies that funds have been properly handled.

3. Determine Income

A program's resources, be they cash revenue or in-kind donations, strongly influence wage levels and the type of program offered. It is important to understand the difference between restricted and unrestricted funds. Unrestricted funds, such as parent fees or monies derived from fundraising, have no particular limitations on how or when they are to be used.

Restricted funds, such as parent fee subsidies and wage enhancement grants from governments, often come with very specific requirements that dictate how and when the funds may be used. (Program income is elaborated on later in the chapter.) Be conservative about forecasting income. Some directors factor in under-enrolment of 10%.

4. Compare

This step is also known as the "read 'em and weep" step. There is often too much expense and not enough income. Decision makers must act responsibly and only undertake what the program can pay for.

5. Set Priorities

It is time to debate which programs and activities will be included in the budget. This step can be very challenging. Priority setting should be linked to the philosophy—the organization's reason for being. Decision makers must determine what is best for the organization and meets the needs of the children and families. During discussions of the budget, some may defend a special project that they feel must be included whereas others may reject any new activity.

6. Balancing the Budget

If the projected expenses exceed the projected income, the budget is not balanced. Decision makers will need to reduce expenditures or increase income. To reduce expenditures, review variable and irregular expenses to determine areas where money can be saved. In the area of payroll, it may be determined that there are times in the day when staffing could be reduced while maintaining ratios. Or, a director might review those areas in which the program is exceeding licensing standards. If the shortfall is small, the staff may review the supplies requested or program plans.

An alternative strategy for balancing the budget is to increase income. Soliciting parents' input on the budget and keeping them informed of the financial situation will help families understand the costs of quality early childhood development. Most programs hold meetings annually to discuss the budget and give parents the opportunity to ask questions and provide input on alternative sources of funding. Questions such as, How much must parent fees be raised in order to balance the budget? Could all the families afford this increase? and, How will the program deal with a number of families withdrawing their children because they cannot pay the increased rates? are considered.

7. Get Budget Approval

After all the initial groundwork is completed, there must be approval of the budget. In a small commercial program, this will involve the owner reviewing all the computations. In a larger corporation, the approval step may involve submitting the budget to a corporate office, whereas in a non-profit community centre, the budget will be approved by the board of directors, usually first by the finance committee. It is necessary to document decisions in minutes and keep financial statements. Given that so much time is spent developing the budget, some may assume that this step is just a formality. However, the decision makers need to be responsible and assure themselves, for example, that all the projected revenues will be forthcoming, particularly those funds that will have to be raised.

8. Monitor and Amend

Most budgets need to be amended and modified over time to accommodate new information and conditions that occur over the year. It is necessary to create a mechanism for ongoing budget review. There needs to be an approach that allows some flexibility, yet requires approval for any significant changes.

The advantage of doing a monthly cash-flow analysis is that the director can predict serious cash problems throughout the year and act to prevent a surprise dip in the bank balance. It is the responsibility of the decision makers to review the budget on a regular basis and make adjustments as necessary. Cowperthwaite and Mehta (1996) acknowledge that, while preparing an annual review of revenue and expenses is important, cash flow must also be monitored, because due to fluctuations in monthly revenue and expenses, a program could run out of money in August even though the budget suggests that the program will be solvent until December. Programs can experience significant fluctuations in outlays for salaries and benefits due to months in which three pay periods occur. Also, the timing of some receipts, such as operating grants, may not coincide with biweekly pay periods.

Sources of Program Income

A program's resources strongly influence wage levels and the type of program offered. A large multi-state US study found that in-kind donations, such as subsidized rent, enable programs to allocate a large portion of their revenue to staff wages and programming (Hepburn 1995). *You Bet I Care!* found that, on average, 49.2% of program revenue comes from parent fees, 30.5% from government fee subsidies, and 17.5% from other government grants such as operating or salary-enhancement grants (see Table 10–1). Forty-two percent of programs engage in their own fundraising, although nationally, this activity accounted for less than 2% of program revenue. Fifty-one percent of programs reported that they receive some type of in-kind donation. Non-profit programs reported receiving more than twice the amount of donations than did commercial centres. *You Bet I Care!* found considerable variation across provinces in the proportion of revenue coming from each source (Doherty et al. 2000a). Other income may include GST rebates and interest. Parent fees and subsidies provide a significant portion of a program's revenue; consequently, the director should ensure this area gets time and attention.

Income is related to the number of children enrolled in the program and the fees per child. Parent fee and subsidy revenue is calculated by multiplying the number of children in the program by the fees to be charged. It is recommended that this figure be calculated separately for each age group served. The calculation itself is not difficult; however, predicting the actual revenue can be challenging as enrolment fluctuates substantially over the course of the year. It is not possible to operate a program at 100% enrolment. When children leave, others will not always take their place on the same day. A well-run program operates at between 95 and 98% enrolment. Careful attention to attendance records is key

TABLE 10-1	Average Percentage of Revenue from Three Primary Sources by Province, 1998			
Province/Territory	Parent Fees	Fee Subsidy	Other Gov't Grants	Totals
British Columbia	49.4%	38.5%	8.9%	96.8%
Alberta	53.8%	36.2%	7.5%	97.5%
Saskatchewan	38.3%	35%	21.7%	95%
Manitoba	33.9%	40.3%	21.6%	95.8%
Ontario	46.9%	34.1%	16.6%	97.6%
Quebec	45.8%	18.9%	33%	97.7%
New Brunswick	68.7%	26.9%	1.9%	97.5%
Nova Scotia	72.7%	20.5%	5.2%	98.4%
Prince Edward Island	66.8%	26.1%	6.3%	99.2%
Newfoundland	82.1%	14.4%	0%	96.5%
Yukon/N.W.T.	not reportable	not reportable	not reportable	not reportable
Canada	49.2%	30.5%	17.5%	97.2%

1. Information for the Northwest Territories and the Yukon is not reportable because of small sample size.

2. Quebec's phase-in of $7.00/day fees will alter the current relative reliance on parent fees and government grants.

3. Newfoundland announced April 1998 that it will be spending $4.6 million annually on improving and expanding licensed child care centres. When implemented, this should reduce reliance on parental fees.

Source: G. Doherty, D. Lero, H. Goelman, J. Tougas, and A. LaGrange, *You Bet I Care! Caring and Learning Environments: Quality in Regulated Family Child Care across Canada* (Guelph, ON: Centre for Families, Work and Well-Being, University of Guelph, 2000). Reprinted by permission.

to ensuring that non-attendance is not non-enrolment. The previous year's budget and current year's financial statements can be helpful. Enrolment variations, such as a drop in enrolment during the summer months, should be expected. As well, factor into revenue estimates some allocation for uncollected fees.

To have full enrolment, a few programs are considering a flexible approach. Lowe (2001a) notes one example, King's Park Centre in Ottawa, which was having trouble filling 32 full-time spaces. It decided to retain 24 full-time spaces and create eight flexible ones, accommodating up to 20 more part-time children. As the director noted, this flexible approach serves the families as well as the bottom line.

Parent Fees   Setting parent fees involves a complicated set of decisions. If the director sets the fees based on what parents can afford to pay, this will not likely generate enough income to cover the costs of operating the desired program. This may force the staff to subsidize the program through wages that are too low. The simplest way to increase income and achieve a balanced budget is to raise parent fees. However, careful consideration must be given to the impact on families in the program. It is helpful to know what other programs in the community are charging. Know what the families are willing to pay. Programs may be able to charge more if their program is unique and meets parents' needs. The Canada-wide median fee charged for full-time infant care in 1998 was $531 per month with a high of $783 in Ontario. For toddler care, it was $477 per month with a high of $603 in Ontario, and for preschoolers, $455 with a high of $541. There were substantial parental-fee increases in many parts of the country between 1991 and 1998 (Doherty et al. 2000a).

Fee Subsidy   Government **fee subsidy** is intended to purchase care for a particular number of children. The director should check with the government agency regarding the reimbursement schedule. It may be necessary to arrange credit or a short-term loan to facilitate cash flow. In 1998, fee subsidization provided over a third of centre revenue in Manitoba (a high of 40.3%), British Columbia (38.5%), Alberta (36.2%), Saskatchewan (35.0%), and Ontario (34.1%). The lowest level (14.4%) was in Newfoundland and Labrador where the rates have been capped since 1993 (Doherty et al. 2000a).

Other Government Grants   Nationally, government operating/equipment grants accounted for 9.6% of program revenue. Recurring annual operating grants are important to a program's viability since they can provide a certain degree of financial stability. However, operating grants have been the source of real insecurity for some time. It depends upon the political will of the party in power.

Wage enhancement grants were received by 43.5% of centres on a national basis, but they accounted for less than 6.5% of centre revenue. Ontario received the most, amounting to 12.7% of revenue. Although most programs include at least one child with special needs, the receipt of specific government grants to assist in the child's integration was only noted in British Columbia, Saskatchewan, Manitoba, and Quebec, with grants amounting to less than 0.4% of revenue in any jurisdiction. The government in Quebec implemented major programs to make child care more affordable for parents. In Quebec, parents pay a standard $7-per-day fee and the government covers the remaining costs.

Fundraising   Increasingly, early childhood development programs are seeking ways to expand financial resources beyond parent fees and government grants. Fundraising strategies are becoming more crucial to the economic survival of programs. In the past, fundraising was synonymous with bake sales and selling candy door to door. Although most directors recognize the need for fundraising, they often lack experience in fundraising and an understanding of professional techniques for executing a successful campaign. Before involving the program in fundraising, it is important to consider the amount of work required.

These activities must have the full support of the operators and the commitment of dedicated volunteers. The quality of this commitment will define the scope of the fundraising campaign. When launching a fundraising effort, the purpose for the funds must be identified. It is easier to generate support for building an outdoor playground than to raise funds for general operating expenses. In fact, raising funds for operating expenses is strongly discouraged and even viewed by some as dangerous; fundraising cannot always be sustained, and operating funds need to be regular. However, carefully executed, an annual fundraising campaign will not only generate ongoing financial support for capital and special expenditures, it will enhance the program's presence in the community.

Other Sources of Revenue   *You Bet I Care!* found that assistance from corporate sponsors is rare in Canada, accounting for less than 0.5% of centre revenue nationally. Nationally, 51.3% of programs reported that they received in-kind resources such as subsidized rent or rent-free space (Doherty et al. 2000a). Other kinds of support included donated toys and equipment or free or subsidized utilities and janitorial/maintenance services. An in-kind donation is any good or service donated to the program. There are many reasons why these resources should be identified. Complete information about all the resources a program has makes it easier to compare costs from one program to another and contributes to determining the full costs of care.

Financial Record Keeping

After creating a balanced budget, it is important to develop an effective system for keeping track of income and expenses. The director is responsible for overseeing or preparing this information, generally with an accountant's assistance. The director should inform everyone authorized to make purchases of the budget limitations. Early childhood practitioners, cooks, and housekeeping staff must know the allowable monthly expenditures for budget categories for which they are responsible.

Directors who have had little or no experience with record keeping can improve their financial management skills by taking courses at a local college or using information available through websites (such as those listed at the end of the chapter). They may employ a local accounting firm. Either way, it is essential for the director to be familiar with basic accounting methods and terminology. Accounting entries recorded by the program should include all income and expenditures regardless of the source. The entries should reflect all financial transactions and be recorded at appropriate intervals (daily, weekly). Poor record keeping may cause errors or deletions. This can result in an inability to borrow funds or lead to questions about the program's financial standing. Almost any accountant or computer package will provide monthly balance and income statements. Computer generated reports can be revised readily so that the most current information is available.

In some cases, the cost of keeping records and budgets may actually be reduced through computer use (fewer employees, less time). Small programs may be able to handle their record keeping more easily without a computer; larger programs will find a computer a necessity. Additional benefits may be increased accuracy and availability of information. Computers can be used to monitor financial transactions (e.g., income and expenses, fee payments, payroll, tax payments). It is useful to contact other directors of similar programs to ascertain their experience with financial software programs. Computer software can save administrative time, enabling directors to spend more time with families and staff or observing the program. Relevant computer applications include budget templates and systems for maintaining individual payroll records and preparing the payroll, writing cheques and making receipts, recording daily transactions, reviewing cash flow, and summing figures. A number of ECEC professional organizations offer software programs and support (see the section later in this chapter on building financial stability for programs).

The basic accounting systems necessary for all businesses are accounts receivable and accounts payable, described below. In addition to using a system for payroll that tracks the hours worked, deductions, rate of pay, and vacation time for each employee, there should be a general ledger or computer program that posts both expenses and deposits. These categories should be tracked monthly, quarterly, and annually to determine whether or not the budget is working.

- **Accounts receivable.** Accounts receivable are all monies owed that have not been paid. Accounts receivable records keep track of any payment received, generally on a weekly basis. The director needs to know who is not paying and why. There will always be a few uncollected fees, primarily from those families who withdraw their children without warning, perhaps owing the program for several days. However, prompt attention to those families who are behind in payments can reduce the bad debt expense (a **bad debt** is a receivable that will never be collected). A weekly report should list families by name and the amounts that they owe. Such a list can be generated automatically by a computerized accounts receivable program.

- **Accounts payable.** These are the records of bills or invoices that have been received by the program for goods and services received but not yet paid. When a bill is received, it should be stamped with the date. In general, bills should be paid promptly so that they can be reflected in the monthly expenses. It is important to develop accurate record keeping systems. Once a bill is paid, mark the invoice with the cheque amount, date, and number and note any partial payments.

Financial Policies and Procedures
Salary Schedules

Program directors need to invest limited resources wisely in order to maintain a high quality organization. Even with a limited budget, there are some ways programs can improve performance. One is by how the program structures its salary schedule. Although people don't gravitate to the early childhood development field for its financial benefits, even the most committed staff will become discouraged if they do a great job and are paid no more or even less than staff in other programs. To determine competitive wage rates, programs should consult salary surveys in their community approximately every two years (see Table 10–2). Some early childhood organizations conduct salary surveys and make them available to members.

TABLE 10–2 City of Toronto 2003 Salary Schedule*			
Program staff	Hours/week	Annual salary (261 days)	Hourly rate
Untrained staff	35	$30 912	$16.92
Trained teaching staff (ECE grade 2)	35	$37 797	$20.69
Trained teaching staff (ECE grade 1)	35	$47 992	$26.21
Centre supervisor	35	$68 986	$37.76
Casuals/supply staff:			
Trained with 4% vacation			$19.94
Untrained with 4% vacation			$11.75
Cook/housekeeper	40	$37 974	$17.91
Dietary aide	40	$34 974	$16.75
Administration	35	$78 101	$42.75

(Amount is pro-rated for operating capacity; maximum is for 90 children.)

* including all wage grants

Source: Used with permission. Children's Services Division, Toronto.

Administration of salaries is not a simple mechanical procedure. It is a direct expression of the values of an organization. When hiring a staff member, a program is paying for time, skills, and/or results. If the program is paying for time, the hiring premise may be paying for a warm body to fulfill ratio requirements over a period of time. Consequently, wage levels only need to attract and retain staff who meet minimum legal requirements. When the program is paying for skills, individuals who are knowledgeable and practised in early childhood development are hired in the belief that they will perform significantly better than persons without training and experience. The salary scale may also reward them for continuing acquisition of knowledge and skills. If the program is paying for results, the assumption is that what really matters is who performs well on the job, and effective performers are rewarded. In setting salary scales, Neugebauer (1994) recommends giving a combination of **cost-of-living adjustment (COLA)** and merit raises to acknowledge individual efforts.

Family Fee Policies

Programs for young children are expensive. Although families seldom pay absolute costs, early childhood development programs can still represent a large portion of the family budget—particularly for middle- and low-income families. For many families, quality ECEC programs are simply not affordable. There is tremendous variation in the rates programs charge. These variations reflect regional cost-of-living factors, staff:child ratios, competition, family incomes, and outside financial support.

When determining fee policies, directors should consider the following points:

- *Fee levels.* Set realistic fee levels. The fee charged should be based on what it costs to provide a level of quality that the program believes in. If the fees are set to be in line with what other programs in the community charge, they may not be high enough to cover costs. Some directors keep their fees too low because they fear that parents may not be able to afford higher fees. By doing so, they are dooming the program to a mediocre level of quality. It is best to base the fees on what quality care costs and finds ways to assist families to be able to afford the program.

- *Charging for absences.* Program policies often include lengthy and complicated explanations for why parents are charged when their child is absent. When setting policies in this area, programs must strive for a balance between the program's need for financial stability and being sensitive to the needs of families.

- *Payment terms.* Programs today require fee payment in advance. In bygone days, collecting after the delivery of service was common. This often resulted in cash flow stresses as expenses were incurred ahead of income. Currently, most programs collect on a monthly basis, which keeps the number of collections to a minimum and gives the program greater flexibility in managing cash flow. In some communities, parents cannot afford to pay a month in advance. Therefore, some programs collect on a weekly basis. Most programs prefer to receive payments by automatic bank account deductions and some even have policies against receiving payments in cash. Some programs permit payments by credit card.

- *Late fee payments.* A chronic problem for programs is fee collections. It is important to confront the problem early and work out solutions that meet the program's needs as well as those of the families. Encourage families who are experiencing financial difficulties to let the director know as soon as possible about problems they may have with fee payments. Work out a schedule of payments that will help the family and ensure that the payments are eventually made. Some programs arrange for an individual from the finance committee to collect late fees, not the staff who have relationships with the parents.

- *Late pickups.* This issue poses a problem for the child as well as the staff. Most programs realize that being totally inflexible regarding lateness imposes even more pressure on families who are living stressful lives. Impress upon parents the importance of calling the program if they are going to be late so the child knows why. In endeavouring to implement family-friendly policies, some programs allow up to two late pickups per year before any penalty is allotted. The newsletter *Caregiver Connection*, published by Western Canada Family Child Care Association of BC, cautions that if a staff member is paid directly for late fees owed, she or he is not covered by Worker's Compensation for the time period. This is because a late fee is not treated as taxable income. The association recommends that the program bill the parent directly and pay the staff through regular methods.

- *Withdrawal policies.* Most programs spell out specific procedures for withdrawing a child. These are designed to give the program adequate notice so it can collect what is due from the outgoing family and find a new child to fill the vacancy. In addition, programs spell out specific policies for temporary withdrawals for a family vacation or illnesses. Everything must be paid for. For example, if a program allows for two weeks' vacation, this means higher fees throughout the year to cover lost revenue. Often a program will place an absent child on a priority waiting list so the child can fill the first available vacancy when she or he is ready to return.

It is important to set fee policies that can be enforced consistently. Directors should also consider the following points regarding fee policies:

Parents must be aware of policies. At intake, directors should carefully review key policies on withdrawals, absences, late pickups, and late payments so parents clearly understand in advance what the rules are. Many programs require a parent to sign a statement or contract agreeing to these policies.

Be sensitive to language when writing policies. Programs want to set family-friendly policies that convey respect for parents. When wording policies, assume good intentions on the part of the parents. Their perspective should be taken into account. Policies ought to be stated in a straightforward, non-judgmental fashion. Avoid using a negative, legalistic tone.

Ensure that policies are clearly written. Policy writers should keep policies simple and have them reviewed by people from outside the staff, such as parents. To assist with this task, the *Financial Policies and Procedures Manual Workbook* (Draper 1997) provides a compact disc with a template for writing financial policies for ECEC programs.

Provide help to parents. Provide parents with advice on how to apply for fee subsidies and information on receiving tax credits.

It takes thoughtful planning to set fee policies that are flexible enough to accommodate the needs of parents yet firm enough to protect the program from financial hardship.

Building Financial Stability for Programs

Early childhood organizations tend to be small. Small businesses often do not have the financial stability or expertise necessary to take advantage of many financing strategies. Some ECEC programs form a management services organization, where a group of programs consolidate administrative costs and operations. These organizations may function as purchasing alliances for insurance and benefits, perform other functions such as facilities management, and represent programs in contract negotiations. Another model is an administrative services organization, which is an entity that serves as a bridge between insurers and early childhood programs. Many insurers do not find it cost effective to insure individual service organizations of less than 10 employees, which is the size of many early childhood programs. Administrative service organizations may perform a variety of functions, including enrolment of children in the program, eligibility determination for fee subsidy, finding providers for families, claims for staff benefits, payment of salaries, and other tasks. Finally, other small businesses have developed joint marketing programs to gain new clients, offer space to clients, or take advantage of purchasing opportunities that may be too expensive for one program alone. These kinds of partnerships can help small businesses look, act, and feel larger.

Similarly, a group of family child care homes or providers can come together in a structure similar to a management services or administrative services organization. Providers can jointly contract for such administrative costs and operations as billing and fee collection,

It is important to build financial stability for programs.

accounting, purchase of equipment and supplies, staff development, transportation, marketing, and so forth. Additionally, forming this type of alliance might allow a group of providers to provide services to an employer or group of employers. These are but a few of the possibilities. (Chapter 5 provides more information on provider networks and family child care agencies.)

Family Child Care Budgets

Family child care providers are self-employed business operators. It is important to manage the business aspects of care. Often providers find dealing with the business aspect extremely stressful. Unit 8 of the *Family Child Care Training Program* (CCCF 2000a), "Financial Planning and Management," provides tremendous assistance in learning about budgeting. Some family child care providers follow a strict budget, divided into categories such as food, play materials and equipment, household supplies, and administrative supplies. Consequently, they know exactly how much they have to spend on play equipment each year. If they decide to purchase a playground climber that costs more than their annual play materials budget, they may borrow from another budget category where they expect to underspend.

Standard

Financial Management, Family Child Care

Manage the family child care business's financial resources so they are used effectively, by:

- developing an annual operating budget and effective procedures for tracking income and expenses on an ongoing basis and taking corrective action as indicated;

- developing and implementing procedures to obtain government funding and meet all reporting requirements for same; and

- taking into account all future financial needs when considering new enrolments, in order to maintain the income that will enable the child care service to continue to function.

Source: Gillian Doherty, in Canadian Child Care Federation (CCCF), *Partners in Quality: Tools for Practitioners in Child Care Settings* (Ottawa: CCCF, 2000).

Other providers have no idea exactly how much they spend each year on specific budget categories, but they have an intuitive sense of their overall budget. They know how much they can afford to spend and stay within guidelines. If they do not, they will go out of business. Revenue fluctuates for a variety of reasons, including ill children who miss days, giving a discount to a family with more than one child, or bad debts, where a family leaves without paying the provider. It is wise to follow a budget closely during the first couple of years of operation. With this approach, even if the provider changes her plans about what is spent, there will be more financial security from knowing where to cut (or increase income) to make up for unexpected operating expenses. Once the business is operating with greater financial security, the provider can reduce the financial planning by keeping track of monthly expenses and comparing them to average monthly expenses.

You Bet I Care! found provider gross income for those who had worked for 48 weeks or more in the previous year ranged from $15 000 to $24 999. Sixty percent of all providers spent between 30% to 59% of their income on child-related expenses such as food and toys (Doherty et al. 2000b). Thus, the net income before taxes of providers is considerably lower than their gross income. However, since they are treated as self-employed persons for tax purposes, on their tax return they can deduct business expenses and a portion of home maintenance costs when calculating the amount of income tax owed. For more information on this, check the website hosted by Canada Customs and Revenue Agency, found at www.ccra-adrc.gc.ca.

The chapter "The Business of Family Child Care" in the Family Child Care Training Program (CCCF 2000a) and Bush (2000) provide additional information on the development of budgets.

FAMILY CHILD CARE BUDGET

Income
- Parent fees
- Other

Expenses
- Food
- Children's toys and materials
- Office supplies
- Copying
- Computer
- Postage
- Household supplies
- Maintenance and repairs
- Assistant caregiver
- Accountant
- Utilities
- Insurance (liability, accident, motor vehicle)
- Professional development
- Membership

Parent Fees and Subsidy

It is essential that the family child care provider determine the rates parents will be charged before she or he searches for clients. In some cases, the agency or licensing office (the office or agency primarily responsible for licensing centres and family child care agencies in individual provinces and territories) may set the rates. As with group care, fees need

TABLE 10–3   **Median Daily Fees Charged for Full-Time Family Child Care, by Jurisdiction, 1999**

Jurisdiction	9-month-old infant cared for from 8:00 a.m. to 5:30 p.m. Monday to Friday	3-year-old child cared for from 8:00 a.m. to 5:30 p.m. Monday to Friday	7-year-old child with care provided for four hours a day
British Columbia	$31.15	$27.69	$15.00
Alberta	$16.15	$16.00	$10.95
Saskatchewan	$19.61	$18.07	$13.15
Ontario	$22.00	$20.00	$9.57
Quebec	$21.00	$20.00	$11.23
New Brunswick	$17.00	$15.00	$8.00
Yukon	$27.69	$24.00	$11.54
Total Sample	$20.77	$19.35	$12.69

Source: G. Doherty, D. Lero, J. Tougas, A. LaGrange, and H. Goelman, *You Bet I Care! Policies and Practices in Canadian Family Child Care Agencies* (Guelph, ON: Centre for Families, Work and Well-Being, University of Guelph, 2001). Reprinted by permission.

to be high enough to cover expenses for food, toys, and equipment. Other factors that should be considered include average rates charged by other providers in the community, the training and experience of the provider, the quality of the program, and the number and ages of children in care. In addition to setting rates, providers should determine when they will review parent fees.

Table 10–3 shows the average fees reported by providers. Nearly two-thirds of providers reported that the fees charged to full-fee parents had risen in the past three years.

You Bet I Care! notes that, in all jurisdictions, fee subsidy for low-income parents is paid directly to the provider. In the agency model, the agency usually looks after fee subsidy claims for its providers. However, individually licensed providers have to handle this administrative task themselves. Seventy-one percent of licensed providers provided care for at least one child whose parents were receiving subsidy (Doherty et al. 2000b). Administering fee subsidies adds significantly to the individually licensed provider's workload.

Summary

Early childhood development programs in Canada have become an extremely important component in the social infrastructure that supports healthy child development, economic security for families, and social cohesion in communities. In addition to providing care and early education for young children, the majority of programs offer other services. Programs vary in the populations they serve, the resources available to them, and the economic and policy contexts that affect their operation.

Handling the finances of these settings is complex. To provide a quality program for children, programs must maximize limited resources. Goals must be achieved; boards of directors/owners, families, and funders must be satisfied. Most early childhood directors and family child care providers need more training in financial matters. Budgets must be prepared carefully, monitored regularly, and modified thoughtfully. Good record keeping helps with the preparation of future budgets. Programs are accountable to governments for spending grants as intended.

A program's ability to provide high quality services is strongly influenced by the characteristics of the staff—number, qualifications, ability, dispositions, and stability—and the characteristics of the environment. Each of these aspects is associated with costs and the need for adequate resources. Personnel costs are the largest component of an ECEC program budget.

Assuming that a quality early childhood development program is too expensive to achieve passes the burden on to children, who ultimately pay the price of a lower quality program. In addition, ever growing challenges in recruiting and retaining qualified staff are being experienced in a number of communities in Canada. However, like all good investments, an expenditure in quality early childhood programs for children will reap dividends many times the original cost.

Key Terms and Concepts

Accounts payable, p. 234

Accounts receivable, p. 233

Bad debt, p. 234

Benefits, p. 227

Budget, p. 224

Cash flow, p. 223

Cost-of-living adjustment (COLA), p. 235

Fee subsidy, p. 232

Fixed costs, p. 225

Incremental budgeting, p. 225

Maintenance, p. 228

Operating budget, p. 224

Operations, p. 224

Personnel policies, p. 227

Revenue, p. 223

Start-up budget, p. 224

Variable costs, p. 225

Zero-based budgeting, p. 225

Activities

1. In order to increase awareness of the sources of income for a program budget, make arrangements to interview a director. Assure her that all information gathered will be kept confidential. Gather responses to the following questions:

    •   What are the weekly rates for the following age groups: infants, toddlers, preschoolers, school-age children?

    •   How much of the total budget is covered by parent fees?

    •   What are other sources of funding (operating grants, wage enhancement grants, etc.)?

    •   Is the program involved in fundraising? What are the activities? Approximately what percentage of the total budget is raised through fundraising?

2. Investigate how community ECEC programs pay their employees (i.e., weekly or monthly, hourly wage or salary). Does the program prepare its own payroll or does it use a service?

3. Review provincial/territorial funding programs available in your region. For which are ECEC programs eligible? What is the procedure for applying for funds?

4. Develop a detailed budget for a family child care program. Identify what items should be included.

5. Survey three programs in your community to determine the salary ranges for caregivers. Is there much difference? If so, why do you think there is a difference?

Recommended Reading

Bush, J. *Dollars and Sense: Planning for Profit in Your Child Care Business*. Albany, NY: Delmar, 2000.

Canadian Child Care Federation. *Family Child Care Training Program, Level 3*. Ottawa: Canadian Child Care Federation, 2003.

Draper, N. *Board Orientation Manual: A Key to Effective Governance*. Belleville, ON: Family Space Quinte Inc., 1997.

Morgan, G. *Managing the Day Care Dollars: A Financial Handbook*. Rev. ed. Cambridge, MA: Steam Press, 1992.

Neugebauer, R. and B. Neugebauer, eds. *Managing Money: A Center Director's Guidebook*. Redmond, WA: Exchange Press, 1997.

Stevenson, M.F. *Fundraising for Early Childhood Programs: Getting Started and Getting Results*. Rev. ed. Washington, DC: National Association for the Education of Young Children, 1995.

Willer, B. *Reaching the Full Cost of Quality in Early Childhood Programs*. Washington, DC: National Association for the Education of Young Children, 1990.

Weblinks

www.187gerrard.com
Cowperthwaite Mehta
Cowperthwaite Mehta provides administrative services to over 150 non-profit organizations. This valuable website has information available in the following categories: financial management, governance, technology, taxation, and registered charities, as well as child-care-specific information. Its newsletter, *Financial Management,* is available online.

www.cfc-efc.ca/wcfcca
Western Canada Family Child Care Association of BC
This site provides a wealth of information including links to Child and Family Canada, current British Columbia legislation for operating a family child care home, and a list of resources— both print resources and community groups—for parents and providers.

Advocating for Canada's Children

chapter 11

Objectives

- **Identify the need for advocacy.**
- **Examine the role of the ECEC practitioner in advocating for young children and families.**
- **Define types of advocacy.**
- **Increase awareness of media portrayal of early childhood development.**
- **Define the need for public education.**
- **Identify personal and collective approaches to advocating for early childhood development and its workforce.**
- **Identify the skills needed to promote an awareness of early childhood development issues.**
- **Recognize the advocacy role of organizations in addressing issues of quality, compensation, and accessibility.**

Rationale for Advocacy

The research is clear: the early years matter. Quality early childhood education and care makes a difference for young children. When it is done right, ECEC benefits families and communities as well as the children themselves. We need to get the message out. Early childhood practitioners need to set aside their ambivalence about **advocacy**, identify community partners, develop message strategies, and advocate for better funding. This chapter examines this public responsibility, suggests strategies to achieve it, and summarizes some advocacy success stories.

To effectively advocate, practitioners require first-hand knowledge of the issues facing children, families, and staff. Some important messages to communicate include:

- Early childhood is an important time for brain development. It is crucial for infants and toddlers that we have knowledgeable practitioners and responsive environments to stimulate children's learning. The pathways and connections made in the brain during the early years affect the brain's capacity in future.

- High quality early childhood services need to be maintained as well as expanded. The gap between supply and demand is significant. Families have great difficulty finding quality environments for their infants, toddlers, and school-age children.

- The education of caregivers is a major determinant of how well children do in early childhood settings. One of the most important components of high quality programs is education and the ongoing professional development of the staff. In programs where the caregivers have preparation in early childhood development, the children behave more positively, are more co-operative, and are more involved in the program (Doherty 2000a).

- Early childhood development is not only an issue for women. Both men and women feel the stress of work and family responsibilities.

- Early childhood development is not only a concern of the individual family. It affects the economy and society as a whole. Employers are becoming increasingly aware and, in some cases, attempting to respond to the problems that arise when families are unable to make adequate child care arrangements. Many Canadians experience frustration and disappointment in their efforts to find quality early childhood environments for their children. For their minds to be at ease while they work or

Early childhood practitioners must speak out on behalf of young children.

study, parents need settings that provide reassurance and inspire confidence. Regulated care continues to be largely unavailable, unaffordable, or unsatisfactory; in some cases, all three problems exist. Even when a quality setting is located for one child in the family, the service may not offer care for the older or younger child in the family. In some situations two—or even three—child care arrangements are required to meet the needs of one family.

Few employers have responded adequately to the changing needs of families. In parts of the country, regulated services are almost non-existent for parents working shifts and irregular hours, or for those needing part-time, seasonal, or emergency care. Specialized services for First Nations children, children with special needs, and other children from diverse backgrounds are often lacking (Irwin, Lero, and Brophy 2000). In some places, long waiting lists for subsidized spaces exist alongside full-fee vacancies in established programs. The list of issues is long, and every item poses challenges. Many Canadians have little understanding of these crucial issues, and it is critical to increase public awareness. The results will be:

- happier, healthier, and more competent children;
- families who can concentrate on their jobs or studies, knowing that their children are well cared for;
- increased opportunities for optimal early childhood development;
- decreased number of settings/transitions needed by one family;
- reduction in unnecessary travelling time for families;
- siblings who are able to see each other for parts of the day; and
- reduction in the stress many families are experiencing balancing work/family responsibilities.

Taking on an Advocacy Role

Child advocacy is political or legislative activism—by parents, professionals, or other interested groups—who urge the consideration of social issues affecting children. It is a personal commitment to active involvement in the lives of children, beyond remunerated professional responsibilities, with the goal of enhancing the opportunities for children to achieve optimal growth and development. Early childhood practitioners have a responsibility to become activists for children and families. Activism does not imply radicalism, only a firm belief in the value of early childhood development and a commitment to influence children's lives for the better.

When caregivers become child advocates, they move beyond the boundaries of their immediate employment situations into the greater society. Many must overcome feelings of powerlessness, which are related to the low value sometimes placed on the profession by the public and lack of public understanding of the importance of early childhood development. Feelings of powerlessness can also stem from low salaries. *You Bet I Care!* found that only a few staff felt that their job was respected by the general public. Some early childhood practitioners must also overcome a lack of knowledge of the intricate workings of government and fear of the political process (Doherty et al. 2000a). Kagan (1988) lists several additional reasons why early childhood practitioners tend to be ambivalent about advocacy. Many practitioners believe curriculum planning and caregiving are their chief responsibilities. Some may be cynical and believe that political action is fruitless. Others question the use of political forces for child advocacy. Kaiser and Sklar Rasminsky suggest "we may feel safer inside the familiar world of the centre with the children and parents" (1999a, 10).

It is essential to incorporate advocacy into one's professional self-image and envision advocacy as a problem-solving tool. When governments reduce funding, cut ratios, or freeze subsidies, there is an immediate impact on the quality of service that is provided.

RATIONALES FOR ADVOCACY

Advocacy in the field of early childhood development has four main rationales, all of which are critically important to practitioners:

- Preserve programs and safeguard spaces for children.

- Increase service capacity, enhance program quality, or demonstrate that a new idea or program type can increase quality or accessibility.

- Change the infrastructure of the field, making early childhood development programs more accessible, affordable, and equitable.

- Generate public awareness of issues facing the early childhood development field and the families of young children.

Types of Advocacy

Given the urgent need for advocacy for young children and their families, how does an early childhood practitioner go about this? Caldwell (1987) identifies three types of advocacy—personal, professional, and informational.

Personal advocacy can be as straightforward as helping a neighbour understand what you do at your job. It is based on the way practitioners carry out their daily practice and communication with others. For example, when someone refers to an early childhood practitioner as a "babysitter," gently but firmly correct them. Help friends to understand why caring for children costs as much as it does, and how it can help them in their own jobs. Enlighten them on the critical importance of the early years for learning; explain how early experiences benefit children. Correct the assumption that child care is a custodial service for the poor by making clear that care for children is a service used by families of all income groups.

The more practitioners learn about the importance of child development and appropriate practices, the more they will resist pressure to accept less than optimal environments in early childhood settings. Keeping informed and making changes to improve children's health and well-being is part of personal advocacy.

Personal advocacy is generally carried out on one's own time. Some employers, such as public institutions, do not support advocacy efforts by employees. In such situations, make it clear that you are speaking as a citizen, not as a public employee.

Professional advocacy is often called "lobbying." Like personal advocacy, its aim is to benefit the profession and the children and families it serves. This type of advocacy attempts to challenge and reform public systems that affect children and families and is directed toward legislative, administrative, and budgetary processes.

There are many groups that advocate for quality early childhood development programs. A climate of deregulation and deficit cutting serve as powerful motivators for practitioners to be involved in public policy. Public policy **advocates** try to change policies, practices, and budgets to make them more responsive to children's needs. The study *A Matter of Urgency* affirms that the primary responsibility for ensuring all children, have access to quality early childhood development programs lies with all three levels of government (Irwin, Lero, and Brophy 2000). The study recommends "that the federal, provincial and territorial, and municipal governments make specific public commitments to ensure the equitable inclusion of children with special needs in all child care programs and other early childhood development services that receive public funding or preferential tax treatment."

Broadening the base of support to include groups such as health professionals and the business community is essential if widespread public understanding and support for high quality, inclusive ECEC programs is to be attained. In the past decade, the field has gained strong allies such as the Canadian Paediatric Association, the Canadian Teachers' Federation, Family Service Canada, and the National Council on Crime Prevention, to name a few.

Informational advocacy, or educative advocacy, is directed to raising public awareness of the importance of the period of early childhood and the capacity of high quality programs to strengthen families and provide opportunities for optimal growth and development of young children.

Practitioners can start by educating the families at their own program about high quality care and education. Some families send their child to a program because of convenience rather than the superb care offered. They may take quality for granted. However, once they have a real understanding of what good early childhood development is and its importance for their child's future, they will more likely demand it—both from the program and from the government. Families can have a large influence on policy, through their votes and by speaking out. Helping parents to become effective advocates for their children is essential. Whenever early childhood development is advocated for in the media, articles should be posted on the parents' bulletin board as examples of this advocacy approach.

What Can Be Done?

When you commit yourself to being an advocate for the creation of environments that support optimal child development, there is a lot of work ahead. The task isn't simple. The best place to start is in your own program.

1. Increase Staff Awareness Regarding Advocacy

At staff meetings, directors can provide regular updates on advocacy initiatives and discuss implications, report on meetings attended, and share information and resources. Staff may need to be encouraged to join professional and advocacy groups. The board of directors can be encouraged to contribute to professional development opportunities and/or memberships in early childhood organizations for staff. To build skills and confidence, opportunities for participation and leadership experience should be provided. Directors can inspire and encourage staff to participate. These collective efforts can build bonds among the staff and a sense of solidarity with other concerned people. The action taken by young parents in the Prospects for Young Families in Toronto Project demonstrates the feelings of empowerment that can be achieved by collective action.

Case Study

Prospects for Young Families in Toronto Project

This group is working to improve circumstances faced by young families. Data was collected and compared with information from a similar study conducted a decade ago. Statistics showed that between 1981 and 2001, poverty rates for young families in Toronto jumped by an alarming 56%. During the same period, the median income for these families fell by more than 20%, representing a much larger decline than that of older families. Clearly, decision makers were not hearing what young families needed and ensuring that they got it. The project's organizers recognized that parents know what they need to support their children and themselves, and this initiative gave them the opportunity to express their ideas, hopes, and frustrations about how to improve their quality of life. A variety of family structures were represented: single parent families, aboriginal families, families new to Canada, same-sex couples, and adolescent parents. Their insights and experiences are a testament to their commitment to building a future for their children. To endeavour to change these patterns, a number of community-based organizations met with 58 young parents (under 35) to see how they were doing socially and economically and to explore their experiences and ideas on:

- work
- barriers to employment such as lack of child care, education, and training
- managing the system for those living on social assistance
- finding safe and affordable housing
- accessing adequate and appropriate health care
- improving opportunities for young families

The families involved with the Prospects for Young Families in Toronto Project were brimming with ideas about how to effect change and are ready to put their energies into action. Many of the recommendations outlined in the project's final report (Wilson 2004), came from the ideas put forward by these families. Several parents who participated in the project are involved with other groups advocating for changes to housing, income security, and child care policies. Some participated in the media conference to release the reports produced by the project and are pressing for action on the recommendations contained in them. Decision makers are listening. In the days following the release of the project's reports, the Mayor of Toronto said he supported one of the key recommendations made by the *Prospects* report—to convene a "summit on good jobs." There is no doubt that the city's young parents will be watching ensure that policy makers at all levels of government follow through on these ideas, stop the downward spiral facing them, and improve the quality of life for Toronto's young families.

Michele Lupa, Coordinator
Growing Up Healthy Downtown

(a partnership of multi-service agencies, part of the Family Service Association of Toronto)

2. Choose the Issue

There are many issues needing attention and it is easy to feel overwhelmed. Most practitioners do not look for ways to become involved in public issues. As citizens we hope and expect that elected officials will do a reasonably good job of governing. However, it has been apparent for some time that there are many unresolved issues in our chosen field. There is a need to target efforts.

In defining the issue, it is important to propose solutions as well as protest problems. It is necessary to identify small, incremental goals. It is less daunting to try to achieve small goals, and results are easier to measure.

What happens to families when they don't have high quality ECEC programs available?

Families suffer, but more importantly, society suffers. We won't have a productive, pleasant society if we don't properly prepare our youngest citizens.

What is the connection between practitioners' salaries and the quality of ECEC that children receive?

Practitioners who are better paid tend to stay longer in their jobs, and they can form consistent relationships with the children and foster in them the emotional stability that they need to learn and grow. Highly qualified, experienced, well-educated teachers are leaving the profession because they cannot afford to stay at current wages. The report *Working for Change: Canada's Child Care Workforce* (Beach et al. 2004) noted there was high turnover and a limited career ladder.

What would an educationally-oriented ECEC program look like?

Education for young children is rooted in relationships, emotional health, and bonding. Learning takes place through play and active exploration. This play needs to be guided and supported by consistent, knowledgeable, caring practitioners, who can provide children with the emotional stability and confidence to explore the world. The love of learning can be nurtured through the early years. Consistent caregiving is essential for children, so they can feel emotionally comfortable in learning. The key ingredient in educationally appropriate care is the knowledgeable, responsive staff.

3. Gather the Facts

After the issue has been chosen, the case must be presented in a convincing way. For this, information is needed. Before one can speak confidently and capably about the issues facing families and their children in a changing and demanding society, one must understand the issues and be able to articulate them clearly in one's own mind. One must be aware of the research and gather facts, placing them in a coherent order, and draw conclusions from them. It is essential to know the numbers of people affected by the problem. The Childcare Resource and Research Unit provides demographic fact sheets, information kits, bibliographies, and background papers to aid in this task. (Many are available online; website addresses are included later in the chapter.) A number of organizations, such as the Vanier Institute of the Family and Canadian Policy Research Networks, conduct research on child and family issues. When using research to guide policy recommendations and make persuasive arguments, it is important to critically investigate the information used. The document "Understanding Research: Top Ten Tips for Advocates and Policymakers" offers some useful guidance on this subject. It is available online at www.childadvocacy.org.

As well, practitioners should monitor the media to find out what has been reported and how the issue was reported. Track who was interviewed and the names of reporters who cover the issue. This information can identify potential allies. Most reporters will gladly listen to an insider's point of view, and once you have shown that you are informed and articulate, they might repeatedly call upon your expertise. It is also important to be familiar with those who have opposing viewpoints. Understanding their arguments helps increase your effectiveness as an advocate when responding to their concerns. However, it is not enough to get in the news; it must be portrayed in a way that lets policy makers know what they must do to improve the situation. How the story is covered has a huge impact on how the public and policy makers perceive and address it. The publication *Making the Case for Early Childhood Education and Care: A Message Development Guide for Advocates* (Dorfman et al. 2004) provides invaluable information to enable success.

4. Work with Others

The challenges faced in providing optimal development opportunities for children are multi-faceted. They require the involvement and coordination of numerous groups in all levels of government, private sector organizations, and related professions. A host of barriers needs to be bridged, between health care and child care, economic development and human development, and the child care and child welfare systems.

An organization made up of peers, such as staff from other programs, is an obvious place to start. Target local associations, anti-poverty groups, trade unions, women's groups, child welfare organizations, advisory councils, and government agencies that are actively addressing early childhood issues. Monitor the work of these groups online, attend a couple of meetings, and when you are familiar with the organization and feel at ease, share your ideas.

At your ECEC program, keep a list of pertinent provincial/territorial and local agencies. Provide the names, telephone numbers, and e-mail addresses of appropriate contact persons to parents who express concern over issues and are prepared to lobby.

5. Take Action

A fundamental step in developing an advocacy strategy is to figure out under which jurisdiction the concern in question falls. Pinning responsibility where it belongs can be more complicated than one might expect. Sometimes demands must be presented to two levels of government, such as provincial/territorial and municipal governments. Start a list of individuals who have responsibility for an issue. Look at your community and find out how the government structure will allow you to have input into municipal, regional, provincial, and federal decision making on early childhood issues.

> ### CHECKLIST: KEY QUESTIONS WHEN CHOOSING A TARGET
>
> Who or what institution has the power to solve the problem and pass the desired policy?
>
> Who has the power to influence the target person or institution? (Voters, consumers, taxpayers, stockholders)?
>
> What is their interest? For example, if the person or institution is elected, how many voting parents are in their constituency?

6. Enlist More Child Advocates by Informing Others

A key task is to be heard by the right group. Advocates direct their lobbying toward decision makers. Decision makers can range from heads of government to families to boards of directors to employers. Politicians are decision makers. They need to hear from voters before they will put an issue at the forefront of policy. Policy can be changed through pressure applied by large groups of voters. Task force committees, commissions, and public hearings present opportunities to communicate policy recommendations and respond to budget allocations and government policy initiatives. Position papers and briefs outline each group's perspective and recommendations on a particular issue.

There are a number of ways in which advocates can convey these messages. It is essential to get accurate images of the field of early childhood education and care to the public and government. This requires personal efforts and professional supports.

Membership in a professional organization provides an effective channel for communication with the public and to government. Many local, provincial, and national groups are actively involved in public education and advocacy efforts, and it is beneficial to be aware of the objectives of these groups and to work with them. (Provincial early childhood organizations are listed in the appendix.) The Canadian Child Care Federation publishes a comprehensive directory of provincial and local early childhood organizations on the Child and Family Canada website at www.cfc-efc.ca/cccf. This list provides a good starting point for contacting others who are concerned with quality services for children and families.

Individuals you might talk with about your program include legislators, members of the business community, politicians, media representatives, parents, and other professionals.

Call or write the minister responsible for young children (see appendix), the member of parliament for the riding where you work or reside, your provincial representative (MLA), and/or your municipal councillor. Contact MPs in the Opposition—they long to hear of voter dissatisfaction and welcome ideas, particularly near election time. Describe your program, explaining the service it provides for children and families. Take the opportunity to explain the support you require in order to improve the service. Politicians are often interested in knowing the number of children served by the program and their ages. It is useful to have photographs of the children engaged in positive activities. Encourage prearranged visits to the program. Include families and staff in presentations.

Remember, no one strategy will always work. Each advocacy experience is unique because the people and issues involved vary. Advocates must be prepared to use a variety of techniques and be persistent. Change takes time, and developing any new skill takes time. Some people have special areas of interest. People should take on the jobs they are most comfortable doing. Some will be speakers, others writers, planners, researchers, or envelope stuffers. Each role is valid and necessary.

The Need for Public Education

There are many misconceptions about early childhood education and care and the needs of Canadian families. Some continue to believe that the "traditional family" of two parents, two children, with a mother at home, is typical. A few continue to think a mother's involvement in the workforce will harm her children. Some Canadians question their tax dollars being spent on caring for children and ask why these services are so expensive. Some people believe that children do not learn much when they are young, so the education of caregivers is unnecessary. Sometimes we need to focus on why early childhood development programs are good for children in order to change the public perception that only parents' needs are met.

A concerted public and government education effort will need to be made to meet the never-ending challenge of achieving comprehensive, high quality early childhood environments in Canada. This effort is hampered, in part, by non-standardized nomenclature in the field. For example, there is little consensus on what we should call ourselves: "early childhood educators," "child care workers," "caregivers," "early childhood professionals," or "providers," to mention a few. Some groups have developed a glossary of terms, but no one title has been universally adopted. The discussion paper *What's in a Name?* (CCCF 2004) suggests that the debate can best be approached through a framework of child care merging with education.

The public's image of early childhood development needs clarification and improvement. Highly knowledgeable and committed staff are crucial for the delivery of quality programs for children. A very high proportion of staff love the day-to-day aspects of their job. However, the study *You Bet I Care!* (Doherty et al. 2000a) as well as working for change found poor morale and the potential for high turnover rates.

The perception of being undervalued or not respected contributes to poor staff morale and high turnover and impedes recruitment of new workers into the field. There is an urgent need for a public information campaign that ties the increasing evidence of the importance of the early years to a recognition of the value of the people who work in early childhood development. As discussed in chapter 1, practitioner education in early child development is linked to high quality care. Practitioners with appropriate education deserve to receive adequate wages. Instead, early childhood practitioners have often had their already inadequate salaries frozen. The true cost of ECEC continues to be poorly understood. Public education campaigns help garner increased public support for the investment of government funds in early childhood development and the education of young children and for adequate remuneration for caregivers and family child care providers.

The governments of Manitoba and Quebec have each undertaken public education campaigns to attract more individuals to the field of ECEC. As well, campaigns such as the Worthy Wage Campaign carried out by the Manitoba Child Care Association, and the Parade of Promises by Nova Scotia's Child Care Connection NS draw attention to early childhood practitioners' inadequate compensation and the value of the work itself. The public becomes informed of the wide discrepancies between the responsibilities and skills required to do the job and the compensation levels. In order for these efforts to succeed, all early childhood practitioners must make it their business to understand the issues and solutions—more government support and greater public education—and recruit others to join the undertaking.

Case Study

Child Care Worker Appreciation Day

The Ontario Coalition for Better Child Care (OCBCC) has introduced a day of celebration, held in November each year, to acknowledge the work of child care practitioners. This important event is an opportunity for parents, boards of directors, supervisors, community members and politicians to show their thanks to practitioners who work with young children on a daily basis. Ten thousand OCBCC members, six union partners, and over 80 municipalities passed resolutions to support this annual event. Part of the focus was on making government and the public at large aware of the challenges faced by practitioners and on publicly recognizing the important work carried out by child care workers—who are amongst the poorest paid professionals in society. The provincial government could demonstrate their respect for this important work by adequately funding the sector, including providing funds to further enhance wage subsidies and money for professional development.

On this year's Child Care Worker Appreciation Day, boards of directors showed their appreciation through a variety of events, such as taking the staff to dinner and sharing stories and laughter. In one community, a local politician brought home-baked treats. Some staff received gift baskets while others received a poem and merit bonuses. In *Working for Change: Canada's Child Care Workforce* (Beach et al. 2004), practitioners voiced the need for better understanding of their roles and responsibilities, a valuing of the service, and required expertise to ensure the well-being of children. Events such as Child Care Worker Appreciation Day serve as a step to building the necessary support to establish progressive public policy and expand public investment.

Kira Heineck
Ontario Coalition for Better Child Care

Framing Media Portrayal of Early Childhood Development

Television, radio, newspapers and magazines, and the Internet are powerful influences. An earlier approach to stories in the media was the framing of government support for ECEC as a necessity as a support to working parents rather than as a child development issue. Consequently, parents, rather than children were portrayed as the key benefactors of ECEC. More recently, the message emphasizes child care as a social benefit, particularly for poor children. Another message, is that child care is an economic benefit for parents enabling them to work or study. This serves as a desired message for employers who have access to a broader base of talented employees. For society, good and available child care has the ultimate potential of enlarging the tax base and creating more prosperous communities. Not only is it important that we keep child care in the news, it is critical that we are sending the right message: that high quality child care benefits children, families, and communities.

Advocacy Strategies

Use anecdotes from your program or community as an effective way to build awareness of early childhood concerns. As a caregiver, you see first-hand the issues that face children and their families. The following questions may help you to think about the kinds of information you could provide through public education endeavours:

- How available is regulated child care in your community? Are there waiting lists for care? Is part-time care available for school-age children?
- Is funding available to assist families with the cost of child care? What percentage of a family's total income is needed for child care?
- What are the average salaries of caregivers in your community?
- Are there professional development opportunities for early childhood staff in your community?
- Are salary levels affecting staff retention and the quality of programs? Are salary levels attracting appropriate candidates to the field?
- Do families have access to good information about early childhood services?
- Are provincial/territorial licensing standards adequate?
- Is there support for early childhood development from your business community?
- Is there a need for care for the children of parents who work shifts?
- Is care available for children with special needs?

It is important to recognize that early childhood practitioners can and do make a difference in improving the quality of programs for young children and their families. Some early childhood practitioners need to consider running for local, provincial/territorial, or national office. Only by working diligently together can we hope to continue to change public attitudes toward early childhood development. This change is required to get the critical mass of support needed to provide a comprehensive, high quality early childhood development system that responds to the diverse needs of Canadian families. As you become more aware of the need to take a stand in improving the field, you will continue to add effective strategies to your list.

ADVOCACY STRATEGIES

- Share with others anecdotes about experiences in the program (real stories of children and families) and information about its significance in the community.
- Speak to community groups and the local media.
- Arrange for decision makers to visit your program.
- Write letters to the editor of your local newspaper or popular magazines.
- Write for professional newsletters or journals.
- Speak on radio programs and make television appearances.
- Prepare a press release.

(continued)

- Call or write the minister responsible for young children, your MP and MPs in the Opposition, your MLA, and/or your municipal councillor.
- Speak with government staff at both informal and formal meetings.
- Get involved in interactive conferences on the Internet.
- Provide leadership at workshops or conferences.
- Prepare a deputation to policy makers on an issue affecting children, families, or staff in your program.

To turn business leaders and politicians into advocates for early childhood development programs, use the following strategies:

- Educate them about the fact that child care has an important educational component.
- Talk investment rather than spending. Early childhood development truly is an investment in the future—boosting children's school readiness and success in school and on the job. There are plenty of examples to document this.
- Be specific. Nothing turns off a business person faster than talking in generalities. You need to have a concrete proposal with concrete goals and a way to achieve those goals. Be concise and focused, using only the facts you need for a winning case.
- Start small, be patient. There's a learning curve to every new venture, and turning a business person/politician into an advocate can take time. It pays to approach people who have already shown an interest in children's issues and then educate them and bring them along. Take them to visit local programs.

Working with Unions

Overall, unionized ECEC workplaces contribute to higher quality programs and more knowledgable staff. Unions support professional development and regulation of the occupation. They are long-standing advocates of women's equality and a publicly funded ECEC system. The paper "The Union Advantage in Child Care: How Unionization Can Help Recruitment and Retention" (Kass and Costigliola 2003) elaborates on the supports and services provided by unions.

In September 2003, thousands of Quebec child care workers walked off their jobs to pressure the provincial government to honour their pay equity commitment in their collective agreement. The contract signed in March 2003, called for a 2% pay increase, and set a deadline for the implementation of pay equity. Although the government did increase the wages as promised, they had not followed through on the pay equity clause. The Confederation des Syndicates Nationaux represents the majority of centre-based caregivers who are predominately women. The strike was the first of four one-day strikes to improve wages. Although actions such as this—or even becoming unionized—are not the only strategies to solve workers' issues, this has proven to be an effective way to get measurable results that improve the lives of practitioners and the quality of the service for children and families.

Summary

This final chapter acknowledges the many caregivers who witness the plight of the increasing numbers of children and families who face abject poverty and recognize that this must be brought to the public's consciousness. Yet the social problems reach beyond families who are poor to parents with moderate incomes who are beset by the scarcity of affordable, high quality early childhood development programs. Advocacy and professional empowerment are necessary roles for all practitioners. Early childhood practitioners need to take a stand to improve early childhood development so that current and future generations—both families and practitioners—will benefit. The potential of early childhood environments must be communicated. Advocacy activities include active membership in child care organizations, writing letters to influence policy makers, writing informational articles, and speaking to the media.

Key Terms and Concepts

Advocacy, p. 243

Advocates, p. 247

Child advocacy, p. 245

Informational advocacy, p. 247

Personal advocacy, p. 246

Professional advocacy, p. 246

Activities

1. Identify an organization in your community that is working for better early childhood development services. Make arrangements to attend a meeting, interview staff about the goals of the organization, or subscribe to their newsletter.

2. If you were given three wishes to bring about changes for children and their families, what would they be? Share your choices with others in the class. Identify priorities from the compiled list. Develop strategies you might use to advocate for these issues.

3. Review daily newspapers to identify statements of public policy related to early childhood development. What are the issues involved? In what ways do you support or disagree with these positions?

4. Review popular publications to assess how often child care is portrayed in the media. What views are held by the general public and are these views consistent with media portrayals?

Recommended Reading

Dorfman, L., K. Woodruff, S. Herbert, and J. Ervice. *Making the Case for Early Care and Education: A Message Development Guide for Advocates.* Berkeley, CA: Berkeley Media Studies Group, 2004.

Fennimore, B. *Child Advocacy for Early Childhood Educators.* New York: Teachers College Press, Columbia University, 1989.

Goffin, S. and J. Lombardi. *Speaking Out: Early Childhood Advocacy.* Washington, DC: National Association for the Education of Young Children, 1988.

Guy, K., ed. *Our Promise to Children.* Ottawa: Canadian Institute of Child Health, 1997.

Jensen, M. and M.A. Hannibal. *Issues, Advocacy, and Leadership in Early Education.* Needham Heights, MA: Allyn & Bacon, 2000.

Weblinks

The national organizations listed below are among a number in Canada that provide assistance, publications, and/or technical support to professionals and members of the general public concerned about the well-being of children and families. Weblinks, where available, are included to facilitate accessing further information about publications and services.

www.cfc-efc.ca/cccf
Canadian Child Care Federation

The Canadian Child Care Federation is a national non-profit organization working to improve the quality of child care for Canada's children through its membership of provincial/territorial organizations, caregivers and providers, and programs. It plays a leadership role in research and policy development, provision of information services and publications, and facilitating communication in the field.

www.cfc-efc.ca/nca
National Children's Alliance

The National Children's Alliance is a group of national organizations with an interest in the well-being of children and youth. The group meets monthly to share information, work co-operatively, devise strategies to promote a national children's agenda, and respond to concerns and issues affecting children and their families. Since 1996, it has been promoting the discussion of policy issues through the document *Investing in Canada's Children—A Framework for Action,* available on the site.

www.cfc-efc.ca/ccrc
Canadian Coalition on the Rights of Children (CCRC)

The CCRC has a membership of over 45 non-governmental agencies (NGOs) committed to promoting the rights of children in Canada and abroad. The mandate of the coalition is to ensure a collective voice for Canadian organizations and youth concerned with the rights of children as described in the United Nations Convention on the Rights of the Child and the World Summit for Children declaration. The CCRC was responsible for preparing a report on Canada's compliance with the UN Convention in 1999. The CCRC has coordinated input into the Special United Nations Session on Child and Youth scheduled for 2002.

www.childcarecanada.org
Childcare Resource and Research Unit (CRRU)

The Childcare Resource and Research Unit (part of the Centre for Urban and Community Studies, University of Toronto) focuses on early childhood education and care policies and resources. Its mandate is to promote universally accessible and high quality settings in Canada. CRRU provides public education and policy analysis and publishes papers and other resources on child care policy, many of which are available online.

www.campaign2000.ca
Campaign 2000

Campaign 2000 is a non-partisan, cross-Canada coalition of over 70 national, provincial, and community organizations. Its mandate is to raise awareness of and support for the 1989 all-party House of Commons resolution to eliminate child poverty in Canada by the year 2000. This non-partisan group urges all Canadian elected officials to keep their promises to children. It publishes an annual report card on child poverty in Canada and organizes events to aid public education and advocacy.

www.frp.ca
Canadian Association of Family Resource Programs

This is a national organization whose mission is to promote the well-being of families by providing national leadership, consultation, and resources to those who care for children and support families.

www.childcareadvocacy.ca
Child Care Advocacy Association of Canada

This organization promotes comprehensive, high quality non-profit child care programs. It provides focus and leadership to social policy activists, labour groups, women's organizations, and the early childhood community through ongoing campaigns designed to improve the accessibility, availability, and quality of child care services across the country.

www.childadvocacy.org
Child Advocacy Institute

The Child Advocacy Institute page on the Voices for America's Children website offers a number of publications to help advocates be more effective in getting their message out to policy makers and the media. Some of the valuable fact sheets include "Understanding Research: Top Ten Tips for Advocates and Policymakers."

Appendix
Provincial Legislative Offices, Regulations, and Early Childhood Organizations

Alberta
Department Governing Early Childhood Programs

Ministry of Family and Social Services
Director, Service Support
Alberta Family and Social Services
7th Street Plaza
10030–107th Street, 9th Floor
Edmonton, Alberta
T5J 3E4
www.gov.ab.ca/cs

Provincial Organizations

Alberta Association for Young Children
Avonmore School, Room 31
7340–78th Street
Edmonton, Alberta
T6C 2N1

Alberta Association for Family Day Home Services
11411–54th Avenue
Edmonton, Alberta
T6H 0V8

British Columbia
Department Governing Early Childhood Programs

Child Care Team
Family Services, Child Day Care
P.O. Box 9965
836 Yates Street, 4th Floor
Stn Provincial Government
Victoria, British Columbia
V8W 9R4
www.sdes.gov.bc.ca/programs/childcar.htm

Provincial Organizations

Early Childhood Educators, British Columbia (ECEBC)
210 West Broadway, 3rd Floor
Vancouver, British Columbia
V5Y 3W2
www.cfc-efc.ca/ecebc

Western Canada Family Child Care Association of British Columbia
c/o 11861–88th Avenue, Suite 101
Delta, British Columbia
V4C 3C6
www.cfc-efc.ca/wcfcca

Manitoba
Department Governing Early Childhood Programs

Department of Family Services & Housing
Child Day Care
114 Garry Street, Suite 219
Winnipeg, Manitoba
R3C 4V6
www.gov.mb.ca/fs

Provincial Organizations

Manitoba Child Care Association, Inc.
2350 McPhillips Street, 2nd Floor
Winnipeg, Manitoba
R2V 4J6
www.cfc-efc.ca/mcca

New Brunswick
Department Governing Early Childhood Programs

Provincial Day Care Consultant
Family and Community Services
P.O. Box 6000
551 King Street, 2nd Floor, Carleton Place
Fredericton, New Brunswick
E3B 1E7
www.gov.nb.ca/hcs-ssc/english/services/fcss/index.htm

Provincial Organizations

Early Childhood Care and Education NB
770 Main Street, 8th Floor
Moncton, New Brunswick
E1C 1E7

Newfoundland
Department Governing Early Childhood Programs

Provincial Director of Child Care Services
Division of Child, Youth and Family Programs
Department of Health and Community Services
3rd Floor, Confederation Building, West Block
P.O. Box 8700
St. John's, Newfoundland
A1B 4J6
www.gov.nf.ca/health

Provincial Organizations

Association of Early Childhood Educators of Newfoundland and Labrador (AECENL)
P.O. Box 8657
St. John's, Newfoundland
A1B 3T1
www.cfc-efc.ca/aecenfld

Family Home Child Care Association of Newfoundland and Labrador
25 Canada Drive
St. John's, Newfoundland
A1E 4H2

Northwest Territories
Department Governing Early Childhood Programs

Early Childhood Coordinator
Education, Culture & Employment
Government of the NWT
P.O. Box 1320
Yellowknife, Northwest Territories
X1A 2L9
siksik.learnet.nt.ca

Territorial Organizations

Currently there are no active child organizations in the NWT.

Nova Scotia

Department Governing Early Childhood Programs

Director
Community Services
Family & Children's Services
Early Childhood Development Services
P.O. Box 696
Halifax, Nova Scotia
B3J 2T7
www.gov.ns.ca/coms

Provincial Organizations

Certification Council of Early Childhood Education of Nova Scotia
1200 Tower Road
Halifax, Nova Scotia
B3J 1C2
www.cfc-efc.ca/ccens

Child Care Connection NS
1200 Tower Road, Suite 100
Halifax, Nova Scotia
B3J 1C2
home.istar.ca/-cccns

Nunavut

Department Governing Early Childhood Programs

Early Child Development Manager
Department of Education
Government of Nunavut
P.O. Box 1000, Station 980
Iqaluit, Nunavut
X0A 0H0

Territorial Organizations

Currently there are no active child organizations in Nunavut.

Ontario
Department Governing Early Childhood Programs

Director, Early Years & Healthy Child Development Branch
Integrated Services for Children Division
4th Floor, Hepburn Block
80 Grosvenor Street
Toronto, Ontario
M7A 1E9
www.gov.on.ca/css

Provincial Organizations

Association of Early Childhood Educators, Ontario (AECEO)
40 Orchard View Boulevard, Suite #211
Toronto, Ontario
M4R 1B9
www.cfc-efc.ca/aeceo

Ontario Coalition for Better Child Care
726 Bloor Street West, Suite 209
Toronto, Ontario
M6G 4A1
www.childcareontario.org

Home Child Care Association of Ontario
c/o Network Child Care Services
756 Ossington Avenue
Toronto, Ontario
M6G 3T9
www.cfc-efc.ca/hccao

Prince Edward Island
Department Governing Early Childhood Programs

Director, Children's Secretariat
Social Policy Development
Department of Health and Social Services
16 Garfield Street, P.O. Box 2000
Charlottetown, Prince Edward Island
C1A 7N8
www.gov.pe.ca/hss/cfacs-info/index.php3

Provincial Organizations

Early Childhood Development Association of PEI
129 Kent Street, Suite 205
Charlottetown, Prince Edward Island
C1A 1N4
www.cfc-efc.ca/ecdapei

Quebec
Department Governing Early Childhood Programs

Conseillière en affaires internationales
Ministère de la Famille et de l'Enfance
425 rue St-Amable
Québec City, Québec
J1R 4Z1
www.famille-enfance.gouv.gc.ca

Provincial Organizations

Association de l'éducation préscolaire du Québec
Montréal, Québec
H1K 4L1

Concertations inter-régionale des centres de la petite enfance du Québec
438, rue Victoria
St-Lambert, Québec
J4P 2J4

Saskatchewan
Department Governing Early Childhood Programs

Child Day Care Division
Department of Community Resources & Employment
1920 Broad Street
Regina, Saskatchewan
S4P 3V6
www.gov.sk.ca/govt/socserv

Provincial Organizations

Saskatchewan Early Childhood Association, Inc.
510 Cynthia Street
Saskatoon, Saskatchewan
S7L 7K7
www.cfc-efc/ca/scca

Yukon Territory
Department Governing Early Childhood Programs

Manager, Early Childhood & Prevention
Department of Health and Social Services
Government of Yukon
P.O. Box 2703 (H-12)
Whitehorse, Yukon
Y1A 2C6
www.yukonweb.com/government/womensdir/directory/whitehorse/hss.ht

Territorial Organizations

Yukon Child Care Association
Box 5439
Whitehorse, Yukon
Y1A 5H4
www.cfc-efc.ca/ycca

Glossary

Accountability   To be responsible for one's actions, reporting to funders.

Accounts payable   Bills to be paid by the program.

Accounts receivable   All monies owed by a person or organization to the program that have not been paid.

Accreditation   A type of quality control for programs, building on regulations and licensing standards; often involves self-study and validation by outside professionals.

Adult:child ratio   The number of children for whom an adult is responsible, calculated by dividing the total number of adults into the total number of children. A "high" ratio means there are fewer children per caregiver, a "low" ratio means there are more children.

Advisory board   An advisory board suggests policies and procedures or provides information to those who administer the program; it has no power to enforce its recommendations.

Advocacy   Lobbying for a cause. In the field of early childhood development, the cause may be services for children and families, recognition of quality services, or improved wages and working conditions for early childhood **practitioners**.

Advocates   Individuals or groups speaking out on behalf of others. Advocates pursue or define a program believed to be in the best interests of children and families.

Affordability   The ability of parents to pay for programs; the costs of providing a quality program.

Allergies   Physiological reactions, such as asthma, hives, or hay fever, to environmental or food substances. Allergies can affect or alter behaviour.

Altruism   The work is service-oriented and child-focused—not for financial rewards.

Annual general meeting (AGM)   A yearly meeting of shareholders of a corporation or members of a non-profit organization, especially for holding elections and reporting on the year's events.

Anti-bias curriculum   A method of presenting curricula that helps children to understand and respect differences such as race, gender, culture, and physical ability.

Auspice   Refers to the legal incorporated status of the program. In Canada, ECEC services operate under the auspices of **non-profit** or **for-profit** (commercial) organizations and **corporations**, municipalities, or schools.

Bad debt   An **accounts receivable** item that will never be collected.

Benefits   All the money and in-kind insurance, vacations, and other benefits offered to an employee over and above wages. There are both mandatory benefits, such as the Canada Pension Plan and Employment Insurance, and voluntary benefits, such as extended health and dental programs or paid recreational programs.

Best practices   Professional **standards**, elements, and principles that guide the education of early childhood **practitioners**. The basic principles include: encouraging active learning, addressing individual needs, recognizing different learning styles, providing hands-on learning experiences, and designing an environment in which children are responsible for their own learning.

Board of directors   A policy-making board that holds the ultimate responsibility for **non-profit** programs; also known as "governing board."

Budget   A statement of goals for one year stated in financial terms.

Bylaws   Rules made by a body subordinate to a legislature; rules made by an organization for its members describing such things as how a

corporation will do its business, its power structure, and how power may be transferred.

Career ladder   A way to describe a continuum of **professional development**. Each rung represents predetermined criteria for advancement to a new step, objective, or opportunity for **practitioners** to take on new roles.

Career lattice   Incorporates multiple, interlocking **career ladders** providing for the multiple roles and settings within the **early childhood profession**. Each step requires greater preparation, involves increased responsibility and compensation, and allows movement laterally.

Cash flow   The movement of cash used to operate a business or organization; cash inflow compared with cash outflow.

Centre   A group program licensed by the province or territory.

Certification   Professional recognition of an individual's **competency** to practice within a given occupation. This process recognizes that the individual has met the established occupational **standards** of knowledge, skills, and abilities needed to perform required tasks. The term "credentialling" may also be used.

Child advocacy   Political or legislative activism by **parents**, **practitioners**, or other interested groups who urge the consideration of social issues affecting children.

Child-centred   An educational philosophy that facilitates children selecting activities themselves.

Children with special needs   Children whose development and learning do not follow typical patterns. These children may need modifications to their environments and in their caregiver's style of interaction.

Clarity   The extent to which policies, procedures, and responsibilities in an early childhood setting are defined and communicated.

Code of ethics   A document that maps the dimensions of the **early childhood profession's** collective social responsibility and acknowledges the obligations individual

practitioners share in meeting the profession's responsibilities.

Colleague   Any other adult working in the program as well as professionals from the community.

Collective agreement   A negotiated agreement between an employer and employees' representatives (union) outlining the rate of pay and conditions of employment.

Collegiality   The extent to which staff work together as equals, co-operating rather than competing with one another.

Competency   The state of being adequately qualified or able to meet agreed-upon **standards of practice** relevant to the profession.

Conflict resolution policy   A written statement informing employees that they have the right to express complaints and a right to expect the employer to review and respond to the complaint.

Continuity   The way and degree to which aspects of a program relate to one another for the benefit of the children. The term can also refer to strategies among programs to communicate with each other.

Contract   A legally binding agreement, either written or oral, entered into by two parties. To be legally enforceable, a contract must have something offered by one party, accepted by the other party, and agreed upon "consideration."

Corporation   A legal entity with certain powers and responsibilities; a group of individuals who voluntarily join together under the law to form a **for-profit** or **non-profit** enterprise.

Cost-of-living adjustment (COLA)   A change in salary based on the government cost-of-living index.

CPE   Centre de la petit enfance. The primary administrative structure for regulated child care in Quebec. These are not-for-profit, community based organizations administered by parents that provide both centred-based care for children newborn to age 4 and regulated family child care.

Criminal reference check   A review of provincial or federal databases to determine if a job applicant has any outstanding criminal charges, criminal charges in front of the courts, or any criminal history.

Decision making   The degree of autonomy given to the board or staff and the extent to which they are involved in program-wide decisions.

Developmentally appropriate   A Developmentally Appropriate Program (DAP) is one designed and based on the principles of developmentally appropriate practice. The program incorporates play-based activities and experiences where the child is an active learner. The activities selected and the physical environment, material, and equipment must be age appropriate and correspond to the developmental level of each child.

Director   An individual administering, supervising, and/or managing an early childhood service, including group child care centres, **family child care** programs, nursery schools, child care support, and family resource programs. The director is usually responsible for overall administration and **supervision** of staff and, in some situations, may work with the children.

Early childhood education and care   All programs and services for children and families including group child care, **family child care**, kindergarten, family resource programs, and primary grades. This term is used by the Organisation for Economic Co-operation and Development (OECD) and the government of Canada.

Early childhood profession   The group of individuals who have acquired the pedagogical knowledge necessary to provide quality care and education to young children. Pedagogical knowledge is an organized body of knowledge forming the basis of the profession's **occupational standards** and influencing the concept of **best practice**. It includes core principles, relevant subject matter, theories of child development, and related methodology.

Early childhood setting   A setting other than a child's home in which care and education is provided for the child by a person who is not a member of the child's immediate family.

Ecological model   A framework for viewing childhood development that takes into account the various interconnected contexts within which an individual exists—for instance, the family, neighbourhood, and community.

Employee records   A collective term for all records containing information about employees and their employment.

Ethical dilemma   A moral conflict that involves determining appropriate conduct when an individual faces conflicting professional values and responsibilities.

Ethics   Moral principles; the study of right and wrong, duty and obligation. Ethics involves critical reflection on morality.

Ex officio member   A person who, although not a member of the board of directors, always attends board meetings by virtue of her or his office or status.

Exosystem   According to ecological theory, that part of the environment that includes the broader community—government, media.

Family-centred   A philosophy encompassing all aspects of family involvement and acknowledging the family as the focal point of care.

Family child care   Care in a private home, by a non-relative. This type of care is sometimes referred to as "home child care."

Family child care agency   The organization responsible for overseeing the individual home and ensuring the implementation of government **regulations**.

Family child care provider   One who offers care in her or his own home to a small group of children. In most provinces, care is limited to six or fewer children. Other terms also used include "caregiver" and "**practitioner**."

Family involvement   Expands the focus beyond the child by providing education and social services to the entire family.

Fee subsidy   Financial assistance from the government to help **parents** with low incomes pay for child care fees.

First Ministers   The premiers of Canada's provinces and territories.

Fiscal monitoring   Standards associated with funding.

Fixed costs   Those expenditures that tend to stay constant in the short term.

For-profit   An organization run with the aim of making a profit (although in reality it may not); a for-profit organization may be a sole proprietorship (i.e., one individual owns the business), **corporation**, partnership, or co-operative. Any profits may be distributed to investors or reinvested in the program.

Goal consensus   The degree to which staff agree on the goals and objectives of the early childhood development program.

Governing board   Makes and enforces policy that is then implemented by the program **director**.

Governing body   The group or person (**board of directors**, owner, parent/advisory committee) legally responsible for the actions of the program.

Grievance procedure   A process to be followed by an employee to settle a dispute, generally identifying who to contact.

Group size   The total number of children in a group.

Human resources policies   A set of written guidelines covering employer–employee relations. Policies describe conditions of employment and may include job descriptions, advancement opportunities, and procedures for termination of employment, conflict resolution, and so on.

In-service training   On-the-job training that adapts material or topics to meet the needs of a particular group. Workshops or seminars are conducted at the workplace.

Inclusion   The active involvement and participation of **children with special needs** into early childhood programs, which recognizes their rights as children first and affords them the same choices and opportunities granted to any child.

Incremental budgeting   Relying on information contained in the budget for the prior year.

Informational advocacy   Efforts to raise public awareness of the importance of early childhood development and the benefits to children and families.

Innovativeness   The extent to which an organization adapts to change and encourages staff to find creative ways to solve problems.

Legislation   Rules defined by government; the laws under which organizations operate.

License   A permit given to operators that meet the minimum requirement set by government.

Licensed program   A facility that has been assessed to ensure it provides a minimum quality of care so that children are not harmed.

Licensing   A process of applying **standards** or rules (Acts, **regulations**, or guidelines) to a facility to determine whether or not the licensee provides a minimum quality of care so that children are not harmed.

Macrosystem   According to ecological theory, the broadest part of the environment that includes cultural, political, and economic forces.

Maintenance   Major expenditures on the physical plant: painting, alterations, repair.

Mentor   Someone who can serve as a role model to help less experienced staff members gain new skills and knowledge.

Mentoring   A nurturing process wherein a more experienced practitioner serving as a role model, teaches, encourages, and counsels a less experienced staff member to promote the individual's professional and/or personal development.

Mesosystem   According to ecological theory, the linkages between family and the immediate neighbourhood or community.

Microsystem   According to ecological theory, that part of the environment that most immediately affects a person, such as the family, child care setting, school, or workplace.

Mission statement   A statement to clientele and the public at large stating the nature and purpose of the organization. This term may be used instead of "**philosophy**."

Mixed-age groupings   See **multi-age groupings**.

Monitoring   Official observation after licence issuance to determine ongoing or continued compliance with **licensing** requirements.

Multi-age groupings   Placing children who are at least a year apart in age into the same playgroup.

Non-profit   An organization not involved in making a profit. A non-profit organization is a legal entity that is intended to break even. It cannot issue dividends; it is required to invest any excess revenues in the program.

Nutrition   Encompasses both the quality and quantity of food consumed for healthful living.

Occupational standards   Skills, knowledge, and abilities needed to perform competently in the workforce and the **standards** that identify, describe, and measure the abilities individuals must possess. These standards form the basis for the **accreditation** and **certification** processes within the **early childhood profession**.

Operating budget   Used when programs become operational and annually thereafter.

Operations   Recurring day-to-day activities involved in the upkeep of a facility, including cleaning and sanitation.

Organizational climate   Collective, rather than individual, perception of the staff regarding the culture, atmosphere, and conditions in the workplace.

Organizational structure   Framework for administration and daily operation of early childhood services, including the process and procedures used in decision making and the handling of information. Components of the organizational structure include sponsorships, provincial/territorial **regulations**, funding, and **parent involvement**.

Parent   Any adult who has primary responsibility for the child. The term is intended be inclusive and to encompass not only biological and adoptive parents but also legal guardians and foster parents.

Parent conferences   One-on-one meetings between early childhood **practitioners** and **parents** to discuss a child's progress and resolve problems.

Parent involvement   Parents sharing in the education and care of their children through participation in activities in the early childhood program.

Performance appraisal   A process to assess how well the staff is meeting the program standards, fulfilling their job responsibilities and contributing to the realization of the program vision, reaching the program goals and meeting the program objectives.

Personal philosophy   One's beliefs and attitudes related to **early childhood education**; one's ideas about how children learn and how caregivers interact.

Personal advocacy   Involves talking with acquaintances about the importance of early childhood development.

Personnel policies   (currently referred to as **human resources policies**) A set of written guidelines covering employer–employee relations. Policies describe conditions of employment and may include job descriptions, advancement opportunities, and procedures for termination of employment, conflict resolution, and so on.

Philosophy   A statement of beliefs reflecting one's value system. It is often based on theory and guided by research.

Policy   A course of action that guides decisions.

Practitioner   An adult who works in the field of early childhood development, including early childhood educators, family child care providers, family resource personnel, and resource and referral personnel.

Prior Learning Assessment and Recognition (PLAR) Formal process for determining equivalent academic credit for college-level knowledge and skills acquired through a variety of past learning opportunities, both formal and informal.

Probationary period The period of time at the beginning of a new employment relationship, usually three to six months.

Procedure A series of steps to be followed, usually in a specific order, to implement policies.

Process quality Refers to interactions, the provision of **developmentally appropriate** activities, caregiver consistency, parent involvement, and warm, nurturing, sensitive caregiving.

Professional advocacy Efforts to challenge and reform public systems that affect children and families. This type of **advocacy** is also known as "lobbying" and is directed toward legislative, administrative, and budgetary processes.

Professional development Participation in activities such as courses, conferences, and workshops; a process of continuous learning for the purposes of enhancing an individual's competencies and/or professionalism by enhancing their skills and knowledge based on current research and pedagogical development in the field.

Professional ethics The moral commitments of a profession. Professional ethics require reflective thinking about the profession's responsibilities, values, and practices that extends and enhances the personal morality that **practitioners** bring to their work. Professional ethics concern the kinds of actions that are right and wrong in the workplace and help individuals resolve the moral dilemmas that they encounter in their work.

Professional judgment Assessing events and estimating consequences of decisions and actions based on specialized knowledge.

Professionalism The skill or qualities required or expected of members of a profession.

Ratio See **adult:child ratio**.

Rating scale An instrument for assessing specific skills or concepts based on some qualitative dimension of excellence or accomplishment.

Reflection A natural process that facilitates the development of future action from the contemplation of past and current behaviour.

Registration A process that requires **family child care providers** to certify that they have complied with **regulations** and maintain records.

Regulations The rules, directives, statutes, or standards that prescribe, direct, limit, or govern early childhood development programs.

Resource and referral programs These community organizations provide a variety of services such as a volunteer registry of care providers, lending libraries, training for caregivers, and access to liability insurance.

Resource teacher An individual who assists early childhood **practitioners** with the **inclusion** of **children with special needs** into **early childhood settings**.

Revenue Income received by the program, including parent fees, government grants, and funds raised.

Staff:child ratio See **adult:child ratio**.

Staff development A broad term that refers to all processes that encourage employees to engage in professional growth and development.

Stakeholders Individuals or groups that have an investment in a particular system or organization. In early childhood development, the stakeholders include the children, parents, **practitioners**, **directors**, **licensing** inspectors, government, funding agencies, advisory bodies, policy makers, and students.

Standards Degrees of excellence along a continuum, with some regulations only specifying baseline standards for acceptability below which a program's quality is unacceptable (possibly leading to criminal sanctions) and other regulations indicating excellent quality.

Standards of practice   Benchmarks, or points of reference, against which occupations and the proficiency of people in those occupations are measured or assessed. These standards are also known as **occupational standards**.

Start-up budget   One-time-only costs that are incurred prior to starting a program.

Structural quality   Variables that can be regulated, including **adult:child ratio**, **group size**, and the education and training of caregivers.

Supervision   The process of communicating performance expectations and supporting individual staff members to fulfill their job responsibilities and to reach their full potential during the performance of their jobs.

Support staff   Anyone working under a **director** in an early childhood development program who is not directly involved with the children, including clerical, cooking, and cleaning personnel as well as home visitors and others involved in a supervisory capacity.

Task orientation   The emphasis placed on good planning, efficiency, and getting the job done.

United Nations Convention on the Rights of the Child   An agreement to do what is best for children that has been endorsed by almost every country in the world.

Values   The qualities or principles individuals believe to be intrinsically desirable or worthwhile.

Variable costs   Those expenditures that increase as the number of children served increases.

Work Environment   The physical and social environment in which work takes place. It includes how people are treated, how they feel, and how they relate to each other plus the conditions under which work is done: health and safety; supervision, accountability, and opportunities for personal and professional development; and communication, conflict resolution, and problem solving.

Zero-based budgeting   Requires that each expenditure be newly calculated.

Bibliography

Abbreviations
NAEYC   National Association for the
    Education of Young Children
CCCF   Canadian Child Care Federation

Abbott-Shim, M., and A. Sibley. 1986. *Child care inventory.* Atlanta: Humanics.

Alberta. 1990. Day care regulation: Alberta regulation 333/90. Edmonton: Publication Services.

Albrecht, P. 2002. *The right fit: Recruiting, selecting, and orienting staff.* Lake Forest, IL: New Horizons.

Allred, K., R. Briem, and S. Black. 1998. Collaboratively addressing needs of young children with disabilities. *Young Children* 55 (5): 32–36.

Almy, M. 1975. *The early childhood educator at work.* New York: McGraw-Hill.

American Academy of Pediatrics. 1999. *Handbook of pediatric environmental health.* American Academy of Pediatrics.

American Academy of Pediatrics, and American Public Health Association. 2002. *Caring for our children: National health and safety standards - Guidelines for out of home programs.* 2d ed. Washington, DC: American Academy of Pediatrics & American Public Health Association,

Anthony, M. 1998. Stages of director development. *Child Care Information Exchange* 9, 81–83.

Association of Early Childhood Educators of Ontario (AECEO). 1993. *Final report for the feasibility study regarding legislative recognition of early childhood educators in Ontario.* Prepared by Levy-Coughlin Partnership. Toronto: AECEO.

Avataq Cultural Institute. 2004. *Unikkaangualaurtaa Let's tell a story.* Montreal: Avataq Cultural Institute.

Bachmann, Kimberley, and Judith MacBride-King. 1999. Is work-life balance still an issue for Canadians and their employers? You bet it is!, Work-life balance series no. 1. Ottawa: Conference Board of Canada.

Baines, C., P. Evans, and S. Neysmith. 1991. *Women's caring: Feminist perspectives on social welfare.* Toronto: McClelland & Stewart.

Baker, M. 1995. *Canadian family policies: Cross-national comparisons.* Toronto: University of Toronto Press.

Baker, M. 1999. Child care and family policy: Cross-national examples of integration and inconsistency. Paper presented at the Good Child Care in Canada symposium, Toronto.

Barnett, W.S. 2003. *Better teachers, better preschools: Student achievement linked to teacher qualifications. Preschool policies matter, 2.* New Brunswick, NJ: Rutgers University, National Institute of Early Childhood Research.

BC Aboriginal Child Care Society (BCACCS). 2004. Elements of quality child care from the perspectives of Aboriginal peoples in British Columbia, draft standards. Vancouver: BCACCS.

Beach, J., J. Bertrand, and G. Cleveland. 2004. *Our child care workforce, from recognition to remuneration: A human resources study of child care in Canada.* Ottawa: Human Resources Development Canada.

Beach, J., J. Bertrand, B. Forer, D. Michal, and J. Tougas. 2004. *Working for change: Canada's child care workforce. Labour market update study.* Ottawa: Child Care Human Resources Sector Council.

Beach, J., and J. Bertrand. 2000. More than the sum of the parts: An early childhood development system for Canada. Occasional Paper 12. Toronto: Childcare Resource and Research Unit, Centre for Urban and Community Studies, University of Toronto.

Becker, S. 2001. The good, the bad, and the few: Men in childcare. *Interaction* (CCCF) 14 (5).

Bennett, H. 1989. *Parent education programs: Growing healthy children.* Ottawa: Canadian Association of Family Resource Programs.

Berk, L. 1985. Relation of a caregiver education to a child-oriented attitude, job satisfaction and behaviours towards children. *Child Care Quarterly.*

Berk, L.E., and A. Winsler. 1995. *Scaffolding children's learning: Vygotsky and early childhood education.* Washington, DC: NAEYC.

Bernhard, J., M. Lefebvre, G. Chud, and R. Lange. 1995. *Paths to equity: Cultural, linguistic, and racial diversity in Canadian early childhood education.* Toronto: York University.

Bertrand, J. 1990. *Childcare management guide: A comprehensive resource for boards of directors.* Toronto and Ottawa: Ontario Coalition for Better Child Care and Canadian Day Care Advocacy Association.

Bertrand, J. 1991. *George Brown College guide to workplace child care: Health care facilities manual.* Toronto: George Brown College.

Boutte, G., D. Keepler, V. Tyler, and B. Terry. 1992. Effective techniques for involving "difficult" parents. *Young Children* 47 (3): 19–22.

Bredekamp, S., and C. Copple, eds. 1997. *Developmentally appropriate practice in early childhood programs*, rev. ed. Washington, DC: NAEYC.

British Columbia. 1989. *Community Care Facility Act*: Child care regulation. Regulation 319/89. Victoria: Queen's Printer for British Columbia.

Bronfenbrenner, Urie. 1979. *The ecology of human development.* Cambridge, MA: Harvard University Press.

Bronfenbrenner, Urie. 1986. Ecology of the family as a context for human development: Research perspectives. *Developmental Psychology* 221, 723–742.

Bronson, M.B. 1995. *The right stuff for children birth to 8: Selecting play materials to support development.* Washington, DC: NAEYC.

Buchanan, T., and D. Burts. 1995. Getting parents involved in the 1990s. *Day Care and Early Education* (Summer), 18–22.

Bush, J. 2000. *Dollars and sense: Planning for profit in your child care business.* Albany, NY: Delmar.

Caldwell, B. 1984. What is quality care? *Young Children* 39 (3): 3–8.

Caldwell, B. 1987. Advocacy is everybody's business. *Child Care Information Exchange* (March), 29–32.

Campaign 2000. 2003a. *Diversity or disparity? Early childhood education and care in Canada (ECEC): Second report, Community Indicators Project.* Campaign 2000, Toronto.

Campaign 2000. 2003b. *Honouring our promises: Meeting the challenge to end child and family poverty: 2003 report card on child poverty in Canada.* Campaign 2000, Toronto.

Campaign 2000. 2004. *One million too many: Implementing solutions to child poverty in Canada: 2004 report card on child poverty in Canada.* Campaign 2000, Toronto.

Canada. 1987a. *Sharing the responsibility: Federal response to the report of the special committee on child care.* Ottawa: Health and Welfare Canada/Queen's Printer.

Canada. 1987b. *National strategy on child care.* Ottawa: National Day Care Information Centre/Health and Welfare Canada.

Canada. 1988b. *Child care initiatives fund.* Ottawa: National Day Care Information Centre/Health and Welfare Canada.

Canada. 1991. *Status of day care in Canada.* Ottawa: National Day Care Information Centre/Health and Welfare Canada.

Canada. 1992a. *The child benefit: A white paper on Canada's new integrated child tax benefit.* Ottawa: Health and Welfare Canada/Queen's Printer.

Canada. 1992b. *Canada's guide to healthy eating.* Ottawa: Health and Welfare Canada/Supply and Services Canada.

Canada. 1992c. *The 1992 budget and child benefits.* Ottawa: National Council of Welfare/Supply and Services Canada.

Canada. 1993. *Where are the children? An analysis of child care arrangements used while parents work and study,* by A. Pence, H. Goelman, and D. Lero. Ottawa: Statistics Canada.

Canada. 1994a. *Agenda: Jobs and growth: Improving social security in Canada: A discussion paper.* Ottawa: Human Resources Development Canada/Supply and Services Canada.

Canada. 1994b. *Improving social security in Canada: Child care and development: A supplementary paper.* Ottawa: Supply and Services Canada.

Canada. 1994c. *Canadian child care in context: Perspectives from the provinces and territories.* Ottawa: Statistics Canada.

Canada. 1995. *Budget in brief.* Ottawa: Department of Finance Canada.

Canada. 1996a. *Child care: Where we stand.* Ottawa: Human Resources Development Canada.

Canada. 1996b. *National longitudinal survey of children and youth: Growing up in Canada,* by D. Keating and F. Mustard. Ottawa: Statistics Canada.

Canada. 1998a. *Perspectives on Labour and Income.* Vol. 9 (4). Ottawa: Statistics Canada.

Canada. 1998b. *Women's support, women's work: child care in an era of deficit reduction, devolution, downsizing and deregulation,* by G. Doherty, M. Friendly, M. Oloman, and J. Mathien. Ottawa: Secretary of State/Status of Women Canada.

Canada. 1999a. *National child benefit progress report 1999.* Ottawa: Human Resources Development Canada/Federal-Provincial-Territorial Council of Ministers on Social Policy Renewal.

Canada. 1999b. *A national children's agenda: developing a shared vision.* Ottawa: Human Resources Development Canada/Federal-Provincial-Territorial Council of Ministers on Social Policy Renewal.

Canada. 1999c. *Preschool children: Promises to keep.* Ottawa: National Council of Welfare/Public Works and Government Services Canada.

Canada. 2000a. *Using your home for day care.* Ottawa: Revenue Canada/Canada Customs and Revenue Agency, available online: www.ccra-adrc.gc.ca. eliminate? more recent version – Canada 2003?

Canada. 2000b. *Women in Canada 2000: A gender-based statistical report.* Ottawa: Statistics Canada.

Canada. 2001a. *Children and the hill* 20 (Spring). Ottawa: Senate of Canada.

Canada. 2001b. *Federal/provincial/territorial early childhood development agreement: Report on government of Canada activities and expenditures 2000–2001.* Ottawa: Government of Canada.

Canada. 2002. Women in Canada: Work Chapter Updates. Ottawa: Statistics Canada.

Canada. 2003. *Using your home for day care.* Ottawa: Revenue Canada/Canada Customs and Revenue Agency, available online: www.ccra-adrc.gc.ca.

CCCF. 1991a. Issues in post-secondary education for quality in early childhood care and education. Discussion paper. Ottawa: CCCF.

CCCF. 1991b. *National statement on quality child care.* Ottawa: CCCF.

CCCF. 1995. *Towards excellence in early childhood care and education training programs: A self-assessment guide.* Ottawa: CCCF.

CCCF. 2000a. Family Child Care Training Program, Level 1. Ottawa: CCCF.

CCCF. 2000b. *Partners in quality: Tools for practitioners in child care settings.* Ottawa: CCCF.

CCCF. 2000c. *Partners in quality: Tools for administrators in child care settings.* Ottawa: CCCF.

CCCF. 2001a. Convention on the rights of the child. In *Research connections Canada,* vol. 7. Ottawa: CCCF.

CCCF. 2001b. Supporting children and families. In *Research connections Canada,* vol. 7. Ottawa: CCCF.

CCCF. 2004. What's in a name? Discussion paper. E. Elaine Ferguson, author; Lana Crossman and Anne Maxwell, eds. Ottawa: CCCF.

CCCF, and CCAAC (Child Care Advocacy Association of Canada). 2003. *Perceptions of quality child care: Final report.* Submitted by Espey & Good Company, national survey carried out by Millward, Brown and Goldfarb for CCCF and CCAAC, Ottawa.

CCCF, and CICH (Canadian Institute of Child Health). 2001. "Supporting Breastfeeding in Child Care," resource sheet No. 57 from the "Nourish, Nurture and Neurodevelopment Resource Kit," Neurodevelopmental Research: Implications for caregiver practice, on nourishing and nurturing the child's brain for optimal neurodevelopmental health. Ottawa: CCCF and CICH.

Canadian Day Care Advocacy Association (CDCAA), and Canadian Child Day Care Federation (CCDCF). 1992. *Caring for a living: A study on wages and working conditions in Canadian child care.* Ottawa: CCDCF.

Canadian Institute of Child Health (CICH). 2000. *The health of Canada's children: A CICH profile.* 3d ed. Ottawa: Canadian Institute of Child Health.

Canadian Pædiatric Society. 1996. *Well beings: A guide to promote the physical health, safety and emotional well-being of children in child care centres and family day care homes.* Toronto: Creative Premises Ltd.

Canadian Standards Association. 2003. *Children's play spaces and equipment.* Mississauga: Canadian Standards Association.

Carter, M., and D. Curtis. 1998. *The visionary director: A handbook for dreaming, organizing, and improvising in your center.* St. Paul, MI: Redleaf Press.

Carter, M., and E. Jones. 1990. The teacher as observer: The director as role model. *Child Care Information Exchange* (Sept.).

Cartwright, S. 1998. Caregivers of quality. *Child Care Information Exchange* 3: 18–21.

Caruso, J., and M. Fawcett. 1999. *Supervision in early childhood education: A developmental perspective,* 2d ed. New York: Columbia University, Teachers College Press.

Chandler, K. 1988. Accreditation: One route to professionalism. Presentation at the annual conference of the Alberta Association for Young Children.

Chandler, K. 1994. Voluntary accreditation and program evaluation: Background paper. Ottawa: CCCF.

Chandler, K. 1997. What do we know about ECE training in Canada? Background paper for Steering Committee of Early Childhood Care and Education Training in Canada. Ottawa: Association of Canadian Community Colleges and CCCF.

Chandler, K. 1999. Professional development. In *Research connections Canada,* vol. 3. Ottawa: CCCF.

Chandler, K. 2001. The director's role in staff development. *Interaction* (CCCF) 15 (2): 18–20.

Chandler, K., and P. Hileman. 1986. Professionalism in early childhood education. Association for Early Childhood Education Newsletter.

Chapman, E. 1990. *Supervisors' survival kit.* New York: Macmillan.

Cherry, C., B. Harkness, and K. Kuzma. 1987. *Nursery school and day care center management guide.* Belmont, CA: Fearon.

Child Care Advocacy Association of Canada (CCAAC). 2004. *From patchwork to framework: A child care strategy for Canada.* Ottawa: CCAAC.

Child Care Employee Project. 1990. *Taking matters into our own hands: A guide to unionizing in the child care field.* Berkeley, CA: Child Care Employee Project.

Child Care Information Exchange. 2001. Employer family policy solutions. *Child Care Information Exchange* (March).

Children's Services Division. 1998. Multi-age operating criteria. Children's Services Division, City of Toronto.

Children's Services Division. 2004. Operating criteria for child care centres providing subsidized care in Toronto, rev. ed. Toronto: Community Services, Children's Services Division, City of Toronto.

Child's play/Jeu d'enfant: A Playground safety video for daycares, schools, and communities. 1997. Videocassette. In French and English. Canadian Standards Association, Toronto.

Chud, G., and R. Fahlman. 1995. *Honouring diversity with child care and early education: An instructor's guide.* Victoria: British Columbia Ministry of Skills, Training and Labour.

Clark, S. 1995. Marketing when your creativity is high and your budget is low. *Child Care Information Exchange* (July).

Cleveland G., and M. Krashinsky. 1998. *The benefits and costs of good child care: The economic rationale for public investment in young children.* Toronto: Childcare Resource and Research Unit, Centre for Urban and Community Studies, University of Toronto.

Cleveland G., and M. Krashinsky. 2001. *Our children's future: Child care policy in Canada.* Toronto: University of Toronto Press.

Click, P., and D. Click. 1990. *Administration of schools for young children.* Albany, NY: Delmar.

Cooke, K., et al. 1986. *Report of the task force on child care.* Ottawa: Supply and Services.

Cowperthwaite, P., and R. Mehta. 1996. The art of budgeting. Available online: Cowperthwaite Mehta Chartered Accountants, not-for-profit administration web page: www.187gerrard.com.

Cryer, D., and L. Phillipsen. 1997. Quality details: A close up look at child care program strengths and weaknesses. *Young Children* 52 (5): 51–61.

Culkin, M., ed. 2000. *Managing quality in young children's programs: The leader's role.* New York: Teachers College Press, Columbia University.

Decker, C., and J. Decker. 2001. *Planning and administering early childhood programs,* 7th ed. New York: Prentice Hall.

Deiner, P., L. Dyck, and L. Hardacre. 1999. *Resources for educating young children with diverse abilities—birth through twelve.* Toronto: Harcourt Brace.

Denholm, C., R. Ferguson, and A. Pence. 1987. *Professional child and youth care: The Canadian perspective.* Vancouver: University of British Columbia Press.

Derman-Sparks, L. 1993–94. Empowering children to create a caring culture in a world of differences. *Childhood Education* (Winter): 66–71.

Derman-Sparks, L., and the ABC Task Force. 1989. *Anti-bias curriculum: Tools for empowering young children.* Washington, DC: NAEYC.

Doherty G. 1998. *Program standards for early childhood settings.* Ottawa: CCCF.

Doherty, G. 1999. Elements of quality. In *Research connections Canada,* vol. 1. Ottawa: CCCF.

Doherty, G. 2000a. Issues in Canadian child care: What does the research tell us? Part 5, Funding child care. In *Research connections Canada,* vol. 5. Ottawa: CCCF.

Doherty, G. 2000b. Standards for quality child care programs; Standards of practice for administrators/directors. In *Partners in quality: Tools for administrators in child care settings.* Ottawa: CCCF.

Doherty, G. 2003. Occupational Standards for Child Care Practitioners. Ottawa: Canadian Child Care Federation.

Doherty, G., and B. Forer. 2004. Unionization and quality in early childhood programs. In *Research connections Canada: Supporting children and families,* vol. II. Ottawa: Canadian Child Care Federation, 33–52.

Doherty, G., R. Rose, M. Friendly, D. Lero, and S. Irwin. 1995. Child care: Canada can't work without it. Occasional Paper 5. Toronto: Childcare Resource and Research Unit, Centre for Urban and Community Studies, University of Toronto.

Doherty G., D. Lero, H. Goelman, A. LaGrange, and J. Tougas. 2000a. *You bet I care! A Canada-wide study on wages, working conditions, and practices in child care centres.* Guelph, ON: Centre for Families, Work and Well-Being, University of Guelph.

Doherty G., D. Lero, H. Goelman, J. Tougas, and A. LaGrange. 2000b. *You bet I care! Caring and learning environments: Quality in regulated family child care across Canada.* Guelph, ON: Centre for Families, Work and Well-Being, University of Guelph.

Doherty, G., D. Lero, J. Tougas, A. LaGrange, and H. Goelman. 2001. *You bet I care! Policies and practices in Canadian family child care agencies.* Guelph, ON: Centre for Families, Work and Well-Being, University of Guelph.

Doherty-Derkowski, G. 1995. *Quality matters: Excellence in early childhood programs.* Don Mills, ON: Addison-Wesley.

Dorfman, L., K. Woodruff, S. Herbert, and J. Ervice. 2004. *Making the case for early care and education: A message development guide for advocates.* Berkeley, CA: Berkeley Media Studies Group.

Draper, N. 1997. *Board orientation manual: A key to effective governance.* Belleville, ON: Family Space Quinte Inc.

Dunster, L. 1994. *Home child care: A caregiver's guide.* Ottawa: Child Care Provider's Association.

Early Childhood Education. 1999. *Best practices for supervisors.* Toronto: George Brown College, Faculty of Community and Health Sciences.

Early Childhood Education. 2000. *Best practices for cooks.* Toronto: George Brown College, Faculty of Community and Health Sciences.

Early Childhood Educators of British Columbia (ECEBC). 1995. *The early childhood educators of British Columbia code of ethics.* Vancouver: ECEBC.

Eiselen, S.S. 1992. *The human side of child care administration: a how-to manual.* Washington, DC: NAEYC.

Ekos Research Associates. 2000. *National survey of children's issues: Final report.* Prepared for the Strategic Policy Communications Branch: Human Resources Development Canada.

Endsley, R., P. Minish, and Q. Zhou. 1993. Parent involvement and quality day care in proprietary centers. *Journal of Research in Childhood Education* 7 (2): 53–61.

Esbensen, S.B. 1984. *Hidden hazards on playgrounds for children*. Hull, QC: Université du Québec à Hull.

Esbensen, S.B. 1987. *The early childhood education playground: An outdoor classroom*. Ypsilanti, MI: High/Scope Press.

Essa, E., and R. Young. 2003. *Introduction to early childhood education*, 3d Cdn. ed. Toronto: Nelson.

Evans, E.D. 1975. *Contemporary influences in early childhood education*. New York: Holt, Rinehart & Winston.

Feeney, S. 1987a. Ethical case studies for NAEYC reader response. *Young Children* 42 (4): 24–25.

Feeney, S. 1987b. Ethics case studies: The working mother. *Young Children* 43 (1): 16–19.

Feeney, S., and R. Chun. 1985. Research in review: effective teachers of young children. *Young Children* 41 (1): 47–52.

Feeney, S., and N.K. Freeman. 1999. *Ethics and the early childhood educator: Using the NAEYC code*. Washington, DC: NAEYC.

Feeney, S., and K. Kipnis. 1985. Public policy report: Professional ethics in early childhood education. *Young Children* 40 (3): 54–56.

Feeney, S., and K. Kipnis. 1989. A new code of ethics for early childhood educators: Code of ethical conduct and statement of commitment. *Young Children* 45 (1): 24–29.

Feeney, S., and L. Sysko. 1986. Professional ethics in early childhood education: Survey results. *Young Children* 42 (1): 15–20.

Feeney, S., B. Caldwell, and K. Kipnis. 1988a. Ethics case studies: The aggressive child. *Young Children* 43 (2): 48–51.

Feeney, S., D. Christensen, and E. Moracvik. 1987. *Who am I in the lives of children?* 3d ed. Columbus, OH: Merrill.

Feeney, S., S. Riley, and K. Kipnis. 1988b. Ethics case studies: The divorced parents. *Young Children* 43 (3): 48–51.

Fennimore, B. 1989. *Child advocacy for early childhood educators*. New York: Teachers College Press, Columbia University.

Ferguson, E. 1997. *Child care administration credentialling: A work in progress*. Halifax: Child Care Connection NS.

Ferguson, E., and T. McCormick Ferguson. 2001. *Maximizing child care services: The role of owners and boards*. Halifax: Child Care Connection NS.

Ferguson, E., K. Flanagan-Rochon, L. Hautmann, D. Lutes, A. Masson, and D. Mauch. 2000. *Toward a best practices framework for licensing child care facilities in Canada*. Halifax: Child Care Connection NS.

Field, H. 1999. The public image of child care: A revealing reality check. *Interaction* (CCCF) (Winter).

Freiner, C., and J. Cerner. 1998. *Benefiting Canada's children: Perspectives on gender and social responsibility*. Ottawa: Status of Women Canada.

Friendly, M. 1994. *Child care policy in Canada: Putting the pieces together*. Don Mills, ON: Addison-Wesley.

Friendly, M. 2000. A national child care program: Now is the time. *Pediatric Child Health* 5.

Friendly, M. 2001a. Child care and Canadian federalism in the 1990s: Canary in a coal mine. In *Good child care for the 21st century: Preparing the policy map*, G. Cleveland and M. Krashinsky, eds. Toronto: University of Toronto Press.

Friendly, M. 2001b. Putting the "S" back in the CHST. *Interaction* (CCCF) 15 (1).

Friendly, M. 2004. Strengthening Canada's social and economic foundations: Next steps for early childhood education and care. *Policy Options* (March).

Friendly, M., J. Beach, and M. Turiano. 2002. *Early Childhood Education and Care in Canada: Provinces and Territories, 2001*. Toronto: Childcare Resource and Research Unit, Centre for Urban and Community Studies, University of Toronto.

Friesen, B. 1995. A sociological examination of the child care auspice debate. Occasional Paper 6. Toronto: Childcare Resource and Research Unit, Centre for Urban and Community Studies, University of Toronto.

Frost, J.L. 1992. *Play and playscapes*. Albany, NY: Delmar.

Galinsky, E. 1988. Parents and teacher-care-givers: Sources of tension, sources of support. *Young Children* 43 (3): 4–12.

Galinsky, E. 1990. Why are some parent/teacher partnerships clouded with difficulties? *Young Children* 45 (5): 2–3, 38–39.

Galinsky, E. 1999. *Ask the children: What America's children really think about working parents.* New York: Families and Work Institute.

Galinsky, E., C. Howes, S. Kontos, M. Shinn. 1994. The study of children in family child care and relative care: Key findings and policy recommendations. *Young Children* 50 (1): 58–61.

Gauthier. 1999. Family policies and families' well-being: An international comparison. Paper prepared for the Good Child Care in Canada symposium, Toronto.

George Brown College. 2000. *Best Practices for Child Care Cooks.* Toronto: George Brown College.

Gestwicki. C. 1999. *Developmentally appropriate practice: Curriculum and development in early education.* Albany, NY: Delmar.

Goelman, H., G. Doherty, D. Lero, A. LaGrange, and J. Tougas. 2000. *You bet I care! Caring and learning environments: Quality in child care centres across Canada.* Guelph, ON: Centre for Families, Work and Well-Being, University of Guelph.

Goffin, S., and J. Lombardi. 1988. *Speaking out: Early childhood advocacy.* Washington, DC: NAEYC.

Goss Gilroy Inc. 1998. *Providing home child care for a living: A survey of providers working in the regulated sector.* Ottawa: CCCF.

Green, B., chair. 1991. *Canada's children: Investing in our future: Report on the standing committee on health and welfare, social affairs, seniors and the status of women.* Ottawa: Queen's Printer.

Greenberg, P. 1989. Parents as partners in young children's development and education: A new American fad? Why does it matter? *Young Children* 44 (4): 61–75.

Greenman, J. 1988. *Caring spaces, learning places: Children's environments that work.* Redmond, WA: Exchange Press.

Greenman, J., and R. Fugua, eds. 1984. *Making day care better: Training, evaluation and the process of change.* New York: Teachers College Press, Columbia University.

Griffen, Sandra. 1994. *Professionalism: The link to quality care.* Ottawa: CCCF.

Guralnick, M. 1990. Major accomplishments and future directions in early childhood mainstreaming. In *Topics in Early Childhood Special Education* 10 (2): 1–7.

Guy, K., ed. 1997. *Our promise to children.* Ottawa: Canadian Institute of Child Health.

Hadley, K. 2001. Unionized women in Canada more likely to earn the equivalent of a man's wage. Paper. Ottawa: National Action Committee on the Status of Women.

Hardy, C., and T.B. Lawrence. 1999. *Swimming with sharks: Managing multi-sector collaboration in the Canadian HIV/AIDS domain.* Melbourne, Australia: Employee Relation and Organization Studies, University of Melbourne.

Harms, T., and R.M. Clifford. 1989a. *Family day care rating scale.* New York: Teachers College Press, Columbia University.

Harms, T., and R.M. Clifford. 1989b. *Family home day care environment rating scale.* New York: Teachers College Press, Columbia University. same book as above?? delete both? later editions are shown below

Harms, T., and R.M. Clifford. 1998. *Early childhood environment rating scale.* rev. ed. New York: Teachers College Press, Columbia University.

Harms, T., and R.M. Clifford. 2004. *Family home day care environment rating scale*, rev. ed. New York: Teachers College Press, Columbia University.

Harms, T., D. Cryer, and R.M. Clifford. 1990. *Infant/toddler environment rating scale.* New York: Teachers College Press, Columbia University.

Harms, T., E. Jacobs, and D. White. 1995. *School-age environment rating scale.* New York: Teachers College Press, Columbia University.

Hawkins, Jim. 1997. *1001 fundraising ideas and strategies.* Toronto: Fitzhenry and Whiteside.

Hayden, J. 1996. *Management of early childhood services: An Australian perspective.* Wentworth Falls, NSW, Australia: Social Science Press.

Health Canada. 1992. *Canada's food guide to healthy eating.* Ottawa: Health and Welfare Canada/Supply and Services Canada.

Helgesen, S. 1990. *Female advantage: Women's ways of leadership.* New York: Doubleday.

Hendrick, J. and K. Chandler. 1996. *The whole child.* 6th Cdn. ed. Scarborough, ON: Prentice Hall Canada.

Hepburn, S., M. Culkin, et al. 1995. Cost, quality, and child outcomes in child care centres: Executive summary. Denver, CO: University of Colorado.

Herr, J.R., D. Johnson, and K. Zimmerman. 1993. Benefits of accreditation: a study of directors' perceptions. *Young Children* 48 (4): 32–35.

Hertzman, C. 2000. The case for an early childhood development strategy. *isuma: Canadian Journal of Policy Research* (Autumn).

High/Scope Educational Research Foundation. 1998. *High/Scope program quality assessment instrument (PQA).* Ypsilanti, MI: High/Scope Press.

Hildebrand, V. 1993. *Management of child development centers.* New York: Macmillan.

Holland, M. 2004. "That food makes me sick!" Managing food allergies and intolerances in early childhood settings. *Young Children* (March), 42–46.

Hollestelle, K. 1994. At the core: Entrepreneurial skills for family child care providers. In *The early childhood career lattice: Perspectives on professional development,* edited by J. Johnson and J.B. McCracken. Washington, DC: NAEYC.

Honig, A.S. 1979. *Parental involvement in early childhood education.* rev. ed. Washington, DC: NAEYC.

Howes, C., and D. Norris. 1997. Adding two school-age children: Does it change the quality in family day care? *Early Childhood Research Quarterly* 12.

Human Resources Development Canada. 2003. Multilateral Framework Agreement on Early Learning and Child Care. Online: socialunion.gc.ca/ecd-framework_e.htm.

Hurst, L. 1992. A death blow for day care: How Tories reneged on their promise to set up a national system. *Toronto Star,* March 15.

Irwin, S., D. Lero, and K. Brophy. 2000. *A matter of urgency: Including children with special needs in child care in Canada.* Sydney, NS: Breton Books.

Janmohamed, Z. 1992. *Making the connections: Child care in Metropolitan Toronto.* Toronto: Metro Toronto Coalition for Better Child Care.

Jensen, J., and R. Mahon. Child care in Toronto: Can intergovernmental relations respond to children's needs? An options paper. Canadian Policy Research Networks, 2001.

Johnson, D.W., and F.P. Johnson. 1991. *Joining together: Group theory and group skills.* Boston: Allyn and Bacon.

Johnson, J., and J.B. McCracken, eds. 1994. *The early childhood career lattice: Perspectives on professional development.* Washington, DC: NAEYC.

Johnson, K.L., D.S. Lero, and J. Rooney. 2001. *Work-Life Compendium 2001: 150 Canadian Statistics on Work, Family, and Well-Being.* Guelph, ON: Human Resources Development Canada and the Centre for Families, Work and Well-Being, University of Guelph.

Jones, E., and L. Derman-Sparks. 1992. Meeting the challenge of diversity. *Young Children* 47 (2): 12–18.

Jones, E., and J. Nimmo. 1994. *Emergent Curriculum.* Washington, DC: NAEYC.

Jorde Bloom, P. 1986. The administrator's role in the innovation decision process. *Child Care Quarterly* 15 (2), 182–197.

Jorde Bloom, P. 1987. *Improving the quality of work life: A guide for enhancing the organizational climate in the early childhood setting.* Evanston, IL: National College of Education.

Jorde Bloom, P. 1989. *Measuring work attitudes: Technical manual for the early childhood work environment survey.* Mt. Rainer, WA: Psychology Press.

Jorde Bloom, P. 1997. *A great place to work: Improving conditions for staff in young children's programs.* rev. ed. Washington, DC: NAEYC.

Jorde Bloom, P. 2000. *Circle of influence: Implementing shared decision making and participative management.* Lake Forest, IL: New Horizons.

Jorde Bloom, P. 2002. *Making the most of meetings: a practical guide.* Lake Forest, IL: New Horizons.

Jorde Bloom, P. 2003. *Leadership in action: How effective directors get things done.* Lake Forest, IL: New Horizons.

Jorde Bloom, P., M. Sheerer, and J. Britz. 1991. *Blueprint for action: Achieving center-based change through staff development.* Lake Forest, IL: New Horizons.

Kagan, S. 1988. Dealing with our ambivalence about advocacy. *Child Care Information Exchange* 61 (May): 31–34.

Kagan, S. 1994. Leadership: Rethinking it—making it happen. *Young Children* 49 (5): 50–54.

Kaiser, B., and J. Sklar Rasminsky. 1995. *HIV/AIDS and child care: Fact booklet; Facilitator's guide.* Ottawa: CCCF.

Kaiser, B., and J. Sklar Rasminsky. 1999a. The child care supervisor as child care advocate. *Interaction* (CCCF) (Winter).

Kaiser, B., and J. Sklar Rasminsky. 1999b. *Partners in quality,* vol. 2, *Relationships.* Ottawa: CCCF.

Kaiser, B., and J. Sklar Rasminsky. 1999c. *Partners in quality,* vol. 3, *Infrastructure.* Ottawa: CCCF.

Kass, J., and B. Costigliola. 2003. The union advantage in child care: How unionization can help recruitment and retention. (July 8). Child Care Connection NS, Halifax NS. Available online: Child Care Advocacy Association of Canada, Home Page, Archives: www.child careadvocacy.ca/archives/archives03b.html.

Katz, L.G. 1972. Developmental stages of preschool teachers. *Elementary School Journal* 73: 50–55.

Katz, L.G. 1992. Early childhood programs: Multiple perspectives on quality. *Childhood Education.*

Katz, L.G., and E. H. Ward. 1993. *Ethical behaviour in early childhood education,* 4th ed. Washington, DC: NAEYC.

Keating, D., and C. Hertzman, eds. 1999. *Developmental health and the wealth of nations.* New York: Guildford Press.

Kilbride, K. 1990. *Multicultural early childhood education: A resource kit.* Toronto: Ryerson Press.

King, P. 1996. The ergonomics of child care: Conducting a worksite analysis. *Work: A journal of prevention, assessment and rehabilitation.*

Kipnis, K. 1987. How to discuss professional ethics. *Young Children* 42 (4): 26–30.

Kome, P. 1989. *Every voice counts: A guide to personal and political action.* Ottawa: Canadian Advisory Council on the Status of Women.

Kontos, S., C. Howes, and E. Galinsky. 1996. *Does training make a difference to quality in family child care.* New York: Teachers College Press, Columbia University.

Kotter, J.P. 1990. *A force for change: How leadership differs from management.* New York: Free Press.

Kritchevsky, S., E. Prescott, and L. Walling. 1983. *Planning environments for young children: Physical space.* Washington, DC: NAEYC.

Kuhn, M. 1994. Quality child care and partnerships with parents. In *Research connections Canada,* vol. 6. Ottawa: CCCF

Kurtz, R. 1991. Stabilizer, catalyst, troubleshooter, or visionary: Which are you? *Child Care Information Exchange* (Jan.–Feb.): 27–31.

Kyle, I. 2000. *Quality in home care settings: A critical review of current theory and research.* Guelph, ON: Centre for Child Care Excellence.

Kyle, I., and D. Lero. 1985. *Day care quality: Its definition and implementation.* Ottawa: Task Force on Child Care.

Lally, R. 1995. The impact of child care policies and practices on infant/toddler identity formation. *Young Children* 51 (1): 58–67.

Lemire, D. 1993. *Services de garde au Québec.* Ottawa: Federation canadienne des services de garde à l'enfance.

Lero, D. 1994. In transition: Changing patterns of work, family life and child care. *Ideas: The Journal of Emotional Well-Being in Child Care* 1 (3): 11–14.

Lero, D., and L. Johnston. 1994. *110 statistics on work and family.* Data produced by Health and Welfare Canada. Ottawa: Canadian Advisory Council on the Status of Women.

Lero, D., and I. Kyle. 1985. Day care quality: Its definition and implementation. Paper submitted to the Task Force on Child Care, Ottawa.

Lowe, E. 2001a. Helping families meet their needs. *Interaction* (CCCF) 14: 4.

Lowe, E. 2001b. When shift work is the norm. *Interaction* (CCCF) 14: 4.

Lyon, M., and P. Canning. 1999. *Child care management study: A study of organizational behaviour in Canadian day care centres.* Halifax: Mount Saint Vincent University.

Manitoba. 1987. The *Community Child Day Care Standards Act:* Child day care regulation.

Winnipeg: Queen's Printer for Manitoba.

Manitoba Community Services Child Day Care. 1986. Competency-based assessment: policy and procedures. Winnipeg: Manitoba Community Services Child Day Care.

Martin, S. 1987. *Sharing the responsibility: Report of the special committee on child care.* Ottawa: Queen's Printer.

Mayfield, M. 2001. *Early childhood education and care in Canada: Contexts, dimensions, and issues.* Toronto: Prentice Hall.

McBride, S.L. 1999. Family-centred practices. *Young Children* 54 (3): 62–68.

McLean, C. 1994. *Regulations, standards and enforcement.* Ottawa: CCCF.

Meyerhoff, M.K. 1994. Of baseball and babies: Are you unconsciously discouraging father involvement in infant care? *Young Children* 49 (4): 17–19.

Miller, K. 1999. *Simple steps: Developmental activities for infants, toddlers and twos.* Toronto: Gryphon House.

Mizrahi, T., and B.B. Rosenthal. 1993. Managing dynamic tensions in social change coalitions. In *Community organization and social administration: Advances, trends, emerging principles.* New York: Haworth Press, Inc.

Modigliani, K., M. Reiff, and S. Jones. 1998. *Opening your door to children: How to start a family day care program.* Washington, DC: NAEYC.

Morgan, G. 1984. Change through regulation. In *Making day care better: Training, evaluation and the process of change,* edited by J. Greenman and R. Fugua. New York: Teachers College Press, Columbia University.

Morgan, G. 1992. *Managing the day care dollars: A financial handbook,* rev. ed. Cambridge, MA: Steam Press.

Morgan, G. 1997. *Imaginization: new mindsets for seeing, organizing, and managing.* San Francisco: Berret-Koehler.

Morris, J. 1995. *Early childhood continuing education certification standards and individual competency-based ECE training and assessment in Newfoundland and Labrador.* St John's, NF: Cabot Institute of Applied Arts and Technology.

Morris, J., and S. Helburn. 1996. How centres spend money on quality. *Child Care Information Exchange* (July): 75–80.

Moss, P. 1994. *Quality targets in services for young children: Proposals for a ten-year action plan.* Brussels: European Commission.

Musson, S. 1994. Key issues in school-age care. *Interaction* (CCCF).

Musson, S. 1999. *School-age care: Theory and practice.* Don Mills, ON: Addison-Wesley.

NAEYC. 1986. Developmentally appropriate practice in early childhood programs serving children from birth through age 8. Position statement. Washington, DC: NAEYC.

NAEYC. 1995. How many ways can you think of to use NAEYC's code of ethics? *Young Children* 51 (1): 42–43.

NAEYC. 1997. Licensing and public regulation of early childhood programs. Position statement. Washington, DC: NAEYC.

NAEYC. 1998a. Accreditation criteria and procedures of the National Academy of Early Childhood Programs, rev. ed. Washington, DC: NAEYC.

NAEYC. 1998b. NAEYC position statement on licensing and public recognition of early childhood programs. *Young Children* 53 (1): 43–50.

Neugebauer, B. 1990. Are you listening? *Child Care Information Exchange* 62 (Sept.–Oct.).

Neugebauer, R. 1984. State of the art thinking on parent fee policies. *Child Care Information Exchange.*

Neugebauer, R. 1994. Is your salary schedule up to speed? *Child Care Information Exchange.*

Neugebauer, R., and B. Neugebauer, eds. 1997. *Managing money: A center director's guidebook.* Redmond, WA: Exchange Press

New Brunswick. 1985a. Day care facilities standards. Fredericton, NB: Queen's Printer for New Brunswick.

New Brunswick. 1985b (Consolidated to June 30, 1985). *Family Services Act* regulations 8385; under family services act. O. C. 83-457. Fredericton, NB: Queen's Printer for New Brunswick.

Newfoundland. 1990. The *Day Care and Homemaker Services Act.* St. John's, NF: Queen's Printer for Newfoundland.

Newman, R. 2000. *Building relationships with parents and families in school-age programs.* Nashville, TN: School-Age Notes.

Northwest Territories. 1987. Child day care standards regulations. Yellowknife: Queen's Printer.

Northwest Territories. 1988. Northwest Territories *Child Day Care Act*. Yellowknife: Queen's Printer.

Nova Scotia. 1989. *Day Care Act* and regulations: Chapter 120 of the revised statutes, 1989. Halifax: Queen's Printer for Nova Scotia.

OECD (Organisation for Economic Cooperation and Development). 2001. *Starting strong: Early childhood education and care*. Paris: Education and Training Division, OECD.

OECD. 2004. *Early childhood education and care policy: Canada, country note*. OECD Directorate for Education.

Ontario. 1987a. *Initial steps in starting a day nursery in Ontario*. Toronto: Ministry of Community and Social Services.

Ontario. 1987b. *New directions*. Toronto: Ministry of Community and Social Services.

Ontario. 1988. *Day nurseries manual*. Toronto: Queen's Printer for Ontario.

Ontario. 1990a. *Day Nurseries Act* (Revised Statutes of Ontario, 1980: chapter 11). Toronto: Queen's Printer for Ontario.

Ontario. 1990b. Ontario regulation 760/83. (Under the *Day Nurseries Act*).

Ontario. 1996. *Early childhood education program standards*. Toronto: Ministry of Education and Training/College Standards and Accreditation Council.

Ontario. 1999. *The early years study: Reversing the real brain drain*, by F. Mustard and M. McCain. Toronto: Ministry of Community and Social Services/Ontario Children's Secretariat.

Pence, A., and H. Goelman. 1991. The relationship of regulation, training and motivation to quality of care in family day care. *Early Childhood Research Quarterly* 2: 315–334.

Penn, H. 2000. How do children learn: Early childhood in a global context. In H. Penn, ed., *Early childhood services: Theory, policy, and practice*. Buckingham, UK: Open University Press.

Peters, D. 1988. The child development associate credential and the educationally disenfranchised. In *Professionalism and the early childhood practitioner*. New York: Teachers College Press, Columbia University.

Phillips, D., ed. 1987. *Quality in child care: What does research tell us?* Washington, DC: NAEYC.

Pimento, B., and D. Kernsted. 2004. *Healthy foundations in child care*, 3rd ed. Toronto: Nelson.

Prentice, S. 2004. *Time for action: An economic and social analysis of child care in Winnipeg*. Winnipeg, MB: Child Care Coalition of Manitoba.

Prince Edward Island. 1987. *Guiding principles for the development of child care services*. Charlottetown: Acting Queen's Printer.

Prince Edward Island. 1988. Prince Edward Island's *Child Care Facilities Act* regulations. R.S.P.E.I. Cap. C-5. (including any amendments to December 31, 1990). Charlottetown: Acting Queen's Printer.

Pruissen, C.M. 1993. *Start and run a profitable home day care: Your step-by-step business plan*. North Vancouver: Self-Counsel Press.

Québec. 1992. Loi sur les services de garde à l'enfance L. R. Q., chapitre S–1 1979 (incluant les modifications apportées jusqu'au 1er octobre 1992, à jour au 1er décembre 1992). (An act respecting child care.) Quebec: Editeur Officiel du Québec.

Québec. 1993. Règlements sur les services de garde en garderie, dernière modification: 17 octobre 1991, à jour au 16 février 1993. (Regulations respecting child care centres.) Quebec: Editeur Officiel du Québec.

Radomski, M.A. 1986. Professionalization of early childhood educators: How far have we progressed? *Young Children* 41 (5): 20–23.

Read, M. 2000. Early childhood care and education learning outcomes. In *Research connections Canada*, vol. 4. Ottawa: CCCF.

Reiniger, A., E. Robinson, and M. McHugh. 1995. Mandated training of professionals: A means for improving reporting of suspected child abuse. *Child Abuse and Neglect* 19: 63–70.

Rhomberg, V. 2000. Nourishing with the brain in mind: Professional development for cooks in early childhood settings. *Interaction* (CCCF) 14 (3).

Rimer, P., and B. Prager. 1998. *Reaching out: Working together to identify and respond to child victims of abuse*. Toronto: Nelson.

Roberts-DeGennaro, M. 1997. *Conceptual framework of coalitions in an organizational context*. New York: Haworth Press, Inc.

Roeher Institute. 1992. *Quality child care for all: A guide to integration*. North York, ON: Roeher Institute.

Rood, J. 1998. *Leadership in early childhood*, 2d ed. New York: Teachers College Press, Columbia University.

Ruopp, R., H. Travers, F. Glantz, and C. Coelen. 1979. *Children at the center: Final report of the national day care study,* vol. I. Cambridge, MA: Abt Associates.

Safe Kids Canada. 1997. *Child's play: A playground safety guide for daycares, schools and communities.* Toronto: Safe Kids Canada.

Saifer, S. 1990. *Practical solutions to practically every problem: The early childhood teacher's manual.* St. Paul, MI: Redleaf Press.

Sargent, P. 2002. *Real men or real teachers? Contradictions in the lives of men elementary school teachers.* Harriman, TN: Men's Studies Press.

Saskatchewan. 1990a. An act to promote the growth and development of children and to support the provision of child care services to Saskatchewan families. Regina: Queen's Printer for Saskatchewan.

Saskatchewan. 1990b. The child care regulations 948/90. Chapter C-7.3 REG. 1 Section 27. Regina: Saskatchewan Social Services.

Schaeffer, S. 2001. Understanding research: Top ten tips for advocates and policy-makers. Fact sheet. National Association of Child Advocates, Washington, DC.

Schiller, P. 2001. Brain research and its implications for early childhood programs. *Child Care Information Exchange.*

Schom-Moffat, P. 1992. *Caring for a living: National study on wages and working conditions in Canadian child care.* Ottawa: CCCF and Canadian Day Care Advocacy Association.

Schweinhart, L.J, and D.P. Weikart, eds. 1985. *Quality in early childhood programs: Four perspectives.* High/Scope Early Childhood Policy Papers. Ypsilanti, MI: High/Scope Press.

Schweinhart L.J., H.V. Barnes, and D.P. Weikart. 1993. *Significant benefits: The High/Scope Perry Preschool Study through age 27.* Ypsilanti, MI: High/Scope Press.

Sciarra, D.J., and A.G. Dorsey. 2002. *Leaders and Supervisors in Child Care Programs.* Albany, NY: Delmar.

Sciarra, D.J., and A.G. Dorsey. 2003. *Developing and administering a child care center,* 5th ed. Albany, NY: Delmar.

Senge, P.M. 1990. *The fifth discipline: The art and practice of learning organizations.* New York: Doubleday.

Senge, P.M., et al. 1999. *The dance of change: The challenges of sustaining momentum in learning organizations.* New York: Doubleday.

Shimoni, R., and J. Baxter. 2005. *Working with families: perspectives for early childhood professionals,* 3d ed. Don Mills, ON: Pearson Addison-Wesley.

Shonkoff, J., and D. Phillips, eds. 2000. *From neurons to neighborhoods: The science of early childhood development.* Washington, DC: National Research Council.

Shore, R. 1997. *Rethinking the brain.* New York: Families and Work Institute.

Siegel, D. 1999. Relationships and the developing mind. *Child Care Information Exchange.*

Sissons, B., and H.M. Black. 1992. *Choosing with care: The Canadian parent's practical guide to quality child care for infants and toddlers.* Don Mills, ON: Addison-Wesley.

Spodek, B., O. Saracho, and D. Peters, eds. 1988. *Professionalism and the early childhood practitioner.* New York: Teachers College Press, Columbia University.

Spodek, B., O. Saracho, and D. Peters, eds. 1990. *Early childhood teacher preparation.* New York: Teachers College Press, Columbia University.

Steinhauer, P. 1999. How a child's early experiences affect development. *Interaction* (CCCF) 13 (1).

Stevenson, M.F. 1995. *Fundraising for early childhood programs: Getting started and getting results,* rev. ed. Washington, DC: NAEYC.

Swick, K.J. 1995. What parents really want from family involvement programs. *Day Care and Early Education* (Spring): 20–23.

Taylor, A., L. Dunster, and J. Pollard. 1999. And this helps me how? Family child care providers discuss training. *Early Childhood Research Quarterly* 14 (3): 285–312.

Tertell, E., S. Klein, and J. Jewett, eds. 1998. *When teachers reflect: Journeys toward effective, inclusive practice.* Washington, DC: NAEYC.

Toronto. 2001. Operating criteria for child care centers providing subsidized care in Metropolitan Toronto. Toronto: Metro Community Services, Children's Services Division.

Townson, M. 1986. *The costs and benefits of a national child care system for Canada.* Halifax: DPA Group Inc.

UNICEF. 2000. *The state of the world's children 2000*. New York: UNICEF Publications

Van der Gaag, J., and Jee-Peng Tan. 2001. The benefits of early childhood development programs: An economic analysis. Washington, DC: World Bank Publication, online: www.worldbank.org/children.

Vander Ven, K.D. 1988. Pathways to professional effectiveness for early childhood educators. In *Professionalism and the early childhood practitioner*, edited by B. Spodek, O. Saracho, and D. Peters, 137–160. New York: Teachers College Press, Columbia University.

Vanier Institute of the Family. 2000. *Profiling Canada's families*. Ottawa: Vanier Institute of the Family.

Wallach, Frances, and Afthinos, I. 1990. *An analysis of the state codes for licensed day-care centers: Focus on playground and supervision*. New York: Total Recreation Mangement Services, Inc.

Walsh, P. 1988. *Early childhood playground: Planning an outside learning environment*. Melbourne, Australia: Martin Educational, in association with Robert Andersen and Associates.

Westcoast Child Care Resource Centre. 2001. *Towards partnership/Vers un partariat: Multi-language resources for families in child care/Ressources multilingues pour les familles ayant un enfant en garderie*. Vancouver: Westcoast Child Care Resource Centre.

Whitebook, M., L. Sakai, E. Gerber, and C. Howes. 2001. *Then & now: Changes in child care staffing, 1994–2000, Technical report*. Washington, DC: Center for the Child Care Workforce.

Whitebrook, M., and D. Bellm. 1996. Mentoring early childhood teachers and providers: Building upon and extending tradition. *Young Children* 52 (1): 59–64.

Whitebrook, M., C. Howes, and D. Phillips. 1990. *Who cares? Child care teachers and the quality of child care in America. Final report of the National Child Care Staffing Study*. Oakland, CA: Child Care Employee Project.

Willer, B. 1987. *The growing crisis in childcare: Quality, compensation and affordability in early childhood programs*. Washington, DC: NAEYC.

Willer, B., ed. 1990. *Reaching the full cost of quality in early childhood programs*. Washington, DC: NAEYC.

Willer, B. 1994. A conceptual framework for early childhood professional development. In *The early childhood career lattice: Perspectives on professional development*, edited by J. Johnson and J.B. McCracken. Washington, DC: NAEYC.

Wilson, Beth. 2004. *Community voices: Young parents in Toronto speak out about work, community services and family life*. Toronto: Community Social Planning Council of Toronto and Family Service Association of Toronto.

Wilson, L. 2005. *Partnerships: Families and communities in Canadian early childhood education*, 2nd ed. Toronto: Nelson.

Winter, S. 1994–95. Diversity: a program for all children. *Childhood Education* (Winter): 91–95.

Workers Health and Safety Centre. 1999. Health and safety module for child care workers in Ontario. Don Mills, ON: Workers Health and Safety Centre.

Worotynec, S. 2000. The good, the bad and the ugly: Listserv as support. *CyberPsychology and Behavior* 3 (5) 797–809.

Yankelovich, D. 2000a. What grown-ups understand about child development: A national benchmark survey. *Zero to Three*.

Yankelovich, D. 2000b. Parents speak: Findings from focus group resources on early childhood development. *Zero to Three*.

Yukon. 1990a. *Child Care Act*. Bill 77. (Statutes of the Yukon.) Whitehorse: Commissioner of the Yukon.

Yukon. 1990b. Child care centre program regulations, O.C. 1990/115. Whitehorse: Commissioner of the Yukon.

Yukon. 1990c. Child care subsidy regulations. Order-in-Council, 1990/116. (Pursuant to section 40 of the Child Care Act.) Whitehorse: Commissioner of the Yukon.

Yukon. 1990d. Family day home program regulations. Order-in-Council, 1990/117. (Pursuant to section 40 of the Child Care Act.) Whitehorse: Commissioner of the Yukon.

Index